Nature of Polyexistentials

Basis for Abolishment of
the Western Intellectual Property Rights Regime

And Introduction of
the Libre-Halaal ByStar Digital Ecosystem

Mohsen Banan

Email: plpc-120033@mohsen.1.banan.byname.net

PLPC-120033.p1bsi

First US Edition – July 2023 – Version 1.042

Available on-line at:
https://github.com/bxplpc/120033

Access Information

The primary URL for this document is:
`https://github.com/bxplpc/120033`. The pdf format is authoritative.

Distribution of this document is unrestricted. We encourage you to copy and forward it to others.

This is the US Edition of this book. The International Edition of this document, PLPC-120074, is available at:
`https://github.com/bxplpc/120074`.

ISBN-13: 978-1-960957-00-9

The manifest of other forms and formats of this document can be found in Section E.1 and Table E.1.

Copying Information

This book is a Libre-Halaal polyexistential.

Without objecting to verbatim copying of his book, Ali-ben-Hossein, a famous historian of third and fourth Islamic lunar century (15th and 16th century AD) in the introductory section of his book writes:

any person who
distorts any part of my book
or destroys any part of it
or distorts any point that I had clarified
or changes any of my descriptions
or attributes my writings to himself
or attributes my work to others
or pretends that others participated in it
should receive God's anger!

Short Contents

Detailed Contents

V **Formulation of Libre-Halaal Oriented Societal Policies**   **321**

18 **Societal Adoption of Libre-Halaal Strategies**   **323**

List of Figures

Preface

Economics is full of externalities. Horrible things happen when market value deviates from true value. The harm is even more horrific when economics is the main pillar of societies.

Often it takes time to understand correct new true values and correct new market values. It can even take longer to correct such divergences. In the case of fossil fuels and global warming, we may well be too late in correcting the relevant economic deviations.

Divergence of market value from true value may have various reasons and various dynamics. The deviation is particularly devastating when it is through ownership rules. Ownership rules are man-made constructs which can be slanted to economically benefit one group at the expense of another group.

Rules for ownership of Africans by Americans and Europeans, resulted in reduction of the economic value of labor to the benefit of Americans and Europeans. This was accomplished by deemphasizing true value of Africans as human beings. Horrible things happened when the market value of Africans deviated from the true value of Africans. Some three hundred years or so later, this is even mostly clear and generally recognized by the old masters (Americans and Europeans), but no corrective economic measures (reparations) have been made. The repercussions of such economically motivated ownership rules are vast and may remain uncomprehended in parts.

Something similar is happening today with respect to the Western Intellectual Property Rights (IPR) regime. This time, things are more complicated. The victims are not easily identifiable, and the harm is not immediately recognizable. Yet, the scope has become global and long-term ramifications are perhaps even more disastrous.

Knowledge, know-how, uses of know-how, ideas and information are inherently non-scarce. They are **polyexistentials**. Unlike **monoexistentials** which exist in singular, polyexistentials naturally exist in multiples and are inherently not scarce.

What is abundant in nature is being made artificially scarce through man-made ownership rules called copyright and patents. These ownership rules then permit a certain group which usually take the form of corporations to economically profit from these unnatural and economically motivated artificial scarcities. The market value of the use of the know-how for making the Covid vaccine is artificially inflated compared to the true non-scarce value of the use of that know-how, so we ended up with less of the more expensive Covid vaccines. This has caused a divergence between the market value of the use of know-how and its true value. As a result, horrible things have been happening, but people have been conditioned not to worry about these. The power of corporations has been amplified. Autonomy and privacy of the individuals has been diminished and rendered irrelevant. Professions are being marginalized. People all over the world are being subjected to the Americanization process. Humanity is being destroyed.

In this book we analyze the topic of Intellectual Property Rights (IPR) from a new perspective. The topic of restriction of polyexistentials and Western IPR are one and the same. Yet, the concept of polyexistentials has not appeared in prior discussions of this topic. This is the very first time that the concept and the word "polyexistentials" are being introduced.

The model of polyexistence makes it easy to prove that the concept of Intellectual Property is erroneous. This proof is based on logic that is rooted in nature of existence and nature of possession and the requirement for ownership to be in harmony with nature of possession and existence.

Based on philosophy, nature and logic we present a case that makes it clear that the Western IPR regime is in conflict with nature and is obviously fraudulent. The logic that demonstrates polyexistentials are unownable is sufficient to persuade anyone who thinks with his brain and whose interests do not conflict with the natural conclusions of our discourse.

But human rationality is a myth. Both individually and in groups people don't think with their brain. People think with their character. Dominant aspects of their character that impact their thinking are self-interest and their value system.

Over the past two hundred years or so a great deal has been invested to cultivate the myth of the merits of Western IPR regime. Many generations have been born inside of this mistake. Very many are so very vested in preservation of the myth of IPR that our logic will likely not prove sufficient. So, we spend a good part of this book debunking various arguments that have been put forward to preserve and further cultivate IPR.

We are asked to believe that the artificial competitive environment that Western IPR regime creates is superior to the natural collaborative environment. What Westerners see in others is a reflection of their own **self-toxication**. We are asked to believe that people are economic creatures.

We, humans, are more than economic creatures.

The detrimental effects of the Western IPR regime include the obstruction of engineering creativity, a distortion of the competitive business environment, and denial of the benefits thereof to the public. Our profession, the software and internet engineering profession, is hindered by the Intellectual Property Rights (IPR) regime. As engineers instead of being able to freely collaborate, we are enticed to compete. Instead of collectively inventing and innovating towards the good of society, the Western IPR model pushes us to individually reinvent. Our intimacy and knowledge of internet application services has positioned us to better understand the harms of IPR on privacy and autonomy of individuals. Our profession, has a responsibility to society, and we have a responsibility to our profession. It is towards the fulfillment of our responsibilities to our profession and our profession's responsibility to society and humanity that we have prepared this book.

Having rejected the Western IPR regime as a wrong model for governance of polyexistentials, towards **proper governance of polyexistentials** we first introduce the potent and sensitive word "Halaal". We then introduce the **Libre-Halaal** label for the **halaal manner-of-existence of polyexistentials** through which we facilitate **conviviality of tools**. Based on that, we then provide definitional criteria for **Libre-Halaal Software,** **Libre-Halaal Content** and **Libre-Halaal Internet Services.**

We use the metaphor of a societal disease to highlight the harms of Western IPR regime and trace the roots of this disease to "**Americanism.**"

The American internet is based on American values and the American digital ecosystem is a product of American corporatocracy. In America, the user's autonomy and privacy is now the implicit internet currency and American corporations have established necessary mechanism to translate that to hard cash — they call it "Surveillance Capitalism." Outside of America, American internet corporations function as the surveillance and propaganda arms of the U.S. government and its American values. As of 2022, almost 90% of Facebook's daily active users come from outside the US. When necessary, American internet corporations happily collaborate with the US government towards foreign espionage and foreign exploitations. Together, these two then put on a charade. From time-to-time the government speaks of antitrust and regulation of monopolies. And Facebook says we need more privacy guidance! In the meantime, people are being conditioned to accept more of loss of autonomy and privacy as side effects of American surveillance capitalism. As if the American Internet can be fixed on its fringes.

No. The American internet cannot be fixed. Instead, the American internet model should be fully rejected, and a different model is needed. We have built **The Libre-Halaal By* (ByStar) Digital Ecosystem**, as a moral alternative to the existing models for internet services and software. Equipped with a **multidisciplinary blueprint**, we offer our initial implementation of the

ByStar digital ecosystem as a starting point towards concrete solutions.

Today's American internet is mostly a business construct. The current basic model of the internet is rooted in the rise-of-the-middle model of corporations exploiting the individual. The engineering architecture of the proprietary internet application services is very central. Proprietary American corporations the likes of Google, Facebook, Amazon, Microsoft and Apple are positioned in the middle and monitor, control and exploit citizens of the world.

The engineering architecture of Libre-Halaal ByStar Digital Ecosystem is distinctly different. The multidisciplinary blueprint that we have provided can be the basis for de-Americanization, de-IPR-ization and **redecentralization** of internet application services. Unlike the central and rise-of-the-middle model of American internet application services, ByStar design is highly distributed, decentralized and end and edge oriented.

We need non-proprietary digital ecosystems. And that is what ByStar is. ByStar's primary offerings are real, tangible and practical autonomy and privacy — on a very large scale. The scope of ByStar is everything. The "*" in By* comes from Unix's glob expansion symbol. ByStar is rooted in the model of mediated and direct interactions of autonomous edges. For this to function properly, software of autonomous edges must be internally transparent and un-owned. Software of ByStar is and must be publicly owned — it is Libre-Halaal Software.

ByStar individual services represent real individuals in the real world. In ByStar, real individuals have real autonomy, real control and real ownership of their own ByStar individual services. ByStar individual services are edge-oriented and can be externally-hosted or self-hosted. Each citizen of the world is offered his/her own **Possession Assertable Libre-Halaal Service (PALS)**. Through guarantees of possession assertability, PALS provide for tangible autonomy and privacy for individuals and for societies.

In the ByStar model each nation and each culture adopts and nationalizes the publicly owned (humanity owned) global ByStar digital ecosystem software consistent with its own values — while preserving the universal ByStar model of autonomy and privacy of the individual. This is very different from the proprietary American model of exploitation, and this is also very different from national reactions and responses to the proprietary American model.

The core software of ByStar Libre-Halaal Services is the **Universal BISOS (ByStar Internet Services Operating System)**. The entirety of BISOS is Libre-Halaal Software. The engineering design of BISOS is towards redecentralization of internet application services and privacy and autonomy of the individual. This book is not just a book. It is backed by software and internet application services. As Libre-Halaal Software, the software of

ByStar is publicly available and some ByStar internet application services are functional and in use.

We are devout monoexistential bounded-corporations capitalists. We are pro-business. The existing capitalist model for monoexistentials is generally correct, in both philosophical and economic terms. But the extension of the monoexistential capitalist model into the domain of polyexistentials, based on the Western IPR regime, is a grave mistake. To address this mistake of American Capitalism, we introduce the model of
Global Polyexistential Capitalism as an **Attribution Based Economy**
towards correcting the existing Ownership Based Economy of
American Capitalism. Deep understanding of the strategy that we outline in this book, makes it clear that Polyexistential American Capitalism is very vulnerable.

What we are trying to do in this book is distinct and different from the many other books and articles that have been written on this topic. First, most books on this topic are written by Western lawyers, politicians, economists, journalists, sociologists and academics. We are engineers and we are not Western. Second, this is the very first time that the philosophical concept of polyexistentials is being used to analyze this topic and this domain. Third, our treatment of this subject is genuinely independent. We are not doing it for money or hype. Fourth, we have tried to be comprehensive and precise in this book. All the key concepts that are emphasized in bold in the above text have concrete and precise definitions. Finally, unlike most other writings on this topic which amount to naggings of impotents, we are putting a multidisciplinary blueprint for a cure on the table. As engineers, we are offering explicit multidisciplinary solutions.

Our ultimate goal for all of this has been to influence societal policies towards adoption of halaal manner-of-existence of polyexistentials. We recognize that adoption of such societal policies in America is likely not possible and their adoption in the West is likely very difficult. Therefore, we focus on Eastern societies in general and Iran and China in particular.

It is only through full rejection of the Western IPR regime and its deep roots in Americanism that humanity can be rescued.

Mohsen BANAN
April 2023
Bellevue, WA, USA and
Isfahan, Iran

Chapter 1

Introduction

That which exists in nature in multiples, we call "polyexistentials". That which exists in nature in singular, we call "monoexistentials". All material objects exist in singular and are monoexistentials. Ideas, information and knowledge exist in nature in multiples — not in singular. Ideas, information and knowledge are polyexistentials. Much of our world is actually a mixture of monoexistentials and polyexistentials, which we call mixed-existentials.

In this document we analyze the topic of Intellectual Property (IP) from a new perspective. The topic of monopolistic ownership-oriented restriction of polyexistentials and Western Intellectual Property Rights (IPR) are one and the same. Yet, the concept and terminology of polyexistentials has not appeared in prior discussions of this topic. This is the very first time that the concept and the word "polyexistentials" are being introduced.

The traditional perspective on Intellectual Property is that it is debatable. Some good arguments have been made in its favor and some good arguments have been made opposing it. Some are for it and some are against it. It is perceived to be economically more profitable to be for it, than to be against it. So, in the West, a whole lot more people are in its favor.

The model of polyexistence makes it easy to demonstrate and prove that the concept of Intellectual Property is erroneous. This proof is based on logic that is rooted in nature of existence and nature of possession and the requirement for ownership to be in harmony with nature of possession and existence. Unlike other writings on this subject, we do not consider this as part of any debate. In this document we prove that the basic concepts of Intellectual Property are invalid.

The IPR regime is about extending the model and concept of ownership of monoexistentials to the realm of polyexistentials by creating artificial scarcity. This is against the nature of polyexistence.

Ownership of polyexistentials impacts their manner-of-existence towards being monopolistically controlled and towards becoming internally opaque. Monopolistic oriented restriction of polyexistentials has ramifications on autonomy and privacy of the individual and health of societies. Natural dynamics of Western IP restrictions result in reduced autonomy and privacy of the individual and result in transfer of more power to corporations and Corpocracy. Any digital ecosystem that is rooted in Western IPR puts humanity in danger. A moral alternative to the American proprietary digital ecosystem (Internet as we know it today) is called for.

The first part of this document is concerned with ontology of polyexistentials. We construct the "Polyexistentials Reference Model" in order to analyze the nature of what Intellectual Property restricts. Polyexistentials are naturally un-scarce and naturally multi-possessable and naturally un-territorial. Therefore, polyexistentials are unownable. Western IP regime is about ownership (monopolistic restriction) of polyexistentials. The concept of polyexistence through the polyexistentials reference model makes the fraudulence of Western IPR regime clear and obvious.

In the second part of this document, we engage in discrediting of the IPR regime through debunking the arguments that have been put forward in its support and we address the false beliefs surrounding Western consensuses. We also put on the table the character of those who originated it and who are pushing it. Westerners are vested in their IPR regime. It is not in their interest to understand the invalidity of IPR. We point out that when a given society gets its fundamental ownership rules wrong, the consequences are severe. When most of the world gets its fundamental ownership rules wrong, the consequences are catastrophic.

The third and fourth part of this document are about solutions and cures. We advocate full rejection of the Western IPR regime. We then advance a specific replacement strategy which includes societal and global governance models that require halaal manner-of-existence of polyexistentials. We then propose construction of a complete ethics oriented digital ecosystem which has autonomy and privacy of the individual at its core. We then introduce a starting point for such a digital ecosystem called: The Libre-Halaal ByStar Digital Ecosystem. Finally, in the fifth part, we postulate a set of societal strategies that in theory can cure Eastern societies and do an economic number on Western IPR vulnerabilities.

This document is vast in scope and in ambition. And this public version is just a beginning. The first and second parts are mature and complete enough to deserve scrutiny. The third, fourth and fifth parts are less ripe. We draw the contours of what needs to be addressed and convey intent and direction. We have explicit plans for future editions that focus more on the cure parts. Throughout, our main goal is to underscore the importance of this topic and to agitate towards further discussions.

1.1 The Nature of Polyexistentials Makes Them Unownable

A thesis of this document is that polyexistentials are unownable. Polyexistentials cannot be proper private property — or any other type of property. Our analysis revolves around the relationships among:

1. Existence

2. Possession

3. Ownership

Existence is a key term in ontology and has been subject of much analysis and debate. "I think an almost unbelievable amount of false philosophy has arisen through not realizing what 'existence' means." says Bertrand Russell. Here, we are not going to rehash that topic. Like René Descartes who says: "To know what existence is, all we have to do is to understand the meaning of the word, for it tells us at once what the thing is which the word stands for, in so far as we can know it. There is no need here for a definition, which would confuse rather than clarify the issue", [1] And like Avicenna (Ibn Sina) who says:

> Being is recognized by reason itself without the aid of definition or description. Since it has no definition it has neither genus nor differenzia because nothing is more general than it. Being does not have a description since nothing is better known than it.

Here, by existence we mean existence and by being we mean being.

By possession we mean the act or fact of possessing. Actual holding or occupancy, either with or without rights of ownership.

Existence and possession are aspects of nature, but ownership is a human construct. Ownership, as man-made rules, can in theory be anything. In that sense, anything and everything is ownable. We then draw a distinction between "proper ownership rules" and "improper ownership rules". We consider proper ownership rules as those which are in harmony with existence and possession aspects of nature, and which result in enduring amelioration of society and humanity. An acknowledged recent Western improper ownership rule is Americans' ownership rules for Africans as slaves. Existence of humans as equals makes them unownable. It is in this context that we consider polyexistentials as ownable or unownable.

To a certain extent, each society's ownership rules reflect that society's values and character. Intellectual Property as ownership rules represents the American and Western model for governance of polyexistentials. Since for

Americans, IP is directly sourced from the U.S. Constitution and since analysis of ownership involves both the governed (polyexistentials) and the governor, the American character is on the table. We therefore need to fully consider it within our scope to analyze and understand why these people (Americans) have come up with these ownership rules (IP).

Ownership rules exist to resolve conflicts and to improve order in society. Main ownability requirements are the following:

1. Exclusive Possession — What is to be owned must be possessable by only one possessor at any given time.

2. Scarcity — What is plentiful need not be owned.

3. Territoriality — Assignment of ownership in a given place should not impact other ownerships in other places. Ownership is a definition within the context of a sovereign. Sovereignty is bounded by territoriality.

4. Harmony with the existence of the owned.

The nature of polyexistentials violates these ownership requirements:

1. Polyexistentials (e.g., ideas, formulas, knowledge) can be possessed by multiple possessors at the same time.

2. Each polyexistential can easily be copied and can therefore be plentiful. Each polyexistential is not scarce.

3. Each polyexistential can exist in multiple places at the same time. Each polyexistential can be possessed by multiple possessors in different places at the same time. Polyexistentials are non-territorial.

4. The concept of polyexistence, as derived from nature, leads to their ownership being unnatural.

Polyexistentials are therefore unownable.

Western Intellectual Property Rights regime is an umbrella misnomer to cover the following branches of US and Western laws:

- Copyright

- Patent

- Trademark

Copyright, patent and trademark provide for ownership oriented monopolistic restrictions of polyexistentials. Each of these branches of Western law directly maps to different forms of monopolistic restriction and ownership of different aspects of certain types of polyexistentials.

Since polyexistentials are unownable; copyright, patent and trademark laws as individual branches of law and collectively as Intellectual Property Rights regime are therefore invalid.

Ramifications of incorrect ownership laws can put societies and humanity at risk.

Monoexistentials are bounded by their location. The context of monoexistence is inherently local. Polyexistentials can be in multiple places at the same time. The context of polyexistence is inherently un-territorial, global and universal.

1.2 This Document is in Globish

This document is in Globish. It is not in conventional Anglo-American English.

See the document titled "Introducing Globish into Globish" [6] for a description of Globish. That document also includes references to other specific words and concepts relevant to this document. Briefly, Globish (mixture of Glob-al and Engl-ish) is the language that a Chinese may use to communicate with a Brazilian.

The intended audience for this document is all of humanity.

Some of the concepts developed in this document stand separate from American and Western values. Some of these concepts specifically reject American and Western values. Western readers need to pay extra attention, as many of their assumptions are likely not ours.

So-called Intellectual Property Rights (patent, copyright and trademark laws) are fundamentally Western concepts. They are primarily rooted in the American, English, French and European cultures. Much of our audience has not had these beliefs and should not permit these corrupt beliefs to enter their cultures. That segment of our audience that has patent and copyright traditions in their culture and their belief system need to recognize that these beliefs are by no means universal.

1.3 Relevant Globish Vocabulary

The Intellectual Property Rights regime is a set of societal rules. The IPR regime is a Western construct. The concepts and vocabulary of IPR are Western and are targeted towards justification, protections, promotion and propagation of the Western IPR regime.

The basis of analysis of this document is Eastern. Many of the concepts that we use to invalidate Western IPR regime are not rooted in Anglo-American English. Throughout this document, there are also a number of important words and concepts that we use in their Globish sense and not in the Anglo-American English (Western) sense.

The concepts behind these words, to a large extent, have directed our analysis and as such are key to understanding this document. Recognizing the specific contexts for our use of these words is essential for understanding our exposition. Here we provide a short list of some of the key words and concepts that are essential for our exposition.

Libre:

Libre is a substitute for the word free in English which distinguishes the freedom sense from the gratis sense. Libre in Globish refers to the sense of freedom in the word "free". The other and dominant sense of the word free is gratis (free of charge). In the context of this document our use of Libre is in the scope of freedom from Western societal restrictions that come as a result of IPR regime's restrictions. This scoping of Libre is different from FLOSS's (Free and Libre Open Source Software) scope of the user's freedom as it applies to Free Software.

Conviviality Of Tools

By conviviality we refer to the concept of "Tools for Conviviality" as Ivan Illich introduced it.

Briefly, in Illich's words:

> To the degree that an individual masters his tools, he can invest the world with his meaning; to the degree that he is mastered by his tools, the shape of the tool determines his own self-image. Convivial tools are those which give each person who uses them the greatest opportunity to enrich the environment with the fruits of his or her vision. Industrial tools deny this possibility to those who use them and they allow their designers to determine the meaning and expectations of others.

Western IPR model of polyexistentials leads to industriality of tools where the tool maker is more in charge.

The Libre-Halaal model of polyexistentials leads to conviviality of tools where the tool user is more in charge.

We expand on this in Section 16.2.3.1 — Tools for Conviviality.

Halaal and Haraam — «حلال و حرام»

In English, halaal and haraam are over simplified Orientalist adoptions that map onto "permitted" or "prohibited" and which come with negative Islamophobia connotations.

In Globish, philosophical halaal is "manifestation" of "moral sensibilities" relevant to a specific topic where "the set of actions" map to "right."

We use the words halaal and haraam as vehicles for expression of ethics and morality as we have formally defined them in:

> **Introducing Halaal and Haraam into Globish**
> **Based on Moral Philosophy of Abstract Halaal**
> **And Defining The Libre-Halaal Label**
> http://mohsen.1.banan.byname.net/PLPC/120039 — [7]

Section 11 — Introducing Halaal and Haraam Into Globish, is a digest of that document.

A particular focus of this document is to identify halaal and haraam manner-of-existence of polyexistentials. We conclude that the Western IPR regime leads to the haraam manner-of-existence of polyexistentials.

We elaborate on this in Section 4 — Proper Governance of Polyexistentials.

Libre-Halaal

Libre-Halaal is the label that we apply for the halaal manner-of-existence of polyexistentials. A necessary condition for conviviality of polyexistential tools is their Libre-Halaalness.

In Section 4.2.2 — The Libre-Halaal Label — we expand on this.

In Section 12.1.3 — The Right Label for Correct Manner-of-Existence of Software — we describe why Libre-Halaal is superior to "Free Software", "Open Source", and other FLOSS attempts at labeling Halaal manner-of-existence of software (and other polyexistentials).

East and West

Political East and political West represent labels for spheres of consensus.

Some of the important concepts that the Western sphere of consensus focuses on are: supremacy of markets, economics, competition, dominance, exploitation and freedoms of the individual and the corporation and separation of religion from governance.

Some of the important concepts that the Eastern sphere of consensus focuses on are: supremacy of family and society, social cohesion, societal harmony, ethics, morality and sanctity of speech and the intertwinedness of religion and governance.

The fundamental difference in perspective between East and West is in the context of individual and society. An Eastern Iranian may communicate this to a Western American with the following phrases: "The largest societal unit in America is the individual. The smallest societal unit in Iran is the family."

East and West have been engaged in "Models Wars". The West considers its models as universal and has been imposing them on the East. Some Eastern societies have been resisting. Resisting the Western IPR regime is an important battle ground in these Models Wars.

Orientalism

Orientalism, as defined by Edward Said in his book of the same name [40], is an agenda-driven definition of Eastern concepts, customs, and characteristics by Westerners, aimed at establishing a sense of difference and superiority in order to exploit the East and Easterners.

This history of Orientalism has led to a false belief among Westerners that the Western intellectual property rights (IPR) regime is universal. This belief, combined with the belief of Western superiority, has led to the imposition of IPR on Easterners as a natural next step.

West-toxication — «غرب زدگی»

West-toxication is a term that Iranians have created and use to denote pernicious Western influence that is to be rejected.

West-toxication represents the impact of Orientalism on some Easterners which has led to their belief that the Western model is superior to the Eastern model in almost all respects.

We use the word West-toxication in the context that Jalaal Al-Ahamad introduced it in his Gharbzadegi book in 1966 [16].

The history of West-toxication has led some Easterners to believe that the Western IPR regime is universal, because it is Western.

We expand on this in a Section titled "Western IPR Regime: An Instrument of Neocolonialism".

Americanism and Americanists

In English, Americanism is the self-congratulatory celebration of the likes of: free markets, rugged individualism, capitalism, the corporation, free speech, free Facebook friends, the national rifle association, debt driven education, market driven health care and TV advertised prescription drugs.

In Globish, Americanism is the model of corporatized economic creatures existing in an industrial context. The Americanism model is focused on economic and industrial dominance. Americanism results in the core of the character of the Americanists to become that of morally bankrupt self-absorbed bullies. In that context, with Americanists, everything is always just about money.

Because governance of polyexistentials are man-made constructs, analysis of Americanism versus Eastern humanity oriented models needs to be an essential part of our discourse.

The Globish's Americanism contrasts against the English's Americanism in humanity's context. Governance of polyexistentials in a humanity-oriented model, naturally leads to the label of Libre-Halaal.

A key part of our analysis is to compare and contrast Americanism's focus on self-toxication «خود زدگی» and economics versus the Eastern humanity-oriented model of focusing on the greater good and halaal and haraam. Thus, we identify Americanism as the root of the Western IPR problem. Furthermore, we recognize Americanism as a contagious disease, and we recognize IPR as an agent for propagation of Americanism.

We expand on this in Section 9 — Americanism: Root of the IPR Mistake.

Unbounded Corporations — Corporatization — Western Corpocracy

When properly bounded, limited and controlled, there is nothing wrong with a group of people creating a legal entity called a corporation in order to generate economic profit for themselves.

But society faces grave risks of harm when corporations are not properly bounded. Unbounded Corporations are a pillar of Americanism. In that model, in due course humans become corporatized economic creatures existing in an exploitative industrial context. The American/Western legal system then kicks in and formalizes the Western legal notions of "corporate personhood". Americanism then amounts to a complete collection of economic creatures (people and corporations alike) where money fully rules and humanity is suppressed.

The scope of corporatization in Americanism is vast, encompassing all aspects of life and professions. This includes academia, universities, medicine, medications and agriculture, which are either already under the control of large corporations or are in the process of being corporatized.

By definition, Corporations exist for the sole purpose of generating profit. The character of such a "corporate personhood" is then like that of a psychopath where empathy and remorse are impaired and egotistical traits rule.

It is inside of Americanism that the Western IPR regime has thrived. Copyright and patents have become instruments for amplification of power of corporations and dominance of corporations over individuals.

After all is said and done, the overwhelming majority of copyright and patents are controlled by large, unbounded corporations.

We expand on this in Section 8.1 — Amplification of Power of Corporations and Corporate-Personhood.

So-Called Western IPR Regime

The IPR regime was contrived to facilitate the Americanism goals of economic and industrial dominance by few and by corporations. Corporatized economic creatures (Americanists) have chosen intellectual property as a model for governance of polyexistentials in order to create unnatural exploitable environments. They then hyped it up as legal and moral!

In Anglo-American English, "Intellectual Property Rights (IPR)" has become revered and chic terminology, which is often portrayed as moral, ethical and universal.

In Globish, we reject all of that. The entirety of what some call "Intellectual Property Rights" is a rigged misnomer. Western copyright and patent artificial laws are not about property or rights or intellectuality.

For this reason, we usually prefix IPR with "Western" and "so-called."

We expand on this in Section 6.2 — So-Called Western IPR: A Rigged Misnomer.

Understanding of polyexistence plus the above concepts and words, very simply and naturally lead to the obvious recognition of fraudulence of the Western IPR regime. Yet, because it is not in the interest of many to recognize fraudulence of the Western IPR regime we need to apply more than just logic. Throughout this document we further develop the above concepts for those who have difficulty putting aside their interests in favor of logic and reason. Many of these concepts resonate in the East and are suppressed in the West.

These concepts and these words permit us to change the center of gravity of this topic from individualism and economics to ethics and harmony with nature.

1.4   Dynamism of This Document

Copying of this book is unrestricted. We encourage you to copy and forward it to others.

You can obtain this book in both digital and paper forms. The primary URL for this document is:

https://github.com/bxplpc/120033. The pdf format is authoritative.

This is the US Edition. Our audience in this edition of the book is primarily Americans and Americanists. Americans are often offended by how they are regarded internationally. In the US Edition we take some care to see that Americans are not overly offended. There is also an International Edition of this book. In the International Edition, we look at Americanism and Americans as it is genuinely seen throughout the world by non-Americanists. The primary URL for the International Edition of this document is: https://github.com/bxplpc/120074.

The analysis presented in this book is multidisciplinary. We have had to dabble in chemistry, physics, biology, information theory, computer science, logic, philosophy, ethics, theology, sociology, law and economics. Clearly, we are not experts in all of these fields.

Core concepts have been adequately developed and our conclusions are correct. However, the cures that we introduce require a great deal more cultivation and development. This book is evolving, and we plan to follow up with future updates and enhancements.

This book is much broader in scope than other books on this topic. We introduce the concept of polyexistentials, establish the invalidity of the Western IPR regime, call for its abolishment, and recognize the negative ramifications of IPR on privacy and autonomy of the individual, as well as the emergence of surveillance capitalism and its potential for destruction of humanity. Unlike other books on this topic, we do not limit ourselves to the scope of naggings of impotents.

As engineers, we are committed to providing solutions. In the digital domain, we are proposing a multidisciplinary blueprint for replacing the existing model of proprietary American internet application services with a model for Libre-Halaal privacy and autonomy-oriented set of non-proprietary internet application services. This book provides a starting point for describing the engineering and societal aspects of this solution.

In Part IV − Libre-Halaal ByStar Digital Ecosystem, we introduce the engineering design of a specific Libre-Halaal digital ecosystem called "ByStar". In this regard, this book is not just a book, but is backed by software and internet application services. As Libre-Halaal software, the software of ByStar is publicly available and some ByStar internet application services are functional and in use. But, ByStar is not just backed by its software and its internet application services. We have also created some of the needed structures so that others can join, participate, and profit. We point to the ByStar Open Business Plan in various places, but the purpose of this book is not to promote ByStar and our plans. We want to rescue humanity from the eventualities of the Western IPR mistake, and the ByStar attempt is part of that comprehensive effort.

We can benefit from your feedback. Please let us know your thoughts. You

can send us your comments and criticisms by email to:
mailto:plpc-120033@mohsen.1.banan.byname.net

1.5   Our Motivations and our Purposes

We are software engineers. The Western IPR regime has crippled our profession by prohibiting collaboration and transferring more power to corporate businessmen. This has led to dominance of internally opaque software and internally opaque internet services. Internally opaque software and internally opaque internet services foster a competitive model which stifles engineering collaboration. Internally opaque software and internally opaque internet services in turn lead to deterioration of individual's autonomy and privacy.

Our profession, software and internet engineering, has a responsibility to society and we have a responsibility to our profession. It is towards the fulfillment of our responsibilities to our profession and our profession's responsibility to society and humanity that we have prepared this document.

Because we have been close to writing of software and creation of internet services, we understand the ramifications of the Western IPR regime better than many others. Dynamics of the Western IPR regime are such that they put society and humanity at risk.

We have concluded that the Western IPR regime is a colossal mistake.

Let's say that based on solid logic we could demonstrate that the bases for establishment of IPR regime is fundamentally wrong and that IPR regime results in serious harm to society and humanity. What impact would that have? Contemporary global mistakes often result in entrenched vested interests. Many powerful people and entities are deeply vested in Western IPR. Such deep economic interests often prevent people's willingness to hear and follow basic logic.

The Western IPR regime is a sphere of consensus that cannot be changed based on logic and reason alone. Therefore, the scope and purpose of this book should not be limited to logic and reason alone.

The consequences of the IPR Western ownership mistake may even be more grave than the previous Western ownership mistake — that of slavery of Africans by Americans based on formal Western laws of ownership of human beings. This time ramifications of the mistake are broader than just America or the West, they put all of humanity in danger.

Ramifications and harm of the Western IPR regime are far broader than they are generally understood. Western IPR regime indirectly impacts the individual's autonomy and privacy and distorts the relationship between individuals and corporations.

In this document we address much of what surrounds IPR. Our goal is to open the subject wide towards tangible results.

1. We introduce the concept of polyexistentials and based on that we evaluate the validity of the Western IPR regime. From that analysis we conclude that all basis for establishment of Western IPR regime are invalid.

2. It is clear that polyexistentials should not be owned and it is clear that the Western IPR regime should be abolished. But abolishment of IPR regime should not lead to ungoverned polyexistence. Polyexistentials should be regarded as "public goods" and as such deserve legal protection because of negative externalities which arise if polyexistentials are not properly governed.

   We frame the question of correct governance of polyexistentials in their halaal and haraam manner-of-existence.

3. We then recognize digital as the most potent form of polyexistentials and put forward concrete definitions for halaal manner-of-existence of software and internet Services and label them as Libre-Halaal.

4. In Part 2, we debunk common arguments in favor of validity of the Western IPR Regime. We recognize and illustrate that it is not reasonable to expect that Americanists could be awakened. This disease cannot be stopped in the West. Our hope is with the East.

5. In Part 3, our focus then shifts towards solutions. We propose a number of abstract cures towards replacing the current Western IPR traditions.

6. In Part 4, having confined ourselves with halaal manner-of-existence of software and internet application services, we move towards creation of a complete parallel Libre-Halaal digital ecosystem.

   In a document titled:

   The Libre-Halaal ByStar Digital Ecosystem
   A Unified and Non-Proprietary Model For Autonomous Internet Services
   A Moral Alternative To The Proprietary American Digital Ecosystem
   http://www.by-star.net/PLPC/180016 — [11]

   and also at the web site:

   http://www.by-star.net

   which is partially reproduced in Chapter 16 — The Libre-Halaal ByStar Digital Ecosystem —, we describe the contours of a cure.

7. Equipped with a tangible initial Libre-Halaal digital ecosystem, we then turn our attention to economics and business.

   In Chapter 13 — Global Polyexistential Capitalism —, we analyze and distinguish dynamics of Monoexistential Capitalism vs Polyexistential Capitalism.

8. Our ultimate goal is to influence formulation of national policies and adoption at societal level of halaal manner-of-existence of polyexistentials in general and Libre-Halaal Software and Libre-Halaal Internet Services in particular.

   In Part 5, we focus on the formulation of societal policies.

   In the Western context in general and in the American context in particular, in this domain, at best such a goal is academic.

   In the Eastern context in general and in the Iranian context in particular, with these understandings, we believe it is possible to move towards governance of polyexistentials based on their halaal manner-of-existence.

   To this end, in Chapter 20 — Eastern Societal Libre-Halaal Strategies —, we have proposed a set of software and internet services national policies for Iran and China that are equally applicable to other Eastern societies.

Each part of this document has a particular tone and a specific style. The parts that introduce the concept and terminology of nature of polyexistentials are scholarly, formal, logic based, and persuasion oriented.

The parts that deal with exposure of the Western IPR regime mistake are by choice inflammatory and aggressive. Our philosophical analysis is that nature of polyexistentials leads to the natural right to copy and the natural right to apply knowledge without any monopoly oriented restrictions. This in turn naturally leads to full rejection of the restrictive IPR regime. The context of polyexistentials is inherently universal. It is the responsibility of those who wish to restrict our (humans) natural rights, to make a case for their model. The burden of proof is on them not on us.

A meaningful case for IPR has never been made. So, where appropriate we mock, and we ridicule the Western status quo. We frequently toy with the self-absorption and overly individualistic aspects of Western cultures. Logic and persuasion alone are ineffective against the entrenched Western IPR disease. Exposure of the Western IPR regime mistake also involves the clarification that IPR is a Western and mostly American mistake. As such our tone may come across as anti-American and anti-Western. Western readers need to recognize that the intended audience of this document is all of humanity and that the scope of this topic is all of humanity. The nature of this topic is inherently global.

The purpose and scope of this document is not limited to analysis of Western IPR disease. We also offer theoretical recipes for cures. The parts of this document that deal with the cure occasionally go beyond persuasion and are prophetic. The cure part is broken into Western cures and Eastern cures — each with their own flavor.

This document is the product of our independent thoughts and has not been funded in any way. We have not written this document in the traditional context of the Western IPR where the result of our work is expected to bring economic rewards. We have something to say and we want others to read it and discuss it — towards the progress of science and useful arts. We believe that collaboration is the best way to motivate engineers, scientists, and artists to create meaningful work.

We are law abiding. While we underscore the corrupt nature of Western IPR regime, we do not advocate illegal or unauthorized copying in applicable territory. We advocate the abolishment of the Western IPR regime. In the meantime, we encourage authors and inventors to subject their work to non-restrictive copyright and no patents or non-restrictive (defensive) patents in applicable territories. We advocate full rejection of the Western IPR regime in territories where they may be under consideration.

If there were to be any civil disobedience, we would follow Martin Luther King's model.

> I hope you are able to see the distinction I am trying to point out. In no sense do I advocate evading or defying the law, as would the rabid segregationist. That would lead to anarchy. One who breaks an unjust law must do so openly, lovingly, and with a willingness to accept the penalty. I submit that an individual who breaks a law that conscience tells him is unjust, and who willingly accepts the penalty of imprisonment in order to arouse the conscience of the community over its injustice, is in reality expressing the highest respect for law.

The anti-Americanist tone and our focus on curing Eastern societies is not towards a market-oriented agenda. It is reality and logic that has taken us there. In Appendix C — About the Author — we include our profile for those curious about the tone of this document.

1.6 The Libre-Halaal Manner-of-Existence of This Document

Not only is this document a Libre-Halaal polyexistential, but it has been produced, published and distributed by pure Libre-Halaal Software and Libre-

Halaal Internet Services. In Appendix E — Manifest and Colophon —, we
provide a summary of how purely Libre-Halaal convivial tools can produce
results that surpass their Proprietary-Haraam competitors.

1.7   You, Your Choices and Your Responsibility

Our primary focus in this book is governance of polyexistentials. Therefore,
both the governed (polyexistentials) and the governor (economic creatures vs
humans) need to be subjects of our analysis. In the context of governance,
throughout this book, in parallel with the model of polyexistence, we draw a
clear and explicit distinction between being an economic creature and being
a human.

In a sense then, you are part of the governance. Governance of polyexistentials
by humans for humanity would be distinct and different from governance of
polyexistentials by economic creatures for economic creatures. We have a
choice. Ownership is a human construct. We are in charge.

As Ursula K. Le Guin puts it:[2]

> Books aren't just commodities; the profit motive is often in con-
> flict with the aims of art. We live in capitalism, its power seems
> inescapable – but then, so did the divine right of kings. Any hu-
> man power can be resisted and changed by human beings. Resis-
> tance and change often begin in art. Very often in our art, the art
> of words.

Americanism as a model for self-toxicated economic creatures existing in an
exploitative industrial context has led to the creation of the artificial-scarcities
and artificial competition oriented environments that are rooted in the Western Intellectual Property Rights regime. Humanism as a model for humans living in societies leads to the natural collaboration-oriented Libre-Halaal polyexistential regime. Americanism vs Humanism lies at the center of the conflict
for governance of manner-of-existence of polyexistentials.

Where do you fit in all of this? Are you a participant? Or are you just an
observer? Are you an "Intellectual Worker"? Do you "own" any patents or
copyright? Are you an economic creature or are you a human? What are
your responsibilities in these regards?

By an "Intellectual Worker", we are referring to those involved in production,
organization and propagation of polyexistentials. Professions related to: software, engineering, teaching, research, arts, journalism, medicine, pharmacy,
plant biology, etc. — all involve production or propagation of polyexistentials.
As a medical doctor, when you prescribe patented medications, you are propagating patents. As a software engineer working for the likes of Microsoft,

when you write code, you are producing copyrighted material. Today, large parts of many societies are intellectual workers. Enlarging of numbers of intellectual workers throughout the world is a clear trend.

It is very convenient for intellectual workers to assume the validity of IP and become accomplices. Status quo is often very profitable for intellectual workers. It may well not be in your economic interest to understand or to advocate that the basic concept of Intellectual Property Rights is invalid.

If you are an intellectual worker, you are a participant. And if you are not just an economic creature, as a human, you have responsibilities.

Your responsibilities start by being willing to understand — even when it may not be in your economic interest to understand.

It could well be the case that you, on your own, cannot do much to impact the situation. But collectively perhaps we can.

Part I

Polyexistence

Chapter 2

Nature of Polyexistentials

Here we categorize our world into two:

1. Monoexistentials

2. Polyexistentials

There are things in nature that exist in singular and there are things that exist in multiples.

That which exists in nature in singular, we call monoexistential. Examples of monoexistentials include: tangible physical objects, a pencil, land, Internet domain names, bandwidth. Chemistry and physics are the realm of monoexistentials.

That which exists in nature in multiples, we call polyexistential. Examples of polyexistentials include: knowledge, ideas, information, the digital entities.

This natural categorization then permits us to revisit the question of ownership of polyexistentials which simply maps to the Western Intellectual Property Rights (IPR) Regime. The topics of Western IPR and ownership and restriction of polyexistentials are one and the same.

Our analysis is from the perspective of the possessed. Traditional Western IPR analysis has always been from the perspective of owner/creator/author. The perspective of the possessed represents societal and human liberties.

This is the first introduction of the concept of polyexistentials which leads to a different way of looking and analyzing Western IPR regime. This duality of analysis based on the perspective of author/owner vs. the perspective of possessor/owned perspectives is similar to time domain analysis vs frequency domain analysis or the dual nature of light as particle or light as wave. They are different bases of analysis for the same thing. Results of correct analysis in each domain are equally valid and incorrect analysis in each domain are equally invalid.

There is ample historic precedence for our approach. In the 13th century Ibn-Sina «بو علی سینا» produced "Daneshnamh Alaei" «دانشنامه علایی», [43], in which he classified his world. Based on those classifications, he then used logic to conclude. Ibn-Sina's work became a basis for much of the Western scholarly beginnings. In a sense, what we are doing here is extension of that type of classification and logic for the digital era.

2.1   Polyexistentials Reference Model

In this chapter we begin to develop a reference model. Let us call it the "Polyexistentials Reference Model." Our goal is to introduce a set of concepts and a terminology that can then be used to evaluate merits of Western Intellectual Property laws and to assist us to understand the proper governance model that is needed for polyexistentials. The polyexistentials reference model is independent and outside of the Western IP traditions. This reference model is based on nature. It reflects science, not beliefs, faith and opinions. This model is independent of societal consensus and is equally valid in the East and the West.

We then put the Western IPR model against the polyexistentials reference model and see that the two are in conflict. When nature and man-made conventions conflict, it is the man-made conventions that are wrong. The polyexistentials reference model permits us to **prove** that Western copyright and patent laws are invalid as any form of property. Such proof is then no longer subject to any dispute because it is rooted in nature and logic – not beliefs and opinions.

We then conclude that the Western IPR model is erroneous. Based on that, we advocate that the Western IPR model should be abolished.

Such analysis needs to start with a clear categorization of monoexistentials, polyexistentials and mixed-existentials.

2.2   Monoexistence, Polyexistence and Mixed-Existence

Examples of monoexistentials are:

Material Monoexistentials: (things, spoon, touchables)

Non-Material Monoexistentials: (spectrum, internet domain name, view)

Rivalry Monoexistentials: [economic term] (Rival Goods: spoon, spectrum)

Non-Rivalry Monoexistentials: [economic term] (Non-Rival Goods: air, fish in the ocean, view) – non-Rivalry goods are often confused with polyexistentials – (e.g., Wikipedia and Jewish analysis have made that mistake).

Public Monoexistentials: [economic term] (Public Goods: roads, national parks)

Examples of polyexistentials are:

Pure Polyexistential: (recording/s, disclosed formula, disclosed idea, text, recipe, algorithm, knowledge)

Digital Polyexistential: (recording/s, formula, idea, text, recipe, software source, software binary)

Polyexistential Content: (mp3, book, cd, video, cookbook, software on a cd)

Polyexistential Service: (Google, By*, Facebook – Polyexistential drived service – monoexistential aspect not dominant)

Examples of mixed-existentials are:

Polyexistential Product: (tivo, viagra, sauce-bechamel, Mixed-Existentials as polyexistential drived products)

We present the concept of "Expressed Formula" as the general form of "primary polyexistential". The digital format presents a "pure polyexistential" form.

Polyexistentials and monoexistentials do mix. Sometimes the dimension of polyexistence is dominant and sometimes the dimension of monoexistence is dominant.

Much of our world is actually a mixture of monoexistentials and polyexistentials – mixed-existentials. In the case of mixed-existentials, the dominant aspect of polyexistence or monoexistence is sometimes clear. In such instances, we will refer to the mixed-existentials based on its dominant aspect.

Consider a book. A traditional book is mixed-existential. The paper and the ink are monoexistentials. But the content of the book (its information) is polyexistential. In the case of a book, clearly the dominant aspect is usually (not always) polyexistential. When you read a book, you are reading its content. A book can easily be digitized, in which case it becomes a pure polyexistential. But, if the book was a rare historic manuscript, then the dominant aspect could have been its monoexistential dimension.

In the case of a given factory generated spoon, the dominant aspect is usually the material spoon which is monoexistential and not polyexistential instructions supplied to the numerically controlled machine that produced that particular spoon.

2.3 Monoexistentials

Monoexistentials are bound by their location. At any given time they exist in one and only one specific location. Material monoexistentials can be moved (transported) at physical speed.

2.3.1 Categories of Monoexistentials

In the context of monoexistence versus polyexistence, all that is material is monoexistential. Some non-materials are also monoexistential.

We categorize monoexistentials in the following 4 categories.

- Nature's Material Monoexistentials

- Man Made Material Monoexistentials

- Nature's Non-Material Monoexistentials

- Man Made Non-Material Monoexistentials

In the following sections we describe each of these.

2.3.1.1 Nature's Material Monoexistentials

Anything material is monoexistential.

Matter is the stuff around us. Atoms and molecules are all composed of matter. Matter is anything that has mass and takes up space.

A substance is matter which has a specific composition and specific properties. Every pure element is a substance. Every pure compound is a substance. For example, iron is an element and hence is also a substance. All substances are monoexistentials.

Chemistry allows us to categorize material monoexistentials into: chemical elements, chemical compounds and organic and inorganic.

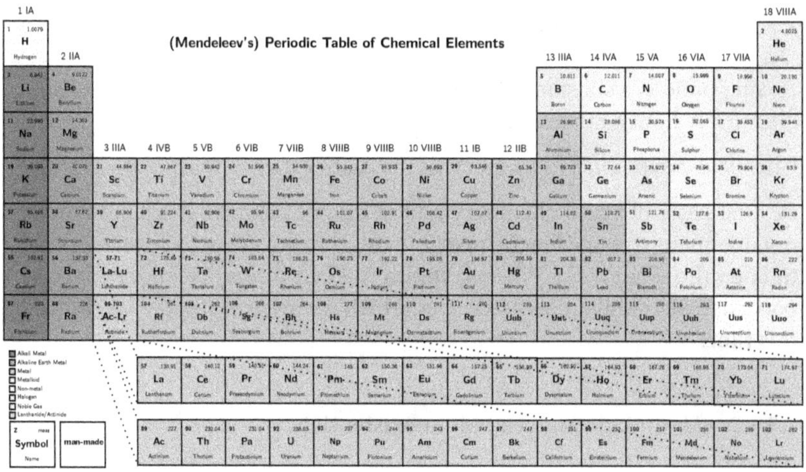

(Mendeleev's) Periodic Table of Chemical Elements

Figure 2.1: Periodic Table of Chemical Elements

2.3.1.1.1 Chemical Elements

Each stable chemical element is a monoexistential. This is illustrated in Figure 2.1.[3]

Our understanding of the periodic table itself is a polyexistential.

Our understanding of the periodic table allowed us to predict the existence of elements in nature prior to having discovered them.

Mendeleev used the patterns in his table to predict the properties of the elements he thought must exist but had yet to be discovered. He left blank spaces in his chart as placeholders to represent those unknown elements. The four predicted elements lighter than the rare-earth elements, eka-boron (Eb, under boron, B, 5), eka-aluminium (Ea or El,[2] under Al, 13), eka-manganese (Em, under Mn, 25), and eka-silicon (Es, under Si, 14), proved to be good predictors of the properties of scandium (Sc, 21), gallium (Ga, 31), technetium (Tc, 43), and germanium (Ge, 32) respectively, each of which fill the spot in the periodic table assigned by Mendeleev.

Monoexistence of those undiscovered elements was independent of us. Our discovery created new polyexistentials. The monoexistential existed before being discovered.

2.3.1.1.2   Chemical Compounds

A compound is a substance formed when two or more chemical elements are chemically bonded together.

Chemical compounds form much of the matter that is around us.

Beyond basic physical chemistry and inorganic chemistry, when it comes to organic chemistry and biochemistry, at this time we are not adequately equipped to open those analysis. When it comes to DNA in particular, there are some polyexistence similar characteristics which we are not prepared to address at this time.

2.3.1.2   Man-Made Material Monoexistentials

A whole lot of the stuff around us is man-made.

Man-made monoexistentials involve a manufacturing process. The manufacturing process is a polyexistential but what gets produced can have a dominant monoexistential characteristic. When mass produced, each is monoexistential.

If the manufacturing process is relatively simple (say cutting of a tree), then we would consider the result of the manufacturing process monoexistential because the polyexistential component of the end result is insignificant.

If the manufacturing process is complex (say building a gun) then we would consider the result of the manufacturing process a mixed-existential. See Section 2.5 — Mixed-Existentials —, for details.

Strictly speaking one could take the position that all man-made material results are mixed-existentials. There are no pure man-made material monoexistentials.

2.3.1.3   Nature's Non-Material Monoexistentials

Beyond matter there are other things in nature we experience. It is easy to recognize that matter is monoexistential. But it is a mistake to equate matter with monoexistentials. Some monoexistentials are not matter.

There have been many attempts in putting all of our experienceable understandings of the universe into one equation. Figure 2.2 is one such attempt.[4] This equation is annotated by attribution of aspects of knowledge to primary contributors.

All such forces and all such phenomena is monoexistential. They are bound by time and place and exist in singular.

Forces such as gravity and electromagnetic forces are bounded by location. So, things such as radio broadcasting and spectrum are monoexistentials.

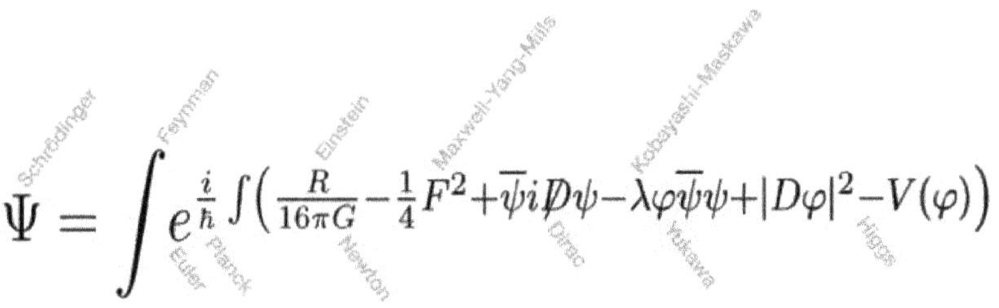
$\Psi = \int e^{\frac{i}{\hbar}\int\left(\frac{R}{16\pi G}-\frac{1}{4}F^2+\bar{\psi}i\not{D}\psi-\lambda\varphi\bar{\psi}\psi+|D\varphi|^2-V(\varphi)\right)}$
Schrödinger
Feynman
Einstein
Maxwell-Yang-Mills
Kobayashi-Maskawa
Euler
Planck
Newton
Dirac
Yukawa
Higgs

Figure 2.2: Unified Physics Equation With Inventors Labels

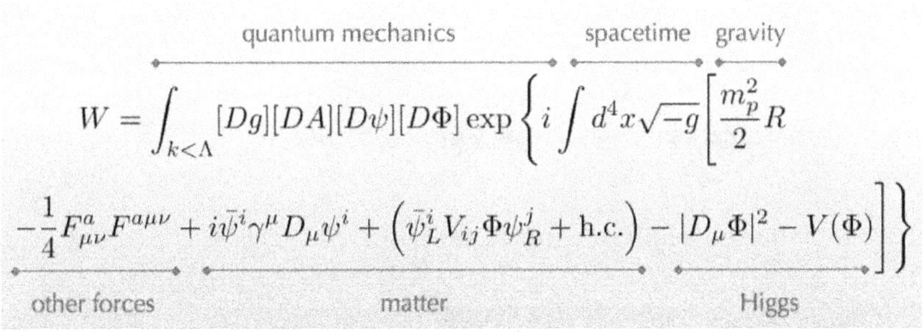
$W = \int_{k<\Lambda} [Dg][DA][D\psi][D\Phi] \exp\left\{ i \int d^4x \sqrt{-g} \left[\frac{m_p^2}{2} R - \frac{1}{4} F^a_{\mu\nu} F^{a\mu\nu} + i\bar{\psi}^i \gamma^\mu D_\mu \psi^i + \left(\bar{\psi}^i_L V_{ij} \Phi \psi^j_R + \text{h.c.} \right) - |D_\mu \Phi|^2 - V(\Phi) \right] \right\}$
quantum mechanics
spacetime
gravity
other forces
matter
Higgs

Figure 2.3: Unified Physics Equation With Subject Matter Labels

Figure 2.3 is another such attempt.[5] This equation is annotated by subject matter labels.

The knowledge of such equations are polyexistentials.

2.3.1.4 Man-Made Non-Material Monoexistentials

Man-made non-material monoexistentials fall into two categories. Man-made physical non-material monoexistentials and man-made social monoexistentials.

Examples of man-made physical non-material monoexistentials are over the air television and radio broadcasts. These all involve energy, electricity, magnetism and waves and they are all bound by time and place.

Social monoexistentials involve creation of uniqueness and scarcities. Social structures and interactions often require uniqueness. As such, humans create non-material monoexistentials. Some examples of man-made non-material monoexistentials are: domain names and national identification numbers such as American social security numbers.

While many copies of an instance of a digital (polyexistential) exist, it is possible to create an association between a specific instance of that digital as its genesis (which we label as original) and its creator (which we label as originator or original assignee). Such associations can then be recorded in public ledgers. This allows for the tracking of all further assignments, so that at any given time it is possible to know the association between the original and the current assignee. This is the concept behind digital assets. An example of digital assets is Non-Fungible Tokens (NFTs). NFTs are typically used to represent digital art, collectibles and gaming items. They are stored on a blockchain and can be bought, sold, and traded on digital marketplaces.

2.3.2   Scarcity of Monoexistentials

Monoexistentials can be scarce or plentiful. Scarcity and plentifulness are relative concepts and depend on the environment and time. It is scarcity of monoexistentials that make them rivalry or non-rivalry.

2.3.2.1   Monoexistentials Rivalry Goods

"Rivalry Goods" is an economic concept.

In economics, a "good" is said to be rivalrous or rival if its consumption by one consumer prevents simultaneous consumption by other consumers.

In general terms, almost all private goods are rivalrous.

A good can be placed along a continuum ranging from rivalrous to non-rivalrous.

2.3.2.2   Monoexistentials Non-Rivalry Goods

"Non-Rivalry Goods" is an economic concept.

Non-rival goods may be consumed by one consumer without preventing simultaneous consumption by others. A good can be placed along a continuum ranging from rivalrous to non-rivalrous.

Many examples of non-rival goods are intangible.

Some broad examples of Non-Rivalry Goods are: air, fish in the ocean, view, roads, national parks, television broadcasts, wind and sunshine.

Non-Rivalry goods are often confused with polyexistentials (e.g., Wikipedia and Jewish IPR analysis make that mistake). Introduction of the concept of polyexistentials fully eliminates this common confusion.

The concept of polyexistentials is a philosophical concept. The concept of Non-Rivalry Goods is an economic term. Basing economics as the primary basis for structuring human laws is wrong. Inclusion of IPR in the US constitution by businessmen (founding fathers of America) is another example of the confusion which amounts to an attempt in creating rivalry goods from polyexistentials – based on artificial scarcity.

Goods that are both non-rival and non-excludable are called "public goods." It is generally accepted by mainstream economists that the market mechanism will under-provide public goods, so these goods have to be produced by other means, including government provision. Polyexistentials are inherently public goods.

The Western IPR regime is the opposite of "Public Goods". In the US constitution we have government provisions creating artificial scarcity against the public good.

2.4 Polyexistentials

We present the concept of "Expressed Formula" as the general form of "primary polyexistential". Each formula forms a class of polyexistentials. Each possession of a formula forms an instance of a polyexistential. The digital format presents a "pure polyexistential" form. Unless expressed a formula is not a polyexistential.

The full emergence of digital technology in the middle of the 20th century has moved humanity into an arena where the dominance of monoexistentials ended. We now live in a world where polyexistentials impact nearly every aspect of life. Restrictions on polyexistentials has been harming nearly every aspect of life.

Pure polyexistentials are kept in some form of memory. Polyexistentials are "remembered", "retrieved" with memory. Memory relates to object permanence. While memory is usually material, polyexistentials are always non-material. Memory can be a human's brain or handwritten ink on a piece of paper, machine produced ink on paper (traditional books), digitized information on hard disk. Memory functions as a minimal substrate and is the container of polyexistentials.

An animal can be the producer of the polyexistential and an animal's memory can be the memory for a polyexistential. But polyexistentials are for the most part the result of human activity. Polyexistentials are often expected to be useful. The value of the polyexistentials comes from the impact that they can have on human condition.

Polyexistentials can be re-instantiated. Two copies of the Expressed Formula are two instances of the same formula. The mechanism that surrounds storage of the pure polyexistentials (e.g.; brain (human's or animal's), paper, digital memory) can facilitate copying, transmission and dissemination of the pure polyexistentials to varying degrees. The digital form in particular makes copying, transmission and dissemination of pure polyexistential extremely practical and as such the digital era has made understanding the nature of polyexistentials most critical.

Unlike monoexistentials, polyexistentials are not bound by location. At any given time, multiple instances of the same polyexistential could be in different places. Unlike monoexistentials, polyexistentials can be transmitted or broadcasted over distances at the maximum theoretical speed of light. The digital form of polyexistentials permits for error-free and exact transmission and error-free and exact copying of polyexistentials. This ability to make exact transmission and exact copying of polyexistentials is a new human capability that occurred in 20th century. It is this new capability that has made the need for a polyexistential reference model more acute.

Expressed Formula is either for human consumption (idea, knowledge, software source code) or for machine consumption (binary software, paper tape for NC machines, Music CDs). When Expressed Formula is for machine consumption, we call it a program or software. Machines consume the binary form of software. Humans produce the source form of software. When the source form is publicly available, it is called open-source software. When the source form is only privately available, it is called closed-source software. With open-source software, the software engineering profession can know what the software does and can inform the public of potential harm. With closed-source software, we simply cannot know exactly what the software does. The Western IPR regime slants availability of software towards being closed-source and proprietary. The Libre-Halaal model slants availability of software towards being open-source and a public asset.

Propagation, replication and copying of polyexistentials is as simple as memory transfer. Restricting propagation of polyexistentials is counter to nature. New existence (instantiations) of polyexistentials have no impact on previous existence. Additional existence of polyexistentials can make them more useful. Monopolistic ownership-oriented restriction of polyexistentials is counter to nature and creates harmful artificial scarcities. Monopolistic ownership-oriented restriction of polyexistentials is morally wrong and should be abolished. Attribution of Expressed Formula to its producer is called for.

For monoexistentials possession and ownership is one-to-one. For polyexistentials, possession is many-to-many and therefore ownership is not possible.

2.4.1   Categories of Polyexistentials

Below we enumerate some categories of polyexistentials:

- Data

- Information

- Content

- Knowledge

- Application of knowledge

- Code – Software

- Execution of code

- Remote execution of code – Internet Services

- Productization of code

Later, we expand on some of these categories of polyexistentials.

2.4.2   Model of Birth of Polyexistentials

The moment of "divulging" is the moment of birth of polyexistentials. In the context of the concept of polyexistential as "expressed formula" we are drawing a distinction between a formula and an expressed formula. Divulging is expression of the formula.

The act of divulging a polyexistential is that of putting the polyexistential in the possession of others without adequate measures for prevention of its further possession.

It is only prior to divulging that there can be ownership.

The following is a simple look at the stages of transformation of polyexistentials.

Producing: Ballet, Acting, Authorship, Human Activity.

Divulging/Capturing: Expressing the formula. Can be by producer or others.

Polyexistential: Moment of birth of polyexistential is the moment of divulging.

Polyexistential Possessors: Any dissemination of the polyexistential may further result in independent and unrelated possessions.

When producers and divulgers are different and have different interest, the polyexistential is born as a "leak."

On August 13, 1813 in a letter to Isaac McPherson, Thomas Jefferson writes:[6]

[...] by an universal law indeed, whatever, whether fixed or move-
able, belongs to all men equally and in common, is the property,
for the moment, of him who occupies it; but when he relinquishes
the occupation the property goes with it. stable ownership is the
gift of social law, and is given late in the progress of society. it
would be curious then if an idea, the fugitive fermentation of an
individual brain, could, of natural right, be claimed in exclusive
and stable property. if nature has made any one thing less sus-
ceptible, than all others, of exclusive property, it is the action of
the thinking power called an Idea; which an individual may exclusively possess as long as he keeps it to himself; but the moment
it is divulged, it forces itself into the possession of every one, and
the receiver cannot dispossess himself of it.

It is the "Model of Birth of Polyexistentials" that Jefferson is trying to communicate.

2.4.3   Model of Evolution of Polyexistentials

Once a polyexistential is born, it can proliferate widely. The analogies of
"river" which flows and "fire" which spreads has been used to highlight these
characteristics of polyexistentials – without explicit recognition of polyexistence.

In that same letter of August 13, 1813 to Isaac McPherson, Thomas Jefferson
writes:

it's peculiar character too is that no one possesses the less, because every other possesses the whole of it. he who receives
an idea from me, receives instruction himself, without lessening
mine; as he who lights his taper at mine, receives light without
darkening me. that ideas should freely spread from one to another over the globe, for the moral and mutual instruction of man,
and improvement of his condition, seems to have been peculiarly
and benevolently designed by nature, when she made them, like
fire, expansible over all space, without lessening their density in
any point; and like the air in which we breathe, move, and have
our physical being, incapable of confinement, or exclusive appropriation. inventions then cannot in nature be a subject of property. society may give an exclusive right to the profits arising
from them as an encouragement to men to pursue ideas which
may produce utility. but this may, or may not be done, according to the will and convenience of the society, without claim or
complaint from any body. accordingly it is a fact, as far as I am

informed, that England was, until we copied her, the only country on earth which ever by a general law, gave a legal right to the
exclusive use of an idea. in some other countries, it is sometimes
done, in a great case, and by a special and personal act. but generally speaking, other nations have thought that these monopolies
produce more embarrassment than advantage to society. and it
may be observed that the nations which refuse monopolies of invention, are as fruitful as England in new and useful devices. [...]

It is the natural model of proliferation of polyexistentials that Jefferson is trying to communicate.

During the process of proliferation, polyexistentials have the potential to evolve.
Ideas can be refined, modified, and subsequently replicated. This inherent
process is so natural that precise individual attribution becomes inadequate.
Instead, blurred and shared collaborative attributions are more reflective of
reality.

The shared characteristic of polyexistentials in terms of both creation and
possession holds great significance. Based on this premise alone, Ayatollah
Motahhari «مطهری» considers polyexistentials as unownable and rejects the
Western Intellectual Property Rights model.

The evolution process of distinct types of polyexistentials varies. Take software, for instance. It is inherently dynamic, and its development relies on
collaboration and accumulation. It is not uncommon for non-proprietary software source code development to involve hundreds of developers, whose contributions and attributions may be unclear in terms of value.

2.4.4   Private and Public Polyexistentials

A polyexistential can be private polyexistential or public polyexistential. Private polyexistential is secret. Public polyexistential is knowledge. Knowledge
is not ownable. Secret is inherently owned – until divulged.

The physical key to most houses is a mixed-existential with a dominant polyexistential characteristic. The house key is usually marked as "do not duplicate."
Because the key should not be shared, it is a *Private Polyexistentials*.

In the context of digital signatures (PKCS), the user's secret key is *Private
Polyexistential* and public key is *Public Polyexistential.*

Confidentiality Agreements are a form of explicit copy restriction which are
fundamentally different from copyright law. Confidentiality Agreements are
in the context of private polyexistentials, Western copyright laws are in the
context of public polyexistentials. We fully reject the Western copyright law
and consider it un-natural. We regard confidentiality agreements as legitimate

and natural – because the parties to Confidentiality Agreements are explicit and the agreement is by choice.

2.4.5   Human Work and Motivations of Authors

Polyexistentials are result of human activity. There are typically two stages of human activity.

- Production of potential polyexistentials. (A Formula)

- Divulging (recording, dissemination, distribution) of the polyexistentials – expressing the formula.

Human activity then results in creation of polyexistentials that are considered desirable or useful by some.

Economic models that can be used to organize human activity towards production and consumption and usage of polyexistentials involve motivating authors towards creation of more and better polyexistentials.

The economic models should be subservient to the nature of polyexistentials. By restricting natural propagation of polyexistentials Western IPR amounts to an unnatural economic model.

The Western IPR regime amounts to extending monoexistential economics to the realm of polyexistentials by restricting polyexistentials and creating artificial scarcity. Any economic model that is based on creation of artificial scarcity is unhealthy, vulnerable and challengable. In the aggregate, the creation of artificial scarcity is counter to general human progress. It creates profits for a few at the cost of loss for many.

Human motivations are not always economically oriented. This is hard to understand for Americanists – economic creatures. Concepts such as Kamikaze, Martyrdom, Libre-Halaal software development and the actions of 911 perpetrators were not economically oriented. Human motivations to produce more and better polyexistentials need not always be economically oriented. The document that you are reading – a polyexistential available to all – is not being produced and distributed for economic motivations.

Because polyexistentials are copy-able, they thrive in a collaborative environment where they go through multiple derived work accumulations. It is unnatural for derived work from public polyexistential to be monopolistically restricted.

Because of possession and ownership differences, economic models for monoexistentials should be fundamentally different. In Chapter 13 – Global Polyexistential Capitalism –, we present the contours of an economic model residing in the Non-Proprietary and For-Profit quadrant.

2.4.6   Polyexistentials as Artificial Rivalry Goods

Polyexistentials are by nature non-rivalry goods.

By nature, one consumption of polyexistentials does not prohibit another consumption. Polyexistentials by nature are "Public Goods".

It is possible to turn polyexistentials into artificial rivalry goods. This amounts to an unnatural and purely economic activity.

That is what the Western IPR regime does. It creates artificial rivalry goods from polyexistentials through government provisions that restrict natural existence of polyexistentials and which violate basic human rights of: "Right to Copy" and "Right to Apply Knowledge"

The Western IPR regime is the opposite of "Public Goods".

The creation of artificial rivalry goods from polyexistentials has major side-effects which put civilization in danger. This often happens when man tries to violate basics of nature.

2.5   Mixed-Existentials

Pure polyexistentials and pure monoexistentials are very often mixed to form mixed-existentials.

With a mixed-existential, a polyexistential is instantiated in the substrata of a monoexistential.

Hence, a mixed-existential has a monoexistential component and a polyexistential component.

We expand on this in the context of an example.

2.5.1   Mixed-Existential Example: A Hypothetical Gun

We are using a hypothetical gun as an example because guns are relatively cohesive products and yet they can be relatively complex to build. Guns have also been the subject of many Western IPR patents.

Consider a gun, a `3d-printer` (or a Numerical Controlled (NC) Machine) and some
`3d-printer-raw-material` (or metal for the NC Machine).

The gun is then the result of running the `gun-program` on the `3d-printer` with the `3d-printer-raw-material`.

The gun is then a mixture of the gun-program (which is a polyexistential) and the 3d-printer-raw-material (which is a monoexistential).

In the context of the gun-program (polyexistentials) component of the gun (mixed-existentials) there are two distinct aspects.

1. The totality of the gun-program.

2. Applying one's knowledge of the gun-building-process to write one's own gun-program.

The Western IPR regime restricts one with copyright law.

The Western IPR regime restricts two with patent law.

This gun (mixed-existential) represents the majority of man-made stuff that is around us (manufactured product). 3d-printer represents the factory equivalent. 3d-printer-raw-material represents the product's raw material. gun-program represents the specific manufacturing steps. Knowledge of gun-building-process represents the knowledge of manufacturing process.

Through controlling the gun-program (polyexistential) and the gun-building-process (polyexistential) the Western IPR regime restricts the totality of gun (mixed-existential) which is the processed 3d-printer-raw-material (monoexistential). Hence, the Western IPR regime can restrict classes of mixed-existentials and limit existing ownership of instances of mixed-existentials.

2.5.2   Scarcity of Mixed-Existentials

Scarcity of mixed-existentials could be based on their monoexistential component or their polyexistential component.

If the polyexistential component of a mixed-existential is not owned or restricted, then scarcity of the mixed-existential is same as its monoexistential component.

If the polyexistential component of a mixed-existential is restricted, then the mixed-existential is more scarce than its monoexistential component.

2.6   Possession of Monoexistentials, Polyexistentials and Mixed-Existentials

Naturally, possession of monoexistentials and possession of polyexistentials work very differently. Possession of monoexistentials is one-to-one. Possession of polyexistentials is many-to-many.

Multi-possessablity is a universal aspect of nature of polyexistentials. Any law that prohibits multi-possessablity is counter to nature.

Here we first analyze possessibility of monoexistentials and possessibility of polyexistentials.

Based on that, we next analyze proper ownership assignments for monoexistentials and polyexistentials.

2.6.1 Natural Law of Mono-possessability of Monoexistentials

Possession is one-to-one for monoexistentials.

At any given time, each possessed has one and only one possessor. A given possession preempts any other possession.

Disassociation of this one-to-one relation can be immediately and tangibly disadvantageous to the possessor.

2.6.2 Natural Law of Multi-possessability of Polyexistentials

Here we enumerate some key attributes relating to possession of polyexistentials.

- It is an inherent characteristic of polyexistentials to be possessed by many at the same time over distance.

- Any new possession of a polyexistential does not impact other possessions of that polyexistential.

- Multi-possessibility is a universal aspect of the nature of polyexistentials. Any law that prohibits multi-possessibility is counter to nature.

- Any agreement not to copy can only be made voluntarily and is only valid among explicitly agreeing parties. This cannot extend to any other person that is not part of the agreement.

- Because copying is a universal human right, no entity is authorized to restrict copying other than in a voluntary bilateral or multilateral manner.

- When a person possesses a polyexistential which is not subject to a voluntary not-to-copy agreement he has the freedom to copy.

2.6.3   Natural Law of Mono-possessability of Mixed-Existentials

Mixed-Existentials are processed monoexistentials and are therefore mono-possessabile.

2.7   Missing From Basic Human Rights: Natural Right to Copy and Apply Knowledge

Multi-Possessibility of polyexistentials is part of nature.

The right to copy and the right to apply knowledge are basic natural human rights.

Yet the Western IPR model amounts to restrictions of these basic natural rights and under Western dominance, these rights are missing from Western declarations.

2.7.1   The Natural Right to Copy

Missing from universal basic human rights is:

> WHEREAS recognition of the inherent dignity and of the equal and inalienable rights of all members of the human family is the foundation of freedom, justice and peace in the world,
> We proclaim
>
> - All human beings have a right to remember.
> - Everyone has the right to share one's memory with others who wish to share. We call this the natural right to copy.
>
> The natural right to remember naturally includes the right to use available tools to better remember without undue restrictions.
> The natural right to share one's memory naturally includes the right to use available tools to disseminate information without undue restrictions.

These universal basic human rights lead to polyexistentials' natural law to be copied, to be shared and to be transmitted without restrictions.

These universal basic human rights are in full conflict with Western Copyright laws.

Western IPR is in conflict with these universal human rights and natural law of polyexistentials.

2.7.2 The Natural Right to Apply Knowledge

Missing from universal basic human rights is:

> WHEREAS recognition of the inherent dignity and of the equal and inalienable rights of all members of the human family is the foundation of freedom, justice and peace in the world,
> We proclaim

> - All human beings have a right to learn.
> - Everyone has the right to apply one's knowledge without restrictions.

These universal basic human rights are in full conflict with Western Patent laws.

Western IPR is in conflict with these universal human rights and natural law of polyexistentials.

2.7.3 The Natural Right to Encrypt

Missing from universal basic human rights is:

> WHEREAS recognition of the inherent dignity and of the equal and inalienable rights of all members of the human family is the foundation of freedom, justice and peace in the world,
> We proclaim

> - All human beings have a right to encrypt relevant polyexistentials (digital entities) that they possess.
> - Everyone has the right to encrypt their communications.

These universal basic human rights are impacted by the Western IPR.

2.8 Ownership of Monoexistentials, Polyexistentials and Mixed-Existentials

Concepts of existence and possession are aspects of nature. Everything that we have presented in this chapter this far has been about analyzing aspects of nature. Such analysis is independent of society, culture and belief systems.

Concept of ownership is man-made and is dependent on society, culture and belief systems. Ownership rules in one society can be quite different from ownership rules in another society.

There are certain general aspects of proper ownership that span societies, cultures and religions. We will start by analyzing basic principles of ownership.

2.8.1   Ownability Criteria

Ownership rules exist to resolve conflicts. Conflicts arise as a result of scarcity and adverse possession. Ownability requires exclusive possessablity. Ownability requires scarcity.

Since ownership is a form of man-made law, it is limited to the territory where the law is applicable.

2.8.1.1   Exclusive Possessablity

Ownership rules are tied directly to possession of what is to be owned.

Tony Honoré puts it this way:

> The right to possess, namely to have exclusive physical control of a thing, or to have such control as the nature of the thing admits, is the foundation on which the whole superstructure of ownership rests.

Monoexistentials and mixed-existentials are mono-possessable. Therefore, monoexistentials and mixed-existentials are ownable.

Polyexistentials are multi-possessable. Therefore, polyexistentials cannot be owned. Western IP laws are about assigning ownership to multi-possessables (polyexistentials), as such Western IP laws are erroneous laws. They are erroneous because multiple possessions of a polyexistential does not lead to any conflict that needs to be resolved and because they are counter to the nature of polyexistentials.

Proper ownership laws should not result in restricting general liberty. Ownership of a monoexistential restricts actions of only those who wish to interact with that particular monoexistential (a unique instance). Ownership of a polyexistential or ownership of the polyexistential component of a mixed-existential put blanket restrictions on liberty of all those who wish to interact with any instance (all instances) of that polyexistential or mixed-existential.

In the context of mixed-existentials and our hypothetical gun example in Section 2.5.1 – Mixed-Existential Example: A Hypothetical Gun –, Western IPR restricts everyone who wanted to make a `hypothetical` gun with their own labor, their own `hypothetical` `3d-printer` and their own `hypothetical` `3d-printer-raw-material`.

Note that assignment of ownership to the polyexistential component of a mixed-existential impacts the ownership of the monoexistential component of the mixed-existential. Hence, assignment of ownership to the polyexistential reduces and muddies monoexistential ownership.

2.8.1.2   Scarcity

Ownership rules exist to resolve conflicts and as such are tied to the scarcity of what is to be owned. Natural scarcity is what gives rise to the need for property rules.

Only naturally scarce entities over which access control is possible are candidates for protection by property rights. Only monoexistentials (and mixed-existentials) are naturally scarce and rivalry. Polyexistentials are naturally non-scarce (naturally abundant) and non-rivalry. For polyexistentials, the only property rights oriented protection possible is that achievable through personal rights, i.e., explicit bilateral or multi-lateral contract.

Bouckaert, correctly notes:

> Natural scarcity is that which follows from the relationship between man and nature. Scarcity is natural when it is possible to conceive of it before any human, institutional, contractual arrangement. Artificial scarcity, on the other hand, is the outcome of such arrangements. Artificial scarcity can hardly serve as a justification for the legal framework that causes that scarcity. Such an argument would be completely circular. On the contrary, artificial scarcity itself needs a justification.

Western IP laws create an artificial, unjustifiable scarcity.

2.8.1.3   Territoriality

Monoexistentials are bounded by territory. At any given time, a monoexistential can only exist in a single place and is subject to a specific legal territory. At any given time, a polyexistential can exist in multiple places and therefore the polyexistential cannot be subject just to a specific legal territory.

In the next section we analyze common aspects of ownership with respect to possession and scarcity of monoexistentials, polyexistentials and mixed-existentials.

In the section after next we map Western IPR to ownership and monopoly and restrictions on polyexistentials and mixed-existentials.

2.8.2   Ownership of Monoexistentials

Since possession of monoexistentials is a one-to-one relationship, assignment of ownership is very simple. The owner is the legitimate possessor. Based on some criteria (e.g., homesteading) an owner is assigned to a monoexistential. Thereafter, only that owner is the legitimate possessor.

Some monoexistentials are scarce (rivalry goods). Some monoexistentials are not scarce (non-rivalry goods). Scarce monoexistentials are subject of proper ownership.

The concepts of theft and stealing are truly clear. Theft is an illegitimate possession. Theft is the denial of possession to the owner.

Judaism, Christianity and Islam all consider stealing a sin.

The economic models that have been built around these are well established and enduring ownership laws are well established. We are devout monoexistential Capitalists – subject to societal health.

2.8.3   Ownership of Polyexistentials

Possession of polyexistentials is many to many. A given polyexistential can have multiple possessors at the same time and in different places.

A new possession of a given polyexistential does not impact previous possessions.

Creation, transfer and dissemination of polyexistentials can be restricted. Such restrictions could be general restrictions or they could be monopolistic restrictions.

In the context of general polyexistential restrictions (in contrast to monopolistic ownership) consider the real situation with porn in Iran. The Iranian society has chosen to prohibit creation, transfer and dissemination of pornographic polyexistentials within its borders. Let's also consider the hypothetical case of some society requiring that the manner-of-existence of any software that is to be made generally available should always be internally transparent (open-source) so that all users could have the option of knowing what the software that they are using is actually doing. Such general polyexistential restrictions are separate from ownership of polyexistentials.

In the context of monopolistic polyexistential restrictions consider the real situation of the Western copyright laws. A given entity is assigned to define its own monopolistic polyexistential restrictions for a given polyexistential. Such monopolistic polyexistential restrictions are sometimes called ownership of polyexistentials. See Section 2.9.2 – Mapping of Copyright to Polyexistentials, for additional details.

Any polyexistential is inherently non-scarce. Assignment of ownership (monopolistic polyexistential restrictions) to a given polyexistential is counter to the nature of polyexistentials.

2.8.4   Ownership of Mixed-Existentials

Possession of mixed-existentials is a one-to-one relationship.

The assignment of ownership to a given mixed-existential based both on its monoexistential component and its polyexistential component results into inherent conflicts. In which case a mixed-existential is to be owned by both by its monoexistential component owner and also by its polyexistential component owner at the same time. In other words, assignment of ownership to the polyexistential component of a mixed-existential causes conflict – as opposed to resolve conflict (which is the purpose of ownership laws).

The Western patent model results in ownership conflicts.

See Section 2.9.4 — Mapping of Patent Law to Polyexistentials, for more information.

2.9   Mapping of Western Intellectual Property Rights to Polyexistentials

Each and every aspect of the Western Intellectual Property Rights directly maps to restriction of one or more category of polyexistential.

The Western IPR is a recent umbrella misnomer to cover the following 4 branches of US and Western laws.

- Copyright

- Patent

- Trademark

- Secrecy (Confidentiality)

Each of these 4 branches are distinct and different.

Copyrights are public restrictions on verbatim (or close to verbatim) copying and partial copying of many types of polyexistentials including books and code (software).

Patents are public restrictions on application of knowledge.

Trademarks are public restrictions on labeling and use of labels.

Secrecy is explicit bilateral or multilateral agreement about restricting copying (transfer, dissemination) of information and other forms of polyexistentials.

As such, it is clear that the subject of the entirety of the Western so-called Intellectual Property Rights are polyexistentials. Therefore, analysis of nature of polyexistentials is analysis of the Western so-called Intellectual Property Rights regime.

Copyright, patent and trademark are monopolistic ownership restriction laws that apply to subjects within a local jurisdiction without explicit agreement from the claimed subjects of that jurisdiction (territory).

Copyright, Patent and Trademark violate people's basic human rights of copying and applying knowledge.

There is no global consensus on the ethical and moral validity or applicability of Copyright, Patent and Trademark. These forms of property law have no basis in any major religion.

There is global general consensus on ethics and morality of property laws related to ownership of monoexistentials. All major religions fully recognize theft as denial of possession to the proper owner.

Any attempt to create parallels between ownership laws of monoexistentials and ownership laws of polyexistentials are a sham. In fact, putting the word "property" inside of the "Intellectual Property Rights" is a huge fraud.

It is the simple perspective of monoexistential vs polyexistential that makes the mistakes and fraud of the Western "Intellectual Property Rights" so very obvious.

2.9.1   About Copyright Laws

Broadly speaking, copyright is a legal concept that grants the creator of an original work exclusive rights to reproduce, distribute, display, perform, or create derivative works based on the original.

Copyright are public restrictions on verbatim (or close to verbatim) copying and partial copying of many types of polyexistentials including, books and code (software).[7]

Copyright believers claim that one of the most visible rights that the author of a work has, is the copyright over his work. In the Western model, almost everything that is published, whether electronically or not, is copyrighted. In general, a work is copyrighted when it is created, and it is not necessary to apply for copyright. Some countries may, however, give extra protection to works that are registered. In any case, when a work is copyrighted, others may not use or redistribute the work without the permission of the author.

Copyrights are considered "territorial rights", which means that they do not extend beyond the territory of a specific jurisdiction. While many aspects of national copyright laws have been standardized through international copyright agreements, copyright laws vary by country.

In the U.S.A., copyright is a right given to authors of "original works," such as books, articles, movies, and computer programs. Copyrights protect only the form or expression of ideas, not the underlying ideas themselves. While a copyright may be registered to obtain legal advantages, a copyright need not be registered to exist. Rather, a copyright comes into existence automatically the moment the work is "fixed" in a "tangible medium of expression," and lasts for the life of the author plus seventy years, or for a total of ninety-five years in cases in which the employer owns the copyright.

2.9.2 Mapping of Copyright to Polyexistentials

Copyright law is a form of monopolistic ownership oriented polyexistential restriction.

Under Western copyright laws, the creator of a given polyexistential (the copyrighted polyexistential) is granted a monopolistic ownership oriented restriction privilege that enables the grantee (copyright holder) to restrict all others within the jurisdiction of copyright law from copying the polyexistential or any mixed-existential whose polyexistential component is the copyrighted polyexistential.

2.9.3 About Patent Law

Broadly speaking, a patent is a form of legal protection granted by a government to an inventor for a limited period of time. It grants the inventor exclusive rights to their invention, which must be novel, non-obvious, and useful. In exchange for this protection, the inventor must publicly disclose the details of their invention.

Patents are monopolistic ownership oriented laws which restrict the public on application of knowledge (polyexistentials). Patents do not restrict knowledge, they restrict the use of knowledge.

A patent is the exclusive right to make, use or sell an invention in a country. In order to get this right, the inventor must apply for a patent at his patent office. Patents provide very powerful legal remedies against infringers, even against infringers who have developed the same invention completely independently.

A patent effectively grants the inventor a limited monopoly on the manufacture, use, or sale of the invention. However, a patent actually only grants to the patentee the right to exclude (i.e., to prevent others from practicing the patented invention); it does not actually grant the patentee the right to use the patented invention.

In the U.S. not every innovation or discovery is patentable. Three categories of subject matter that are unpatentable are: "laws of nature, natural phenomena, and abstract ideas." Reducing abstract ideas to some type of "practical application," i.e., "a useful, concrete and tangible result," is patentable, however. U.S. patents, last from the date of issuance until twenty years from the original filing date of the patent application.

Most countries have a "first-to-file" system for priority. The U.S. system is a "first-to-invent" system.

Under the Western World Trade Organization's (WTO) TRIPS Agreement, patents should be available in WTO member states for any invention, in all fields of technology, provided they are new, involve an inventive step, and are capable of industrial application. Nevertheless, there are variations on what is patentable subject matter from country to country, even among WTO member states. TRIPS also stipulates that the term of protection available should be a minimum of twenty years.

2.9.4   Mapping of Patent Law to Restriction of Mixed-Existentials and Polyexistentials

Western patent law assigns a given entity monopolistic ownership-oriented rights to restrict all others (the public) from incorporating a given polyexistential (subject of the patent) in any mixed-existential whose polyexistential is the subject of the patent.

In the context of patent laws, the restricted polyexistential is the application of knowledge. The patent law then restricts the public from applying their own knowledge to their own monoexistential to become the substrate of mixed-existentials that they desire to create.

In the example of the hypothetical gun, the real owner of the hypothetical raw-material loses its real ownership rights over his/her hypothetical raw-material when he/she wants to mix it with the monopolistic polyexistential restrictions – even when the existence of such restrictions in not known to him/her.

In the case of patents, monopolistic polyexistential restrictions are allowed to interfere with the existing monoexistential real ownership.

Notice that both knowledge and application of knowledge are polyexistentials. It is the application of knowledge as a polyexistential that patents restrict. This restriction in turn impacts the utility of knowledge. These subtleties are often misunderstood.

2.9.5 About Trademark Law

Trademarks are public restrictions on labeling and use of labels.

A trademark is, broadly speaking, any mark that is used for indicating goods or services in commerce. Normally trademarks are words or an image (a logo), although occasionally colors or sounds can also be trademarks. Usually, it is necessary to register the mark with a local trademark office before it gains protection under trademark law. A trademark holder can forbid others from offering particular goods or services using the trademark or a confusingly similar sign. It is also often possible to act against use of the trademark which dilutes its reputation.

2.9.6 Mapping of Trademark Law to Restriction of Polyexistentials

Trademark law amounts to grants of monopolistic polyexistential restrictions on names, symbols, marks and labels.

Trademark laws are not as problematic as copyright and patent. But they are unnecessary. What they set to accomplish can be accomplished by other means – particularly in this day and age.

Kinsella, [33], puts it this way:

> Suppose some Lachmannian changes the name on his failing hamburger chain from LachmannBurgers to Rothbard Burgers, which is already the name of another hamburger chain. I, as a consumer, am hungry for a RothbardBurger. I see one of the fake RothbardBurger joints run by the stealthy Lachmannian, and I buy a burger. Under current law, Rothbard, the "owner" of the RothbardBurgers trademark, can prevent the Lachmannian from using the mark RothbardBurgers to sell burgers because it is "confusingly similar" to his own trademark. That is, it is likely to mislead consumers as to the true source of the goods purchased. The law, then, gives a right to the trademark holder against the trademark infringer.
>
> In my view, it is the consumers whose rights are violated, not the trademark holder's. In the foregoing example, I (the con-

sumer) thought I was buying a RothbardBurger, but instead got a crummy LachmannBurger with its weird kaleidoscopic sauce. I should have a right to sue the Lachmannian for fraud and breach of contract (not to mention intentional infliction of emotional distress and misrepresentation of praxeological truths). However, it is difficult to see how this act of fraud, perpetrated by the Lachmannian on me, violates Rothbard's rights. The Lachmannian's actions do not physically invade Rothbard's property. He does not even convince others to do this; at most, he may be said to convince third parties to take an action within their rights, namely, to buy a burger from the Lachmannian instead of Rothbard.

Western Trademark laws are unnecessary.

2.9.7   About Trade Secret Law (Confidentiality/Secrecy)

A trade secret is a formula, practice, process, design, instrument, pattern, commercial method, or compilation of information not generally known or reasonably ascertainable by others by which a business can obtain an economic advantage over competitors or customers. In some jurisdictions, such secrets are referred to as "confidential information".

Trade secrets are often protected by explicit bilateral or multilateral contracts (agreements) about restricting copying (transfer, dissemination) of information and other forms of polyexistentials.

2.9.8   Mapping of Trade Secret Law to Restriction of Polyexistentials

Trade secret laws are ordinary bilateral or multi-lateral contracts that relate to voluntary restriction of polyexistentials. Trade secrets don't involve grants of monopoly restrictions.

There is nothing wrong with this at all. Applying contract law involves explicit agreed upon restrictions between parties who choose to be restricted.

However, the nature of polyexistentials renders such agreements limited. This will be explained in the following section.

2.9.8.1   Limitations of Contract Law on Polyexistentials

A possessor of a given polyexistential may be able to contractually obligate his purchasers not to copy the polyexistential, but he cannot prevent third parties from publishing and selling the polyexistential, unless some explicit contract prohibits this action.

Third parties, then, who are not parties to the contract and are not in privity with the contractual obligor and obligee, are not bound by the contractual relationship.

For this reason, although a creator of a polyexistential (say an innovator) can use contract law to stop specified individuals from freely using his ideas, it is difficult to use standard contract law to prevent third parties from using ideas they glean from others.

2.10 Fraudulence of the Western IPR Regime

The polyexistential reference model that we presented in this section makes it clear that:

1. The subject of patent, copyright and trademark are polyexistentials.

2. Polyexistentials are multi-possessable and therefore unownable.

3. Polyexistentials are inherently non-scarce and therefore unownable.

4. Polyexistentials are inherently not-territorial and therefore unownable.

Mono-possession and scarcity are fundamental requirements for property and ownership. The underlying subjects of patent, copyright and trademark are polyexistentials. That which is to be patented, copyrighted and trademarked are unownable and therefore cannot be considered property of any sort.

Ownership of polyexistentials in the form of monopolized restriction of polyexistentials and their consideration as any from of property is erroneous and counter to nature.

Therefore, patent, copyright and trademark individually and under the collective label of Intellectual Property are fraudulent. The fraud is that of applying property and ownership to polyexistentials which are inherently not ownable.

Having established that patent, copyright and trademark are not any form of property, we now consider them as societal regulations.

Patent, copyright and trademark in general and patent and copyright in particular are local laws that result in grants of monopoly privileges for restriction of polyexistentials.

These restrictions result in scarcity of polyexistentials which are otherwise inherently non-scarce. Patent, copyright and trademark are local laws that result in the creation of artificial scarcity.

The purpose of patent and copyright laws in creating artificial scarcity is towards the goal of "promoting the progress of science and useful arts" by providing exclusive rights to creators. This amounts to the assumption that by making a particular useful polyexistential scarce it is possible to create an unnatural environment that is superior for creation of more useful polyexistentials. This in turn is based on the assumption that a forced competitive model is superior to the natural collaborative model for progressing science and useful arts. Both of these assumptions were unproven at the time that patent and copyright laws were instituted. We now know that both of these assumptions are wrong.

It is impossible to "prove" a negative – that IP does not have the direct positive economic and innovative effect often claimed. But there is also no conclusive evidence that Western patent and copyright laws have had the direct economic effect often claimed. There is also no conclusive evidence that patent and copyright laws increase incentives for innovation. There are many indications that patent and copyright laws hamper innovation.

2.11   Ramifications of the Western IPR Fraud

After more than 200 years of being in practice in the West, there is no empirical evidence that confirm success of Western IPR in accomplishing its intended goal. However, the harm of Western IPR in the form of restricting natural rights of others is concrete and evident.

Patent and copyright laws are hostile to liberty. Patent and copyright monopolies interfere with the freedom of others. They prevent others to use their own knowledge, their own bodies and their own justly acquired monoexistential properties as they relate to the specific polyexistentials that patent and copyright restrict. Secondary effects of patent and copyright laws result in reduction of autonomy and privacy of individuals.

Grants of patent and copyright monopoly in the wealth maximization utilitarian model end up damaging market foundations. Creation of artificial scarcity for polyexistentials towards mimicking the market process governing monoexistentials results in weakening ownership of monoexistentials. The very same legal foundation from which markets begin.

Patent and copyright laws are in conflict with nature, they do not serve the ideal intended purpose of societal regulations, i.e. to balance rights equitably among conflicting constituencies. On the contrary, they have the effect of enriching a minority of powerful vested interests, to the very great detriment of society at large. The detrimental effects include the obstruction of engineering creativity, a distortion of the competitive business environment, and denial of the benefits thereof to the public.

In practice, natural dynamics of Western IP restrictions result in transfer of power and autonomy away from individuals and to corporations and Corpocracy.

Patent and copyright are laws that have severe harmful ramifications which are not generally understood. In the context of software and internet (digitals – pure polyexistentials), Western patent and copyright laws have directed manner-of-existence of software and internet services to become internally opaque. As a result we don't usually know what the software or internet service that we are using is doing. This has been eroding our autonomy and privacy. That trend is continuing.

Similarly harmful ramifications of patent law are generally misunderstood. Patents restrict the application of knowledge which impact the utility of knowledge. Over time, this can lead to a concentration of specialized skills and competences within a few walled gardens, with long-lasting effects.

The subtleties of patent restrictions are often misunderstood. During the Covid pandemic, Amy Goodman of Democracy Now claimed that if the WTO issued a temporary patent waiver for the Covid patents, more vaccines could be produced quickly. However, this is not how the medical patents environment works. Application of knowledge requires skills, competences, and infrastructures that are built over a long period of time. Prior to the Covid patents, there were already a large number of mRNA related patents, which created a few walled gardens with the necessary skills and competences for applying the knowledge of Covid patents. During the pandemic, although the knowledge of producing the Covid vaccine was publicly available, the skills and competences for applying that knowledge were all concentrated in a few walled gardens. Therefore, the temporary WTO patent waivers could not have a timely impact.

The solution is to permanently abolish the patent system. Without the restrictions on the application of knowledge, the dynamics of creation of walled garden changes and the needed infrastructures and skills and competences become more widespread.

The well-meaning likes of Amy Goodman, should continuously be calling for the abolishment of the patent system and not just for waivers during pandemics — as temporary waivers amount to too little, too late. In preparation for the next pandemic, we should move towards seeing vaccines as public goods.

Notice that knowledge and its application are both polyexistentials. Patents restrict the application of knowledge as a polyexistential, which in turn affects the utility of knowledge. The ramifications and dynamics of patents are different in different fields. Medical, food and agriculture, and software patents all have their own special dynamics. However, the end result in all fields is that of creation of walled gardens and limitation of application of knowledge.

The natural global and universal nature of polyexistentials has required the Western IPR regime pushers to present patent and copyright laws as universal and global. In other words, a local ownership mistake is well on its way to becoming a global ownership mistake.

The Western so-called Intellectual Property Rights regime has put humanity in danger.

Chapter 3

Digital Polyexistence

Sometime in the 20th century humanity entered the digital era. The full emergence of digital technology in late 20th century and early 21st century has moved humanity into an arena where the dominance of monoexistentials ended. We now live in a world where polyexistentials impact nearly every aspect of life.

3.1 Digital: A Practical Pure Form of Polyexistentials

Digital as a practical pure form of polyexistentials permits us to use, apply and produce more potent polyexistentials far more easily.

The aspect of "digital" that we are focusing on in this section is not digital technology or specific digital capabilities. We are concerned with the meaning and ramifications of "being digital". Our focus is the digital as applied math. Digital perspective is that of looking at the world in discrete terms. Analog perspective is that of looking at the world in continuous terms.

Perhaps the most clear moment for our entry into the digital era can be considered the understanding of digital capabilities by the likes of Nyquist and Shannon. We can point to the event that established the discipline of information theory and the digital era, as the publication of Claude E. Shannon's classic paper "A Mathematical Theory of Communication" in July and October of 1948. By then basic physical laws of the digital world were generally understood. Based on that knowledge, we became equipped to convert most information into digital, transfer and broadcast polyexistentials over large distances and store and reproduce exact copies of information.

3.2 Basic Physical Laws of the Digital World

In this section we discuss the basic laws of the digital world that govern data
and information (polyexistentials).

3.2.1 Digitization – Perfect Polyexistential Reconstruction

It is possible to convert some of what we can sense (e.g., sound and images)
into digital form.

Such transformation involves sampling.

Sampling theorem says:

> A signal can be completely reconstructed from its samples
> taken at a sampling frequency F, if it contains no frequencies
> higher than $F/2$:

$$f_{max} < f_{Nyquist} = F/2; \quad \text{i.e.} \quad F > 2f_{max}.$$

This equation is referred to as the Nyquist condition for perfect signal recon-
struction.

The lowest sampling frequency F at which the signal can be sampled without
losing any information must be higher than twice the maximum frequency
contained in the signal; i.e., $F > 2f_{max}$, otherwise aliasing or folding will
occur, and the original signal cannot be perfectly reconstructed.

Human perception is limited, therefore achieving perfect capturing in digital
form is possible.

For example, the maximum frequency that we can hear is 20KHz and sampling at above 40KHz is very feasible. So, audio can reliably become perfect
lossless digital audio which can be digitally encoded, transported, distributed
and encrypted.

3.2.2 Encoding of Information Content

In 1944, Shannon for the first time introduced the qualitative and quantita-
tive model of communication as a statistical process underlying information
theory, opening with the assertion that:

"The fundamental problem of communication is that of reproducing at one
point, either exactly or approximately, a message selected at another point."

With it came the ideas of:

- the information entropy and redundancy of a source, and its relevance through the source coding theorem;

- the mutual information, and the channel capacity of a noisy channel, including the promise of perfect loss-free communication given by the noisy-channel coding theorem;

- the bit—a new way of seeing the most fundamental unit of information.

In information theory, systems are modeled by a transmitter, channel, and receiver. The transmitter produces messages that are sent through the channel. The channel modifies the message in some way. The receiver attempts to infer which message was sent. In this context, entropy is the expected value (average) of the information contained in each message.

Based on the probability mass function of each source symbol to be communicated, the Shannon entropy H, in units of bits (per symbol), is given by equations the like of:

$$H = -\sum_i p_i \log_2 p_i \quad \text{(bits per symbol)}$$

So, at that point the basics of how information can be packed inside of the digital world were understood.

3.2.3 Transmition and Remote Copying of Digitals

Digital entities can be reliably and perfectly transmitted over distances through imperfect and noisy channels. When the received digital entity is stored on the remote end, we have remote copying. We draw a clear distinction between transmission of digital entities and remote copying.

The speed by which digitals/polyexistentials are transferred is very different from the movement of monoexistentials.

Digitals can be transferred at around 70% of the speed of light. The speed of light is about 300,000 kilometers per second or about one billion kilometers per hour. In contrast, the speed of the fastest airplane is about 3500 kilometers per hour. The surface of the earth at the equator moves at a speed of 460 meters per second — or roughly 1,600 kilometers per hour. The speed of transfer of digitals (polyexistentials) can be hundreds of thousand times faster than the speed of movement of monoexistentials.

In information theory, the Shannon—Hartley theorem tells the maximum rate at which information can be transmitted over a communications channel of a specified bandwidth in the presence of noise.

By 1948, theorems and equations such as:

$$\langle v, e_j \rangle, \langle v, x \rangle) \leq 0.5 \log(1 + \text{SNR})$$

expressed our understanding of transmission of digital entities.

We then built on this physical layer understanding and added say six more layers to create the internet.[8] And we now have a global network on which digitals can be transmitted, often without knowing borders.

3.2.4   Cryptography, Encryption and Information Confidentiality

Storage and transfer of digital entities can be in the clear or can be made confidential.

Cryptography, the use of codes and ciphers to protect secrets, began thousands of years ago. Methods of encryption that use pen and paper were used to achieve some secrecy.

By 1949, we had Shannon's theory of perfect secrecy, as a mathematical model for secure communication. It states that if a message is encrypted using a key that is as long as the message itself, then the message is theoretically unbreakable. This is because the key is as long as the message, so it is impossible to determine the key without knowing the message. This means that the only way to decrypt the message is to have the key, which is only known by the sender and receiver.

In parallel with our entry into the digital era, roughly in the 1970s secure cryptography which until then was largely the preserve of governments became a generally available tool. Two events have since brought it squarely into the public domain: the creation of public encryption standards like DES, and the invention of public-key cryptography systems (PKCS). By the 1980s, internationally proposed standards such as X.509 included all necessary knowledge to secure digital information.

Nature believes in encryption. Nature facilitates encryption. It is natural to encrypt.

It is easier to encrypt information than it is to decrypt it.

We have the necessary knowledge to make digital entities private and to make our human communications and human interactions autonomous and private. So, our privacy can be preserved.

3.3 Programming Languages and Manner-of-Existence of Software

One perspective on software and programs is that they are human made set of instructions that computers execute. Another perspective, expressed by Donald Knuth, is: "Programs are meant to be read by humans and only incidentally for computers to execute." Figure 3.1 shows a timeline for the history of high-level-programming languages evolution from 1954 to 2002.[9] Prior to Fortran, most programs were written in Assembly Language. An assembly language is a type of low-level programming language that is intended to communicate directly with a computer's hardware. Unlike machine language, which consists of binary code, assembly languages are designed to be readable by humans. Each computer has its own assembly language and a program written for one computer would not execute on another.[10]

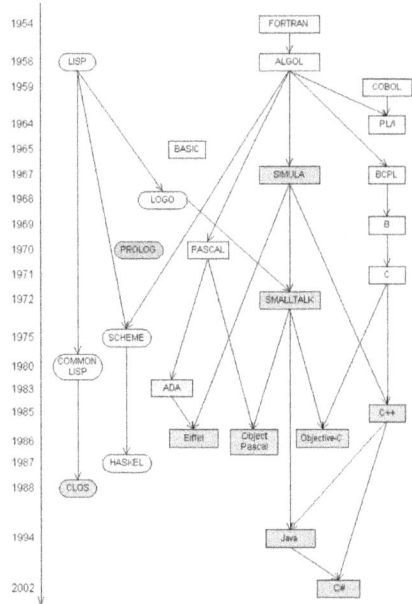

Figure 3.1: A History of Programming Languages

Fortran (FORmula TRANslation) was the first enduring effort in creating a programming language that would produce binaries that would execute on many computers through the use of a Compiler. Fortran was primarily discipline specific. It was for scientific computations.

In our view, the most significant event in the history of programming languages is the publication of the Lisp paper titled: "Recursive functions of symbolic expressions and their computation by machine, Part I" [37] by McCarthy in 1960. Lisp raised programming from the machine domain to human domain. Abstractions of Lisp were no longer computer centric; they were consistent symbols which a programmer could tailor to her subject domain. Various dialects of Lisp continue to be in common use today. In its early days it did not have all the necessary capabilities, but its fundamentals and its structure supported evolution.

Alan Kay has famously described Lisp as the "Maxwell's equations of software". The universality of syntax of Lisp makes it unique in ways that are absent on other programming languages. Lisp is homoiconic. It treats code as data. This means that it is able to create domain specific structures (through a powerful macro system) and become very extensible.

Over the years software engineers have come up with a number of programming languages which emphasize various desired characteristics (efficiency, object orientation, robustness, ease of use, etc.) These have formed families of programming languages which are depicted in Figure 3.1.

From the perspective of polyexistence, what is of significance for us is manner-of-existence of software. Software has two forms, binary and source. The binary form of software is for execution by computers. The source form of software is for use by humans — software engineers.

Based on societal laws, for general use, software can be available in binary form only. Or, software can be available in source form and its resulting binary form. When software is available in source form, based on societal regulations modification and distribution of software can be limited. These types of limitations and permissions define manner-of-existence of software.

Through the Western IPR regime, Microsoft Windows is available in binary form only. This has immense ramifications on health of society which impact the autonomy and privacy of individuals.

Refering to Figure 3.1, we note that in the early days, there were few computers, and most software was custom-developed for in-house applications. At that time, the source code for programs were regarded as part of computer and were available with the computer. It wasn't until the early 1960s that computer programs were being actively marketed by a software industry besides the computer manufacturers. Before widely-marketed software, it was easy to protect by a contract or license agreement any computer program that was being marketed. While a contract restricted what people receiving the software could do with it, particularly limiting their further distribution of the software, it could not bind people who were not parties to the contract. A person finding a computer program on the street could do anything he or she wanted with it. Copyright law, on the other hand, provides protection for a computer program even when no contract exists. [11]

In the United States the Copyright Act of 1976, which became effective on January 1, 1978, made it clear that Congress intended software to be copyrightable.

Also, the number and the types of users of computer programs changed significantly. In the early days of computer programs, both developers and users were typically engineers and scientists. It was not until the early 1980s that Personal Computers (PCs) appeared. In the early days of computer programs it was meaningful to wish for users of software to have the freedom to modify their software. Today, the freedom of users to modify their software is largely theoretical. It is only through the software engineering profession that software in source form has practical significance.

3.4 Manner-of-Existence of Internet Application Services

Internet application services allow for remote execution of software and delivery of the results of that execution. With internet application services, the user has no access to the software that is being executed so the manner-of-existence of software of internet application services is unknown — it is opaque.

To make the manner-of-existence of internet application services tangible, it is necessary to regulate internet application service providers. For example, for some types of internet application services, the service provider may be required to make the service transparent by publishing the entirety of the software of the service and allow users to self-host the service if they wish. Such manner-of-existence of internet application services would then be different from manner-of-existence of unregulated internet application services.

3.5 Human Structures for the Digital World

We can use this natural property to create the laws for a human universe which preserve autonomy and privacy of the individual in the digital era.

Nature permits us to do that. Encryption is in harmony with nature. It is our responsibility to protect our autonomy and privacy.

Julian Assange, put it like this: [12]

> The universe, our physical universe, has that property that makes it possible for an individual or a group of individuals to reliably, automatically, even without knowing, encipher something, so that all the resources and all the political will of the strongest superpower on earth may not decipher it. And the paths of encipherment between people can mesh together to create regions free from the coercive force of the outer state. Free from mass interception. Free from state control.
>
> In this way, people can oppose their will to that of a fully mobilized superpower and win. Encryption is an embodiment of the laws of physics, and it does not listen to the bluster of states, even transnational surveillance dystopias.
>
> It isn't obvious that the world had to work this way. But somehow the universe smiles on encryption.
>
> Cryptography is the ultimate form of non-violent direct action.
>
> Strong cryptography means that corporations, states and corpocracy, even by exercising unlimited violence, cannot violate the

intent of individuals to keep secrets from them.

As corporations and states merge with the internet and the future of our civilization and humanity becomes the future of digital entities and the internet, we must redefine power relationships.

If we do not, the universality of [polyexistentials, digital entities and] the internet will merge global humanity into one giant grid of mass surveillance and mass control.

Our task is to secure autonomy, self-determination and privacy where we can, to hold back the coming dystopia where we cannot, and if all else fails, to accelerate its self-destruction.

The Western IPR regime leads to power dynamics that shape the future of the digital world towards stronger corporations, stronger states and a more dominant corpocracy. Rejecting this regime outside of the West and abolishing it altogether could lead to dynamics that move us towards preservation of autonomy. Nature is on our side, as the physical laws of the digital world permit the preservation of humanity.

Chapter 4

Proper Governance of Polyexistentials: Halaal and Haraam Manner of Polyexistence

Our analysis in the previous chapters makes it clear that polyexistential should not be owned (subjected to monopolistic restrictions). In Chater 2 — Nature of Polyexistentials, we established that monopolistic ownership-oriented restriction of polyexistentials is wrong.

With the question of ownership of polyexistentials aside, we now focus on the question of proper governance of polyexistentials.

Polyexistentials should be regarded as "public goods" and as such deserve legal protection because of negative externalities which arise if polyexistentials are not properly governed.

One of our challenges here is that of terminology. The concepts of "public goods", "commons", "tragedy of the commons", etc. are all rooted in the realm of monoexistentials but have occasionally been extended to polyexistentials without the needed recognitions. Hence, use of the existing terminology for analysis of proper governance of polyexistentials rapidly becomes disorderly.

The types of needed legal protections are dependent on the type of polyexistentials and are to be rooted in the health of professions that correspond to the polyexistential. All of this is to be towards health of society and humanity.

The most basic needed legal protections of polyexistentials is for their manner-of-existence. Because manner-of-existence of polyexistentials is inherently universal and global, it is this most basic aspect of polyexistentials that should eventually be subjected to global governance (legal protections).

Hence, we set the stage for moving towards global definitions and labellings of halaal (ethically correct) manner-of-existence of polyexistentials.

4.1   Manner-of-Existence of Polyexistentials

There are three fundamental aspects to governance of polyexistentials:

- Manner-of-existence of Polyexistentials
- Capabilities (functionality) of Polyexistentials
- Usage of Polyexistentials

By polyexistential capabilities, we mean what the polyexistential is built to accomplish, for good or ill. Examples of software polyexistential built for ill might be spying, tracking, invasion of privacy.

By polyexistential usage, we mean how the polyexistential is used, regardless of its intended purpose. For example, a video player software could be used to watch news or to watch porn.

Regarding the functionality and usage of software and internet services, a sovereign state can and should exercise its own moral sovereignty and define halaal on its own terms. And so, praise and applause to the great firewall of China, and the great firewall of Iran. Clearly, Las Vegas porn should stay in Las Vegas and should remain haraam in Ghom.

Consideration of what constitutes right and wrong regarding capabilities and usage is primarily the domain of ethicists. And these rights and wrongs need not be global in scope.

In contrast to functionality and usage, the definition of halaal manner-of-existence of polyexistentials in general and software and internet services in particular are best dealt with in the global context.

The topic of this section is *manner-of-existence* of polyexistentials. By "manner-of-existence" of polyexistentials we mean everything relating to how the polyexistential exists within society. This includes but is not limited to:

- Is possession of polyexistentials restricted by local law?
- Is possession of polyexistentials restricted by other methods?
- Is the polyexistential assigned to an owner?

- Is the polyexistential attributed to its true author?

- Is copying polyexistentials restricted by local law?

- Is copying polyexistentials restricted by other methods?

- Is use of polyexistentials restricted by local law?

- Is use of the polyexistentials restricted by other methods?

- Are polyexistentials internally transparent?

- Are polyexistentials modifiable and enhanceable?

Global or societal rule governing manner-of-existence polyexistentials can be broadly categorized into the following three:

Monopolistically restricted manner-of-existence of polyexistentials: This is exemplified by the Western IPR Regime.

Lawless Polyexistentials: Some societies allow governance of polyexistentials to be purely based on the nature of polyexistentials and have no laws governing manner-of-existence of polyexistentials.

Halaal manner-of-existence of polyexistentials: Where for each form of polyexistentials a set of requirements for the "right" manner-of-existence of the polyexistential is recognized. By "right" here we really mean "halaal".

4.2   Halaal Polyexistence and Haraam Polyexistence

Therefore, we need to introduce the sensitive and potent word "Halaal."

In a document titled:

> **Introducing Halaal and Haraam into Globish**
> **Based on Moral Philosophy of Abstract Halaal**
> **And Defining The Libre-Halaal Label**
> http://mohsen.1.banan.byname.net/PLPC/120039 — [7]

we precisely define what we mean by "Halaal" and "Haraam".

Section 11 — Introducing Halaal and Haraam Into Globish, is a digest of that document.

Briefly, philosophical halaal is "manifestation" of "moral sensibilities" relevant to a specific topic where "the set of actions" map to "right." And, philosophical haraam is "manifestation" of "moral sensibilities" relevant to a specific topic where "the set of actions" map to "wrong."

4.2.1   Uses of Halaal as a Label

In the context of polyexistence, the primary question is what is the appropriate manner-of-existence for a polyexistential. However, the term "right" is not the most accurate word to describe this concept. Other words such as "moral" or "ethical" may be more appropriate. Unfortunately, English does not have the exact word to describe this concept.

In the context of polyexistence, the primary question then becomes: What is the "right" manner-of-existence of a polyexistential? However, the term "right" is not the most accurate word to describe this concept. Are "moral" or "ethical" better words for the label that we need? Unfortunately, English does not have the exact word to describe this concept.

"Halaal" is the right word for the label that we are looking for.

What makes for Halaal or Haraam manner-of-existence of polyexistentials directly affects and involves professions.

We put forward that for each form of polyexistential, the manner-of-existence that permit professions to safeguard society and humanity are the halaal manner-of-existence for that polyexistential.

4.2.2   The Libre-Halaal Label

As a title for halaal manner-of-existence of polyexistentials we introduce the "Libre-Halaal" label.

In the "Libre-Halaal" label, Libre indicates that:

1. The scope of consideration of Halaal is manner-of-existence of polyexistentials.

2. We reject the Western IPR regime. That the natural right to copy and the natural right to apply knowledge are the basis of our ideology.

In the "Libre-Halaal" label, Halaal indicates that:

1. We are rooted in philosophy, ethics and morality — not just economics.

2. For each form of polyexistential, the manner-of-existence that permit professions to safeguard society and humanity are the halaal manner-of-existence for that polyexistential.

   There are two reasons for this:

   - A: Professions have responsibility to society.

- B: When polyexistentials are man-made tools, the halaalness requirement should empower conviviality of tools.

By conviviality we refer to the concept of "Tools for Conviviality" as Ivan Illich introduced it.

In the document titled:

Introducing Convivial Into Globish
http://mohsen.banan.1.byname.net/PLPC/120037

we introduce the term "Convivial" into Globish.

Briefly, in Illich's words:

> Tools are intrinsic to social relationships. An individual relates himself in action to his society through the use of tools that he actively masters, or by which he is passively acted upon.
>
> To the degree that he masters his tools, he can invest the world with his meaning; to the degree that he is mastered by his tools, the shape of the tool determines his own self-image. Convivial tools are those which give each person who uses them the greatest opportunity to enrich the environment with the fruits of his or her vision. Industrial tools deny this possibility to those who use them and they allow their designers to determine the meaning and expectations of others. Most tools today cannot be used in a convivial fashion.

The dynamics of the Western IPR regime produce industrial tools.

In a sense, tools are extension of human behavior.

The conviviality of tools involves their manner-of-existence, capabilities of the tools, their broader environment and their usage context. The dimension of manner-of-existence of polyexistential tools (their Libre-Halaalness) is necessary but not sufficient to make the tools convivial.

In the context of our own profession (software and internet engineering), we build on this and provide definitional criteria for Libre-Halaal Software and Libre-Halaal Internet Services.

4.3 Ramifications of Manner-of-Existence of Polyexistentials on Professions

We put our finger on Western IPR Regime and label it a central sin of our time because it impacts many professions and many aspects of life. Western IPR regime is the source of much that becomes haraam.

Each profession has a responsibility to society and humanity towards protecting a certain aspect of life. In order to fulfill these responsibilities, professions need and require certain moral understandings and agreements from society.

Here we are using the term "profession" in the way it is understood in the East.

In the West, the concept of a "profession" is largely based on the acquisition of specialized skills and training to perform specialized work for monetary gain. Responsibility to society at large is not a significant factor in this model. Western society is largely, if not entirely, driven by economics, with individuals existing within an exploitative industrial context that only considers money and self-interest. Broader concepts such as society, profession, responsibility, and respect are largely absent from this model.

In the East the word "profession" carries a greater meaning. It includes the Western meaning of a specialized skill set to perform work of value to others. But it also includes an agenda of trust and responsibility. The professional person is entrusted by society to maintain guardianship over an important aspect of life. Based on proper execution of this responsibility, the profession is respected.

The primary author of this essay, attests that: for him as an engineer it is only in Iran that he is called "Mr. Engineer Banan." That has never happened to him in America, Canada, England, France, or anywhere else in his travels throughout the Western world.

So it is in this Eastern sense that we are here speaking of "professional responsibility."

Today, professions know less borders. And these certain moral understandings need to now be certain global moral understandings and agreements from humanity. Such global moral agreements can well take the form of halaal and haraam declarations.

Subject-matter knowledge and application of subject-matter knowledge is at the core of professions. The profession's subject-matter knowledge is often tied to something that is a basic societal need. Farmers and Food, Doctors and Medication, Software-Engineers and Software are some examples. Restriction of knowledge and restriction of application of knowledge through patents amounts to crippling of professions. That crippling of professions in turn makes the manner-of-existence of the thing that the profession is responsible for, a haraam manner-of-existence.

4.3.1 Role of Professions in Declaring Halaal and Haraam

The rapid pace of technology has created an environment where the need for Halaal/Haraam declarations is more urgent.

Because the profession is often closest to the source of the harm and because the profession is sometimes best positioned to understand the harm, the profession should sometimes blow the whistle before the ethicists, theologians, philosophers, sociologists and legislators get to it. Often, by the time that the legislators get to it, it is too late.

The halaal manner-of-existence of what is at the base and core of a profession therefore needs protection. For example:

Halaal Manner of Existence of Medication is fundamental to the profession of Medicine.

Halaal Manner of Existence of Food is fundamental to Farmers.

Halaal Manner of Existence of Knowledge is fundamental to Academics.

Halaal Manner of Existence of Digitals is fundamental to the profession of Software Engineering.

Here we briefly consider, "Medicine and Doctors", "Food and Farmers" and "Knowledge and Academics" as three examples. We then focus on our own profession (Software Engineering) to move towards defining halaal-manner-of-existence of software and internet services.

4.3.1.1 Medication and Doctors

The fact that patented medication in the West restricts healing has ramifications for the profession of medicine in Brazil, in Iran, in China and everywhere. In the Western patent model, the knowledge of the cure for an illness is at hand but applying that knowledge to produce the medication is restricted by the patent regime and the businessman who holds that patent (a monopoly). And the patient has to suffer and perhaps die, unless he is rich enough and he conforms to the Western so-called Intellectual Property Rights economic regime that demands payment to the patent holder who is in control of his cure. In many cases, the cost of a patented medication is almost entirely the cost of the patent. The cost of the ingredients and the cost of making the drug are often a very small fraction of what the patent holder demands for the patent.

In America, the profession of medicine has fully failed society. The American doctor has become quite comfortable being an economic creature existing in an industrial context. The "Patient" has become the "Client". The American "Doctor" has become the "Service Provider". And in that "Client"–"Provider" model, the services and goods being exchanged for money is called "Health Care". In that model, of course there is no place for respect that society owes its doctors.

The nature of the profession of medicine is unique and making it subservient to the economic model damages society and endangers humanity. In America the profession of medicine is fully subservient to economics. This is fully manifest in an exceptionally American phenomena: Prescription Drug Advertising. On national TV, the holder of patents for prescription drugs directly advertises to the public the availability of their goods. The business-man dangles the cure in front of the patient and tells the customer to demand that good from his service provider. That much for the end of the Doctor-Patient relationship! The ugliness of this inhumanity goes straight over the heads of American individualistic economic creatures.

In 2018, the average American was exposed to an estimated 9 advertisements for prescription medications each day. Each of these advertisements were associated with a set of patents, and the prescription medication manufacturers spent more than 6.4 billion dollars in direct to consumer advertising that year.[13]

For a long time, direct-to-consumer television advertising of prescription medication was only legal in United States. Now, as of 2023, it is also legal in Canada, Australia, New Zealand, and the United Kingdom, all of which are part of the Commonwealth.[14] In all other civilized societies, however, it remains illegal.

The profession of medicine and doctors everywhere should do what the American service provider does not comprehend: start with demanding that society, government and moral leaders declare:

Patents for Medications are Haraam.

It is only after the powerful patent based pharmaceutical industry is contained that Medicine may have a chance to be a profession.

4.3.1.2   Food and Farmers

The fact that American agro-business has terminated the American farmer (see Food Inc., [32].) has ramifications for the Brazilian, Iranian and Chinese farmers. A main instrument of American agro-business in terminating the American farmer were patented chemicals and patented organisms. Separate from the American economic model, Brazilian, Iranian and Chinese farmers should put on the table the question of what makes for global halaal agriculture and what makes for global halaal food. Are patented GMOs (Genetically Modified Organisms) haraam? Is patented food haraam?

Farmers everywhere should do what the American farmer failed to do: demand that society, government and moral leaders declare:

Patents for Food are Haraam.

4.3.1.3 Knowledge and Academics

Academics play an important role in the well-being of society. Their role falls into two broad categories:

1. Teaching – dissemination of knowledge

2. Research – discovery and production of knowledge

Teaching prospers when copying is not restricted by the Western copyright regime.

Research prospers when application of knowledge is not restricted by the Western patent regime.

The existence of the patent and copyright debate may be understandable in industry but not in academia. The pursuit of knowledge is in conflict with ownership of knowledge. Being in favor of patents and participating in IPR regime is in conflict with being an academic.

Yet, American Academia loves copyright and patents. There is no shortage of so-called American teachers that compete in producing copyright restricted textbooks and lecture notes. There is no shortage of so-called American researchers that keep restricting application of knowledge with patents.

David Graeber, in "The Utopia of Rules: On Technology, Stupidity, and the Secret Joys of Bureaucracy" [22], captures the evolution of the "Academics" succinctly:

> "There was a time when academia was society's refuge for the eccentric, brilliant, and impractical. No longer. It is now the domain of professional self-marketers. As for the eccentric, brilliant, and impractical: it would seem society now has no place for them at all."

Copyright and patents are tools of self-marketers. The process that has made the American economic model the American societal model has corrupted both teaching and research.

Academics everywhere should do what the American academic has failed to do: demand that society, government and moral leaders declare:

Patents and Copyrighted Information are Haraam.

4.3.1.4   Digitals and Software Engineers

In Section 4.5 — Uses of Halaal and Haraam by Software Engineering we focus on the "Halaal Manner of Existence of Software". There, in addition to providing a formal definition for the halaal manner of existence of software, we put forward a roadmap for realizing it.

Software is a special form of polyexistential that has the most potential for demonstrating the erroneous fundamentals of Western intellectual property rights regime. Software is of essential use. Software is purely digital. Under the halaal manner of existence of software, development of software can be very collaborative and global. Software is inherently cumulative.

The model that we present towards safeguarding the software engineering profession can be mimicked by other professions.

4.4   Manner-of-Existence of Digitals – Halaal and Haraam Digital Existence

By the mid 20th century, one could say that the basic physical laws of the digital world were understood. But what Western technocrats the likes of: Hartley, Nyquist, Landauer, and Shannon; did not pay much attention to is the question of "Halaal manner-of-existence of digital beings".

Without a proper understanding of the halaal manner-of-existence of information, software, and internet services, humanity is doomed. With haraam manner-of-existence, digital beings and the physical laws of the digital world could be used to harm humanity.

For as long as the manner-of-existence of Information, Software and Internet Services are Proprietary-Haraam, there is nothing no one can do.

In the case of digital ecosystems, the Proprietary-Haraam polyexistence model unleashes certain dynamics which result in:

- Amplification of the power of corporation

- Diminishing of role and importance of professions in society

- Loss of the individual's autonomy

- Loss of the individual's privacy

Net cumulative and aggregate result of the above is destruction of civilization and humanity.

With Proprietary-Haraam polyexistence model as the underlying basis of any digital ecosystem, that ecosystem will harm humanity.

Only with Libre-Halaal polyexistence model as the underlying basis for a digital ecosystem, we may have a chance to rescue humanity.

At a minimum we need to properly establish:

- Halaal manner-of-existence of software

- Halaal manner-of-existence of information

- Halaal manner-of-existence of internet services

These writings are towards that.

We happen to be living at a rare inflection point of technological environment. We witnessed the beginning of the information age. It is at this very beginning that our actions and thoughts have most impact. Later the disease will be easier to notice but harder to stop.

4.5 Uses of Halaal and Haraam by Software Engineering Profession

As software engineers, our focus has been one form of polyexistentials and halaal manner-of-existence of that polyexistential. That of: halaal manner-of-existence of software and halaal manner-of-existence of internet services.

Software and internet services are now common, everyday aspects of life, globally. This demands a common set of understandings and agreements regarding their manner-of-existence.

But in contrast to functionality and usage, the definition of halaal manner of existence of software and Internet services is best dealt with in the global context.

4.6 The Manner of Existence of Software

Manner-of-existence of software impacts societal and social structures and autonomy and privacy of the individual.

Today there are two models for the manner-of-existence of software.

1. The Proprietary Software Model.

   This model is exemplified by Microsoft Windows. It is based on a competitive development model and is dominated by American companies.

It is protected and rooted in the corrupt Western so-called Intellectual Property Rights regime, in particular the twin ownership mechanisms of patent and copyright. It is opaque and prevents software users from knowing what their software is doing. Therefore, the user cannot trust the software. Its distribution is controlled by its producer.

2. The Non-Proprietary Software Model.

This model is exemplified by Debian GNU/Linux. It is based on a collaborative development model where software engineers worldwide work collectively to move the software forward. It rejects the corrupt Western so-called Intellectual Property Rights regime of patent and copyright. It is internally transparent and permits the Software Engineering profession to verify the software. Therefore, the user can trust the software. Its distribution is unrestricted.

Though it is not part of popular cultural awareness, there is currently a titanic battle taking place between these two competing ideologies. This is a to-the-death battle, from which there can eventually emerge only a single winner.

The software battle is part of a broader ideological contest, about ownership models for polyexistentials in general (software, but also including literature, music, images, movies, etc.) in the digital era.

The result of this battle has broader ramifications for individuals and society – which impact autonomy, privacy, freedom, and social interaction. The model that any given society chooses for the manner-of-existence of software (and more broadly digital constructs and polyexistentials) impacts social and societal behaviors and shapes what people become.

The scope of usage of the "Libre-Halaal" label is entirety of the domain of polyexistentials. The digital domain as a form of polyexistentials is of particular interest to us as software engineers.

Libre-Halaal Software in particular is of importance in that software is controller of all that is digital. Key attributes of Libre-Halaal Software are that its usage and copying are unrestricted and it is perpetually internally transparent and modifiable.

We want to move towards defining the halaal manner-of-existence of Software and the halaal manner-of-existence of Internet Services and halaal manner-of-existence of Digital Ecosystems. As such we provide our definitions for use of the labels Libre-Halaal for Software, Internet Services and Digital Ecosystems in [3].

The Free Software and Open-Source movements and their combination of the Free and Open-Source software (F/OSS, FOSS) or free/libre/open-source software (FLOSS) have been attempting to address this labeling challenge. Because their philosophical and moral analysis is shallow, all of their labels are problematic in a number of respects.

The FLOSS movement lacks deep recognition of the IPR regime being just Western and does not call for full abolishment of the IPR regime. The FLOSS movement lacks deep recognition of the place of software as a special form of digital polyexistential. The FLOSS movement lacks deep recognition of importance of morality and role of software engineering profession in formulation of definitions and labels.

But since we have the "Libre" label in common, we use the "Libre-Halaal" label when operating in Western authority. Where our rejection of the copyright regime is through FLOSS copyleft public licensing. And where we wish to express common cause with our FLOSS brothers and sisters.

4.6.1   Software and Internet Services as Natural Primary Focus

We are software engineers. Our profession, the Software Engineering profession, is hindered by the Western so-called Intellectual Property Rights (IPR) regime. As engineers instead of being able to freely collaborate, we are enticed to compete. Instead of collectively inventing and innovating towards the good of society, the Western IPR model pushes us to individually reinvent.

Software and Internet Services have become an integral and critical component of societal functioning, and the consequences for humanity are enormous. Of fundamental importance in this regard is what we will call the *manner of existence* of software.

We present the Halaal *manner of existence* of software and Internet services in: "Defining Halaal Software and Defining Halaal Internet Services" [3] – available on-line at:
http://www.bycontent.net/PLPC/120041 . The Western IPR regime adversely impacts our ability to produce Libre-Halaal software and Internet services.

It is for this reason that we are writing this paper. While polyexistentials are far broader than software, we emphasis software in this presentation for two reasons. First, we are software engineers. Second, the collaborative and cumulative and usage orientation of software (as a polyexistential) permits us to demonstrate the natural power of polyexistentials in contrast to Western so-called Intellectual Property Rights (IPR) regime. This of course is demonstrated in success of the Libre-Halaal GNU/Linux in contrast to the proprietary MS Windows.

4.6.2   Libre-Halaal Software — Halaal Manner-of-Existence of Software

So, with the stakes that high, what is the halaal ("right") manner-of-existence of software?

We put forward that for each form of polyexistential, the manner-of-existence that permit Professions to safeguard society and humanity are the halaal manner-of-existence for that polyexistential.

The following criteria are required for halaal manner-of-existence of software, to allow the Software Engineering profession to fulfill its responsibility to society and humanity.

We use the label "Libre-Halaal Software" to convey "Halaal Manner of Existence of Software".

Software is Libre-Halaal Software if it has all of the following attributes:

- **Halaal Criterion 1 — Unrestricted Multi-possessablity.** There are no restrictions in possessing the software by anyone who wishes to possess it — There are no restrictions in copying and redistributing copies.

- **Halaal Criterion 2 — Unrestricted Usage.** There are no restrictions for using (running) the software.

- **Halaal Criterion 3 — Internal Transparency.** The source code of the software is available to all software engineers to examine the software and study how it works. Unless software is internally transparent, the software cannot be trusted.

- **Halaal Criterion 4 — Modifiability.** Software engineers must be able to modify the software, re-install the modified version and use the modified version without restrictions. The available source code of the software permits software engineers to change and enhance it.

- **Halaal Criterion 5 — Proper Authorship Attribution.** The authorship of the software is not misrepresented.

Additionally, the software engineering profession requires from software engineers that the perpetuity of all of the above be applied to all public modifications of the software. In other words, any modification or enhancement that is generally offered as software or service shall also have all of the above attributes. Perpetual internal transparency is a key requirement.

In a document titled:

> **Definition Of The Libre-Halaal Software Label**
> **Defining Halaal Manner-Of-Existence Of Software**
> http://www.by-star.net/PLPC/180044

> http://www.halaalsoftware.org

we provide definitional criteria for Libre-Halaal manner-of-existence of software.

Based on that definition, the manner-of-existence of proprietary software such as Microsoft Windows is not halaal.

Based on that definition, the manner-of-existence of libre software such as Debian GNU/Linux is halaal.

4.6.3 Libre-Halaal Internet Application Services: Halaal Manner-of-Existence of Internet Services

In a document titled:

Definition Of The Libre-Halaal Internet Services Label
Defining Halaal Manner-Of-Existence Of Internet Application
Services
A non-proprietary model for delivery of Internet services
http://www.by-star.net/PLPC/180045

http://www.libreservices.org

we provide definitional criteria for halaal manner-of-existence of internet application services.

The following criteria are required for Internet Services to be considered Halaal, and so to allow the Software Engineering and Internet Engineering professions to fulfill their responsibility to society and humanity:

1. Every software component included in the service must be Libre-Halaal software.

2. The software for the entire service must be Libre-Halaal software. The entire primary source code for the entire service must be available to all software engineers, so that the entire service can be reproduced.

3. All protocols used by the service must be transparent and unrestricted.

Based on the above definition, manner-of-existence of Facebook, Google, Yahoo, MSN and many others are not halaal. Manner-of-existence of these internet application services is haraam.

It accomplishes little to label something as haraam, when a halaal alternative is not offered.

See Chapter 16 — The Libre-Halaal ByStar Digital Ecosystem, for details.

4.7 Overview of Digital Ecosystems

Our use of the term "Digital Ecosystem" is very broad and includes inter-related software, systems, services, content and societal frameworks including: philosophical, moral, societal, social, economic, business and legal practices — that shape it and are shaped by it.

Here we describe digital ecosystems in four parts.

Ideology — Societal Frameworks:
Digital Ecosystems exist within societal frameworks. Digital Ecosystems are shaped by societal norms and Digital Ecosystems shape people and society.

A very important aspect of societal framework which has immediate impact on shape of digital ecosystems are laws and models governing polyexistentials. Societal Agreements governing all that is digital (and more broadly polyexistentials) in the West is based on the IP regime. This has shaped the entirety of Western Digital Ecosystems.

Software and Usage Environments:
Software is the digital form that controls other digital forms. As such, it is the foundation of digital ecosystems.

Internet Services:
Internet Services are a distinct part of digital ecosystems, as they consist of *software execution accessed through a network*, rather than being in the immediate possession of the user.

Information and Content:
A primary purpose of digital ecosystems is to facilitate production and communication of information and content. In addition to the content itself, facilities and rules governing production, publication and access to content are a distinct part of digital ecosystems.

4.8 Manner-of-Existence of Digital Ecosystems

We recognize two basic manner-of-existence of digital ecosystems.

Proprietary Digital Ecosystems: Governed by laws and models for polyexistentials which are:

- rooted in the Western patent regime
- rooted in the Western copyright regime
- internally opaque

Libre-Halaal Digital Ecosystems: Governed by laws and models for polyexistentials which:

- consider knowledge as unownable and fully rejects the Western patent regime
- consider the right to copy a basic human right and fully rejects the Western copyright regime
- are required to be internally transparent

We expand on this in Part IV — Libre-Halaal ByStar Digital Ecosystem.

Part II

The Mistake: Myths and Realities of the Western IPR Regime

Chapter 5

Dynamics of the Western IPR Mistake

There are many things for which right and wrong are very real. When right and wrong can be reached based on logic, they are absolute. Such rights and wrongs are not a matter of opinion, personal, societal or global beliefs.

It is not unusual for global beliefs to be wrong and counter to basic logic. By "global beliefs" or "societal beliefs" we mean spheres of consensus that are global or societal in scope. People are often born into such wrong global/societal beliefs and ordinary people are often unable to follow correct basic logic when they have been brainwashed from birth.

5.1   About Dynamics of Unrecognized Global Mistakes

In due course some unrecognized societal mistakes can be recognized and understood. When looked at in historic terms, they become obvious.

Such historic global and societal mistakes include:

- Earth is center of universe

- Earth is flat

- American ownership rules for African humans

But when we are in the middle of contemporary societal global mistakes, clear vision is often hard to come by. So, there are some global and societal mistakes that remain unrecognized by masses and societies.

Unrecognized global mistakes in due course become faith.

As Hellman puts it:

> Faith-based reasoning led the Inquisition to hold fast to a complex and convoluted Ptolemaic model of the universe rather than accept the simpler explanation proffered by Copernicus.

Faith is not necessarily true, no matter how firmly held.

Some examples of such contemporary global and societal fundamental mistakes include:

- Western Intellectual Property Rights is legitimate and universal

- Global warming is not real or is not serious

By "global fundamental mistakes" we mean the types of mistakes that put all of us in danger. The Western Intellectual Property Rights Regime is one such example.

Some global mistakes are not very harmful – they result in sub-optimum societal/global human environments. "Ill Conception of The Metric System" and "Backwards-ness Of Internet Domain Notation" are some such examples.

Contemporary global mistakes often result in entrenched vested interests. Such deep economic interests often prevent people's willingness to hear and follow basic logic.

In all cases, it is good to follow basic logic and understand these basic global mistakes.

Those for whom recognition of falsehood of such global/societal beliefs is difficult, can profit from remembering the history of American enslavement of Africans. We expand on this in Section 7 — Western Slavery and the Western IPR Regime.

5.2 Historical Genesis of Intellectual Property

Intellectual property originated in grants of monopoly from the state and received its legitimacy from that source, the public debate over its legitimacy shifted radically in the late Eighteenth Century.

The history of Copyright, Patent and Trademark predates by a great deal the collective misnomer of Intellectual Property. See Section 6.2 — So-Called Western IPR: A Rigged Misnomer —, for more information.

Here we provide a summary of the history of Copyright, Patent, Trademark and IP.[15]

5.2.1   History of Trademark Law

In Section 2.9.5 — About Trademark Law —, we provided an overview of trademark law.

The history of trademarks is generally very Western.

In trademark treatises it is usually reported that blacksmiths who made swords in the Roman Empire are thought of as being the first users of trademarks. The first trademark legislation was passed by the Parliament of England under the reign of King Henry III in 1266, which required all bakers to use a distinctive mark for the bread they sold.

The first modern trademark laws emerged in the late 19th century. In France the first comprehensive trademark system in the world was passed into law in 1857. England and The U.S. followed suite shortly after that.

5.2.2   History of Copyright Law

In Section 2.9.1 — About Copyright Laws —, we provide an overview of the Western copyright system.[16]

The history of copyright law is generally very Western.

Copyright came about with the invention of the printing press and with wider literacy. As a legal concept, its origins in Britain were a reaction to printers' monopolies at the beginning of the 18th century. The English Parliament was concerned about the unregulated copying of books and passed the Licensing of the Press Act 1662, which established a register of licensed books and required a copy to be deposited with the Stationers' Company, essentially continuing the licensing of material that had long been in effect.

In the United States Article I, section 8, clause 8 of the Constitution (1787) authorized copyright legislation.

The 1886 Berne Convention first established recognition of copyrights among sovereign nations, rather than merely bilaterally. Under the Berne Convention, copyrights for creative works do not have to be asserted or declared, as they are automatically in force at creation: an author need not "register" or "apply for" a copyright in countries adhering to the Berne Convention. As soon as a work is "fixed", that is, written or recorded on some physical medium, its author is automatically entitled to all copyrights in the work, and to any derivative works unless and until the author explicitly disclaims them, or until the copyright expires. The Berne Convention also resulted in foreign authors being treated equivalently to domestic authors, in any country signed onto the Convention. The UK signed the Berne Convention in 1887 but did not implement large parts of it until 100 years later with the passage of the Copyright, Designs and Patents Act of 1988. Specially, for educational and scientific research purposes, the Berne Convention provides the developing countries issue compulsory licenses for the translation or reproduction of copyrighted works within the limits prescribed by the Convention. This was a special provision that had been added at the time of 1971 revision of the Convention, because of the strong demands of the developing countries. The United States did not sign the Berne Convention until 1989.

Iran is a non-signatory to WTO (Western Trade Organization) copyright laws.

5.2.3   History of Patent Law

In Section 2.9.3 — About Patent Law —, we provided an overview of the patent system.[17]

History of patent law is generally very Western.

Patents were systematically granted in Venice as of 1450, where they issued a decree by which new and inventive devices had to be communicated to the Republic in order to obtain legal protection against potential infringers. The period of protection was 10 years. As Venetians emigrated, they sought similar patent protection in their new homes. This led to the diffusion of patent systems to other countries.

By the 16th century, the English Crown would habitually abuse the granting of letters patent for monopolies. After public outcry, King James I of England (VI of Scotland) was forced to revoke all existing monopolies and declare that they were only to be used for "projects of new invention". This was incorporated into the Statute of Monopolies (1624) in which Parliament restricted the Crown's power explicitly so that the King could only issue letters patent to the inventors or introducers of original inventions for a fixed number of years. The Statute became the foundation for later developments in patent law in England and elsewhere. James Puckle's 1718 early autocannon was one of the first inventions required to provide a specification for a patent.

Important developments in patent law emerged during the 18th century through a slow process of judicial interpretation of the law. During the reign of Queen Anne, patent applications were required to supply a complete specification of the principles of operation of the invention for public access. Legal battles around the 1796 patent taken out by James Watt for his steam engine, established the principles that patents could be issued for improvements of an already existing machine and that ideas or principles without specific practical application could also legally be patented. Influenced by the philosophy of John Locke, the granting of patents began to be viewed as a form of intellectual property right, rather than simply the obtaining of economic privilege.

The English legal system became the foundation for patent law in countries with a common law heritage, including the United States, New Zealand and Australia. In the Thirteen Colonies, inventors could obtain patents through petition to a given colony's legislature. In 1641, Samuel Winslow was granted the first patent in North America by the Massachusetts General Court for a new process for making salt.

The modern French patent system was created during the Revolution in 1791. Patents were granted without examination since inventor's right was considered as a natural one.

In the United States Article I, section 8, clause 8 of the Constitution (1787) authorized patent legislation. The first Patent Act of the U.S. Congress was passed on April 10, 1790, titled "An Act to promote the progress of useful Arts". The first patent was granted on July 31, 1790.

5.2.4 History of Intellectual Property

The term Intellectual Property is an afterthought. The history of trademark, copyright and patent were well established before the very first introduction of the term "Intellectual Property".

The first known use of the term intellectual property dates to 1769, when a piece published in the Monthly Review used the phrase. The first clear example of modern usage goes back as early as 1808, when it was used as a heading title in a collection of essays.

The German equivalent was used with the founding of the North German Confederation whose constitution granted legislative power over the protection of intellectual property (Schutz des geistigen Eigentums) to the confederation. When the administrative secretariats established by the Paris Convention (1883) and the Berne Convention (1886) merged in 1893, they located in Berne, and also adopted the term intellectual property in their new combined title, the United International Bureaux for the Protection of Intellectual Property.

The organization subsequently relocated to Geneva in 1960, and was succeeded in 1967 with the establishment of the World Intellectual Property Organization (WIPO) by treaty as an agency of the United Nations. According to Lemley, it was only at this point that the term really began to be used in the United States (which had not been a party to the Berne Convention), and it did not enter popular usage there until passage of the Bayh-Dole Act in 1980.

5.3   Multi-Disciplinary Discrediting of the Western So-Called IPR Regime

Westerners adopted the IPR regime without much understanding and logic.

To take away those most basic natural human rights of "Applying Knowledge" and "Copying" demands solid logic and proof on the side of those who want to take away these rights. Those who believe in the Western IPR regime need to convince those who reject it. Not the other way around.

In the last 200 years, a colossal mistake has been made by Westerners. Ownership and capitalism were extended into the realm of polyexistentials, creating Intellectual Property Rights.

Many generations have been born into this mistake and now the mistake has become default truth for many Westerners.

So, to deal with Western IPR in the West we need more than logic. Below, we address some of the entrenched fallacies associated with the Western IPR regime.

To those that are not born into the IPR mistake or who can think for themselves, the simple logic of "Nature of Polyexistentials" that we presented above would be more than sufficient. The conclusion is obvious and simple: The Western IPR Regime should be abolished.

But it is naive to imagine that sound logic and correct philosophy can be the basis for abolishment of the Western IPR Regime.

This is because of several reasons, including:

- The Intellectual Property Rights regime is now an integral part of Western cultures. Even after it becomes obvious that the Western Intellectual Property Rights regime is corrupt, economic interests will keep it in place. In many ways this parallels the history of Slavery in America.

- Western societies are primarily economically driven. Correct philosophy, harmony with nature, logic, and Halaal and Haraam; generally (if not always) remain fringe concepts for Westerners.

- The Proprietary model is fully entrenched. And the course for using the proprietary model for internal and external exploitation is already fully charted.

As with any other social structure wherein the benefactors are in power, and the victims see the structure as normal, it is very difficult to change the status quo. Those promoting the Intellectual Property Rights regime have a vested interest in maintaining the system and will do so at all costs. The abolishment of the Western IPR regime must begin with bringing a level of understanding of the exploitation and conflict with nature of the IPR to those being disadvantaged by the system.

Calling for abolishment of the Western IPR regime is reasonable. But in practical terms we should recognize that it won't be abolished anytime soon. So, in parallel for that call we should work on cures to this Western disease.

Our exposition in this part is polemic. This is not a debate. Nature is against the Western IPR regime and we are on the side of nature.

Chapter 6

Debunking the Myth of Western IPR Regime

The Western IPR regime has been in place for over 200 years and has produced a set of economical and societal results.

From a human perspective, these results are generally very negative. But Westerners portray the results as very positive. They point to their exploitative economic success as proof and require that their model be considered universal. They do so by propagating various myths.

In this section we identify such myths and debunk each of them with logic and truth.

To view the Western IPR Regime as any sort of authoritative law or enduring order is unreasonable. It has been in practice for a very short period of time (about 200 years) and the scope of its territoriality is primarily the Western world.

While the self-congratulating Westerners may consider their IPR Regime as some basis, the rest of the world more reasonably views the Western IPR Regime as an experiment. The results of the past 200 years of this experiment have made it clear that despite the hype, it is a failed experiment.

6.1 Westerners Own Recognition of Fallacies of the Western IPR Regime

Some in the West have recognized the fraudulence of Intellectual Property Rights and have pointed out some of the problems.

The Western IPR debate amounts to an individual's rightful claim to the product of his labor vs undeserved monopoly privilege granted by government. In the Western perspective, two important principles are to be balanced as legal protection of intangible works butts up against free expression and exchange of ideas.

Our Eastern perspective is simple and crisp. The "Polyexistentials Reference Model" that we developed in Chapter 2 — Nature of Polyexistentials, permits us to prove that polyexistentials are unownable (through grants of monopoly privileges) and therefore the Western IPR regime should be abolished. There is no need to debate anything.

Some notable examples of Western cases against Western IPR are:

What is Property? by Boudewijn Bouckaert, [15].

Bouckaert correctly points out that scarcity is a fundamental requirement for property rules. The subjects of IP (polyexistentials) are inherently not scarce and therefore IP is un-needed and invalid.

Bouckaert also debunks various arguments that have been put forward to justify IP.

We summarize and include some of his thoughts and his text in this chapter.

Are Patents and Copyrights Morally Justified? by Tom G. Palmer, [39].
— The Philosophy of Property Rights and Ideal Objects

Palmer introduces the concept of "Ideal Objects" in the context of IP analysis. Ideal Objects are similar or perhaps equivalent to pure Polyexistentials. He refers to Monoexistentials as Tangible Objects, Material Objects and Physical Objects.

Palmer, however, fails to fully build the complete model that is needed to surround polyexistentials and does not focus on multi-possessibility and un-territoriality. He also does not acknowledge that the scope of monoexistentials is broader than that of matter. We had fully developed the polyexistential reference model presented in Chapter 2 — Nature of Polyexistentials —, prior to reading [39]. Our model of polyexistentials is independent of Palmer's ideal objects.

Equipped with the concept of "Ideal Objects", Palmer is able to easily and comfortably debunk various arguments that have been put forward to justify IP.

We summarize and include some of his thoughts and his text in this chapter.

Against Intellectual Property by Brian Martin, [36].[18]

> Martin also correctly debunks various arguments that have been put forward to justify IP. We also use some of his thoughts and text.

Against Intellectual Property by N. Stephan Kinsell, [33].[19]

> Kinsell builds on Bouckaert's ideas [15] with respect to scarcity and on Palmer's concepts [39] with respect to "Ideal Objects". For the most part he covers the same thoughts that Bouckaert and Palmer had covered but sometimes more clearly.
>
> We summarize and include some of his thoughts and his text in this chapter as well.

Does intellectual property lead to economic growth?
Insights from a novel IP dataset — by E. Richard Gold, Jean-Frédéric Morin, Erica Shadeed, [17].

> Gold et al. point out that causality of IP on economic growth remains indeterminable and the placebo effects of IP are to be taken seriously.
>
> We summarize and include some of their thoughts and their text in this chapter

Against Intellectual Monopoly by Michele Boldrin and David K. Levine, [14].

> Boldrin and Levine examine both the evidence and the theory of IP. They conclude that creators' property rights can be well protected in the absence of intellectual property, and that IP does not increase either innovation or creation. Intellectual property is an unnecessary evil.

These Western analysis have a number of things in common. They all amount to symptoms analysis and do not go to the root of the problem. They do not explicitly and strongly call for the abolition of IPR. They also do not move towards the right solutions — Halaalness of manner-of-existence of polyexistentials. And in the current Western environment where very powerful entities are in control of economy, legislation and Western society, such opposition amounts to academic naggings. In this document, we want to do more than that.

Nevertheless, it is clear that even in the West there is a large awareness of the notion that the IPR regime is a grave mistake. Many Westerners have reached the correct conclusion that: there is no such thing as a right to own intangible ideas and, therefore, the whole regime of grants of monopoly is an unjust and outdated political construct that should be tossed aside.

Yet these Western awarenesses are not profound. As Demings puts it:

> "A system cannot understand itself. The transformation requires a view from outside."

The profound understanding of the fraudulence of the Western IPR regime needed to come from Easterners. The Polyexistentials Reference Model represents the Eastern perspective of focusing on society (through the possessed) and not the individual (through the artificial owner).

In the next sections, we point to various failures of the IPR experiment and focus on the aspects of the IPR regime that impact our profession — software and internet engineering.

6.2   So-Called Western Intellectual Property Rights: A Rigged Misnomer

The term Intellectual Property Rights is a fashionable collective label for patents, copyright, and trademarks. These are all branches of Western law for restricting polyexistentials.

The widespread use of the term "intellectual property" became "chic" following the 1967 founding of the World "Intellectual Property" Organization (WIPO). The "W" in WIPO is fraudulent. It really stands for "West" and WIPO really represents the pushers of copyrights, patents, and trademarks.

In Section 5.2 — Historical Genesis of Intellectual Property —, we mentioned that history of copyright, patents and trademarks predates the notion of intellectual property. The notion of intellectual property was added later towards a particular agenda.

Palmer in [39] notes:

> Intellectual property originated in grants of monopoly from the state and received its legitimacy from that source. the public debate over its legitimacy shifted radically in the late Eighteenth Century. As Fritz Machlup and Edith Penrose note, "those who started using the word property in connection with inventions had a very definite purpose in mind: they wanted to substitute a word with a respectable connotation, 'property,' for a word that had an unpleasant ring, 'privilege.'"

The switch and shift in the popular conception of patents and copyrights to property of any sort is a trick.

Let's take IPR letter by letter and see how the whole thing is a rigged misnomer.

6.2.1   Intellectual

The general term "Intellectual Property Rights" is meant to appear chic, fashionable and wholesome. The word "Intellectual" is part of that scheme.

Copyright law applies as much to an academic paper as it applies to a pornographic movie.

Now, what is that is Intellectual about porn?

The Copyright aspect of IPR is with regard to act of copying not about what is being copied.

Intellectual Property Rights regime pushers think that by calling it "Intellectual" it becomes Intellectual.

The term "Intellectual" in IPR has been put there to facilitate the usual Western marketing agenda.

6.2.2   Property

The word "Property" in "Intellectual Property Rights" has been deliberately put there to mislead.

Western copyright, patent, and trademark laws are restrictive machineries only applicable to polyexistentials. Property only has a meaningful context with monoexistentials.

The term "property" suggests considerations of copyright, patents and trademarks similar to how we think of property rights for monoexistentials (material things). Anyone familiar with both physical property law and copyright law, patent law, and trademark law knows that the two models are not philosophically compatible.

The term "Property" in IPR has been put there to facilitate the usual Western marketing agenda.

6.2.3   Rights

The term "Rights" in IPR has been deliberately put there as an attempt to legitimize what is inherently illegitimate.

Western copyright, patent and trademark laws from their very beginning were at most an experiment. They amount to restricting natural rights of many in favor of artificial rights of few.

When the Rights that are granted conflict with nature, the whole thing is a sham.

6.2.4   Recognize IPR as a Misnomer — Consider Alternative Names

Since Intellectual Property Rights is a rigged misnomer towards a particular agenda, we should reject it — not use it.

But by now the Intellectual Property Rights (IPR) label has become pervasive.

Throughout this document and elsewhere, we usually qualify it with Western as Western Intellectual Property Rights regime. This clarifies that we are dealing with something that is non-universal and that Intellectual Property Rights involves Western propaganda.

Sometimes we prefix IPR with Western and also postfix IPR with "regime", resulting in "Western IPR Regime", indicating that we are dealing with a West imposed agenda driven set of rules.

Where applicable we simply avoid the IPR term and explicitly refer to the relevant branch of law: copyright, patent, trademark or secrecy.

6.2.5   Intellectual Property Isn't What It Says It Is

In addition to being a rigged misnomer, intellectual property is being falsely promoted as many things it is not.

The IPR propaganda machinary surrounding intellectual property rights asserts that IPR promotes creativity and innovation. However, there is no evidence to support this claim.

Similarly, proponents of IPR claim that it benefits economics and business, but there is no meaningful evidence to support this assertion. Moreover, while there is no evidence to substantiate this claim, there is ample evidence to show that IPR contributes to income inequality.

Furthermore, the IPR propaganda machinery propagates the idea that IPR is ethical, just, and necessary. On the contrary, it is unjust, unethical, and unnecessary.

In this section of the book, we thoroughly debunk all of these claims.

6.3 Promoting Creativity and Innovation: IP is a Failed Experiment

According to the US department of commerce:[20]

> Copyright law in the United States is founded on the Constitutional goal of "promoting the Progress of Science and useful Arts" by providing exclusive rights to creators. Protection by copyright law gives creators incentives to produce new works and distribute them to the public. In doing so, the law strikes a number of important balances in delineating what can be protected and what cannot, determining what uses are permitted without a license, and establishing appropriate enforcement mechanisms to combat piracy, so that all stakeholders benefit from the protection afforded by copyright.

So, the American model is based on the assumption that by restricting and assigning ownership to useful polyexistentials, you can create a competitive environment which is superior (in economic and societal terms) to the natural collaborative environment of multi-possessablity of polyexistentials.

This of course is pure theory. There was no proof of this theory when the US Constitution was written. So, at best IPR in the US Constitution was an experiment. It is a failed experiment in that there is now absolute total proof that, for polyexistentials, the natural collaborative model is superior to the American competitive model.

We present the proof in the domain of software in the general context of "Proprietary Software" vs. "Non-Proprietary Software" and in the specific context of "Microsoft Windows" vs. "Debian GNU/Linux".

So, according to the American model of US Constitution, software engineers would not produce good new code unless they can restrict their code with American copyright law. Indeed, Bill Gates and Microsoft created world's largest software virus the American way — based on the US Constitution. But, how about Debian GNU/Linux? Why did software engineers build that? Why do Debian GNU/Linux software engineers choose to reject the American model of US Constitution? How did they manage to collaborate on such huge scale to stand against the American giant — Microsoft?

The mere fact that Debian GNU/Linux exists demonstrates that the American model of IPR in the US Constitution is a failed experiment.

In terms of functionality, let's say that Debian GNU/Linux is as good as Microsoft Windows — in fact it is superior.

In terms of usage, today, the overwhelming majority of internet infrastructure and internet application services use Linux.

But that is not the whole picture. Separate from functionality, there is the question of manner-of-existence of software and its ramifications for users and society.

There are two basic manners-of-existence of software.

Proprietary-Haraam Software: Governed by Western IPR laws and models which are:

- restricted by the Western patent regime
- restricted by the Western copyright regime
- internally opaque

Libre-Halaal (Non-Proprietary) Software: Governed by Libre-Halaal laws and models of polyexistentials which are:

- Libre-Halaal polyexistentials which are not restricted by the Western patent regime
- Libre-Halaal polyexistentials which are not restricted by the Western copyright regime
- required to be internally transparent

Understanding the net societal ramifications of these models is simple: The opaque and proprietary Microsoft Windows is counter to user interests in terms of autonomy, privacy and conviviality. The transparent and collaborative Debian GNU/Linux supports user interests in terms of autonomy, privacy and conviviality.

The above is the concrete result of 30 years of experimentation where the American model of US Constitution have been supporting the likes of Microsoft.

Imagine where we could be if this failed experiment was recognized for what it is and the US government were to support the unimagined winner – the likes of Debian GNU/Linux.

The notion that copyright and patent law in the American model of US Constitution are promoting creativity and innovation and fostering aggregate economic growth is a total fallacy.

The net result comparisons of Western IPR model of the Proprietary-Haraam software vs the Libre-Halaal (Non-Proprietary) software model in the context of humanity makes it clear that the Western IPR regime is a failed experiment.

6.4 Copying is Neither Theft nor Piracy — Copying is Copying

There is universal consensus on what theft is and what theft is not. All Ibrahimic religions include "Thou shalt not steal."

In the model of monoexistentials and polyexistentials that we described above "theft is denial of possession to the owner." Theft only applies to monoexistentials. Theft does not apply to polyexistentials. If I copy yours, you still have yours. I just have one more.

Large American corporations individually and collectively in the form of associations have been engaging in propaganda towards creating harsh and negative connotations for unauthorized copying.

For example, the Motion Picture Association of America (MPAA) says:

> What is "piracy?"
>
> Piracy is theft and includes the unauthorized copying, distribution, performance, or other use of copyrighted materials. With regard to film and television, the term primarily relates to downloading, uploading, linking to, or otherwise providing access to unauthorized copies of movies, television shows or other copyrighted content on the Internet and making and/or selling unauthorized copies of DVDs and Blue Ray discs. ...

Now, what the Motion Picture Association of America (MPAA) is doing is completely unethical. People at MPAA – and anyone who attempts to equate copying with piracy or theft – should be ashamed of themselves.

Piracy is typically an act of robbery or criminal violence at sea. Piracy has nothing to do with Unauthorized Copying. Even in the silly American legal system, punishment for Piracy is very different from Unauthorized Copying.

Theft does not apply to polyexistentials. Even in the silly American legal system, punishment for Theft is very different from Unauthorized Copying.

In very simple terms, the following song: http://questioncopyright. org/minute_memes/copying_is_not_theft says it.

The lyrics are:

> Copying is not theft.
> Stealing a thing leaves one less left.
> Copying it makes one thing more;
> that's what copying's for.
> Copying is not theft.

If I copy yours you have it too.
One for me and one for you.
That's what copies can do.
If I steal your bicycle you have to take the bus,
but if I just copy it there's one for each of us!
Making more of a thing, that is what we call "copying",
Sharing ideas with everyone.
That's why copying is FUN!

We should not permit the likes of MPAA to define words for us. Any time that you hear anyone use the word "Theft" or "Piracy" in the context that MPAA wants to define these, let them know that we reject their vocabulary.

6.5   Fallacy: Copyright Law Restricts Plagiarism

Martin, in [36], puts it this way:

> Many intellectual workers fear being plagiarized and many of them think that intellectual property provides protection against this. After all, without copyright, why couldn't someone put their name on your essay and publish it? Actually, copyright provides very little protection against plagiarism. So-called "moral rights" of authors to be credited are backed by law in many countries but are an extremely cumbersome way of dealing with plagiarism. Plagiarism means using the ideas of others without adequate acknowledgment. There are several types of plagiarism. One is plagiarism of ideas: someone takes your original idea and, using different expression, presents it as their own. Copyright provides no protection at all against this form of plagiarism. Another type of plagiarism is word-for-word plagiarism, where someone takes the words you've written—a book, an essay, a few paragraphs or even just a sentence—and, with or without minor modifications, presents them as their own. This sort of plagiarism is covered by copyright—assuming that you hold the copyright. In many cases, copyright is held by the publisher, not the author.

> In practice, plagiarism goes on all the time, in various ways and degrees, and copyright law is hardly ever used against it. The most effective challenge to plagiarism is not legal action but publicity. At least among authors, plagiarism is widely condemned. For this reason, and because they seek to give credit where it's due, most writers do take care to avoid plagiarizing. There is an even more fundamental reason why copyright provides no protection against plagiarism: the most common sort of plagiarism

is built into social hierarchies. Government and corporate reports are released under the names of top bureaucrats who did not write them; politicians and corporate executives give speeches written by underlings. These are examples of a pervasive misrepresentation of authorship in which powerful figures gain credit for the work of subordinates. Copyright, if it has any effect at all, reinforces rather than challenges this sort of institutionalized plagiarism.

To frame this in concrete terms, consider the following real case:

> WASHINGTON, Sept. 17, 1987 —Senator Joseph R. Biden Jr., fighting to salvage his Presidential campaign, today acknowledged "a mistake" in his youth, when he plagiarized a law review article for a paper he wrote in his first year at law school. Mr. Biden insisted, however, that he had done nothing "malevolent," that he had simply misunderstood the need to cite sources carefully. And he asserted that another controversy, concerning recent reports of his using material from others' speeches without attribution, was "much ado about nothing."

Note that there is no mention of copyright anywhere in Biden's case. What Biden had done never caused any challenge to anyone's copyright monopoly.

6.6 Fallacy: Western IPR Regime is Universal

Polyexistentials are global and universal in their nature, but monopolistic restriction of polyexistentials in the form of Western IPR regime is not universal and should not become global. Many societies fully reject the basic concept of patents and copyright.

Replicability and multi-possessablity of polyexistentials knows no borders. Therefore unless universal, any national laws of ownership of polyexistentials result into diminishing intersocietal relations.

Polyexistence is global in nature, therefore, Western IPR is extraterritorial. The Western IPR regime has become an instrument of neo-colonialism in the era of global trade. West is issuing its currency and is forcing East to accept it. The "W" in WIPO stands for West not the World.

Outside of the Western model of mostly economic analysis of merits of IPR, there are other considerations.

For Iranians for example, acceptance or rejection of the merits of the Western Intellectual Property Rights regime, above all, is a moral and ethical question. Not a business or economics question.

In the American/Western utilitarian model, the maximand is usually wealth. In the Iranian/Eastern utilitarian model, the goal can usually be characterized as "justice-as-order" – where societal health and justice can be considered the maximand. In the Iranian/Eastern model the perspective is that of no particular maximand but the creation of an overarching order and environment in which people can either individually or through collaboration realize their desired ends with clarities that permit resolution of conflicts over resources.

For a description of the basis for rejection of the Intellectual Property Rights regime by Iranian ethicists, see *Iran's Theological Research on Intellectual Property Rights* [18].

Imam Khomeini's Fatwa in particular is succinct in declaring the fundamental invalidity of Western Copyright and Patent law.

Iran is a non-signatory to WTO (Western Trade Organization) copyright laws, but crisp full rejection of the concept of Copyright and Patent as was explicitly stated by Imam Khomeini has not been asserted again.

Moving towards a society based on halaal manner-of-existence of software requires crisp declarations that fully invalidate the Western Intellectual Property Rights regime. See, www.halaalsoftware.org for an initial formulation.

Western IPR Regime is very American and very Western. Portraying Western IPR Regime as anything other than limited local law is a fallacy.

The internet has become an instrument to exploit other societies and cultures. Patents and copyright are Western constructs that may not be suitable for other societies. Even if they are considered a good fit for Western societies, they may not be applicable to other cultures.

They have been promoted as a universal concept. They are not. Patents and copyright have been pushed on other societies through globalization, neocolonialism and ... Swallowing the IPR regime has become price of entry into the likes of the World Bank. Many West-Toxicated Japanese, Chinese, Indians, Iranians, etc. have taken IPR at face value.

Sharing of knowledge, ideas, poetry, music, etc. are more dominant in many Eastern societies.

6.7   Does Intellectual Property Lead to Economic Growth?

Gold et al. in [17], note:

> While policymakers often make bold claims as to the positive impact of intellectual property (IP) rights on both developed and

developing country economies, the empirical literature is more ambiguous. IP rights have both incentive and inhibitory effects that are difficult to isolate in the abstract and are dependent on economic context.

As Eastern nations grow economically, the West pushes the Western IPR regime in the name of an agent for growth into their economies. So, natural economic growth and IP become intertwined.

Gold et al. in [17], further note:

> Finally, we examined and compared the effect of increased formal IP levels on growth and vice versa. We found that growth has a greater effect on IP than IP on growth, further supporting the idea that politics and belief, rather than direct economic effect, explain the virtuous cycle between IP and growth.

Gold et al. cite a large number of studies which can neither prove nor disprove that IP directly causes economic growth.

6.8 IP Rituals: Formal IP vs Practiced IP vs Enforced IP

Usually, theory and practice are different both in theory and in practice. This also applies to IP.

In the context of any society/country there are three measures for a country's IP protections.

Formal IP: IP protection according to its explicit IP laws

Practiced IP: IP related activities as actually practiced

Enforced IP: IP protection according to if/how it is enforced

In the West in general and in America in particular, IP rituals typically goes like this:

- Some guy comes up with an idea.

- He runs his idea by seed investors and gets some money at which time he becomes more of a formal entrepreneur.

- They then apply for patents.

- With the application for the patents in their hand, they then go to some Venture Capitalists (VCs) to get more money.

- If they get more money they then move their idea forward.

- Sometimes the venture is successful and sometimes it is not.

Very often their patents end up being of no use. Many patents are hardly ever enforced.

In the above IP rituals, note that patents and VCs are directly linked. Entrepreneurs apply for the patents, because VCs require it. Without VCs, patents are usually useless because without the VC's money, a real entrepreneur could not (would not) enforce his patents – as he is not a troll. Patents are an integral part of the VC game.

Another common IP ritual in America is that of patent trolls. The troll company obtains the rights to one or more patents in order to profit by means of licensing or litigation, rather than by producing its own goods or services.

Sometimes patents are actually used in fights amongst companies.

All of these have costs. And we are somehow to believe that in the aggregate these costs are all worth it – because the abstract unproven and theoretical invention incentives make up for the costs.

In Eastern countries, when Formal IP has been established, Practiced IP is often just for foreign investors' comfort and Enforced IP is there just like unused weapons.

In the end, a great deal of potential harm remains dormant – just like unused weapons.

Unused weapons accumulate. And at some point, there will be patent wars just so that unused patent weapons are used. These patent wars will likely not be limited to inter-corporation battles. We may well see patent wars between countries.

6.9   On IP Placebos and Self-Fulfilling Prophecies

Some consider IP as placebos. Gold et al. in [17] note:

> The underlying intuition of a placebo, or self-fulfilling prophecy, is well described by Merton as follows: "A false definition of the

situation evoking behavior which makes the originally false conception come true". The danger with these situations is that they lead to strong claims that are false. As Merton explains, "the prophet will cite the actual course of events as proof that he was right from the beginning". In other words, the defining characteristic of a placebo is that it is the very consequences of the belief that make reality conform to the initial belief and that believers "fail to understand how their own belief has helped to construct that reality". The economics literature has its own treatment of placebos and self-fulfilling prophecies. These arise in economies presenting multiple potential equilibria in which untested expectations non-trivially determine the equilibrium into which they eventually fall. These expectations "are unrelated to the preferences, endowments or production set of any individual, and yet come to influence the forecast and actions of economic decision-makers". We can regard economic outcomes as the sum of two distinct effects: (i) direct (structural) effects and (ii) indirect (behavioral) effects. A growth model with strong indirect effects would exhibit placebo characteristics. Where different groups of individuals hold beliefs based on distinct yet false conceptions —such as one group believing in the effect of sunspots and another in those of "moonspots" —each will find "factual" support for their beliefs, leading to increased faith (and, hence, stability) in the false belief.

A policymaker who knows that economic growth is driven by indirect, rather than direct, effects of IP has greater room to increase growth by exerting influence on individuals' beliefs and behavior rather than through increasing levels of IP protection. For example, she could focus on changing beliefs —through education — or on inducing the same behavior through other means at a lower cost. Yu suggests that a self-fulfilling prophecy lay in China's decision to embrace higher levels of IP protection (facially, at least) in the late 1970s after it opened its markets to foreign trade. He argues that while this increased protection had no direct effect on growth, inevitably some sectors and regions would see economic growth after (but not causally related to) the change. Observers then wrongly attributed this growth to the direct effect of IP and called for even greater levels of IP protection. "And," Yu notes, "the cycle would repeat itself". Our theory generalizes and adds precision to Yu's suggestion. It holds that IP as written in formal laws —rather than how these laws operate in practice — has less of a direct role in influencing growth than thought. Instead, a group of foreign investors, believing (even if falsely) that IP always drives growth, invest in countries that adopt these laws without necessarily engaging the IP system itself (e.g., by actually obtaining, defending, and licensing IP rights). There are various reasons why such actors may hold these beliefs even in the absence of direct economic effects, ranging from the symbolic — higher levels of IP protection signal a pro-investor policy environment —to the mystical —that IP will inevitably lead the country to higher rates of growth. In the end, the result is the same: actors' faith in the growth effects of increased IP protection drives investment and thus leads to growth despite the absence of direct causality.

Gold et al. in [17] conclude that:

> [The presented results] are consistent with the placebo theory that states that a belief in the positive effects of increases in levels of IP protection on growth drive both formal IP and investments made in an economy.

What Gold et al. fail to recognize is that their analogy between IP and placebo is off in one very important respect. With respect to the placebo effect, they make it clear that IP is unnecessary – and they are correct in that regard. However, the placebo is designed to be harmless, but IP is harmful and evil.

Economists should note that economic analysis is always full of externalities. And this economic placebo causes a great deal of societal harm.

6.10   IP as Unnecessary Evil

Even though IP does not have any economic and inventive effect, its negative societal impacts are very real.

In the previous section we focused on pointing out that IP is unnecessary. It acts as a placebo in the context of self-fulfilling prophecies. If it were just that, we could have lived with it.

But the net impact of IP on society and humanity is very negative. IP is hostile to liberty – the credit side of IP is ownership and its debit side is freedom. IP weakens real and tangible property. Indirectly, IP empowers the corporation and enslaves the individual. Indirectly, IP erodes autonomy and privacy.

IP is unnecessary evil.

6.11 Mistaken Justifications for Ownership of Polyexistentials

The laws of ownership of monoexistentials are well established and hardly disputed.

Western IP as laws of ownership of polyexistentials on the other hand are very controversial and disputed. It is for this reason that we needed to create the "Polyexistential Reference Model" to demonstrate invalidity of IP laws.

Credibility of ownership laws for monoexistentials and for polyexistentials are very different.

In a Western context, Bouckaert, in [15] points to this:

> ... Nevertheless, the outline reveals one remarkable characteristic in the evolution of continental legal doctrine: its rather "spontaneous" and international character. By spontaneous I mean that the evolution toward a relative consensus about the property concept was not organized from a single center. It was neither the product of a brilliant Lycurgean legislator or the outcome of the action of an organized social group. The growing consensus about the property concept evolved from a dialogue among learned jurists from different parts of the European continent. This dialogue was an ongoing intellectual process lasting several centuries. The jurists of France, the Netherlands, Spain, Germany, and Italy consulted foreign texts, commented on them, and gradually refined their theoretical approach. Although this spontaneous origin of the property concept does not provide a conclusive argument for its rightness, it reveals at least its intersubjective and intertemporal character. The least we can say is that the property theory of the continental legal tradition passed through a test of a multitude of critical insights of learned and experienced legal scholars. For this reason, it is legitimate to assign to such a gradually evolved theory a presumption of rightness and to charge its opponents with the burden of proof about the contrary.

From the perspective of religions as well, there is universal consensus on ownership of monoexistentials and what theft is and what theft is not. All Ibrahimic religions (and other major religions) include "Thou shalt not steal". Additionally, Eastern perspective on ownership of monoexistentials is same as the Western perspective.

Therefore, with regard to the existing laws of ownership of monoexistentials we start with the presumption of rightness and assign the burden of proof about the contrary to the opponents.

Bouckaert, in [15], further elaborates:

> With regard to the debate on intellectual property, the question arises whether this presumption of rightness by tradition can be extended to this kind of property. Is it possible to allot intellectual property the same traditional weight as corporeal property goods? The history of the origin of the several kinds of intellectual property on the continent suggests a negative answer to this question. The origin of intellectual property rights has its historical roots in deliberate interventions by political authorities rather than in the spontaneously evolved continental legal tradition.

There is nothing approaching the notion of IP in any of the Ibrahimic religions (or any other major religion). Additionally, Eastern perspective on ownership of polyexistentials differs greatly from the Western IP perspective.

Furthermore, IP laws amount to taking away basic natural rights of people. The burden of proof should be on those who wish to take away such basic natural rights.

Additionally, sharing polyexistentials still allows the original possessor to use them. Therefore, the burden of proof should lie on those who argue for intellectual property.

In the following sections, after debunking arguments in favor of IP, we reiterate that we have not been persuaded and that they have failed in fulfilling the burden of proof.

6.11.1   Debunking the Labor Theory of Property

Many defenses of intellectual property rights are grounded in the natural law right to the fruit of one's labor. Just as one has a right to the crops one plants, so one has a right to the ideas one generates and the art one produces.

For monoexistentials, the fruit of one's labor is a monoexistential, which is ownable. It is the work product that may be ownable (property) not the work (labor).

That is not the case with polyexistentials. Neither labor nor polyexistentials are ownable.

Further, IP's claimed protection of labor is problematic in a number of ways. Some of which we describe in the following sections.

6.11.1.1   IP Arbitrarily Protects Some Labor but not Others

The types of labor that is protected by IP are arbitrary.

Kinsella, in [33] points to this:

> One problem with the [labor-based or] creation-based approach is that it almost invariably protects only certain types of creations —unless, that is, every single useful idea one comes up with is subject to ownership (more on this below). But the distinction between the protectable and the unprotectable is necessarily arbitrary. For example, philosophical or mathematical or scientific truths cannot be protected under current law on the grounds that commerce and social intercourse would grind to a halt were every new phrase, philosophical truth, and the like considered the exclusive property of its creator. For this reason, patents can be obtained only for so-called "practical applications" of ideas, but not for more abstract or theoretical ideas. Rand agrees with this disparate treatment, in attempting to distinguish between an unpatentable discovery and a patentable invention. She argues that a "scientific or philosophical discovery, which identifies a law of nature, a principle or a fact of reality not previously known" is not created by the discoverer. But the distinction between creation and discovery is not clearcut or rigorous. Nor is it clear why such a distinction, even if clear, is ethically relevant in defining property rights. No one creates matter; they just manipulate and grapple with it according to physical laws. In this sense, no one really creates anything. They merely rearrange matter into new arrangements and patterns. An engineer who invents a new mousetrap has rearranged existing parts to provide a function not previously performed. Others who learn of this new arrangement can now also make an improved mousetrap. Yet the mousetrap merely follows laws of nature. The inventor did not invent the matter out of which the mousetrap is made, nor the facts and laws exploited to make it work.
>
> [...]
>
> Both the inventor and the theoretical scientist engage in creative mental effort to produce useful, new ideas. Yet one is rewarded, and the other is not. In one recent case, the inventor of a new way to calculate a number representing the shortest path between two points – an extremely useful technique – was not given patent protection because this was "merely" a mathematical algorithm. But it is arbitrary and unfair to reward more practical inventors and entertainment providers, such as the engineer and songwriter, and to leave more theoretical science and math researchers and philosophers unrewarded. The distinction is inherently vague, arbitrary, and unjust.

6.11.1.2   IP Protection of Labor Can be Undercut/Spoiled

Furthermore, even with Western IPR in play, the view that labor should result in ownership is not the case. Consider what Leggett argued, in the case of authorship,

> Two authors, without concert or intercommunion, may describe the same incidents, in language so nearly identical that the two books, for all purposes of sale, shall be the same. Yet one writer may make a free gift of his production to the public, may throw it open in common; and then what becomes of the other's right of property?"

The same argument can be extended, of course, to inventions.

We are not Persuaded

Both Palmer and Kinsella further discredit the merits of "The Labor Theory Of Property Argument" in [39] and [33].

The labor theory of property argument in favor of IP has not persuaded us. The labor theory of property argument in favor of IP is a farce.

We are not persuaded that such arguments justify us limiting our natural rights to copy and to apply knowledge. Hence, the Western IPR regime remains erroneous and invalid.

6.11.2   Debunking the Length of Time Adjustment Argument

Some believe that Western IP regime is generally correct and it just needs to be adjusted with regard to the term of the protection to be less restrictive to better balance rights vs liberties.

This is an arbitrary argument. Adopting any limited term for IP rights requires arbitrary rules.

For example, in the US, patents last for twenty years from the filing date, while copyrights last, in the case of individual authors, for seventy years past the author's death. No one can seriously maintain that nineteen years for a patent is too short, and twenty-one years too long.

How are we going to adjust the term of the protection? Who will be deciding those? Why would they be any better or worse than any other durations?

One problem with any of these approaches to validating IP is that it necessarily involves arbitrary distinctions with respect to what classes of creations (labor) deserve protection, and concerning the length of the term of the protection.

The absurdity of the basic IP argument becomes more clear by widening the scope of IP, and by lengthening its duration to avoid making such arbitrary distinctions.

Kinsella, in [33] addresses this:

> And by extending the term of patents and copyrights to infinity, subsequent generations would be choked by ever-growing restraints on their own use of property. No one would be able to manufacture—or even use—a light bulb without getting permission from Edison's heirs.
>
> [...]
>
> Such unbounded ideal rights would pose a serious threat to tangible-property rights, and would threaten to overwhelm them. All use of tangible property would by now be impossible, as every conceivable use of property, every single action, would be bound to infringe upon one of the millions of past, accreted IP rights, and the human race would die of starvation.
>
> [...]
>
> The remaining advocates of IP all qualify their endorsement by limiting the scope and/or terms of IP rights, thus adopting the ethically arbitrary distinctions noted above.

Consider this "Time Limit Adjustment Argument" in the context of the parallels with slavery that we described earlier. Imagine of an argument that would have gone like this: "slavery is fine, we just need to treat the slaves better and keep them as slaves for not as long."

The time limit adjustment argument is obviously ridiculous.

We are not Persuaded

The length of time adjustment argument in favor of IP has not persuaded us. The length of time adjustment argument in favor of IP is a farce.

We are not persuaded that such arguments justify us limiting our natural rights to copy and to apply knowledge. Hence, the Western IPR regime remains erroneous and invalid.

6.11.3   Debunking the Utilitarian Argument

Advocates of IP often justify it on utilitarian grounds. Utilitarians hold that the "end" of encouraging more innovation and creativity justifies the seemingly immoral "means" of restricting the freedom of individuals to use their physical property as they see fit.

This would be based on the assumption that wealth or utility could be maximized by adopting certain legal rules. Unless this assumption is proved correct no conclusions are of any consequence. In fact, we believe that this assumption is false.

But for now, let us suppose that it is correct.

Kinsella, in [33] addresses this:

> Even then, this does not show that these rules are justified. For example, one could argue that net utility is enhanced by redistributing half of the wealth of society's richest one percent to its poorest ten percent. But even if stealing some of A's property and giving it to B increases B's welfare "more" than it diminishes A's (if such a comparison could, somehow, be made), this does not establish that the theft of A's property is justified. Wealth maximization is not the goal of law; rather, the goal is justice—giving each man his due. Even if overall wealth is increased due to IP laws, it does not follow that this allegedly desirable result justifies the unethical violation of some individuals' rights to use their own property as they see fit.
>
> ...
>
> It is debatable whether copyrights and patents really are necessary to encourage the production of creative works and inventions, or that the incremental gains in innovation outweigh the immense costs of an IP system.
>
> Econometric studies do not conclusively show net gains in wealth. Perhaps there would even be more innovation if there were no patent laws; maybe more money for research and development (R&D) would be available if it were not being spent on patents and lawsuits. It is possible that companies would have an even greater incentive to innovate if they could not rely on a near twenty-year monopoly.
>
> ...
>
> It is not clear that society is better off with relatively more practical invention and relatively less theoretical research and development.
>
> ...
>
> We must remember that when we advocate certain rights and laws, and inquire into their legitimacy, we are inquiring into the legitimacy and ethics of the use of force. To ask whether a law

should be enacted or exist is to ask: is it proper to use force against certain people in certain circumstances? It is no wonder that this question is not really addressed by analysis of wealth maximization.

Utilitarian analysis is thoroughly confused and bankrupt: talk about increasing the size of the pie is methodologically flawed; there is no clear evidence that the pie increases with IP rights. Further, pie growth does not justify the use of force against the otherwise legitimate property of others. For these reasons, utilitarian IP defenses are unpersuasive.

We are not Persuaded

Both Palmer and Kinsella further discredit merits of "Utilitarian IP Argument" in [39] and [33].

The utilitarian argument in favor of IP has not persuaded us. The utilitarian argument in favor of IP is a farce.

We too are not persuaded that such arguments justify us limiting our natural rights to copy and to apply knowledge. Hence, the Western IPR regime remains erroneous and invalid.

6.11.4 Debunking the Reserved Rights Argument

Recognizing the limitations of contract law on polyexistentials that we outlined in Section 2.9.8.1 and recognizing that restricting the polyexistential component of mixed-existential imposes on its monoexistential component, some IP advocates shift from a purely contractual approach to a "reservation of rights" approach in which property rights in monoexistentials tangible resources are seen as a divisible bundle of rights.

Kinsela in [33] describes this in some detail:

> For example, under the standard bundle-of-rights view, a landowner can sell the mineral estate to an oil company while retaining all rights to the surface, except for an easement (servitude) granting passage to a neighbor and a life estate (usufruct) granting use of the surface estate to his mother. Drawing on the bundle-of-rights notion, the "reservation of rights" approach holds that a type of "private" IP can be privately generated by creatively "reserving rights" to reproduce tangible items sold to purchasers. Rothbard, for example, argues that one can grant conditional "ownership" (of "knowledge") to another, while "retaining the ownership power to disseminate the knowledge of the invention." Or, Brown, the

inventor of an improved mousetrap, can stamp it "copyright" and thereby sell the right to each mousetrap except for the right to reproduce it. Like the real rights accompanying statutory IP, such "reservations" allegedly bind everyone, not just those who have contracted with the original seller. Thus, third parties who become aware of, purchase, or otherwise come into possession of the restricted item also cannot reproduce it—not because they have entered into a contract with Brown, but because "no one can acquire a greater property title in something than has already been given away or sold." In other words, the third party acquires a tangible thing—a book or a mousetrap, say—but it is somehow "missing" the "right-to-copy" part of the bundle of rights that "normally" constitutes all rights to the thing. Or, the third party acquires "ownership" of information, from a person who did not own the information and, thus, was not entitled to transmit it to others.

The implications of such a view are troubling. Palmer in [39] writes:

> The separation and retention of the right to copy from the bundle of rights that we call property is problematic. Could one reserve the right, for example, to remember something? Suppose that I wrote a book and offered it to you to read, but I had retained one right: the right to remember it. Would I be justified in taking you to court if I could prove that you had remembered the name of the lead character in the book?

Both Palmer and Kinsella further discredit merits of "Reserved Rights Argument" in [39] and [33].

We are not Persuaded

The reserved rights argument has not persuaded us. The reserved rights argument is a farce.

We too are not persuaded that such arguments justify us limiting our natural rights to copy and to apply knowledge. Hence, the Western IPR regime remains erroneous and invalid.

6.11.5 Debunking the Argument of: It Is Part Of Me, Therefore I Own It

In the Islamic tradition, ownership is categorized into two types:

- "Inherent Ownership" «مالکیت ذاتیه تکوینیه»

- "Logical Ownership" «مالکیت عرضیه اعتباریه»

Inherent ownership pertains to ownership that is inherently linked to nature. For example, you own your fingers because they are an inherent part of your being. Logical ownership is based on reasoning and applies to external entities. It is intended to establish order, justice, and benefit for individuals and society.

According to this model, your thoughts, inventions, and creativity are undeniably part of you as long as they remain exclusively within you. Therefore, as long as they have not been disclosed or separated from you, they inherently belong to you – they are your exclusive property.

But once you have disclosed them, once you have chosen to separate them from yourself, they are no longer solely inherent to you. They become external as well. At that moment, you are no longer the exclusive owner. They are no longer subject only to inherent ownership; they also become subject to logical ownership.

Those who desire to retain exclusive ownership over their inventions should keep them to themselves. Once an idea is exposed, it is no longer solely a part of you and no longer exclusively your property.

Once disclosed, the concept of "It is part of me, therefore I exclusively own it" becomes a fallacy.

Based on the concept of polyexistentials, in Section 2.4.2 — Model of Birth of Polyexistentials, we pointed to the same notion:

> The moment of "divulging" is the moment of birth of polyexistentials.

6.11.6 Debunking the Argument of: I Clearly Came Up With It, Therefore I Own It

The context of ownership is inherently societal. As members of society, our thoughts and inventions do not solely belong to us.

For this reason, Ayatollah Motahhari «مطهری» deems the Western IPR regime invalid.[21] The summary of Ayatolah Motahhari's reasoning is included below:

Invention is not solely the direct product of an individual's intellectual genius,	اختراع محصول مستقیم نبوغ فکری فرد نیست تا او مالک اثر یا اختراع خویش باشد بلکه طبیعت

for nature and society, due
to specific conditions and
circumstances, have played
a significant role in the emergence of such inventions.
Therefore, intellectual properties such as inventions
and creations are consid-
ered a common and col-
lective asset rather than
private ownership.

یا اجتماع به دلیل شرایط و زمینه‌های
خاص در پیدایش چنین اختراعی
مؤثر بوده‌اند. ازاین‌رو، اموال
فکری مانند اختراع و تألیف سرمایه‌ای
عمومی و مملوکی اشتراکی است
نه ملک خصوصی.

Based on the concept of polyexistentials, in Section 2.4.3 — Model of Evolution
of Polyexistentials, we pointed to the same notion:

During the process of proliferation, polyexistentials have the potential to evolve. Ideas can be refined, modified, and subsequently
replicated. This inherent process is so natural that precise individual attribution becomes inadequate. Instead, blurred and shared
collaborative attributions are more reflective of reality.

Chapter 7

Ownership Mistakes: Western Slavery and the Western IPR Regime

Horrible things happen when a society gets its ownership rules wrong.

For the Anglo-American culture, a recent acknowledged ownership mistake is slavery of Africans in America. Rules for ownership of Africans by Americans and Europeans, resulted in reduction of the economic value of labor to the benefit of Americans and Europeans. This was accomplished by deemphasizing true value of Africans as human beings. The repercussions of such economically motivated ownership rules are vast and may remain uncomprehended in parts.

The Anglo-American culture is in the midst of making another ownership mistake: That of the ownership of polyexistentials. This time things are more subtle and more difficult to understand, as the victims and oppressors are less obvious.

The Western so-called Intellectual Property Rights (IPR) regime (Western copyright and patent law) is a sin of our time, the same way that Western slavery was a sin of the West's previous generations.

The history of slavery is a sensitive and contentious topic, particularly for Americans and Westerners. In this chapter, we will not delve into an extensive reexamination of that historical context. Instead, our focus is on drawing parallels between the origins and consequences of chattel slavery and the intellectual property rights regime. In doing so, we may occasionally simplify the complex historical circumstances surrounding the enslavement of Africans and its subsequent development. It is important to clarify that our oversimplifications are centered on the dynamics of mistaken ownership rules and not intended to undermine or trivialize the gravity and harm caused by Western slavery.

7.1   Parallels Between Western Slavery and the Western IPR Regime

The parallel that we draw here is in the context of distorted or proper "ownership rules" — not cruelty or kindness. When we use the words "Slave" and "Slavery", we are purely focused on the property and ownership aspect of a human by another human.

American/Western slavery of Africans is rooted in the American belief of White superiority and Black inferiority. Based on that belief Americans/Westerners could then regard Blacks as subhuman and therefore "ownable". And, the revered United States Constitutional Convention could at most get to the Three-Fifths Compromise.[22] Atrocities and involuntary servitude are then derivatives of ownership mistakes. It is the notion of ownership laws that is our focus here.

In the context of parallels between Western slavery and the Western IPR regime, our focus is distortion of ownership rules first and the cruelty that it cultivates second. In the case of the Western IPR regime, the cruelty is not as immediately visible. Yet it is very real as well.

While the immense harm and suffering caused by Western slavery are now widely acknowledged, the detrimental impact of the Western IPR ownership error is frequently disregarded. We will argue that the harm of the Western IPR regime is also very wide and very deep — as the victims are numerous and that recognition of the cruelty is complex and latent. By exploring the parallels between Western slavery and the Western intellectual property rights regime, our intention is to underscore the profound and ongoing devastation that arises from the IPR ownership mistake.

Slavery had been practiced all over the world for thousands of years, but never before had so many people from one continent been transported to another against their will. Americans' formality and form of ownership was unique. The current size and make up of American prisons are also very unique and exceptional. When we speak of "Western Slavery", it is this particular form of ownership and chattel slavery that we are pointing to.

It is not savagery and lack of humanity of American society that is the point we wish to make in this section. We provide these examples to draw attention to long term ramifications of Western ownership mistakes in general and the current Western IPR regime mistake in particular. American Slavery is the previous now well understood Western ownership mistake.

Below we go through various aspects of these colossal Western mistakes that have obvious parallels and similarities.

7.2   What Should Not Be Owned

Both Western Slavery and the Western IPR regime are about owning what should not be owned.

This obvious simple concept is not one that you arrive at through business and economics. It is based on basic philosophy, logic, ethics and respect for nature.

7.2.1   Ownership of Human Beings

Western Slavery was about very formal ownership of human beings. Despite full formality, Western Slavery was without regard for ramifications of inter-breeding with what you own. And the question of ownership of your own child.

Today, a First Lady of America, Michelle Obama, has no comment about her own genealogy. At the age of six, Melvinia, who was Michelle Obama's great-great-great grandmother, was passed on as **property** (valued at $475) to Pa-terson's daughter and son-in-law — Christianne and Henry Shields — after his death in 1852. Some years later, when she was still a teenager, she gave birth to a boy, Dolphus T Shields. Dolphus was recorded in the census as "mulatto" - denoting one white and one black parent. The identity of the father is not known, though the fact that his surname was Shields suggests he may have been a member of the family that **owned** Melvinia.

In the 19th century, in America, human beings were formally owned. Inter-breeding with one's property was common place and the master's own child became property again. On this scale and in this form, all of this is exception-ally American.

So, now in the 21st century, for the very first time we have the descendants of a slave as America's First Lady. The ancestors of the President himself, Barack Obama, do not seem to have been slaves. Americans have not yet chosen a descendant of their slaves as President.

Note here that the modern term "African-American" is quite confusing. Both Michelle Obama and Barack Obama are called African-Americans. Barack Obama is a descendant of Africans who chose to become American. Just like the Irish-Americans (say John F. Kennedy). Michelle Obama is a descendant of African slaves. Michelle Obama and her ancestors did not have a choice in becoming American.

Human beings should not be owned. The nature of their existence as equals makes them unownable.

7.2.2 Ownership of Polyexistentials

As we have described throughout this book, assignment of ownership to what exists in nature in multiples (polyexistentials) is in conflict with nature and violates nature. Ownership of polyexistentials vioaltes all ownability requirements. Polyexistentials are not subjects of exclusive possessability. Polyexistentials are non-scarce. Polyexistentials are non-territorial. That sort of fundamental violation of nature tears the fabric of humanity.

7.3   Short Term Economic Benefits

Both Western slavery and Western IPR regime have managed to produce benefits to a select few. Consider the following as anecdotes:

7.3.1   Slaves and the Cotton Economy

The rise of "King Cotton" as the defining feature of southern life revitalized slavery. The promise of cotton profits encouraged a spectacular rise in the direct importation of African slaves in the late 18th century and early 19th century. 250,000 new slaves arrived in the United States from 1787 to 1808, a number equal to the entire slave importation of the colonial period.[23]

Cotton also contributed to the national economy. The crop comprised more than half the total value of domestic exports in the period 1815-1860, and in 1860, earnings from cotton paid for 60 percent of all imports. Cotton also built-up domestic capital, attracted foreign investment, and contributed to industrial growth. In the early 1800s, northeastern merchants began channeling commercial profits into industrial production of cloth (using cotton).[24]

So, much American prosperity was built on the back of African slaves. In that economic process, Americans destroyed an entire continent and an entire people (cultures, languages, customs, etc.).

Economics is inherently full of externalities.

7.3.2 Viagra Patents and Pfizer

In the American economic model, the single most revealing measure of an innovation's economic value is the market's response to it. On this measure, Viagra offers a striking example: sales of the drug grew very rapidly after launch, and those of its competitors fell dramatically.

All of Viagra profits are anchored in a set of patents.

The target for Viagra is the 50-year-old man who is having trouble and is very willing to pay for his trouble.

So, we can see how the Western patent system has focused innovation and creativity amongst drug makers to exactly where the money is.

But what about the real patient, the sick, who has to pay for the artificial scarcity that the patent system creates?

Economics is inherently full of externalities.

7.4 Long Term Economic Costs

With economics you usually have to worry about two things. First is externality and second is short term benefits vs long term costs.

These economic considerations apply to both Western Slavery and Western IPR regime.

7.4.1 Descendant of Slaves
and the Make-up of the US Prison System

American slavery ended with American civil war. Long term costs of American slavery of course continued and continues.

Today, descendants of enslaved Africans who Anglo-American culture now labels the African-American men, are close to 14% of the population of men in the U.S.[25] Moreover, black women are the fastest growing prison population in the U.S.

Today, male descendants of Africans made slaves, represent close to 40% of America's prison population. Separate from cruelty, taking care of that large population is costly.[26]

With respect to female descendants of enslaved Africans, consider this: Black moms across the US are three and a half times more likely to die in childbirth than white Americans.[27] It is an understatement to say that this is a stark reminder of the systemic racism that has been deeply entrenched in American society for centuries. There is a cost associated with the knowledge of that cruelty. Aside from the harm, the fact that "Black Lives Matter" has now become a catchphrase illustrates state of morality in America. Anglo-American culture has to live with that shame forever.

All of this is uniquely and exceptionally American.

In contemporary times, the descendants of enslaved Africans, who were once seen as economically advantageous to the old masters, have now become less appealing in economic terms. And yet, the topic of reparations has not even been put on the table.

7.4.2   Never Ending Patent Wars and Aggregate Costs of Artificial Scarcity

Many have come to conclude that patents are stifling innovation.

"patent assertion entities," better known as patent trolls, whose business model consists of holding many low-quality patents and suing infringers, real or otherwise. The trolls threatened to sue more than 100,000 companies in 2012. Some seem like little more than extortion rackets. They prey on smaller businesses by claiming, for example, that a jewelry boutique is violating a patent every time it scans a document. One study concludes that defendants paid $29 billion in 2011 to trolls, four times what they paid in 2005.

Patents have now become a lawyers' game. A zero-sum game that produces nothing. But the cost of just running the game is of course significant. And that is eventually passed to the consumer.

7.5   When Mistakes Become So Very Chic

A common characteristic of a sin of the time is that it becomes common and desirable.

7.5.1   Holding Slaves Was Fashionable Then

The more slaves you had, the more powerful you appeared.

Lawyers specializing in the legalities of Slavery were very well paid.

Many of the American presidents of that era were slave owners.

7.5.2 Holding Patents and Copyright is Fashionable Now

Holding patents and copyright is viewed today as prestigious. Even academics put the list of their patents on their resumes and their web sites.

Lawyers specializing in the legalities of IPR are very well paid now.

Many of the American presidents of this era are copyright holders. Much of President Obama's net worth is through his copyrighted books. Even Bush Junior recognized how he could cash his shares through the Western IPR regime.

As engineers, we hold neither patents nor restrictive copyrights. Instead, we offer our services as Patent Assassins and collaborate in legal defense against patent assertions. That is not considered chic, we know!

7.6 America's Founding Fathers and the US Constitution

Many Americans take the US constitution very seriously and revere "America's Founding Fathers".

The US Constitution has been exceptionally wrong both with respect to Slavery and IPR.

These catastrophic mistakes of the US Constitution are fundamentally rooted in the economic nature of that document. Above all, US Constitution is a business plan – by the business-man for the business-man. "Freedom" is included in that business plan as a business ingredient. Individual Freedom in due course will be extended to include Corporate Freedom. Freedom of the weak is viewed as a source of income.

The American two layer model of law and economics is very simple. And in that simple two layered model, one important purpose of law is to accommodate economics. People are viewed as economic creatures. And society is the collection of economic creatures and their economic dynamics. A very simple and effective business plan.

Human beings born into this colossal American business plan, known as the US Constitution, swiftly transform into economic creatures. They become Americanized.

To pay lip service to any remaining human needs of economic creatures, individualistic freedom becomes the main pillar of American morality. Conveniently, the US Constitution and the American economic model celebrates individual freedoms. Based on those individualistic freedoms, the sophisticated American corporation is then well positioned to manipulate the naive American individual — that simple economic creature. With that form of American morality in place, the American corporation then demands those individual-istic freedoms for itself. The American model then amounts to a complete collection of economic creatures (people and corporations alike). Should such a collection be called a society? What is American society?

Humans are to be first right and wrong (halaal and haraam) oriented and only after that, they can be economically oriented. Right and wrong are often or-thogonal to economics and profit, as externality is an inherent characteristic of economics.

The notion of focusing on right and wrong instead of economics is generally foreign to Americans.

7.6.1   Slavery and the US Constitution

Slavery is seen in the US Constitution in a few key places.

The first is in the Enumeration Clause, where representatives are apportioned. Each state is given a number of representatives based on its population - in that population, slaves, called "other persons," are counted as three-fifths of a whole person. This compromise was hard-fought, with Northerners wishing that slaves, legal property, be uncounted, much as mules and horses are un-counted. Southerners, however, well aware of the high proportion of slaves to the total population in their states, wanted them counted as whole persons despite their legal status. The three-fifths number was a ratio used by the Congress in contemporary legislation and was agreed upon with little debate.

In Article 1, Section 9, Congress is limited, expressly, from prohibiting the "Importation" of slaves, before 1808. The slave trade was a bone of contention for many, with some who supported slavery abhorring the slave trade. The 1808 date, a compromise of 20 years, allowed the slave trade to continue, but placed a date-certain on its survival.

The Fugitive Slave Clause is the last mention. In it, a problem that slave states had with extradition of escaped slaves was resolved. The laws of one state, the clause says, cannot excuse a person from "Service or Labour" in another state. The clause expressly requires that the state in which an escapee is found deliver the slave to the state he escaped from "on Claim of the Party."

So, here we have America's founding fathers, speaking of how all men are created equal during the day and then engaging in the sexual exploitation of their female slaves at night. And who knows who is to own the results of all that banging – their own children.[28]

So, now early in the 21st century, some African Americans are seeking to prove a genetic link to James Madison.[29]

This of course provides a window for understanding the character of Amer-ica's founding fathers — and by extension a window to the character of American society.

7.6.2 Copyright and Patents in the US Constitution

US Constitution Article I, Section 8, Clause 8, reads:

> The Congress shall have power [...] To promote the progress of science and useful arts, by securing for limited times to authors and inventors the exclusive right to their respective writings and discoveries;

The heart of the mistake of the authors of the US Constitution is that writings and discoveries of authors and inventors are polyexistentials.

Restricting polyexistential by grants of exclusive right in fact hinders progress of science and useful arts.

In other words, lack of understanding of America's founding fathers as to how science and useful arts progress has now become a disease that the American society has to live with.

7.7 Role and Place of Religions

Both Slavery and IPR are questions of ownership.

Questions of ownership are proper domain of religions.

7.7.1 Slavery in Christianity vs. Slavery in Islam

To recognize the part played by the Christian churches in the slave trade one may consider the following anecdotes. Many priests themselves carried on slave-trading, especially in Angola, and many others owned slaves in the Americas. The only reason the Catholic church give for its action was that it was trying to save African souls by baptizing the slaves. The Protestants were worse, for they did not even make it clear that they accepted that the Africans had a soul. Instead, they supported the view that the African slave was a piece of property like a furniture or a domestic animal. There is no part of the history of the Christian church which was more disgraceful than its support of the Atlantic slave-trade.

When ships loaded with human cargo sailed from Christian countries to the Western hemisphere, Christian priests used to bless the ship in the name of Almighty and admonish the slaves to be obedient. It never entered into their minds to admonish the masters to be kind to the slaves.

Islam's historical record with respect to slavery is much cleaner than Christianity's record.

Malcolm X said that Islam was the "true religion of black mankind" and that Christianity was "the white man's religion" that had been imposed upon African Americans by their slave-masters.

In a Christian country, Cassius Marcellus Clay, Jr., chose to become Muhammad Ali.

Islam's approach to the question of slavery was more philosophical, ethical and societal. And less economic. All Quranic rules on slaves are emancipatory in that they improve the rights of slaves compared to what was already practiced in the 7th century. Many Moslems have interpreted Quran as gradually phasing out slavery.

One key rule in Islam played an important role in gradually phasing out slavery. A female slave who gives birth to her owner's child becomes an "umm walad" ('mother of a child') and becomes automatically free upon the death of her owner. The child would be automatically free and equal to the owner's other children.

Contrast this Moslem rule against the American/Christian one-drop rule of even the early 20th century which asserts that any person with even one ancestor of Black ancestry ("one drop" of "Black blood") is considered Black (Negro or colored in historical terms).

7.7.2   IPR in Christianity vs. IPR in Islam

For the most part Christianity has been silent on the question of IPR.

Islam on the other hand, and Shiite tradition in particular, has been quite explicit in rejecting the Western IPR regime.

Imam Khomeini's fatwa in particular is succinct in declaring the fundamental invalidity of Western Copyright and Patent law.

For a description of the basis for rejection of the Intellectual Property Rights regime by Iranian ethicists, see *Iran's Theological Research on Intellectual Property Rights* [18].

The Christian clergy needs to wake up. As was slavery, the Western Intellectual Property Rights is a critical ownership topic that needs to be directly addressed by the Church based on morality and theology — not economics.

7.8 Role and Place of Special Professions

Let's view society as a collection of professions. Any harm and threat to society at a given time is experienced by various professions differently. The professions that are specially touched by specific harms and threats we consider special professions.

Consider two examples and parallels for slavery and for IPR. Let's consider the employees of shipping lines as a special profession in the history of slavery in Congo. For IPR, let's consider software engineers as a special profession.

In these examples, members of these professions have been best positioned to understand the harm early on and their actions could have had an impact on preventing the harm early on.

7.8.1 Employees of Shipping Lines and King Leopold

Adam Hochschild is the author of "King Leopold's Ghost, A Story of Greed, Terror, and Heroism in Colonial Africa" [24]. He chooses to start the story with Edmund Dene Morel.

It is Morel and his profession that we want to underscore in this story. Morel's profession positioned him such that he could see slavery in Congo as it was happening. He then exposed what he understood to the rest.

Hochschild is an excellent writer. Here is how he describes it in the very beginning pages of this long book.[30]

> THE BEGINNINGS of this story lie far back in time, and its reverberations still sound today. But for me a central incandescent moment, one that illuminates long decades before and after, is a young man's flash of moral recognition.
>
> The year is 1897 or 1898. Try to imagine him, briskly stepping off a cross-Channel steamer, a forceful, burly man, in his mid-twenties, with a handlebar mustache. He is confident and well spoken, but his British speech is without the polish of Eton or Oxford. He is well dressed, but the clothes are not from Bond Street. With an ailing mother and a wife and growing family to support, he is not the sort of person likely to get caught up in an idealistic cause. His ideas are thoroughly conventional. He looks—and is—every inch the sober, respectable businessman.
>
> Edmund Dene Morel is a trusted employee of a Liverpool shipping line. A subsidiary of the company has the monopoly on all transport of cargo to and from the Congo Free State, as it is then called, the huge territory in central Africa that is the world's

only colony claimed by one man. That man is King Leopold II of Belgium, a ruler much admired throughout Europe as a "philanthropic" monarch. He has welcomed Christian missionaries to his new colony; his troops, it is said, have fought and defeated local slave-traders who preyed on the population; and for more than a decade European newspapers have praised him for investing his personal fortune in public works to benefit the Africans. Because Morel speaks fluent French, his company sends him to Belgium every few weeks to supervise the loading and unloading of ships on the Congo run. Although the officials he works with have been handling this shipping traffic for years without a second thought, Morel begins to notice things that unsettle him. At the docks of the big port of Antwerp he sees his company's ships arriving filled to the hatch covers with valuable cargoes of rubber and ivory. But when they cast off their hawsers to steam back to the Congo, while military bands play on the pier and eager young men in uniform line the ships' rails, what they carry is mostly army officers, firearms, and ammunition. There is no trade going on here. Little or nothing is being exchanged for the rubber and ivory. As Morel watches these riches streaming to Europe with almost no goods being sent to Africa to pay for them, he realizes that there can be only one explanation for their source: slave labor.

Brought face to face with evil, Morel does not turn away. Instead, what he sees determines the course of his life and the course of an extraordinary movement, the first great international human rights movement of the twentieth century. Seldom has one human being—impassioned, eloquent, blessed with brilliant organizing skills and nearly superhuman energy—managed almost single-handedly to put one subject on the world's front pages for more than a decade. Only a few years after standing on the docks of Antwerp, Edmund Morel would be at the White House, insisting to President Theodore Roosevelt that the United States had a special responsibility to do something about the Congo. He would organize delegations to the British Foreign Office. He would mobilize everyone from Booker T. Washington to Anatole France to the Archbishop of Canterbury to join his cause. More than two hundred mass meetings to protest slave labor in the Congo would be held across the United States. A larger number of gatherings in England—nearly three hundred a year at the crusade's peak — would draw as many as five thousand people at a time. In London, one letter of protest to the Times on the Congo would be signed by eleven peers, nineteen bishops, seventy-six members of Parliament, the presidents of seven Chambers of Commerce, thirteen editors of major newspapers, and every lord mayor in the country. Speeches about the horrors of King Leopold's Congo would be given as far away as Australia. In Italy, two men would fight a duel over the issue. British Foreign Secretary Sir Edward Grey, a man not given to overstatement, would declare that "no external question for at least thirty years has moved the country so strongly and so vehemently."

This is the story of that movement, of the savage crime that was its target, of the long period of exploration and conquest that preceded it, and of the way the world has forgotten one of the great mass killings of recent history.

Through his profession, Morel understood what was going on. He recognized that he had to act on that understanding. Communication of the understanding of the harm to the rest of the society is a responsibility.

Hochschild then continues:

I knew almost nothing about the history of the Congo until a few years ago, when I noticed a footnote in a book I happened to be reading. Often, when you come across something particularly striking, you remember just where you were when you read it. On this occasion I was sitting, stiff and tired, late at night, in one of the far rear seats of an airliner crossing the United States from east to west.

The footnote was to a quotation by Mark Twain, written, the note said, when he was part of the worldwide movement against slave labor in the Congo, a practice that had taken eight to ten million lives. Worldwide movement? Eight to ten million lives? I was startled.

Statistics about mass murder are often hard to prove. But if this number turned out to be even half as high, I thought, the Congo would have been one of the major killing grounds of modern times. Why were these deaths not mentioned in the standard litany of our century's horrors? And why had I never before heard of them? I had been writing about human rights for years, and once, in the course of half a dozen trips to Africa, I had been to the Congo.

That visit was in 1961. In a Leopoldville apartment, I heard a CIA man, who had had too much to drink, describe with satisfaction exactly how and where the newly independent country's first prime minister, Patrice Lumumba, had been killed a few months earlier. He assumed that any American, even a visiting student like me, would share his relief at the assassination of a man the

United States government considered a dangerous leftist trouble-maker. In the early morning a day or two later I left the country by ferry across the Congo River, the conversation still ringing in my head as the sun rose over the waves and the dark, smooth water slapped against the boat's hull.

It was several decades later that I encountered that footnote, and with it my own ignorance of the Congo's early history. Then it occurred to me that, like millions of other people, I had read something about that time and place after all: Joseph Conrad's Heart of Darkness. However, with my college lecture notes on the novel filled with scribbles about Freudian overtones, mythic echoes, and inward vision, I had mentally filed away the book under fiction, not fact.

I began to read more. The further I explored, the more it was clear that the Congo of a century ago had indeed seen a death toll of Holocaust dimensions.

At the same time, I unexpectedly found myself absorbed by the extraordinary characters who had peopled this patch of history. Although it was Edmund Dene Morel who had ignited a movement, he was not the first outsider to see King Leopold's Congo for what it was and to try hard to draw the world's attention to it. ...

It is one thing to understand what is going on. It is another thing to deeply understand the scope, extent, scale and importance of what is going on. Let's focus on one of Hochschild's observations. He writes: "The further I explored, the more it was clear that the Congo of a century ago had indeed seen a death toll of Holocaust dimensions." Notice two things in his observation. One is use of upper case "H" in Holocaust, the second is limitation of comparison to Congo.

While it is the responsibility of professions to blow the whistle early on. It is a collective responsibility to deeply understand the scope, extent, scale and importance over time and in due course.

7.8.2   Software Engineering Profession and Copyright

Based on the particular aspect of our professions' relationship to patents and copyright, many of us are "Intellectual Workers".

Our professions — be it: software, engineering, teaching, research, arts, journalism, medicine, pharmacy, plant biology, etc. — all involve production or propagation of Intellectual Property. As a medical doctor, when you prescribe patented medications, you are propagating patents. As a software engineer working for the likes of Microsoft, Google, Amazon, Facebook, etc. when you write code, you are producing copyrighted opaque, restricted and proprietary software and internet services.

Hence, the way that the patent and copyright systems operate impacts our professions. The impact of Intellectual Property on our professions is always negative. IPR impedes our ability to share and to collaborate. Each of our profession's responsibilities towards the health of society and the responsibilities of each of us towards our profession demands that we reject the Western IPR regime.

This responsibilities-oriented model is distinct and different from the generally economic American model. If you do not believe in the notion of the responsibilities that we mentioned, then you are likely part of the problem.

With respect to IPR, among all professions of Intellectual Workers, Software Engineers hold a special place. Software is inherently collaborative and cumulative. We are software engineers. The negative impacts of the Western IPR regime on our profession have been significant. And we have been well positioned to understand the harm.

Over the past 40 years or so, we have done various things to address these harms. Inside of the Western IPR regime, some of us have produced public software licenses that revert us back to the natural collaborative environment which the traditional Western copyright regime replaces. In Chapter 12 — Digital Non-Proprietary Movements, we describe these strategies in some detail.

Then, based on the public software licenses, over the past 40 years, collaboratively we built a whole lot of non-propietary (Libre-Halaal) software. Today, the overwhelming majority of internet infrastructure runs on non-proprietary software. In the realm of internet software, there is no debate. The Libre-Halaal model is superior to the Western IPR based Proprietary-Haraam model. We have demonstrated that for software development, the natural collaborative environment is superior to the artificial competitive environment that Western IPR regime wants to create.

The notion of superiority of the natural collaborative environment over the artificial competitive environment that Western IPR regime attempts to create is in no way limited to just software. It applies to all polyexistentials. It should then be clear that the entirety of the Western IPR regime is a failed experiment.

Yet hardly any of these understandings are widespread in mainstream belief systems. So, books like this need to be written. It is towards the fulfillment of our responsibilities to our profession and our profession's responsibility to society and humanity that we are writing this book.

7.9   Core of the Character of the Origin — Americans and Westerners

Without any doubt, slavery in general as it was practiced by all throughout history is very different from American Slavery as it was practiced in the last 500 years. Recognition of the validity and emphasis on IPR throughout the world is also very different from the American IPR regime.

There must be something very unique and exceptional about the American character that has produced these results.

7.9.1   Core of the American Character in the 18th Century — Slavery

With a snapshot of the American society in the late 18th century we make the following observations:

- A strong belief in extreme individualism

- A strong belief in business and economics leading to raw capitalism and supremacy of markets

- A strong belief in American exceptionalism and moral superiority

7.9.2   Core of the American Character in the 21st Century — Intellectual Property

American characteristics have really not changed much over time. If anything, the inhuman side of those characteristics have gradually grown.

With a snapshot of the American society in the 21st century we make the following observations:

- A strong belief in extreme individualism

- A strong belief in raw capitalism and supremacy of economics and markets

- A strong belief in American exceptionalism and moral superiority

- A strong belief in freedom of corporations and the unbound power of corporations

- A strong belief in the American right for imperialism and neo-colonialism

Above all, copyright and patents have become vehicles for accumulation and concentration of wealth and power in corporations.

The American model is in fact quite simple. It is that of economic creatures existing in an exploitative industrial context governed by raw capitalism and a legal system whose purpose is to protect that economic model. There is a big distance between this American model and humanity.

It is very natural for all of that to progress to the point where much of the rest of the world views the core of the American character as that of a morally bankrupt self-absorbed bully.

As an imperialist and neo-colonialist strategy, Americans are now imposing the Western Intellectual Property regime as the universal regime.

With respect to IPR, should the rest of the world subscribe to the American model or should it be rejected in full?

Does the rest of the world want to be like Americans?

Do other societies want to end up where the American society is today?

7.10   Ownership Mistakes Always End Badly

Ownership mistakes result in great vested interests over time. Even when the mistake is well understood, those with vested interests will fight corrections every step of the way. Ownership mistakes result in divergence of market value from true value. Ownership mistakes result in gradual growth of the divergence over time. So, ownership mistakes always end badly.

7.10.1   End of American Slavery

The historical reality reveals a disturbing pattern where the offspring of enslaved individuals and their slave masters became a source of social upheaval. Across generations, male slave masters frequently engaged in the sexual exploitation of their female slaves, resulting in the birth of children who were considered property rather than acknowledged as their rightful offspring according to the American concept of ownership. Over time, this accumulation of such individuals reached a critical mass, causing a significant challenge for the existing social order.

This of course is an oversimplification of the complicated historical circumstances that led to the end of slavery. Our oversimplifications here revolve around the dynamics of mistaken ownership rules. The negative impacts of chattel slavery grew to the point that it was no longer manageable.

There was no other way but to end it. And even then, there was a war.

American Slavery did not end because American masters were persuaded or because they understood any mistake.

And after its end, the magnitude of its real harm and the significance, the scope and the scale of this mistake has never been recognized and acknowledged by the Westerners. The crimes were never acknowledged. The criminals were never punished, and the victims were never recognized and compensated. The African holocaust has never been acknowledged by Americans and Westerners.

Those are part of cost and consequences of the previous American ownership mistake.

7.10.2   End of American IPR

The American IPR is now the basis of much of the American economy (which in this case is same as American society).

American presidents can't wait to get out of the office, have a book written and receive their copyright royalties. That is entrenched at a very high level and very widely.

Through Western IPR more and more power and capital is being concentrated in Western corporations. Corpocracy is the model that rules America.

The American IPR regime will not end because Americans would be persuaded. The American IPR regime will not end because Americans would understand their mistake.

Similar to American Slavery which ended with the American civil war, Western IPR will likely end with a war. The nature of that war will likely be very different. It will likely start as an economic war. Let's hope that the scope of that war remains limited to economic adjustments.

Cost and consequences of the IPR mistakes will be very large as well. With IPR, the scope of the damage is not limited to any locality. Another holocaust is in the making. This time it is our souls — not our bodies — that are being gradually exterminated and the scope of the extermination is global.

Humanity is at risk.

Chapter 8

Ramifications of the Western IPR Mistake

Ramifications of ownership mistakes are deep and are often not understood even after the mistake has been understood. We pointed to some of the ramifications of the American Slavery mistake in Chapter 7. With the Western IPR ownership mistake, things are even more complicated. Ramifications of Intellectual Property Rights (IPR) ownership mistakes are very grave.

8.1 IPR Ramifications: Amplification of Power of Corporations and Corporate-Personhood

In an abstract sense, the victim is the polyexistential which is being restricted. More tangibly, it is the people who suffer from the artificial scarcity of the polyexistential.

This artificial scarcity takes the form of the ill person whose life depends on the medication whose patent holder makes it unaffordable; of Indian farmers to whom access to their most versatile resource, the neem tree, is being restricted by chemical companies' patents; and of all the people who want to access and share digital literature or music or art or software who are unable to because of restrictive laws surrounding ownership of polyexistentials.

Thus, all of humanity is victimized and oppressed by the scarcity created by patent and copyright holders.

It is in humanity's interest to abolish the Western IPR regime.

Widespread adoption of IPR in America and in the West has created certain environments and certain trends which have already destroyed many human institutions in Western societies.

Such destructions are often not pure ramifications of the IPR regime. The IPR regime is being used by Corporations to destroy individuals and professions.

Corporations are major players in control of patents and copyright. In this model, IPR has become a vehicle for concentration of wealth and power in corporations.

8.2   IPR Ramifications: Economic Inequality

It is widely recognized and evident that intellectual property protection can contribute to the exacerbation of economic inequality due to several compelling reasons.

However, establishing a direct causal relationship between intellectual property rights and economic inequality can be challenging, as it involves proving a negative, which can be difficult to provide definitive evidence for. While it may be challenging to demonstrate the absence of economic inequality in the absence of IPR, there are areas where we can observe significant differences.

For instance, comparing the models of Microsoft Windows and Linux provides ample evidence. Microsoft Windows operates within the Western IPR regime, relying on copyright and patents under a competitive corporate model. In contrast, Linux is built on the copyleft and no-patents models, emphasizing international collaboration among software engineers.

Recognizing that the societal benefits of Microsoft Windows and Linux are equal, or even favoring Linux, let's examine their economic ramifications. For a considerable period, Bill Gates, the co-founder of Microsoft, held the position of the world's richest individual, with a net worth of around 120 billion USD in 2023. On the other hand, Linus Torvalds, the creator of Linux, also possesses substantial wealth but with a net worth of around 120 million USD in 2023.

In this particular case, there is a substantial factor of 1000 in economic inequality between the two models. This demonstrates that IPR indeed contributes to economic inequality. Clearly, this example simplifies the measurement of magnitude. Nonetheless, it is evident that IPR plays a significant role in fostering income inequality.

The influence of IPR in perpetuating income inequality is a gradual process, and if left unchecked, it can have disastrous consequences. The current situation in America highlights how income inequality has endangered various societal structures.

Dean Baker, the author of "Rigged: How Globalization and the Rules of the Modern Economy Were Structured to Make the Rich Richer", [2]. elaborates on these concepts. We include some of his key related points below:[31]

> [...] The upward redistribution of wealth arising from intellectual property (IP) is typically disguised in public debates as being the result of "technology." But blaming technology attributes it to an impersonal force. When we point out that it is due to intellectual property, we make it clear that inequality is a policy choice.
>
> To take my favorite example, without Microsoft's government-granted patent and copyright monopolies, Bill Gates would probably still be working for a living. Many other billionaires and millionaires would be far less wealthy if we had different rules for intellectual property.
>
> By my calculations, the amount of money transferred from the rest of us to those in a position to benefit from IP comes to more than $1 trillion annually. This transfer comes in the form of higher prices for prescription drugs, medical equipment, software, and many other products. This amount is almost half the size of all before-tax corporate profits, and roughly one-third larger than the current military budget. In other words, it is real money.
>
> [...] As a practical matter, very few of us receive any substantial income, either directly or indirectly, from intellectual property. That means that we don't stand to lose anything if companies in China don't honor Pfizer's patents on a drug or Microsoft's copyrights on software. In fact, if we are bothered by inequality, we really should not be upset that those at the top will have somewhat less income because China is not honoring their intellectual property claims. [...]

It is crucial for civilized societies to be wary of the effects of IPR on their communities, particularly through the lens of income inequality. A strong defense against these dangers lies in the complete rejection of the Western IPR regime.

8.3 The Paralyzing Effects of Western IPR on Health of Professions

Each profession has a responsibility to society towards protecting a certain aspect of life.

Here we are using the term "profession" in the way it is understood in the East.

The Western IPR regime has had an indirect consequence of empowering financiers, corporations and corpocracy. This has come at the expense of professions, society and individuals.

Intellectual Property is a powerful tool used by businesses to dominate and crush professions. By rejecting Patents, Copyrights, and trade secrecy, professions can protect themselves from business dominance. Unfortunately, this recognition is often absent in many professions.

Journalism can be more productive and resistant to business corruption by rejecting copyright and adopting copyleft. Pharmaceutical, Bio-Medicine and Medicine can be more productive and resistant to business corruption by rejecting patents and adopting the patent-free model.

The software engineering profession has already demonstrated how by adopting the copyleft and patent-free models it can resist dominance by business. GNU/Linux has stood up against the Microsoft monopoly.

The principles of the software engineering profession's collaborative model can be reapplied to many other professions.

In essence the solution is in properly defining polyexistential capitalism.

Consider the Software Engineering profession which is hindered by the Western so-called Intellectual Property Rights (IPR) regime. As engineers instead of being able to freely collaborate we are enticed to compete. Instead of collectively inventing and innovating towards the good of society, the Western IPR model pushes us to individually reinvent towards corporate profit.

Software and internet services have become an integral and critical component of societal functioning, and the consequences for humanity are enormous. Of fundamental importance in this regard is what we will call the *manner-of-existence* of software.

We present the Halaal *manner-of-existence* of software and Internet services in:
"Defining Halaal Software and Defining Halaal Internet Services" [3]
– available on-line at: http://www.bycontent.net/PLPC/120041 .

The Western IPR regime adversely impacts our ability to produce Libre-Halaal software and internet services.

It is for this reason that we are writing this document. While polyexistentials are far broader than software, we emphasis software in this presentation for two reasons. First, we are software engineers. Second, the collaborative and cumulative and usage orientation of software (as a polyexistential) permits us to demonstrate the natural power of polyexistentials in contrast to Western so-called Intellectual Property Rights (IPR) regime. This of course is demonstrated in success of the Libre-Halaal GNU/Linux in contrast to the proprietary MS Windows.

8.4 Loss of Autonomy and Privacy

The dynamics and the environment that Western patents and copyright have created naturally leads to the creation of proprietary software and proprietary internet services.

Westerners have not recognized the important connection between Intellectual Property Rights (IPR) and autonomy and privacy. The use of proprietary software and services leads to a reduction of ownership and control over one's possessions and services, resulting in a loss of autonomy and privacy for the individual. Regulations such as the European General Data Protection Regulation (GDPR) and the Californian Consumer Privacy Act (CCPA) fail to recognize that data and service are often intertwined, and that possession, control, and ownership of both should be transferred to the user, not just the ownership of data.

In the Proprietary American Digital Ecosystem (Internet Application Services as they exist today), the individual's autonomy and privacy are being crushed. A deal has been made. Users free-of-charge get: email, calendar, address book, content publication, and Facebook friends. In return, American corporations get: semantic analysis of email, spying with consent, traffic, logs and trail analysis and behavior cross referencing.

A new currency has been created. The user's autonomy and privacy is now the implicit Internet currency. For now, the established business model is that of translation of the individual's privacy into targeted advertising. That business model will naturally grow in scope. The debit side of this new currency is civilization and humanity.

Today, the world is largely unaware of this. The public is completely oblivious to the perils of the proprietary Internet model, and happily entrusts its personal data, its privacy, its freedoms and its civil liberties to proprietary business interests. And the people whose responsibility it is to safeguard the public interest — government, and the engineering profession — are asleep at the wheel.

The existing proprietary digital ecosystem is well on its way towards the destruction of humanity. Under immediate threat of destruction are the privacy and autonomy of the individual.

At societal level, autonomy and privacy cannot be preserved just with new technology. There are no band-aid technical solutions.

8.5 Corporate Artificial intelligence

Earlier we underscored that the Western IPR regime indirectly amplifies the power of corporations and that the Western IPR regime indirectly leads to loss of autonomy and privacy of the individual.

Unchecked social media data collection by the likes of the American Facebook has been used to threaten people's opportunities, undermine their privacy, or pervasively track their activity — often without their knowledge or consent. The American Google has been collecting people's email through Gmail for decades. The American Microsoft has been monitoring and tracking professional activities and relationships through the likes of LinkedIn and Github.

The collected data of individuals has been stored but is yet to be fully exploited. With the emergence of Artificial Intelligence (AI), the potential for better exploitation of personal data has opened up. One potential use of this data is to create large language models that simulate specific individuals. These models can then be trained using collected Gmail emails, WhatsApp messages, Facebook and LinkedIn relationships, and other information of specific individuals. This could potentially lead to the creation of Artificial Individuals.

Here we are not speaking of general Artificial Intelligence and training of models by public data. Instead, we are speaking of training of models by private data towards full exploitation of individuals by corporations. In due course, corpocracy will kick in and spying as we know it will take a different form. Nuanced nationality and sub-population attitudes and beliefs will be simulated and exploited.

The real danger that AI poses is not necessarily in its training by public data. It is customized training of AI models by private data that we should be afraid of — and that is right around the corner. Based on your private emails and social network interactions, pre-trained large language models can go through additional supervised fine-tuning trainers producing *your artificial inteligence* for the benefit of the corporations who possess your private information. By *your artificial inteligence* we mean corporate owned and controlled computer programs (Artificial Individual models) that know what you know — about your family, your relationships, etc.

Are you using Gmail? Are you on Facebook? etc. How complete do you think your Artificial Individual model is?

The exploitations of your private data by American companies will take different forms, depending on the target. For US citizens and Westerners, the exploitations will be mostly economic in nature. For Easterners, the exploitation will be mostly political and societal, with the goal of Americanization. The overwhelming majority of Facebook and Gmail users are not US citizens.

8.6   Western IPR Regime: An Instrument of Neocolonialism

Westerners have been exploiting their fake so-called intellectual assets (copyrights and patents) as an instrument to dominate other peoples and cultures.

Polyexistence is global in nature, therefore, Western IPR is extraterritorial. The Western IPR regime has become an instrument of neo-colonialism in the era of global trade. West is issuing its currency and is forcing East to accept it. The "W" in WIPO stands for West not the World.

Outside of the Western model of mostly economic analysis of merits of IPR, there are other considerations.

For Iranians for example, acceptance or rejection of merits of Western Intellectual Property Rights Regime, above all, is a moral and ethical question. Not a business or economics question.

Iran is a non-signatory to WTO (Western Trade Organization) copyright laws, but crisp full rejection of the concept of Copyright and Patent as was explicitly stated by Imam Khomeini has not been asserted again.

Moving towards a society based on halaal manner-of-existence of software requires crisp declarations that fully invalidate Western intellectual property rights regime. See, www.halaalsoftware.org for an initial formulation.

The Western IPR Regime is very American and very Western. Portraying Western IPR Regime as anything other than limited local law is a fallacy.

The exploitation starts by demanding that Western IPR be considered universal. Most forms of umbrella economic relationships with the West demand recognition of the Western values of copyrights and patents.

The exploited economically weaker nations are then subjected to these flawed beliefs through West-Toxication at societal level and through economic strong-arming.

The net result is that the exploited are now forced to recognize West's fake currencies of Patents and Copyrights, which the Westerners have plenty of and in which the exploited are poor.

Americans/Westerners are imposing these mistaken views on the East.

American digital colonialism has two fundamental fronts. One is surveillance, where American internet corporations watch over the rest of the world. The second is digital Americanization, where American internet corporations propagate American norms and American values through the American internet.

Chapter 9

Americanism: Root of the IPR Mistake

Based on philosophy, nature and logic we have made a case that makes it clear that the Western IPR regime is in conflict with nature. The logic that demonstrates polyexistentials are unownable is sufficient to persuade anyone who thinks with his brain and whose interests do not conflict with the natural conclusions of our discourse.

But human rationality is a myth. Both individually and in groups people don't think with their brain. People think with their character. Dominant aspects of their character that impact their thinking are self-interest and their value system.

So, to understand the root causes of the Western IPR mistake we should ask who are the people who have come up with these unnatural ownership rules that are designed to create artificial scarcities? And what is the character of the people who have come up with IPR and who are protecting IPR?

Unlike existence and possession that are aspects of nature, ownership is a man-made construct. Ownership rules can therefore directly be associated with the people who made them. As a set of ownership rules, IPR regime is a Western and American construct.

To better understand the Western IPR regime we may profit from better understanding the culture of those who created and who are promoting IPR. We label the ideology of those who created and are promoting IPR, "Americanism". Our use of Americanism is not as a nationality label, it is based on a character type and it is a label for a belief system.

By Americanism, we are referring to a particular established model of economic creatures existing in an exploitative industrial context. We will refer to the American spheres of consensus that we describe in this section which has shaped the core of American character as "The Proprietary American Regime" – and sometimes just "The American Regime" or "Americanism". We refer to the model as Americanism and we call those who believe in and exercise this model "Americanists". We draw a clear distinction between being an American National and being Americanist. It is the belief system and not Americans as individuals that we are referring to – while recognizing that the core of character of most American individuals shapes the American Regime and is shaped by it. Furthermore, the belief system that we call Americanism physically and geographically spans far further than the United States of America. Many throughout the world have been inflicted by this disease and have become "Americanized".

9.1   Americanism and the Economics of IPR

Western IPR assumes that human beings are essentially economic creatures and that if they are not economically rewarded, they will not engage as much in activities that progress science and useful arts. Western IPR regime assumes that human beings are competition oriented and that collaborative values are inferior to competition for advancement of science and useful arts.

Economics is the study of what people do when nothing more important than money is at stake. In the 21st century, economics is the primary governing force on planet Earth, but there are variations in the role it plays in different societies. Western IPR is fully rooted in economics. The Western IPR regime was created and is being promoted in this American and Western context.

To the extent that it can be considered a culture, the American culture understands this – and is proud of it. In the movie "Killing Them Softly", the actor Brad Pitt, in a key scene, puts it like this:

> This guy [Obama] wants to tell me we are living in a community. Don't make me laugh. I'm living in America and in America you are on your own.
>
> America is not a country. America is just a business.
>
> Now, just [.......] pay me.

It is in this pure business sense that Western Intellectual Property exists.

Right and wrong are often orthogonal to economics and profit, as externality is an inherent characteristic of economics. In the spirit of combating westtoxication «غرب زدگی», [16], Imam Khomeini, captured this difference in a short crisp sentence: "basis of everything for the donkey too is its economics" «الاغ هم زیربنای همه چیزش اقتصادش است».[32] Our model for humanity is inherently complex and intertwines: religion, morality, ethics, economics, business, law, language, culture, society and nature. Western IPR regime is not rooted in harmony with nature, morality or ethics.

To pay lip service to any remaining human needs of economic creatures, individualism and individualistic freedom becomes the main pillar of Western morality. Conveniently, the Western economics model celebrates individual freedoms. Based on those individualistic freedoms, the sophisticated Western corporation is then well positioned to manipulate the naive Western individual. With that form of Western morality in place, the Western corporation then demands those individualistic freedoms for itself. The American/Western legal system then kicks in and formalizes the Western legal notions of "corporate personhood". The Western model then amounts to a complete collection of economic creatures (people and corporations alike). Should such a collection be called a society? What is Western society? It is inside of this model that the Western IPR regime has thrived.

9.2   Proprietary Americanist Values

The concepts and laws of IPR have been shaped by proprietary American values. And this is the root cause of the problem. In particular, the proprietary American model is based on:

- Supremacy of business and economics – Leaving no room for societal, social, philosophical or moral considerations in the base fabric of society.

- Unbounded Corporations. The Corporation, an entity whose sole purpose is to generate profit is permitted to do all that it pleases and in many respects is considered equivalent with human individuals. This model reduces humans to the level of Corporations – greed driven psychopaths.

- Elimination or marginalization of role of professions (e.g., Internet Engineering) in society.

- Corpocracy – Where collaboration of Corporation and Government results in manipulation and control of the People.

- Extreme Individualism – Rampant self-toxication at epidemic levels. The stressing of personal freedoms, out of balance against significance of health of society and humanity plays well into manipulation of individuals by corporations.

- Uses of IPR as an instrument to exploit other societies and cultures. Based on American Exceptionalism.

These dynamics are such that the proprietary American model puts not just America, but the entirety of human civilization in danger.

The American model is being portrayed to the world as universal. It is not. There is more to the world than the American regime. The American regime has produced well understood results for other crucial aspects of life that the civilized world has fully rejected. Much of the world wishes to be separate from the American regime.

Americanism is inherently exploitative. It often results into short term prosperity for its practitioners at a cost to others. Sometimes the practitioners don't recognize that they are also the others.

Consider how Americans eat. The American food system, as depicted in the documentary "Food Inc," has transformed the role of the American farmer from a producer of food into instruments of agribusiness machinery of patented economic processes. Eating has become a form of economic manipulation, with humans reduced to economic creatures existing in an exploitative industrial context for the purpose of consumption. This system has led to a prevalence of obesity among the poor in America.

Consider how Americans take care of their sick. Health and medicine have been fully subjected to capitalism. Everyone for himself. The doctor-patient relationship has become a fully economic transaction. Insurance business has been placed on the top and the patient at the very bottom while the American doctor has become nothing more than a tool of business. The rich think that this works very well for them. In the aggregate, it is a miserable failure. For example, Cuba, with a fraction of resources produces an infant mortality rate that compares very well against the American Regime's. The obvious human model of universal health care which is practiced throughout the civilized world is considered nasty socialism in America.

Consider how Americans view prescription medications. The Anglo-American culture permits advertising of prescription drugs on Television. Nowhere else in the world is this permitted. The exclusive producer of the patented medication is permitted to dangle the cure in front of the sick in public – and hardly any American recognizes this as a clear sign for the road to end of civilization and humanity. The profession of medicine is bypassed by the business where the sick is encouraged to tell the doctor what to do.

Consider how Americans consider university education. The average American graduate comes out $35K in debt. The American higher education system is for the rich and the indebted. The purpose of education has become preparation for economic activity. American academia has been fully corporatized. In the American model, learning too has become a purely economic activity.

Consider how Americans view sports. Sports are undoubtedly big business in America, with a total market size of over $70 billion in 2021. This revenue comes from four main sources: ticket sales, media rights, sponsorships, and merchandising. American sports are all organised as cartels. The cartels (they call themselves "leagues") are the holders of "media rights" under the Copyright Act of 1976, which grants copyright protection to the live broadcasts of sporting events. Contrast all of this with pahlevani and zoorkhaneh rituals in Iran.

Consider how Americans view their guns. When extreme individualism is at the center, ridiculous arguments for ridiculous freedoms become the norm. The distance from there, to "going postal", "Columbine", "Sandy Hook", etc. is very little. American savagery is truly exceptional!

Consider how Americans view relations with other societies. America's short history points to exploitation, colonialism, dominance and imperialism as clear trends. The natives are now concentrated in reservations. The African continent has been destroyed and the African languages and cultures were bulldozed into oblivion. Descendants of those African slaves now make up about one third of the population of American prisons.[33] The use of the atomic bomb, the ultimate weapon of mass destruction, was initiated by Americans. The CIA's clandestine coups to manipulate and exploit Iranians, Arabs, South-Americans, etc. are celebrated and glamorized through the American Hollywood. The patterns of Vietnam, Iraq, Afghanistan, Libya and Syria point to the inability of Americans to listen, understand and learn.

Much of the civilized world has looked at these American models and has fully rejected them.

When Americans try to impose their models for monoexistentials on others, rejections of these American models by the rest of the world, often takes the form of: "Yankee Go Home", "Go to Hell Yankee" and "Death to America" chants followed by physical rejection and separation. And that has kind of worked for some – e.g., the 1979 Iranian Revolution.

But rejection of Americanist models for polyexistentials is more complicated.

9.3   Recidivism Patterns of Americanist Offenses

It is naive to imagine that sound logic and advocacy of morality, ethics and philosophy can stop the exploitative patterns and offenses that Americanists have established as a pattern.

The Americanists don't believe in repentance. They have never acknowledged and apologized for the genocide of the natives, the destruction of Africa and its cultures and languages, use of the atomic bomb or any other of their atrocities. The concept of the need for reparations for the damages that they have caused is foreign to Americanists. The notion of reviewing their actions and feeling contrition or regret for past wrongs is not part of Americanism.

Americanists are unwilling to recognize and acknowledge their mistakes.

Left to the Americanists, there is every reason to expect that the above-mentioned self-toxications, bullying, destruction and uncivilized patterns of exploitation will continue and will be repeated.

9.4   Exclusion of Americanism From Human Oriented Polyexistentials Governance

Given these trends, should the world accept the American regime's model of IPR for polyexistence and polyexistentials which Americanists propagate in the form of so-called Intellectual Property as tools for continued exploitation?

The Japanese/Brazilian/Iranian/Chinese/French/Cuban/Indian/Russian/etc models for food, medicine, sports, university education and guns are distinctly different from the American model. Much of the civilized world looks at the American model and sees a purely economically oriented savage model. This of course is very different from what Americans see when they look in the mirror. This degree of self-absorption and these extremes of American mono-cultures of the mind are genuinely exceptional.

Unlike food, guns and medicine (monoexistentials) which are inherently local, the inherent polyexistential nature of IPR restriction is global.

Rejection of the American proprietary model of the Internet is far more complicated than rejecting the local American models of food, medicine, guns, etc. Slogans and chants are ineffective and complete physical separation is impractical. A large segment of the planet has already come to recognize that the greatest threat to humanity is Americanism. It is wholly wrong to allow the Proprietary American IPR to become a propagation vehicle for Americanism. It should not be permitted.

The Americanist's Intellectual Property Rights model of governance of polyexistentials is rooted in extreme individualism and self-toxication. Instead, we want to adopt a human oriented model for governance of polyexistentials.

Saadi, «سعدی» , has well expressed this distinction between self-toxicated economic creatures and humans:

Human beings are members of a whole   بنی آدم اعضای یک پیکرند

In creation of one essence and soul
If one member is afflicted with pain
Other members uneasy will remain
If you have no sympathy for human pain
The name of human you cannot retain

که در آفرینش ز یک گوهرند
چو عضوی به درد آورد روزگار
دگر عضوها را نماند قرار
تو کز محنت دیگران بی غمی
نشاید که نامت نهند آدمی

It is in the context of a human model for governance of polyexistentials that we are fully rejecting The Americanist's Intellectual Property Rights model.

Our Anti-American tone here is not against Americans as individuals. American individuals who disagree with our root cause analysis may continue their use and support of their proprietary model.

The cure that we offer in the next part is for all of humanity and is equally applicable to Americanists and American nationals who recognize the disease.

Part III

Contours of Cures

Chapter 10

Dynamics of Cures

Proper analysis of the Western IPR regime leads to a clear and obvious conclusion, the IPR regime should be abolished. We are IPR abolitionists. We want to persuade all to join us and demand the abolishment of the Western IPR regime.

However, the purpose of writing this document has not been just to analyze the IPR problem and just demand its abolishment. Proposing and analyzing solutions are an equally important aspect of this document.

What can be done? By Whom? How?

For any of the proposed solutions to be significant, solutions need to be at societal level and exposition of concepts in this document are geared towards establishing societal relationships.

We view the Western so-called IPR Regime as a disease. It is a sick way of thinking and a sick way of behaving that becomes an inherent condition. It is abnormal in that it is against the nature of polyexistentials. This disease can spread from one society to the next. It is like alcoholism, it brings short term pleasure but long-term despair, not just for the alcoholic but for all concerned.

We therefore label our effort to restore societal behavior to its normal condition (Libre-Halaal Polyexistentials) not a solution to a problem but a cure for the disease.

In context of cures, there are 3 dimensions of scope that need to be recognized:

1. What types of polyexistentials (corresponding/mapping to professions) should be initial primary focuses? By types of polyexistentials we are referring to digitals, software, internet services, knowledge in general, knowledge of medications, etc.

2. Which societies should we focus on? Eastern cures are inherently different from what may be applicable to the West. Furthermore, in the IPR context economic interests of East and West are different. It is possible for the Libre-Halaal model to do an economic number on the Western IPR based Proprietary model.

3. What general type of activities do we focus on? By type of activities we are referring to informative, academic, promulgative, tangible, or theoretical.

Prior to selecting our focal points, we need to analyze the battleground.

10.1   Dynamics of the Proprietary-Haraam vs. Libre-Halaal Battle

Endorsement of the Western IPR model leads to the Proprietary-Haraam manner-of-existence of polyexistentials which then usually leads to the competition oriented internally opaque digital entities.

Rejection of the Western IPR model can lead to the Libre-Halaal manner-of-existence of polyexistentials which then leads to the collaborative oriented internally transparent digital entities.

In software's context, though this is not part of popular cultural awareness, there is currently a titanic battle taking place between two competing ideologies: the Proprietary-Haraam model (exemplified by Windows), and the Libre-Halaal model (exemplified by GNU/Linux). This is a to-the-death battle, from which there can eventually emerge only a single winner.

Of course, this battle is part of a broader ideological contest, about ownership models for polyexistentials in general (software, but also including ideas, knowledge, literature, music, images, movies, etc.) in the digital era. Current ownership models are rooted in the historical conventions and institutions of material products and materially-based services. In the case of abstract constructs such as software, these conventions appear in the form of the existing Intellectual Property (IP) regime, where proprietary ownership is asserted by means of patents and copyright.

But the inherent nature of software, Internet services and other polyexistentials is fundamentally at odds with these historical conventions of physical property (monoexistentials) ownership. Such constructs have the inherent potential for unlimited replicability and dissemination, and in the age of the Internet this potential is now fully realized.

As a result, the existing Western Intellectual Property conventions are coming under increasing stress, as the internal forces of replicability clash with the externally constraining Intellectual Property framework. The Intellectual Property regime is also coming under formal intellectual attack, as the dysfunctionality and true costs of this regime become increasingly apparent.

10.2   Tear Points of Libre-Halaal and the Proprietary-Haraam Tussle

We have analyzed the forces in nature that work against Proprietary-Haraam model and those which are in harmony with the Libre-Halaal model — and have identified a number of "tear points". Our execution is focused on these tear points.

Some of these tear points are more applicable to Eastern societies and some are more applicable to Western societies.

We present and analyze these tear points with the goal of providing a cure in the context of formulation of national policies for Eastern societies and ad-hoc adoption among Westerners.

10.2.1   Initial Focus: Digital Cures

The domain of polyexistentials is vast. The digital domain in particular is an area where we can explicitly focus on. In other words, the initial scope of the cure is that of a "Digital Ecosystem".

Software is a unique form of polyexistentials. In the context of an alternative to the American digital ecosystem, software has the best chance of illustrating and correcting the Western IPR mistake because it has the following attributes:

- Software is practical and useful. It plays a pervasive role in our daily lives.

- Software controls other digital entities and therefore it impacts internet services and content.

- Software development is highly collaborative in nature.

- Software is inherently cumulative in nature.

For these reasons we believe that the software battle is the best initial front against the proponents of the Western IP regime. Other fields and professions – pharmacists, physicians, plant biologists, farmers, academics/students, and others – can build on our efforts and mimic our approach.

In the realm of software and internet, we offer the creation of the Libre-Halaal ByStar digital ecosystem as a moral alternative to the Proprietary-Haraam American digital ecosystem.

10.2.2   Global/Eastern Tear Point: Inherently Collaborative vs Inhernetly Competitive

The Libre-Halaal model creates an entirely new environment in terms of competition, collaboration, and value chain relationships. Libre-Halaal software and Libre-Halaal Internet Services are genuine public resources, not owned by anyone, freely available for reuse by anyone. They are created by society, for society.

This general proven collaborative model permits for collective efforts for replacing American Proprietary Software which from the perspective of an Eastern society is far more cost effective than the proprietary competitive model.

10.3   Promgulative, Tangible and Theoretical Cures

Informative cures are the types of things that can be done to propagate global understanding and awareness of fraudulence and harm of the Western IPR regime. At a minimum, we are hoping that this book will function as part of informative cures.

Academic cures are the types of things that we all should do even when we know that they won't amount to real cures. We call these academic, because even if they were understood, their impact is unrealistic.

Promulgative cures are the high level things that sources of imitation and legislators should do.

Tangible cures have real assets and capabilities that can be brought to bear.

Theoretical cures are targeted combinations of Informative, Promulgative and Tangible cures. These are cures that could be offered based on the offered understandings.

Thus far all national and societal direction setting related to any aspect of polyexistentials has been reactive. In many cases, we need to move towards proactive regulation as reactive regulation often is a day late a dollar short.

Much of this part of this document is towards formulation of the contours of such proactive regulations.

10.4   Spearhead:
Libre-Halaal ByStar Digital Ecosystem

In order to cure this disease, we need to conceptualize it in its totality — that of a "Digital Ecosystem".

The Proprietary American Digital Ecosystem cannot be fixed. Its dynamics are taking it to a particular eventuality — destruction of civilization and humanity.

Instead, we need to erect an alternative digital ecosystem to stand against it. We properly introduce "The Libre-Halaal ByStar Digital Ecosystem" later in this book.

Chapter 11

Introducing Halaal and Haraam Into Globish

In this chapter we introduce the terms "halaal" «حلال» and "haraam" «حرام» into Globish. [34] Halaal and haraam are facilities that assist with expression of moral sensibilities. It is a good thing for people to be better equipped to express their moral sensibilities. It is a good thing for different societies to move towards consensus on moral topics through dialogue. The inclusion of halaal and haraam in Globish assists with that.

11.1 Shortcomings of English in the Domain of Morality

English is strong in some domains and weak in others.

The strength and weakness of English in various domains is of course directly related to the culture and value system of the native speakers of this language, most notably the Americans and the British. Culture and language are intertwined. Syntax and semantics are adjuncts.

In the domain of business, economics and finance (that is to say, money) English is very strong. In the domain of money English is rich with terms such as: MBS (Mortgage-Backed Securities), shorting, margin, hedge fund, haircut, reverse mortgage, EPS, P/E, dead cat bounce, double down, bubble, pyramid scheme, day trading, pump-and-dump, spin-and-flip, and many others. In Anglo-American English, the term for the world's largest casino is "the stock market." Equivalents for most of these terms do not exist in most other languages, because these concepts do not exist in other cultures. Values, thinking and behavior influence language; and conversely, language influences values, thinking and behavior.

Economics is the study of what people do when nothing more important than money is at stake. Even though twenty first century planet earth is too primitive to be governed by anything but economics, there are variations for the place of economics in societies. With its purest form, Americans have ended up with a collection of economic creatures existing in an industrial complex, which they call American society. And in that context, English, the language of Americans and the British, has ended up being very economically oriented. It is towards evolution beyond economic creatures that we want to introduce halaal into Globish.

In the domain of morality, ethics and philosophy, English is extremely weak. Fundamental human concepts from other cultures such as Halaal and Haraam, Mottainai (もったいない), Esraaf «اصراف» or Ghanawt «قناعت» are entirely absent from English. And previous attempts to translate these terms into English have been miserable failures. This is because these are complex concepts that do not exist within the value system of the Americans and British.

11.2   Current Orientalist Appropriation of Halaal in English

Looking up the words "halaal" and "haraam" in Wikipedia, or in Encyclopedia Britannica or Webster's dictionary, provides at best an over-simplification, or at worst complete garbage. Viewing haraam as meaning just "prohibited" and viewing halaal as meaning just "permissible" is shallow and simplistic. Limiting the scope of applicability of halaal and haraam to Islamic dietary laws and then trying to simplify halaal based on parallels between halaal meat and kosher meat are sophomoric at best. The concepts of halaal and haraam are far more complex than that.

Not only is Anglo-American English weak in regard to expression of morality, but the culturally egocentric Americans (and Westerners generally) are allergic to the expression of morality by others. In Anglo-American English, the word halaal is loaded with connotation. More than anything else, it evokes immediate feelings of Islamophobia.

Westerners tend to define Eastern terms and concepts in their own context and for their own benefit. And not just that, Western definition of Eastern terms and concepts are often intended to degrade Eastern and Moslem concepts in the spirit of establishing Western superiority and towards Western exploitation of the East and Moslems. Edward Said has labeled this Western model of looking at the East and Moslems as: "Orientalism", [40]. In English, halaal and haraam have been subjected to Orientalism. The scope of applicability of halaal for the most part has been reduced and the concept has been overly over simplified.

Our definition of halaal rejects the current Orientalist appropriation in English and focuses on introducing the real concept of halaal in Globish. The Western and the West-toxicated readers should in particular recognize the distinction that we are drawing between English and Globish and the distinction that we are drawing between the Orientalist appropriation of halaal in English and the real meaning of halaal that we are introducing into Globish.

Halaal is a fundamental, deep and broad concept among Moslems which addresses the question of right and wrong about everything and about all aspects of life. The purpose and meaning of life could well be understandings of what should be Halaal and what should be Haraam. Trying to stick to halaal in action could well become life's primary challenge.

11.3 Halaal: the Native Context

Halaal is a word with Arabic origins. Halaal is a word with Islamic origins.

In Arabic and in Persian/Farsi the word halaal has several contexts and usages. It is a pervasive concept, appearing in multiple contexts: in the form of formal decrees for what is prohibited or permitted; in daily language as an individual statement of moral values; in the content of proverbs and stories; and in many other usages. The particular shading of meaning in any particular usage depends on the context and how the term is used.

For Moslems and for Iranians; language, religion, morality, economics, law, culture and society are very intertwined. This leads to a complex model for humanity.

In contrast, the Western two layers model of law and economics is very simple. And in that simple two layered model, one important purpose of law is to accommodate economics. In that context, the word and concept of halaal is clearly non-essential for simple economic creatures.

To pay lip service to any remaining human needs of economic creatures, individualism and individualistic freedom become the main pillars of Western morality. Conveniently, the Western economics model celebrates individual freedoms. Based on those individualistic freedoms, the sophisticated Western corporation is then well positioned to manipulate the naive Western individual. With that form of Western morality in place, the Western corporation then demands those individualistic freedoms for itself. The American/Western legal system then kicks in and formalizes the Western legal notions of "corporate personhood". The Western model then amounts to a complete collection of economic creatures (people and corporations alike). Should such a collection be called a society? What is Western society?

The span of the word halaal does include the individual's freedom. Halaal subsumes freedom. The concept of halaal is far broader and far stronger than freedom. The span of the word halaal in Persian and in the Shia tradition and in the Iranian culture is illustrated below with five examples:

Religious Decree: One of the purposes of religion is to declare "rights" and "wrongs". In Islam that is accomplished with Halaal and Haraam declarations.

> For example, consider the following.

> "Gambling is haraam"   «قمار حرام است»

Here we have Islam, in its entirety, explicitly declaring that gambling is wrong and prohibited.

Fatwa by your Source-of-Imitation: One of the responsibilities of one's source-of-imitation «مرجع تقلید» is to figure the ethics and morality of new complex topics and provide Halaal and Haraam declarations for his followers and on behalf of society. Very often, societal consensus and source-of-imitation's declaration are consistent. In such cases, the source-of-imitation's declaration is still extremely important as it seals societal consensus.

> For example, consider the following fatwa by Grand Ayatollah Sayyid Ali Khamenei.

> «آیت الله العظمی علی خامنه‌ای، رهبر ایران، در سال ۲۰۰۵ طی فتوایی سلاح های اتمی را حرام اعلام کردند»
> "In 2005, Grand Ayatollah Sayyid Ali Khamenei, Iran's leader, issued a fatwa declaring nuclear weapons haraam."

The fatwa includes the following:

> We believe that using nuclear weapons is haraam and prohibited and that it is everybody's duty to make efforts to protect humanity against this great disaster.

Such a declaration by the Iranian leader, using this most strong word "Haraam", is in stark contrast with America's actual use of nuclear weapons, its threats of re-using it in the form of "all options are on the table" and the American belief system of: "might makes right".

Were Halaal and Haraam on the table when in August 1945, on American leader's (Truman's) orders, two atomic bombs were dropped on Japanese civilians in Hiroshima and Nagasaki?

The significance of Iran's leader, a Grand Ayatollah, declaring nuclear weapons haraam seems not to have been understood by Westerners.

If the Westerner's lack of understanding of halaal and haraam plays a role in the failure of dialog between Iran and the West, perhaps this document can prove useful in that regard.

Societal Consensus: In addition to religious decrees and fatwas by sources-of-imitation, the society through consensus can provide halaal and haraam declarations.

Consider the following example.

> "One's manner of earning a living must be halaal."
> «نان حلال خوردن»

Here we have a usage of halaal which is more in the context of society and culture. Where halaal as a label is applied to income.

An Individual and Her God: In a popular song, Hayedeh «هایده» sings:

> «بیا ای سوته دل ساقی به مستی بی ملالم کن»
> «خدایا امشب این می را حلالم کن، حلالم کن»
> "God, tonight make this wine be halaal for me. Make it be halaal for me."

Here we have usage of the word halaal in context of the relationship between an individual and her God – which need not even be necessarily all that religious.

A Mother's Ultimate Threat: A mother's most severe threat to her child may take the form of:

> «شیرم را حلالت نمی‌کنم»
> "I won't make my milk be halaal for you."

Interpersonal Relations: It is easy to imagine the following exchange between an Armenian-Iranian and a Jewish-Iranian.

> «هر چه بدی از من دیدی، حلالم کن»
> " Whatever badness you have seen from me, please make it be halaal for me."

This is a common saying in Farsi that often occurs between good friends when they say good bye to one another for an extended period of time.

Here we have a usage of halaal that is completely outside of religion. It can be used by non-Moslems and is purely cultural. Here the Armenian and Jew's exchange is rooted in their use of Farsi and their being Iranians.

In the above examples halaal and haraam include two distinct contexts. One is the context of manifestation of moral sensibilities and the other is the context of permissibility of actions.

Islamic law is rooted in actions. In the context of permissibility of actions, five categories (a pentad –«الأحكام الخمسة») are enumerated:

1. واجب / فرض (farḍ/wājib) - Compulsory - obligatory, necessary.

2. مستحب (mustaḥabb) - Recommended.

3. مباح (mubāḥ) - Permitted - neither obligatory, recommended, nor dis-liked - neutral.

4. مكروه (makrūh) - Discouraged - abstaining is recommended.

5. حرام (ḥarām) - Forbidden - opposite of «واجب / فرض» wājib, Compul-sory - abstaining is obligatory.

Halaal's context of manifestation of moral sensibilities is associated with (mubāḥ – Permitted) «مباح» context of permissibility of actions. Haraam's context of manifestation of moral sensibilities is associated with (ḥarām – Forbidden) «حرام» context of permissibility of actions – note the two different senses of the single word ḥarām in the different contexts.

The scope, span and depth of halaal is far broader than its common simplistic Western translation of "permissible in Islam" or its limited parallels with the Jewish Kosher in the context of properness and conformity.

The intertwined nature of language, religion, morality, economics, law, culture and society for Moslems leads to uses of halaal and haraam where the source of declaration and the manner of declaration need not always be totally clear. Aside from religious authority, the power of the word halaal can be based on its widespread acceptance and may be rooted in logic, persuasion and consensus.

In all the above examples, the word halaal functions as a facility for declamatory expression of moral values. It is this general concept that is at the heart of the word halaal.

11.4 Philosophical Halaal: a Wordly Framing

The word halaal is loaded in many ways. It carries a number of strong connotations, in both its native context, and in non-native contexts. In its roots it is theological, originating in and tied directly to Islam. It is a sensitive word in its native context (Arabic and/or Islamic cultures), and evokes strong reactions in the West.

In a non-native context the word halaal evokes negative reactions. In particular it is viewed as a direct expression of Islam; at best unwelcome and at worst evoking strong feelings of Islamophobia.

But in this document, we are using this term without these theological/Islamic connotations. The scope of the word here is philosophical and wordly, to be used in day-to-day affairs, including those of business and technology. We are using it as a philosophical term, to address worldly concerns.

Thus, we are introducing a new context for this word, without the native Islamocentrism, and without the non-native Islamophobia.

We considered the word secular as an appropriate qualifier, as in "secular halaal," but this is not correct for our purposes. Secular implies a complete separation from Islamic/theological meaning, but we wish to retain a reference to these theological origins. Thus, we are shifting the center of gravity of the word from theological to wordly, but retaining the origins of the concept as a theological formulation of morality. Thus, we are coining the terms "philosophical halaal" and "abstract halaal" to represent this.

11.5 Philosophical Halaal: the General Concept

Here we provide an overview description of halaal. We will then follow with a more rigorous dialectical definition.

The word halaal has several contexts and usages. Generally speaking one can say it is a term for the declamatory expression of moral values.

The word halaal is a facility for expressing general moral sensibilities which map to "right." The word haraam is a facility for expressing general moral sensibilities which map to "wrong."

In order for the above to be meaningful we need a framework for moral philosophy in the abstract.

11.6 Locating an Abstract Moral Philosophy for Expressing Philosophical Halaal

The Western model has produced its own brand of philosophers and ethicists. Various of these have produced frameworks and structures that come close to recognizing the need for halaal and haraam. For example, Jeremy Bentham and John Stuart Mill (and others) have put forward the ethical theories of Utilitarianism. Utilitarianism is an effort to provide an answer to the practical question "What ought a man to do?" It goes towards rightness and wrongness analysis and the greater good, but does not quite reach the point where the need for the concepts and the words halaal and haraam become obvious. Another Western example is Kantian ethics. Kant gets to principle of the Universalizability and laws of hypothetical kingdoms but does not recognize that he is actually searching for the concepts of halaal and haraam.

From the perspective of those for whom halaal is a natural part of their language and their culture, such Western philosophers and ethicists are not playing with a full deck. Lacking the essential concept of halaal, Western philosophers are benighted without it, and so they flounder when trying to come to grips with moral questions.

To express philosophical halaal we are not going to use any of the well-known existing models. Instead, we will use a set of precise abstractions presented by a fellow electrical engineer. A Western colleague and friend, Dr. Andrew Hammoude, has written an essay which provides a good basis for explicit definition of philosophical halaal.

Hammoude's essay is titled *Moral Philosophy: An Abstract Approach* [23]. The full text of his essay is available at:

`http://andrew.1.hammoude.byname.net/PLPC/150020`

Hammoude's work does not in any way touch on the words halaal or haraam. But the framework he has created is a useful basis for the definition of philosophical halaal.

In this document we are using Hammoude's work extensively. Here we will restate the key ideas, definitions and vocabulary from his essay. For complete details, refer to the original essay titled, *Moral Philosophy: An Abstract Approach*.

The present document is completely separate and independent from Dr. Hammoude's work.

11.7   Definition of an Abstract Morality

Hammoude defines something he calls an *abstract morality*. This is a completely artificial construct, making no formal reference to real-world moral concepts, but it provides a framework and a way of thinking about moral constructs. His definition is as follows:

> An **abstract morality** is a mapping from the *set of actions* into the two-element abstract set {*right, wrong*}.

The set of actions consists of all actions that may be considered to have moral consequence; that is, they are all actions that affect the welfare of others in some respect. The two-element set {*right, wrong*} is a pair of symbolic tokens with no meaning assigned to them—they are merely arbitrary tokens that we may associate with actions. Thus, an abstract morality as defined by Hammoude is a function from the set of actions into this pair of token symbols.

The token words *right* and *wrong* are distinct from the natural language terms "right" and "wrong." To distinguish the two pairs of words clearly the abstract terms are written italicized, while the natural language terms are written unitalicized, and frequently within quotation marks.

Refer to his essay for complete discussion and examples.

11.7.1 Vocabulary for Real-World Morality

Hammoude also establishes a vocabulary to make reference to moral constructs in the real world. He defines a number of terms for this purpose: an "individual moral sensibility" referring to individual persons, an analogous "group moral sensibility" referring to groups of individuals, a "manifestation" of such sensibilities, and a "real-world morality," defined in terms of such manifestations.

We summarize his definitions below:

- An **individual moral sensibility** is defined as "an innate sense of aversion by an individual to certain kinds of behaviour, or to the commission of certain acts."

- A **group moral sensibility** is defined as an analogous concept for groups of individuals; it is a cultural formulation of sensibility, representative of the majority individual sensibilities within the group.

- Hammoude notes that these sensibilities have externally observable "manifestations," and he gives a number of examples of this, including, "avoidance or relative rarity of acts or behaviour that offend the sensibility; explicit verbal expression such as the use of natural language terms like "right" and "wrong" to acts or forms of behaviour that do or do not offend the sensibility; strong forces of dissuasion against offending acts or behaviour; and explicit codifications of the sensibility in the form of religious or legal doctrine."

- He then defines the **real-world morality** associated with a moral sensibility as "a data set, consisting of the set of actions, and for each element in the set of actions, the set of all manifestations of the sensibility regarding that action." Thus a morality is the complete characterization or cataloging of an underlying moral sensibility, in terms of its observable manifestations.

11.7.2 Duality between abstract and real-world moralities

Having defined an abstract morality, and a real-world morality, Hammoude then notes that there is a duality between these two constructs, stating as follows:

> For any abstract morality we define, there is a real-world morality that may exist, or that we can imagine. And for any real-world morality, we can define a corresponding abstract morality. Thus every abstract morality has a real-world counterpart, or doppelganger, and *vice versa*.

11.8 Defining Abstract Halaal and Abstract Haraam

This now provides the framework and vocabulary needed to define philosophical halaal. In particular, we have definitions for following terms:

- The two-element set {*right, wrong*}

- The set of actions

- A mapping

- A moral sensibility

- A manifestation

- An abstract morality

Note that these definitions span both abstract morality and real-world morality contexts. In particular, the *right* and *wrong* definitions taken from abstract morality remain purely symbolic.

Based on this, we now can properly introduce the concepts of philosophical halaal and philosophical haraam.

Philosophical halaal is "manifestation" of "moral sensibilities" relevant to a specific topic where "the set of actions" map to "*right.*"

Philosophical haraam is "manifestation" of "moral sensibilities" relevant to a specific topic where "the set of actions" map to "*wrong.*"

Philosophical halaal and haraam can then be applied to different topics, providing in large part an abstract morality.

Abstract halaal and haraam are powerful enough concepts to become basis of defining one's religion – separate from God and even without a name.

11.9 Uses Of Halaal As Labels

In addition to the description of an act as halaal or haraam, halaal and haraam are also used as labels.

For example amongst Moslems, a well known usage of halaal as a label is "Halaal Meat", where a specific manner-of-existence of meat is considered halaal. This halaal manner-of-existence of meat demands respect for the animal, engagement of the creator at the time of killing of the animal by the human and demands prevention of such a delicate act becoming industrial.

This topic's equivalent in the American and Western cultures is driven by efficiency and economics leading to Food Inc., [32]. Where the animal becomes just a commodity.

The label of Halaal in "Halaal Meat" communicates a great deal in a single word. It demands adherence to specific processes and rituals – specific to the animal. It is not a single act or a single aspect of meat that makes it "Halaal Meat". It is the entirety of the specific process that warrants use of the label. That specific full process is of course well defined.

Uses of halaal as labels are equally applicable in the context of abstract (philosophical) halaal. Throughout this document and elsewhere, we make use of capitalized Halaal/Haraam when we are referring to use of these words as labels. When we are referring to the concept of halaal/haraam we use the uncapitalized form.

11.10 Authority for Halaal and Haraam Declarations and Role of Religions

Early in our exposition of the concept of halaal and haraam, very deliberately, we divorced halaal and haraam from its religious origins. We now want to revisit the role and place of halaal and haraam in religions and the place of religions with regard to halaal and haraam.

Uses and introductions of halaal and haraam by individuals here and there are of some importance and significance. But it is broad consensus and widespread acceptance of halaal and haraam that results in significant moral impact.

To the extent that religions can be considered vehicles for promotion of morality and ethics, religions should concern themselves with halaal and haraam declarations.

In Chapter 14, we discuss the Moslem model for declarations of halaal and haraam by sources of imitation with regard to IPR in more detail.

11.11   Putting Abstract Halaal to Good Use

Globish is often primarily thought of as the language of global trade and global business. On some topics, Globish needs to also be the language for consensus towards common morality.

With a proper description of abstract halaal and haraam in place, we now encourage you to use these in Globish and in your native language.

If a certain aspect of your profession puts you in a position, ahead of the rest of society, to see a need for specific considerations of halaal and haraam; bring them up and move towards defining those. Try to build consensus on those halaal labels. Have those who have authority for halaal and haraam declarations, consider use of the labels.

Our motivation in writing this document has been to facilitate better discussions of global aspects of morality and ethics.

With halaal and haraam in it, the world will be better equipped to be a better world.

Chapter 12

Digital Non-Proprietary Movements

Throughout our discourse, we have been emphasizing some key points. These include:

- For progress of arts and sciences, the natural collaborative model of polyexistentials is superior to the artificial competitive environment that Western IPR creates.

- Professions have guardianship responsibilities to societies. Professions should be empowered to fulfill those responsibilities.

- Humans are more than economic creatures.

While it is true that Westerners in general and Americanists in particular don't take the above key concepts seriously, some individuals and some groups in Western societies intuitively get those concepts. Clearly, not all Westerners are pure economic creatures.

These individuals and these groups have come up with various ways of creating collaborative environments within the Western IPR framework. Strategies for accomplishing this spans copyright and patent law in one dimension and content, software and services in another dimension. All of this has a short history that spans only about 40 years or so.

With respect to copyright, the strategy revolves around the notion of public licenses where authors grant certain permissions and impose certain restrictions on the public use of content, software and services through copyright law. This way authors apply their chosen public licenses to their work. Tens of such public licenses exist and various factions and cults have been created around these public licenses, each representing certain beliefs and characters. All of this has resulted in the creation of a great deal of very valuable non-proprietary software and content which now exists in the collaborative environment.

With respect to patents, things are more complicated. Several anti-patent strategies are in practice. Some simply don't patent their innovations and their inventions are naturally public. Some publish their innovations without regard to patents, such publications then become prior art. Some obtain patents with the intention of never asserting — in theory this prevents others from obtaining the same. Some sabotage patent applications of large corporations from within. Some patent-assassins function as expert witnesses in defense of patent assertions. Some watch over the Standards Essential Patent processes. In the larger picture, none of these have had material impact.

Those Westerners who point to the incredible accomplishments of the open-source movement through open-source public licenses should ask themselves: what if polyexistentials were governed properly to begin with? What if there was just one Libre-Halaal public software license? What if there was no public proprietary software? What if society was aligned with Libre-Halaal software?

In Section 15.2 — Definitions for Libre-Halaal Governance, we provide explicit definitions that address these what-ifs. What we have in the ad hoc open-source model is a small fraction of what we should have.

We have structured this section in 3 parts.

1. Software Public Licenses and Movements

2. Content Public Licenses and Movements

3. Standards Essential Patent Processes and Groups

12.1   Software Public Licenses and Movements

In the realm of software and digital entities, the Western IPR regime promotes internally opaque and proprietary outcomes that are the result of commercial competition.

Advocates of Western IPR believe that software engineers will produce better and more software in a proprietary and closed and competitive (not collaborative) environment because of the resulting economic rewards.

Those rejecting Western IPR believe that software engineers produce better and more software in a non-proprietary and open and collaborative environment.

Those who produce software know that software is inherently collaborative and cumulative. It has long been obvious to them as to which model is correct and superior.

Today, the overwhelming majority of internet infrastructure runs on non-proprietary software.

In the realm of software, there is no debate. The Libre-Halaal model is superior to the Western IPR based Proprietary-Haraam model.

For software, the Libre-Halaal model has defeated the Proprietary-Haraam model in the West despite of the fact that all Western structures have been favoring the Western IPR based Proprietary-Haraam model. Just imagine what the success of the Libre-Halaal model if societal structures were in its favor — not opposing it.

Because software is a pure form of polyexistentials and because the Western IPR regime applies to all polyexistentials, it becomes clear that the entirety of the Western IPR regime is a failed experiment.

In opposition to the Proprietary-Haraam model, the structures of Libre-Halaal software engineering movements have all been ad hoc, spontaneous and ad lib.

Here we review the dynamics of some Libre-Halaal software engineering movements from three perspective.

1. The nature of these Libre-Halaal engineering movements

2. The results that they have produced

3. Their evolution and trajectory

12.1.1 Overview of Non-Proprietary Engineering Movements

There have been various engineering efforts to oppose the Western IPR Proprietary-Haraam model. Because these efforts are mostly just engineering centric, ad hoc, generally unsupported and spontaneous; at best, they have proven to be limited in scope and at most peripheral.

Most of these efforts are Western in origin and focus on "freedom", and are limited in their analysis and scope.

Here we provide a summary.

Free Software Movement:

> The Free Software movement is a social movement with the goal of obtaining and guaranteeing certain freedoms for software users, namely the freedoms to run the software, to study the software, to modify the software, and to share copies of the software (whether modified or not).[35]

Open Source Movement:

The open-source movement manages to share the same short-term goals as the Free Software movement but ideologically it is quite different. The mission of the Open Source Initiative says:

Open Source enables a development method for software that harnesses the power of distributed peer review and transparency of process. The promise of open source is higher quality, better reliability, greater flexibility, lower cost, and an end to predatory vendor lock-in.[36]

FOSS/FLOSS (Free/Libre/Open-Source Software) Movement:

The Free Software movement and the open-source movement often join forces to offer an alternative to the proprietary model.

Free and Open Source Software (F/OSS, FOSS) or free/libre/open-source software (FLOSS) is software that is both free and open source.

Some software engineers have instinctively recognized that the open-source manner-of-existence of software is advantages to software engineers and software engineering.

These groups of software engineers have attempted and mostly failed to frame this topic at societal level.

In the meantime, proprietary corporate America has figured out various ways of bastardizing FOSS and its fruits. Some such examples include, Tivoization, Appleization and Servicization.

Linux Foundation:
The Linux Foundation provides a neutral, trusted hub for developers and organizations to code, manage, and scale open technology projects and ecosystems.[37]

Linux Distros — Debia/Ubuntu/etc Distros:
Over time FOSS/FLOSS movement have produced a complete operating system, where in the software arena, we now have a complete solution that can compete with proprietary software.

But, in the meantime the arena has shifted from software to services.

Upstream Freedom Oriented Component Projects (Tor, etc.) :

Various projects provide some useful partial solutions at component level.

For example, the Tor software protects you by bouncing your communications around a distributed network of relays run by volunteers all around the world: it prevents somebody watching your Internet connection from learning what sites you visit, it prevents the sites you visit from learning your physical location, and it lets you access sites which are blocked.

FreedomBox Project:

FreedomBox is an example of various efforts to transform open-source software into Libre Services by combining the results of various freedom oriented component projects, the FreedomBox attempts to create an umbrella profile. Yet it fails to recognize that what is needed is not just the box but a full digital ecosystem.

None of these attempts have recognized that the problem needs to be addressed as the complete digital ecosystem level and at societal level. Most of these attempts fundamentally come from the American and Western model of thinking and analysis.

12.1.2   Software Public Licenses

The various above-mentioned engineering movements have produced a good number of Software Public Licenses. Broadly speaking these licenses fall into two categories. One category is typically called "Copyleft", the other category is typically called "Permissive". Copyleft licenses attempt to keep the source code of the software perpetually open. Permissive licenses only require that original source code of the software be open.

Copyleft licenses are associated with the free software movement. Permissive licenses are associated with the open-source movement.

Earlier versions of Copyleft licenses, for example GNU General Public License, version 2 (GPLv2), had various loopholes. We discuss these loopholes in Section 12.1.4 — Proprietary Culture's Bastardizations of FOSS.

In the context of mapping of copyright-based software public licenses to governance of proper manner-of-existence of software as a polyexistentials, we only consider one license. That one license is: Affero General Public License Version 3 (AGPLv3).

From our perspective, in a civilized and just society all software will be governed by the equivalent of the single AGPLv3 license. For us, the label of "Libre-Halaal Software" maps into the AGPLv3 of Software Public Licenses. See Section 15.2.1 — Definition of Libre-Halaal Software — for details.

12.1.3   The Right Label for
Correct Manner-of-Existence of Software

In Chapter 4 — Proper Governance of Polyexistentials —, we emphasized the following:

- After rejecting the Western IPR regime, our focus should become the identification and definition of correct manner-of-existence of polyexistentials.

- We then introduced the label of "Libre-Halaal" for the identification of correct manner-of-existence of polyexistentials.

- We then provided our formal definition of "Libre-Halaal Software."

- Based on that definition we then provided a formal definition for "Libre-Halaal Internet Services."

These definitions require perpetual internal transparency and modifiability of manner-of-existence of software towards two goals:

1. Global collaborative software and internet services development

2. Guardianship of society by the software engineering profession

In opposition to the Western IPR regime, there have been various attempts at creating global collaborative software and internet services development models. But the need for guardianship of society by the software engineering profession has never been recognized in the West.

FOSS/FLOSS is liberally licensed to grant users the right to use, copy, study, change, and improve its design through the availability of its source code. In the context of free and open-source software, free refers to the freedom to copy and re-use the software, rather than to the price of the software.

The Western FOSS Movement has produced the GNU/Linux operating system and has demonstrated the viability of free software as a development model for creating large-scale, complex, relevant software systems. GNU/Linux is a fully viable free software alternative to the proprietary Microsoft Windows operating system, against which it continues to make steady inroads. And apart from such well-known and high-profile projects, behind the scenes the free software movement has become a flourishing creative environment, generating a constant stream of new and better software packages, duplicating and surpassing the capabilities of an ever-increasing portion of proprietary software territory.

FOSS is rooted in Western values of liberty and individuality. Free software focuses on the philosophical freedoms it gives to users, whereas open source software focuses on the perceived strengths of its peer-to-peer development model.

The Free Software and Open Source movements and their combination of the Free and open-source software (F/OSS, FOSS) or free/libre/open-source software (FLOSS) have been attempting to address this labeling challenge. Because their philosophical and moral analysis is shallow, all of their labels are problematic in a number of respects.

The FLOSS movement lacks deep recognition of the IPR regime being just Western and does not call for full abolishment of the IPR regime. The FLOSS movement lacks deep recognition of the place of software as a special form of digital polyexistential. The FLOSS movement lacks deep recognition of importance of morality and role of software engineering profession in formulation of definitions and labels towards societal protection.

12.1.3.1   Libre-Halaal Software versus Free Software

Richard Stallman coined the term "Free Software" in the early 1980s. The defining criteria for free software are as follows. This is reproduced from http://www.gnu.org/philosophy/free-sw.html, current as of July 2011.

> Free software is a matter of the users' freedom to run, copy, distribute, study, change and improve the software. More precisely, it means that the program's users have the four essential freedoms:
>
> - The freedom to run the program, for any purpose (freedom 0).
> - The freedom to study how the program works, and change it so it does your computing as you wish (freedom 1). Access to the source code is a precondition for this.
> - The freedom to redistribute copies so you can help your neighbor (freedom 2).
> - The freedom to distribute copies of your modified versions to others (freedom 3). By doing this you can give the whole community a chance to benefit from your changes. Access to the source code is a precondition for this.
>
> A program is free software if users have all of these freedoms.

This definition is concise and understandable, but it is mostly useless to the overwhelming majority of end users. Software engineers may care about having access to the source code, but unless societal responsibilities are taken into account, even they may not be concerned about these freedoms. A Western software engineer who wants to accomplish a task is not likely to choose a free software tool over one that is better in other ways, even if it does not offer the same freedoms. Therefore, for a given user, there is no good reason to choose software that is worse in other ways just because it gives them freedoms that are not relevant to them.[38]

Several decades after promotion of the term "Free Software", hardly any end user has ended up caring about it. Free Software has not managed to establish a material connection with the American society or elsewhere. Even among engineers the connection to Free Software is quite weak.

Some have come to conclude that from the very beginning the politics of Free Software were ill directed. Consider this quote from Melody Horn:

> the free software movement is explicitly political, but its politics suck. it's a movement by and for ideological diehards but the ideology is extremely esoteric. theirs was a losing battle from day one. so what was it that actually killed them? i think in a very real way it was the GPLv3.
>
> [...] the flagship projects of the free software movement are probably Linux and the GNU pile of tools. the Linux kernel being released under a free software license doesn't directly create more free software, though, since even things that tie closely to the kernel aren't obligated to also be free software, and of course user-level applications can have whatever license they want. and also most of the people using Linux right now are using it by accident, distributed as ChromeOS or Android, neither of which is free software. so Linux is a win for the free software movement but a useless one.
>
> [...] the free software movement, in the end, burned itself out, by fighting for a tiny crumb of success and then turning around and lighting that success on fire. the death of free software tells us that we can't use a license to trick corporations into sharing our values: they want to profit, and if good software has a license that puts a limit on how much they can do that, they'll put more resources into writing their own alternative than they would spend complying with the license in the first place.

Based on evolution of the open-source and the Free Software camps, it is reasonable to say that she is expressing a rough consensus.

Definition of Free Software is consistent with our own definition of Libre-Halaal software. So why have we taken the trouble to define Libre-Halaal software, when it turns out to be mostly consistent with free software?

The reason is that the two definitions are ideologically different. They exist in ideologically different contexts, and this ideological difference is reflected in their phrasing.

The term "Free Software" was coined in the early 1980s in America. Their culture and language lacked the word "Halaal". So "Freedom" as the pinnacle of American values became the key word. The label "Free Software" has proven problematic in many respects. Free in English has two meanings, "gratis" and "liberty". For the public at large the "gratis" meaning is dominant, so the "Free Software" label never worked well. To address this, the word "Libre" has been introduced into Globish and "Free Software" and "Libre Software" have become synonyms. But "Libre Software" is also not a good label because it does not focus on the ethical, moral and societal manner of existence of software. The focus of the label needs to be on morality and society. Once "Halaal" is properly introduced into Globish [7], the label "Libre-Halaal Software" will prove crisper and more on the mark.

The Free Software definition exists in the context of Western copyright law, and implicitly accepts that as a reality. The key to free software is the GPL (General Public License), a form of licensing intended to preserve the four definitional freedoms. But this is of course a form of copyright, and so the free software definition resides within and submits to the Western copyright conventions.

The Free Software definition is rooted in the context of Western values and assumptions:

- It is centered on the individual (individual freedom), as opposed to being centered on society (ethics and morality). The concepts of profession and society are absent. The definition is based entirely on the individual, and the individual's freedom.

- It exists in the context of the Western Copyright and Patent regime. Freedom 2 and freedom 3 are written in response to this, and implicitly accept this as a reality. There is no explicit assertion that the ability to copy is a natural law and a human right.

- It does not recognize the Software Engineering profession as a guardian. Freedom 1 makes no distinction between ordinary users (i.e., almost everyone), and software engineering professionals. The implication is that anyone can exercise freedom 1, without need for guardianship by the Software Engineering profession.

The Libre-Halaal software definition on the other hand makes no concession whatever to Western Intellectual Property Rights. We view the Western Intellectual Property Rights regime as a fundamental misconception, and fundamentally invalid.

While operating in countries where Western Intellectual Property Rights regime are law of the land and have deep roots, we subject our own work to the most stringent forms of the General Public License that are available.

While operating in countries where Western Intellectual Property Rights regime have not taken root or are not valid (e.g., China, Iran) we also work towards rejection and abolishment of Western Intellectual Property Rights regime and work towards requiring that all software used in the society be Libre-Halaal Software.

12.1.3.2   Libre-Halaal Software versus Open Source Software

The other branch of the Western FOSS movement is Open Source Software. Open Source demands internal transparency and focuses on a collaborative development methodology.

The primary difference between Open Source Software and Free Software is the intent for keeping software perpetually Libre-Halaal Software through Western copyright law. In that respect Libre-Halaal Software is more aligned with Free Software. The open-source movement was invented to be a friendly, apolitical, pro-corporate alternative to the Free Software movement.

Where Free Software is misguided and quixotic, open-source is spineless and centrist. Open source welcomes and accommodates corporatization of FOSS. And since most Western software engineers are corporatized economic creatures, this arrangement is a match made in heaven and open-source has eaten the world and Free Software has been rendered mostly irrelevant.

12.1.4   Proprietary Culture's Bastardizations of FOSS

The model of Libre-Halaal Software is towards Libre-Halaal Software remaining the Halaal manner-of-existence of software, perpetually.

The open-source branch of the Western FOSS movement does not care much about this. They call their public copyright licenses "permissive". The Free Software branch of the Western FOSS movement attempts to accomplish that perpetuality through the Western Copyright law. They call this technique copyleft.

The desire and intent to keep the software halaal is continuously violated by the proprietary corporate model. We call this "bastardization" of Libre-Halaal software.

Four significant models for bastardizations of FOSS are mentioned below.

12.1.4.1 Appleization: Bastardization Based on Copyleft Ambivalence

Apple's Mac OS X is a derivative of 4.4BSD-Lite2 and FreeBSD. The FreeBSD Copyright license is very loose, very "permissive" and makes no effort towards keeping Libre-Halaal Software, Libre-Halaal Software.

As a result, what used to be Libre-Halaal Software has evolved into proprietary software.

12.1.4.2 Tivoization: Bastardization Based on Copyleft License Holes

Tivoization is the creation of a system that incorporates software under the terms of a copyleft software license (like the GPL), but uses hardware restrictions to prevent users from running modified versions of the software on that hardware. This is in reference to circumstances such as TiVo's use of GNU GPL licensed software on the TiVo brand digital video recorders (DVR).

In such cases the spirit of Libre-Halaal Software is circumvented by exploiting holes in the underlying copyleft license.

So while TiVo has complied with the GPL v2 requirement to release the source code for others to modify, any modified software will not run on TiVo's hardware. GPL v3 attempts to plug that hole in the context of Western IPR regime.

Note that this form of prevention of bastardization takes the analysis outside of software as a pure polyexistential and towards viewing the system as a polyexistential — or not.

12.1.4.3 ASPization: Bastardization Based on Copyleft ASP Loophole

Software is sometimes transformed into services and delivered to users through Application Service Providers (ASP). Transformation of Software into Service permits use of software that often is not covered by copyleft licenses.

This is usually labeled the "ASP loophole." For example, GPL v2 talks about distribution of software and includes a copyleft clause that triggers when you distribute your code. Much software is now accessed as a service which requires no distribution of code.

Large service providers such as Google, use halaal manner-of-existence of software heavily to provide haraam manner-of-existence Internet services.

In the arena of internet services, the basic principles of the FOSS movement have been bastardized, where transparent software is used to provide opaque internet services.

They use the ASP loophole and as parasites on Free Software, abuse the spirit of Libre-Halaal Software.

In the context of Western IPR regime, the Affero General Public License, (AGPL), addresses the problem where use of the software as an exposed service triggers the copyleft provisions. But, private use of the software in the form of a service, does not trigger the copyleft provisions.

Other than the definitions that we provide in Section 15.2.3 — Definition of Libre-Halaal Internet Application Services — there is no clear definition of "Libre Services".

12.1.4.4   Androidization:
Bastardization Through Control of the Development Process

In our model, Libre-Halaal software empowers the entirety of the software engineering profession to collectively develop and to collectively serve humanity.

With Google's Android, adherence to Western FOSS is observed in letter but not in spirit.

Google's mobile platform is a masterful manipulation of open source designed for driving commercial agendas. While profiting from the goodwill surrounding FOSS, the Android model violates the spirit of public collaboration.

The Android governance model is a complex system of control points that allows Google to bundle its own services and dictate the software and hardware components of each device, while still claiming to be open. Current code is tightly controlled and closed, while older code is made open-source. The development process is managed and regulated by Google, creating a Walled-Garden model.

12.1.5   Business and Economics of FOSS

Inside of the IPR model, there are several ways for engineers to generate revenue from FOSS related development. These fall into 3 broad categories.

1. Support for FOSS Software Revenue

2. Grants, Fund Raising and Non-Proprietary Research and Development Organizations

3. Libre Services Repeatable Subscription Fees

We will describe our take on each of these briefly.

12.1.5.1 Revenues From Support for FOSS Software

Proprietary software almost always comes with support from its owner. In the proprietary model the software license is very often bundled with support. Since FOSS's model is non-proprietary, unowned and very often non-commercial, the paradigm for support is different.

As early as 1989, a small company called "Cygnus Support" started providing commercial support for free software. Its tagline was: "Making free software affordable". About 10 years later Cygnus merged with Red Hat. The business model for providing commercial support for FOSS is simple. Large organizations often use a great deal of FOSS and when they do, they need support. The support business arrangements are typically in the form of retainers, consulting and subscriptions for orderly updates.

In due course the scope of software support grew to the totality of operating system distributions and now Red Hat is mostly associated with its enterprise operating system: Red Hat Enterprise. In parallel with Red Hat, Canonical provides enterprise support for Ubuntu (a Debian derivative).

This type of commercial support for enterprises (large corporations) has impacted evolution of FOSS. More emphasis is placed on development and cultivation of the type of software that large organizations use and need. Many of these large organizations operate inside of the Surveillance Capitalism model. As a result evolution of FOSS has been skewed towards central large scale corporate oriented software and systems.

The business of providing support for FOSS in the for-profit, non-proprietary quadrant can be profitable, but it is not as profitable or repeatable as providing support for FOSS in the for-profit, proprietary quadrant.

12.1.5.2 Grants, Fund Raising and Funded Research

There are also opportunities for revenue generation in the in the non-proprietary non-profit quadrant.

Various FOSS organizations emphasize the public good that they are creating and engage in periodic public fund raising campaigns. In America, many of these organizations claim to be "freedom" oriented. We present our perspective on this topic in Section 12.4 — A Cynical Perspective on Freedom Orientation of Americans.

In America, the public sector has not yet realized that investments and support for non-proprietary research outside of academic university settings can have large multiplier effects. This is mostly because of the strong American belief system in their IPR regime. Europeans have invested more heavily in this.

12.1.5.3   Libre Services Repeatable Subscription Fees

The IPR system has created an environment in which the revenue models of non-proprietary (FOSS) software are at a disadvantage compared to the revenue models of proprietary software. However, this does not have to be the case for the revenue models of internet application services.

Thus far, the FOSS movement has failed to extend its definitions to the internet application services realm. The definitions of Libre Services as we describe them in Section 15.2.3 — Definition of Libre-Halaal Internet Application Services — are not widely understood.

At present, there is no clear distinction between proprietary internet application services (Proprietary Services) and Libre-Halaal internet application services (Libre Services).

Extending FOSS into Libre Services should become the primary focus of the business and economics of FOSS.

Libre Services can compete very well against Proprietary Services. In the internet application services domain they are both at equal footing. They both have the repeatability attribute. It is true that with Libre Services the competitive barrier to entry is lower, but on the other hand the collaborative development results are more advantageous.

In 2021, we tried to persuade Mark Shuttleworth, the president of Canonical (Ubuntu) to shift the focus from software and support services to FOSS based consumer oriented internet application services (Libre Services). Below is part of a related email.

The Libre-Halaal ByStar Digital Ecosystem mentioned in this email is described in Chapter 15 — Theory of Libre-Halaal Digital Ecosystems — and also in Chapter 17 — Technology of ByStar: BISOS of Part IV of this book.

> From: Mohsen BANAN <██████████████████████████>
> Subject: Re: ██ ██ ████ ██ █████ █████ ████
> █ ██ ████ ████
> To: Mark Shuttleworth <████████████████████████>
> Date: Tue, 26 Oct 2021 13:58:56 -0700

> ...

> Hi Mark, ...

> Consider what is below as unsolicited feedback about my read on what you have been publicly doing with Ubuntu and Canonical.

> Edwards Deming said:
> "A system can not understand itself. The transformation requires a view from outside."

The short version of my feedback is:

** The competition between Debian and Ubuntu is no longer necessary and productive. The split and having a choice is no longer positive.

** You should reposition Ubuntu-Server to become a layer on top of Debian-Server – not parallel to it. Package whatever you want and load it on top of Debian and call it say, "Debuntu". Provide commercial support services for pure Debian and for Debuntu. You will increase your corporate customer base and you would better compete against RedHat.

** Keep Ubuntu-Desktop as is. But in addition to Ubuntu-Desktop also provide a Debuntu-Desktop. A Debuntu-Desktop boots as a Debian-Desktop and then becomes the equivalent of Ubuntu-Desktop.

Consider the default inclusion of Debian in all Chromebooks. That is a big deal! Debuntu-Desktop strategy as a layer on top (as opposed to in parallel) can keep Ubuntu relevant in such situations. Just that in and of itself, justifies this strategy.

** Focus on building a large scale end-user oriented internet service which can also be self-hosted. Let's call it "Canonical Autonomy-oriented Internet Services (CAIS)" – for now. This is why I had sent you the ByStar information. ByStar can be the beginnings of CAIS. The initial large scale internet service should focus on email and web-publication. Because of the possibility of running a native MUA (as opposed to being just browser based), you should be able to do better that GMail – yet autonomous. The user experience can be superb because you would be in full control of the software-service continuum. The focus of the initial large scale internet service should be artists – writers, musicians, photographers and movie makers. They would self-publish. And you would take care of their syndication and search ...

** Create a rich software-service continuum between Ubuntu-Desktop and CAIS. You are uniquely positioned to do this.

** Grow Ubuntu-Desktop and CAIS together – not independently. A new release's goal should be to improve the software-service continuum end-user experience. Not to just improve one or the other.

** Focus on harvesting as opposed to planting and growing. You learned that through the Unity experience. But still, with Ubuntu proper, you can grow less and harvest more.

** ...

** You have an image problem that you can fix. You made your fortunes during the dotCon era. The caricature image of a dotCon era spin and flipper and pump and dumper who takes himself way too seriously is attributed to you through association. Your previous standings have amplified that caricature.

All of that may well not be true. And if it is not true, you should fix it through humility, statesmanship and healing.

** Focus on healing. The Debian and Ubuntu split is a self-inflicted wound. Make a 180 degrees turn on that. Provide full commercial support for Debian in large data-centers similar to the old Cygnus model. Identify the specific profile of apps and packages that matches your specific software-service continuum and fund that as a non-profit with no strings attached.

...

This question of choosing between Debian vs Ubuntu is silly. They are fundamentally the same. If you are in the business of making free software affordable, why not support them both. Why not see them as one?

...

Today, everything is about creating software-service continuums and from that perspective, much of your past efforts have been ill-directed. On the end-user oriented internet services side, Canonical is behind.

I must confess. I have not written the above just for your benefit. If I am able to influence you in these directions, the greater good is also served.

...

Thanks and regards,

...Mohsen

12.1.6   Corporatization of FOSS

In October of 1998, a number of internal Microsoft documents about threats of FOSS to Microsoft were leaked — some refer to these as Halloween documents.[39]

These documents describe corporate thinking about FOSS and other related open movements. Corporate response towards FOSS and other related open movements has been a mixture of poisoning the well, joining open movements towards controlling and selective open-source participation as a competitive strategy.

Many of these corporate strategies have produced the desired results. For example, IETF is now fully controlled by big corporations, so is Open Source Initiative and many others.

These strategies combined with internal FOSS dynamics have created an environment where much software is available and is being produced but that societal usage and directions come from big corporations — not the engineering profession.

Melody Horn highlights this notion in her Post-Open Source post:

...

> if there's anything corporations love more than rewriting software so it lets them make all the money they can dream of, it's letting other people do that work for them. it took a while to take off, because the conservative approach of "keep things closed source" was pretty solidly entrenched in a lot of places, but now even the once conservative holdouts have accepted the gospel of centrism. corporations have little to nothing to lose by publishing existing source code, and can gain all sorts of unpaid volunteer labor. if they start a new internal project, important enough that they're prepared to put effort into it but not so important that someone could run off with it and compete with them, then now they'll likely open source it. worst case scenario, they do all the work they were already prepared to do. best case scenario, their library turns into the single most popular library of its type, with thousands of unpaid volunteers donating their time to you. more labor for free, community goodwill for having started the project everybody uses, the benefits if it goes well are countless. free software is not in principle anti-corporate, but corporations are very cautious getting caught up in the free software movement, because that actually creates obligations for them. open source gives corporations a shot at improving their code for free, so as long as they don't share so much someone could start a competitor, so there's zero reason for a corporation to not get into open source.

> github itself is arguably the epitome of the open source movement. the platform itself is closed source, because they don't want people to compete with them running their code, and also they sell the very expensive self-hosted version to corporations. opening up the source for github itself would take a chunk out of github's profits. can't have that. but they don't even need to start or adopt an open source component to profit off other people's labor: *literally every project on github* makes github more valuable. popular projects get people in, network effects bring their

colleagues in, and then when it's time for something that you'd rather have closed source you and everyone else are already on github so you might as well spring for the paid tier. if they believed open source was in principle better, they'd be open source themselves. they believe open source is profitable for them, and corporate profit is by definition value generated by labor but not paid to the laborer.

...

Let's consider GitHub a bit further. GitHub has become the defacto international center for open-source collaboration. On January 25th, 2023, GitHub announced:

> Today, I'm excited to share that there are now officially more than 100 million developers using GitHub to build, maintain, and contribute to software projects.

With regard to GitHub and open-source, consider further the American and international dimensions of GitHub as a defacto open-source center.

The overwhelming majority of GitHub developers are non-Americans. [40] Yet, GitHub is owned by Microsoft, a very American corporation. Microsoft has to abide by US law. More and more frequently the US imposes sanctions on various countries and various people. So, here we have large numbers of people engaging in open-source under the surveillance of Microsoft and at the mercy of US government. This is not theoretical, it has happened. For a while, Gitlab (a GitHub competitor) failed to obtain proper sanction exemption for Iran and hundreds of open-source developers could no longer access their own software from Iran.

At this point, American corporatization of FOSS can be considered comprehensive. Free Software ideology has proven irrelevant and corporatized open-source is the defacto model. Many Western FOSS software engineers regard all of this as a fine and cozy relationship.

12.1.7   Open-Source Development as Surrogate Activity

Over time, corporations and the overwhelming majority of FOSS software engineers have come to a convenient consensus that allows for FOSS as a surrogate activity.

First, let's clarify as what we mean by "surrogate" activity. For clarification, consider the entirety of paragraphs 39 and 40 of the 1995 Unabomber's Manifesto: "Industrial Society and Its Future" [31].

39. We use the term "surrogate activity" to designate an activity that is directed toward an artificial goal that people set up for themselves merely in order to have some goal to work toward, or let us say, merely for the qake of the "fulfillment" that they get from pursuing the goal. Here is a rule of thumb for the identification of surrogate activities. Given a person who devotes much time and energy to the pursuit of goal X, ask yourself this: If he had to devote most of his time and energy to satisfying his biological needs, and if that effort required him to use his physical and mental faculties in a varied and interesting way, would he feel seriously deprived because he did not attain goal X? If the answer is no, then the person's pursuit of goal X is a surrogate activity. Hirohito's studies in marine biology clearly constituted a surrogate activity, since it is pretty certain that if Hirohito had had to spend his time working at interesting non-scientific tasks in order to obtain the necessities of life, he would not have felt deprived because he didn't know all about the anatomy and life-cycles of marine animals. On the other hand the pursuit of sex and love (for example) is not a surrogate activity, because most people, even if their existence were otherwise satisfactory, would feel deprived if they passed their lives without ever having a relationship with a member of the opposite sex. (But pursuit of an excessive amount of sex, more than one really needs, can be a surrogate activity.)

40. In modern industrial society only minimal effort is necessary to satisfy one's physical needs. It is enough to go through a training program to acquire some petty technical skill, then come to work on time and exert the very modest effort needed to hold a job. The only requirements are a moderate amount of intelligence and, most of all, simple OBEDIENCE. If one has those, society takes care of one from cradle to grave. (Yes, there is an underclass that cannot take the physical necessities for granted, but we are speaking here of mainstream society.) Thus it is not surprising that modern society is full of surrogate activities. These include scientific work, athletic achievement, humanitarian work, artistic and literary creation, climbing the corporate ladder, acquisition of money and material goods far beyond the point at which they cease to give any additional physical satisfaction, and social activism when it addresses issues that are not important for the activist personally, as in the case of white activists who work for the rights of nonwhite minorities. These are not always PURE surrogate activities, since for many people they may be motivated in part by needs other than the need to have some goal to pursue. Scientific work may be motivated in part by a drive for prestige, artistic creation by a need to express feelings, militant

social activism by hostility. But for most people who pursue them, these activities are in large part surrogate activities. For example, the majority of scientists will probably agree that the "fulfillment" they get from their work is more important than the money and prestige they earn.

Adopting Theodore Kaczynski's terminology, FOSS activity for most software engineers is a "surrogate" activity.

The typical open-source developer does not really care and is perfectly willing to subject his code to what is most convenient for his current or future employer.

So, ethical licenses are out and corporate friendly permissive licenses are in. The profession of software engineering is rendered irrelevant and economic creatures govern through economics.

Of course, what we claim above is not scientific. It is very difficult to understand why people engage in the types of activities that they do. Some research and experimentation have been done in the area of understanding the motivations of software developers. To be considered more scientific, let's also look at MIT Sloan School of Management's 2005 research. Their results were published in a paper titled: "Why Hackers Do What They Do: Understanding Motivation and Effort in Free/Open Source Software Projects"[19]. The abstract from that paper reads:

Abstract: In this paper we report on the results of a study of the effort and motivations of individuals to contributing to the creation of Free/Open Source software. We used a Web-based survey, administered to 684 software developers in 287 F/OSS projects, to learn what lies behind the effort put into such projects. Academic theorizing on individual motivations for participating in F/OSS projects has posited that external motivational factors in the form of extrinsic benefits (e.g.; better jobs, career advancement) are the main drivers of effort. We find in contrast, that enjoyment-based intrinsic motivation, namely how creative a person feels when working on the project, is the strongest and most pervasive driver. We also find that user need, intellectual stimulation derived from writing code, and improving programming skills are top motivators for project participation. A majority of our respondents are skilled and experienced professionals working in IT-related jobs, with approximately 40 percent being paid to participate in the F/OSS project.

Of course, this too should not be taken too seriously. It is likely very outdated; the survey was small and SourceForge[41] was not and is not all that relevant.

Regardless, we believe that for most developers open-source development is either a job or a surrogate activity.

12.2 Content Public Licenses

Earlier, from the perspective of manner-of-existence fo digitals, we created three categories of digitals: (1) software, (2) content and (3) internet application services.

Software controls all forms of digital content. Development of software is inherently collaborative and cumulative. These attributes make software special. The concept of software public licensing started in the early 1980s. Uses of software public licenses were widespread by mid-1980s.

Widespread use of digital content public licenses only started in the mid-2000s. In many ways content public licensing mimics software public licensing.

Let's first define what we mean by digital content. Digital content is any content that exists in the form of digital data. Forms of digital content include information that is digitally broadcast, streamed, or contained in computer files. Types of digital content include: video, audio, images and text. Broadly speaking, digital content is anything that can be digitally published (e. g. digitally updated weather forecasts, GPS maps, and so on).

Use of creative common content copyright licenses have now become widespread. According to the `https://creativecommons.org/licenses` web page:

> The Creative Commons copyright licenses and tools forge a balance inside the traditional "all rights reserved" setting that copyright law creates. Our tools give everyone from individual creators to large companies and institutions a simple, standardized way to grant copyright permissions to their creative work. The combination of our tools and our users is a vast and growing digital commons, a pool of content that can be copied, distributed, edited, remixed, and built upon, all within the boundaries of copyright law.

Creative Commons (CC) organization has released several copyright licenses, known as Creative Commons licenses. These licenses allow authors of creative works to communicate which rights they reserve and which rights they waive for the benefit of recipients or other creators.

In the context of mapping of copyright-based content public licenses to governance of proper manner-of-existence of content as a polyexistentials, we only consider one license. That one license is: Attribution-ShareAlike 4.0 International (CC BY-SA 4.0).

From our perspective, in a civilized and just society all content will be governed by the single CC BY-SA 4.0 license. For us, the label of Libre-Halaal Content maps into the CC BY-SA 4.0 of Software Public Licenses. See Section 15.2.2 — Definition of Libre-Halaal Content — for more information.

12.3   Protocols and Standards Essential Patents

Copyright and patent work very differently.

With copyright, the author wants others to use his work but to pay for the copy that they get. In other words, copying of the polyexistential is prohibited. With patents, in theory, the inventor wants to be the only one who uses the know-how to build things without restrictions. The patent then prohibits other people to use that know-how. The patent holder publishes the know-how and copying of the knowledge polyexistential is not prohibited. It is the use of the know-how (as a polyexistential) for incorporation in other polyexistentials or mixed-existentials that is prohibited. If others end up using that know-how, knowingly or unknowingly, then patent holder can claim damages.

With copyright, the author advertises the work to make it more popular. Or subjects his work to a public copyright license so that more people can use it. The equivalent of a public copyright license does not apply to the patent domain. In some ways the opposite is at work with patents. The patent holder wants others to inadvertently use their patents and then claim damages. A submarine patent is a patent whose issuance and publication are intentionally delayed by the applicant for a long time. Submarine patents stay "hidden" until the industry implements the technology. Trolls making use of submarine patents in patent ambushes are sometimes referred to as patent pirates. Consider how colorful the previous sentence was. The Western IPR system is the source of all this waste and all this ugliness.

If a patent holder could somehow force or encourage inadvertent use of his patent by others, the value of his patent increases. The "somehow" in the above sentence can have the form of applicability of the patent to a public protocol or a public standard.

An essential patent or standard-essential patent (SEP) is a patent that claims an invention that must be used to comply with a technical standard. Standards organizations, therefore, often require members disclose and grant licenses to their patents and pending patent applications that cover a standard that the organization is developing [42].

If a standards organization fails to get licenses to all patents that are essential to complying with a standard, owners of the unlicensed patents may demand or sue for royalties from companies that adopt the standard. This happened for example to the JPEG standard.

Determining which patents are essential to a particular standard can be complex. Standardization organizations require licenses of essential patents to be on fair, reasonable, and non-discriminatory (FRAND) terms.

12.3.1 How Patents Affect Protocols

We use the terms protocols and standards interchangeably. In the broadest sense a protocol specifies an expected behavior and so does a standard.

Patents are applied to software, not to protocols. It is not possible to patent a protocol; in general only a process or an algorithm can be patented. However, a protocol may include a patented algorithm as an integral part of its specification. In this case, *any software implementation of the protocol requires the use of patented software.* That is, a patented process is an inherent part of the protocol.

Even if a protocol does not explicitly decree the use of a specific patented software process, it may still be the case that any practical implementation of the protocol requires the use of patented software components. The protocol could in principle be implemented in a way which avoids the use of patented software; in practice, however, the result would be a significantly inferior implementation, for example in terms of efficiency.

In either case, the protocol effectively implies the use of patented software. We will refer to any such protocol as a **patented protocol**. That is, a patented protocol is any protocol whose practical implementation requires the use of patented software components.

We will use the term **patent-free protocol**, or just **free protocol**, to refer to a protocol which is functionally free from software patents. By "functionally free from software patents", we mean either that the protocol is truly free from patents, or if the protocol does imply the use of patented software, that the patent-holder has granted non-restrictive rights to include the patented software components in implementations of the protocol.

In either case, the result is that the protocol can be freely implemented and used by anyone, without encountering significant restrictions.

12.3.2 Protecting Against Contamination of Protocols by Patents

By the late 1990s IETF (Internet Engineering Task Force) had already been corporatized. Agents of big corporations were now running the show. IETF is the protocols standardization organization of internet. They had codified the rules for the patents in protocols game. How to declare the possibility of patent contamination was codified. And grants of FRAND patent licenses were codified.

Thereafter every standard organization started to mimic the IETF and they sprinkled some of their corporate culture values on top of the standard-essential patent (SEP) policies and procedures. There are now very large databases across various standardization organizations that enumerate which patents may apply to which protocols.

In the early 2000s, we suggested the idea of having a single set of policies and procedures for dealing with patent issues across all standardization organizations. The concept of separating the standards work from the work of decontamination of patents is quite simple. We published details of this concept as:

> **The Free Protocols Foundation Policies and Procedures**
> http://www.freeprotocols.org/PLPC/100201 — [12]

There were no takers. Standard organizations prefer to run their own patent game.

These patents games are very costly. Corporations in turn pass the costs to the consumer. The consumers are utterly unaware that they are paying for the game. Hardly anyone dares to see that without the patent games and without the Western IPR regime, the consumers are going to be much better off.

12.4   A Cynical Perspective on Freedom Orientation of Americans

Copyright laws of the Western IPR regime with its "All Rights Reserved" default left a vacuum. What if it was not in the interest of the authors to keep all the rights?

As Bill Joy, the founder of Sun Microsystems, puts it, "Sometimes when you fill a vacuum, it still sucks."

Though his phrasing leaves much to be desired, his point is beyond debate: even the most appalling solution is better than no solution at all.

In the name of freedom, the concept of public licenses is what has filled that vacuum. And much good has come as a result. But does that really have much to do with freedom?

Freedom always makes for good hype in America.

Consider what happened in February of 2003 in a North Carolina restaurant. Freedom fries was a politically motivated renaming of French fries. That was then widely publicized a month later when the then Republican Chairman of the Committee on House Administration, Bob Ney, renamed the menu item in three Congressional cafeterias. The political renaming occurred in the context of France's opposition to the proposed invasion of Iraq.

Let us consider use of the terms "free" and "freedom" by the groups and movements that we mentioned earlier.

The leader of the Creative Commons is Lawrence Lessig. He is the author of a book titled: "FREE CULTURE" [35].

The historic leader of Free Software Foundation is Richard Stallman. He is the author of a book titled: "Free Software, Free Society" [21].

The historic lawyer of Free Software Foundation is Eben Moglen. He is the founder of "Software Freedom Law Center" and a champion of "FreedomBox".

A historic leader of Open Source is Eric Raymond. Prominent on his web site is: "It's all about freedom..."

But what do these four very American white men mean by "freedom"? The only meaningful freedom in this context is freedom from the restrictions that Western IPR regime imposes on societies. It would make sense to say that copyright law is invalid, explain why it is invalid, call for its abolishment and say that we want to be *free* from the restrictions that copyright law imposes on our societies. It would make sense to say that patent law is invalid, that we want it to be abolished and that we want to be *free* from the restrictions that patent law imposes on our societies.

But none of these four is speaking about that freedom. None of these four Americans have come out to say that the entirety of IPR regime is flawed and invalid and that it should be abolished. If any of them were to do that, they would be subjected to expected backlash from Harvard, Colombia, and other academic and business institutions. Instead, they have chosen to set up non-profit shops on the outskirts of the IPR economy.

In Chapter 7 — Western Slavery and the Western IPR Regime — we draw various parallels between Western Slavery and the Western IPR Regime as ownership rules. Our position is clear and explicit. We argue that the Western IPR Regime should be abolished in the same way that Western Slavery should have been abolished. However, these four Americans are not advocating for abolishment. In the context of the parallels of Chapter 7 they seem to be advocating for better treatment of slaves.

In "FREE CULTURE", Lawrence Lessig says:

> There are many who are skeptical of patents, especially drug patents.
> I am not. Indeed, of all the areas of research that might be sup-

ported by patents, drug research is, in my view, the clearest case where patents are needed.

Lawrence Lessig is dead wrong. As we have established, patent law is invalid because polyexistentials are unownable. There is no evidence to show that for drug research (or any type of research) the artificially created patents-based environment is superior to the natural collaborative model.

Meaningful freedom is complex. Without capability, freedom is shallow. The "Free" in Free Software that Richard Stallman speaks of is about "freedom of users to inspect and modify their software based on available source-code." My aunt, Khaleh, had difficulty using Windows and did not know what source-code is. The four freedoms that Richard Stallman wants to offer my aunt are useless and absurd. Stallman came up with those concepts long ago, when software users were mostly engineers and scientists. So, at best, the definition of Free Software is archaic.

The freedom that Eric Raymond wants to offer is that of doing whatever you want with the source-code. In that model any derivative of open-source software can become closed-source proprietary software. Was it not our goal to get away from proprietary software? Raymond is a member of the American Libertarian Party and an American gun rights advocate. These seem to be the type of freedoms that he believes in.

Stallman has an essay titled "Why Open Source Misses the Point of Free Software" in which he criticizes Eric Raymond's concepts. Eric Raymond in turn has criticized Stallman's rhetoric:

> The "very seductive" moral and ethical rhetoric of Richard Stallman and the Free Software Foundation fails, he said, "not because his principles are wrong, but because that kind of language ... simply does not persuade anybody".

Eben Moglen is an American lawyer, not an engineer. His championship of "FreedomBox" is misguided. We don't necessarily want or need a "Box". What we want is: "Possession Assertable Libre-Halaal Services" (PALS). In software and operating systems, boxes have been rendered irrelevant by virtualization. The option to possess, host and materialize a PALS under one's full control and perhaps in one's own home is of course fundamental. But, based on definition and regulation, PALS can also be externally hosted. Further, the scope of Freedom-Box is overly limited. We should be targeting the totality of a Libre-Halaal digital ecosystem. See Part IV — Libre-Halaal ByStar Digital Ecosystem — for details of what we are suggesting.

If these four Americans really understood freedom, they would be explicitly calling for abolishment of the Western IPR regime. In America, very often, "freedom" hype comes with self-promotion towards cult construction. If we were to be overly cynical, we would say that is what we have here with these four Americans.

We have nothing but respect for the four American gentlemen whose work has enabled us to have access to a great deal of non-proprietary software and content. However, we suggest that they may be conflicted. Perhaps they have not understood the full picture in depth, or perhaps it is not in their interest to understand it, and perhaps their emphasis on free and freedom is superficial.

Compare and contrast what we are saying against the American notions of freedom.

1. We are offering the logic of the nature of polyexistentials to establish invalidity the Western IPR regime.

2. We are explicitly calling for abolishment of the Western IPR regime.

3. We use the label "Libre" to mean freedom from restrictions of the Western IPR regime.

4. We use the label "Halaal" to mean ethical and right.

5. We are offering explicit definitions of Libre-Halaal Software, Libre-Halaal Content and Libre-Halaal Internet Services as models for proper governance of polyexistentials.

6. We offer a multidisciplinary blueprint for a complete digital ecosystem called: "The ByStar Libre-Halaal Digital Ecosystem."

This is all very different from applying band-aids on the fringes of the Western IPR regime.

The topic here is not freedom. This is about right and wrong. It is about philosophy and ethics. It is about halaal and haraam.

12.5   Lessons Learned

Based on our experience with public licenses for software over the past 40 years, collectively we have learned some lessons. Here we will try to summarize some of these lessons.

There are several types of software that result from the application of public licenses to software. The names that we assign here apply to types of software, not to the license types.

Proprietary Software:

Software that is internally opaque and only available in binary form. Microsoft Windows is an example of Proprietary Software.

Source-available Software:

Source-available software is software released through a source code distribution model that includes arrangements where the source can be viewed, and in some cases modified, but without necessarily meeting the criteria to be called open-source.[43]

Permissive Open Software:

Open-source software that is not copyleft. For example, BSD open-source software that became the genesis of MacOS proprietary software.

Opaque Services Software:

The software of opaque internet application services which is likely mostly Permissive Open Software but which we can't know because it is only available as a service. For example GitHub in 2023.

Libre-Halaal Software:

Software that conforms to the Libre-Halaal definition of software. Software that has been subjected to the AGPL license.

Libre Services Software:

Software of Libre Services. See Section 15.2.3 for our definition of Libre Services.

Throughout this book, we use these labels for different types of software.

The inside of IPR open-source software licenses model has established that the collaborative model is superior to the "All Rights Reserved" opaque proprietary competitive software model. This in turn establishes that Western IPR regime's claims of promoting progress of science and useful arts is bogus. Software has progressed much better outside of IPR restrictions.

Many American corporations have understood this. Total proprietary software is no longer the preferred model for many American corporations. American corporations and Western engineers have converged on Permissive Open Software as the pervasive model for software components of American corporations.

The prevalence of corporate-oriented open-source software has had a major effect on the type of open-software that is produced. In particular, the majority of open-source software now consists of components that corporations use to create proprietary services.

The main problem with FOSS movement is that it is aimless. Open source has become primarily component oriented. FOSS movement does not have an ecosystem of its own. What gets produced is untargeted. The FOSS movement needs to target a particular digital ecosystem, distinct from the proprietary American internet application services.

In Part IV — Libre-Halaal ByStar Digital Ecosystem — we put forward the blueprint of an ethics oriented digital ecosystem. The Libre-Halaal philosophy is purposeful. Our components fit in a bigger picture. We select or create components because of their purpose in that bigger picture. Generally, we don't waste time and effort towards making Libre-Halaal software be compatible with Windows and MacOS. Debian Linux is our own platform.

The philosophy, morality and ethics of Libre-Halaal Software repels American corporations and as such is an excellent vehicle for distinguishing genuinely ethical software and services from the software and services of Americanists.

Chapter 13

Global Polyexistential Capitalism

When there is one thing that can only be possessed by one possessor, all wishing to possess that one thing must compete. Hence, monoexistential capitalism is inherently competition oriented.

Thus far, uses of the word capitalism have not been distinguishing between monoexistential capitalism and polyexistential capitalism. Economic models for monoexistentials and polyexistentials should be inherently different. Because monoexistentials lead to mono-possessablity and clear ownership rules but polyexistentials lead to poly-possessablity and no ownership. Rivalry goods are rivalry because of their monoexistence. Polyexistence naturally results in public goods.

We are devout monoexistential bounded-corporations capitalists. We believe in proper ownership rules, free markets and proper regulation. We are pro-business.

The existing capitalist model for monoexistentials is generally correct, in both philosophical and economic terms. But the extension of the monoexistential capitalist model into the domain of polyexistentials, based on the Western IPR regime, is a grave mistake. Philosophically it is wrong. Societally it is harmful to humanity. And economically it is unstable and vulnerable, since it can be displaced by disruptive business models that are based on polyexistential dynamics.

Dynamics of monoexistential capitalism are generally well understood. Americanism is rooted in monoexistential capitalism of unbounded-corporations.

The IPR model of creating artificial scarcity for polyexistentials so that monoexistential economic models remain intact is flawed in the aggregate.

Possession and ownership of monoexistentials and polyexistentials are inherently very different. Economic models that have been established and have worked well in the realm of monoexistentials are not equally applicable to polyexistentials. The basics of monoexistentials and polyexistentials are fundamentally different and monoexistential capitalism and polyexistential capitalism need to be fundamentally different. Unlike monoexistentials that are inherently competition oriented, polyexistential are inherently collaboration oriented.

A competing economic model that is in harmony with polyexistence can easily overtake the IPR economic model. Eastern nations subscribing to polyexistential capitalism can do a number to Western IPR based economies.

Forced extension of economic models of monoexistential into the realm of polyexistentials is unnatural and illogical. The economic ramifications of recognizing the fraudulence of the Western IPR regime are immense. Many people are choosing not to understand the simple logic of polyexistence, which invalidates IPR, because it is not in their interest to do so.

The Western IPR based capitalist model has pushed for proprietary activity in the for profit quadrant and non-proprietary activity in the not-for profit quadrant. This too is artificial. In the context of IPR regime, polyexistential capitalism is about cultivation of the non-proprietary and for-profit quadrant.

13.1   Types of Capitalism

In the Western models, there is no clear distinction between monoexistential capitalism and polyexistential capitalism. Furthermore, there are many different views and models for imposing proper limitations on corporations, with American Capitalism being an extreme case. As a result, the term "Capitalism" has become a tricky one, as it can mean many different things to different people.

For our purposes, we use the following distinctions and terminology.

American Capitalism:
> The type of capitalism that has been practiced in America. A model which only pays lip service to proper limitations of corporations and which fuses corporation and government towards corpocracy. The first phase of American Capitalism was mostly mono-existential and mixed-existential oriented. The second phase of American Capitalism is mostly polyexistential oriented.

American IPR Capitalism:
The second phase of American Capitalism which is deeply rooted in the Western IPR regime and is dominated by digital businesses. It considers foreign and domestic surveillance as non-negative byproducts of the capitalistic economic model.

Monoexistential Capitalism:
The type of capitalism that limits the scope of its economic model to monoexistentials and monoexistential-dominant mixed-existentials.

Libre-Halaal Oriented Polyexistential Capitalism:
The type of capitalism that builds on Monoexistential Capitalism but governs polyexistentials and polyexistential-dominant mixed-existentials differently. It is based on economic models which do not violate Libre-Halaalness of polyexistentials and promote attribution based economy instead of polyexistential ownership.

Notice that the concepts and vocabulary that we have built earlier in this document, allows us to be precise in analyzing the evolution of capitalism as an economic model.

The basic premise of traditional capitalism is that people are economic creatures and through self-interest, the invisible hand brings order through competition. The metaphor of invisible hand, introduced by the 18th-century Scottish philosopher and economist Adam Smith, characterizes the mechanisms through which beneficial social and economic outcomes may arise from the accumulated self-interested actions of individuals, none of whom intends to bring about such outcomes. Adam Smith lived in a world which was an environment of monoexistentials and monoexistential dominated mix-existentials. His theory may have had some validity at that time and in that environment. Things have changed greatly. In the 21st-century we live in an environment where polyexistentials and polyexistential dominated mix-existentials are supreme. It is silly to even imagine that the invisible hand is still applicable. The idea that we can revert back to the 18th-century environment through IPR is equally silly.

Capitalism further suggests that value creation should be primarily economically based through private-sector activity with minimal public-sector interference. Polyexistentials also render these concepts obsolete.

Before digging any deeper, outside of capitalism, let's consider "value creation" in some detail.

13.2 Types of Value Creation Machineries

In the following sections, we will be speaking of "economic value" and "true value." In the broader context, for us, value is a measure of utility. Economic value is the determination of the prices of goods and services. True value is economic value plus the accounting of all externalities.

Now let's consider machineries that create value:

Individuals (non-economic):
> Let's say that this book is of some utility. Let's further say that this book can be obtained at near zero cost. Then as individuals, we have created value — but not economic value.

Non-profit Organizations:
> Groups of individuals, with some declaration of non-profit intent, as an organization can create value.

Private Sector For-Profit Organizations:
> Groups of individuals, with some declaration of profit intent, as an organization can create value.

Public Sector:
> On behalf of a society, governments can create value. Roads and bridges are some examples.

Global Sector:
> Collectively, a number of governments and organizations can create value. International standards (3GPP) for mobile phones for example.

Now let's apply the distinction of monoexistentials and polyexistentials to these types of value creation machineries. And then on top of that, consider ramifications of having IPR as the model of governance of polyexistentials vs ramifications of having Libre-Halaal as the model of governance of polyexistentals.

Clearly, the economic models that we end up with would be very different.

Let's start by re-visiting American Capitalism from this perspective.

13.3   American Capitalism and its Evolution

Sometime in the late 20th century American Capitalism evolved into something far worse and uglier. American Capitalism can be subdivided into two phases. American monoexistential capitalism and American IPR Capitalism. In the 20th century, up until say the Dot-Con era American Capitalism was primarily monoexistential-dominant mixed-existentials centric.[44] Post Dot-Con era, American Capitalism became primarily polyexsitentials and polyexistential-dominant mixed-existentials centric. It is the model of the second phase, "American IPR Capitalism" that is particularly ugly and which endangers humanity.

This recent enhanced ugliness of evolution of "American Capitalism" has been observed by many. Various American academics have focused on various symptoms, each coming up with a catch phrase. Tim Wu's is "The Curse Of Bigness" [47], Ramesh Srinivasan's is "Beyond The Valley" [44], Rana Foroohar's is "Don't be evil" [20], Roger McNamee's is "Zucked" [38], Shoshana Zuboff's is "Surveillance Capitalism" [49], Amy Klobuchar's is "Antitrust" [34], Zephyr Teachout's is "Break'Em Up" and McKenzie Wark's is "Capital Is Dead. Is This Something Worse?" [46]

All of these Americans have recognized that something is wrong. They all have come up with some type of diagnosis. But none of them permits him or herself to identify the American IPR regime as the root cause of the ugliness and none of these thinkers calls for abolishment of the Western IPR regime. Copying of all of the above books by all of these authors is restricted through the US Copyright system. In our view they are accomplices to what causes the ugliness of American Capitalism.

Similar to the situation with guns in the United States, there is general consensus that something is very wrong. So what? Indeed, something far worse than the usual American Capitalism is at work. Solutions and cures exist only outside of Americanism.

13.3.1   Worse Than Capitalism (by McKenzie Wark)

Below we reproduce a verbatim copy of an article titled: "Worse Than Capitalism" by McKenzie Wark which appeared in "Ours To Hack And To Own" [42]. In 2016, that article was subjected to Creative Commons Attribution-ShareAlike 4.0 International license.

Afterwards, we map what she is saying into the model and vocabulary that we have developed in this document. And we compare and contrast our views and positions.

> What if this was no longer capitalism, but something worse? Such a perspective might help explain some of the features of the contemporary political-economic landscape. My argument, odd though it may sound, is that both capital and labor have lost ground to an emerging ruling class, one that confronts a quite different kind of antagonist.

It helps to see capitalism as already a kind of second-order mode of commodified production. First-order commodification emerged in part, at least — through the transformation of the relations between peasants and their lords; the peasants lost traditional rights to arable land and to the commons. In place of the (supposedly) ancient rights and duties that held between landlord and peasant, in which the peasant's duties to the lord were paid directly with a share of the produce, the peasant had to pay rent in cash.

First-order commodification was thus the commodification of land. Pieces of land became abstract pieces of property that could be bought and sold. Peasants lost traditional rights to land and saw much of it enclosed and privatized. A "surplus population" of peasants ended up in the cities, where they were to become the working class, sellers of labor-power.

Capitalism was a second-order mode of commodified production, built on top of the pastoral one that preceded it in the countryside. One can forget that when David Ricardo wrote On the Principles of Political Economy and Taxation, he wrote on behalf of a rising, urban, capitalist ruling class and against the interests of a pre-existing, rural, pastoralist ruling class. It was a study in intra-ruling class studies.

In opposition to the pastoralist ruling class, the capitalist ruling class constructed a rather more abstract mode of production, one in which not only land but labor and the factory could be elaborate forms of fungible private property. With the destruction of the privileges awarded it by the state, the landlord class became a subordinate ruling class within capitalism, still extracting its extortionate ground rents (as indeed it still does today) but unable to claim the whole of the state as its own and to govern exclusively in its own interests.

The peasantry were, of course, no mere spectators upon their own oppression, but resisted the landlord class, every so often rising up against it. However, the peasantry tended toward a politics based on ancient rights. The rise of the modern labor movement was a cultural revolution that replaced the backward-looking peasant politics with a forward-looking one, based on the evident fact of capitalism as the dominant mode of production.

Such might be a more or less orthodox thumbnail sketch of the rise of capitalism in Britain, where it first arose. Of course, elsewhere in the world it followed different paths. But rather than turn toward the complicated business of pluralizing this historical sketch, I want to do something different: to pose the question of whether there is, on top of the second-order commodified mode of production of capitalism, a third-order commodified mode of production—what I will call vectoralism.

First-order commodification, what I call pastoralism, made land into a form of abstract private property relation. Second-order commodification, generally called capitalism, much advanced the abstraction of the private property relation into fungible things. Third-order commodication, which I call vectoralism, extends abstraction much further, subordinating information to whole new kinds of private property rights, and in the process creating new kinds of class relations.

On top of the class relation of landlords and peasants, and of capitalists and the working class, there is a relation between a vectoralist class that owns the vector of information in one form or another, and a hacker class that has to produce new forms of information that can be made into private property.

This emerging class relation does not replace previous layers of commodified abstraction, but it does transform them. Initially, the vectoralist class enabled capital to outwit the working class in the class conflicts of the late twentieth century. The information vector was what enabled capital to route around the power of labor to interrupt production. The information vector enabled capital to draw resources from a variety of sources at short notice. The information vector enabled capital to develop productive resources remote from traditional working class communities, with their historic memory and capacity for self-organization.

In the short term, the vectoralist class was helpful to capital in its struggle against labor, but in the long run, it is trying to subordinate capital to itself. Take a look at the top Fortune 500 companies, or the top "unicorn" venture capital darlings of the moment. With a few exceptions, one finds iterations of the same thing: companies whose power and wealth relies on stocks or flows of information, which control either the extensive vector over space or the intensive vector of an archive of commodified information— so-called intellectual property.

Whether it is finance, tech, cars, drugs, food, or chemicals—often the big companies no longer actually make their products. That can be contracted out to a competing mass of capitalist suppliers. What the vectoralist firm owns and controls is brands, patents, copyrights, and trademarks, or it controls the networks, clouds, and infrastructures, along which such information might move.

The rise of the so-called sharing economy is really just a logical extension of this contracting out of actual material services and labor by firms that control unequal flows of information. This control via the information vector is becoming more granular, working now at the level of individual laborers rather than sub-contracted firms. At first, the vectoral made capitalist firms subordinate. Now, where they can, the vectoralist class replaces them altogether with individual subcontractors.

Like all previous extensions of the abstraction of private property, this one too produces its own internal antagonist. And like all previous antagonists, it never appears in a pure and self-conscious form. Most peasants tugged the forelock and did what they were told, silently cursing the lord under their breath. Most workers settled for some job security and a weekend. Radical class-based movements are rare.

So it comes as no surprise that the hacker class is not particularly conscious or organized or antagonistic either. But its frustrations are real. The hacker class designs the information tools by which all human effort is controlled and organized by asymmetrical flows of information. The hacker can see her or his own job succumbing to this tendency in the end as well.

The organization of the activity of hackers is built into the form of code itself. Their efforts are compartmentalized and separated — black-boxed. They work on alienated tasks just as workers do. Only they do not work from clock-on to knock-off time. Even when they sleep they work for the boss. They might in some cases be well paid, but in many instances they are not. Their skills date quickly, and they are replaced by others.

Hackers won't necessarily respond to the vectoralist class in traditional labor movement terms. A strike would hardly be effective given that hackers can't shut down production. The most frequent forms of antagonism are more likely changing jobs, or stealing time on the job for one's own projects. Of course many dream of start-up glory, but that dream quickly tarnishes when the hacker gets to see firsthand who usually cashes out first in such schemes.

The significance of platform cooperativism is that it is a movement that can place itself at the nexus of the interests and experiences of both workers and hackers. Why not use the specific skills hackers have to create the means of organizing information, but use it to create quite other ways of organizing labor? Cooperatives have a long history in the labor movement; indeed, in their origins, they looked back to forms of peasant self-organization of the commons.

Why not re-imagine the cooperative on the basis of contemporary forms of information vector—but without the information asymmetries that are the basis of vectoralist class power? That seems like the thread of a political-economic project that both honors past struggles and also addresses the distinctive form of commodification in the age of the information vector as a private property relation.

The vectoral political economy is in many ways worse than the capitalist one. It gives the ruling class of our time unprecedented wealth amid growing poverty and despoliation. It enables that ruling class unprecedented flexibility in routing around strikes, blockages, or communal strongholds. It has made the whole planet appear as an infinitely exploitable resource at precisely the moment when it is also clear that the past products of commodified production are coming back to haunt us.

And yet every advance in the abstraction of the form of private property also opens up new perspectives on what may be held in common, and how the common might counter-organize. The practical and conceptual experiments of platform cooperativism are a key moment in the advance of this counter-organizing agenda.

13.3.2 American IPR Capitalism Threatens Humanity

Many of the points made in the reproduced previous section are consistent with what we are saying.

The phase that we call American Monoexistential Capitalism, Wark calls "Capitalism as a second-order mode of commodified production". The phase that we call American IPR Capitalism, Wark calls "vectoralism" — a third-order commodified mode of production. Wark identifies (and refers to it properly) "so-called intellectual property" as part of the problem. We consider intellectual property as the root of the problem in American IPR Capitalism. What Wark calls the "hacker class", we call the "global software engineering profession".

Our objection to the positions of American academics and activists, the likes of Wark, is that they are not seeing the full picture. They don't dig deep enough and don't go far enough. Americans have not recognized the full scope and scale of the harm of their celebrated economic model. That harm is not just to themselves, but to all of humanity — as polyexistentials are non-territorial.

Sure, what we are observing is worse than capitalism. But it is not sufficient to just say that. We should go way deeper and much further, and in this book we do.

13.3.3   Containing the American IPR-Based Capitalism

Economic models are human creations for the purpose of bettering the human condition. But humans should not live just for the purpose of bettering the economic model.

Corporations are created and exist for the sole purpose of generating profit. Consider the equivalent of a person whose sole purpose was accumulation of profit and power. Would you not be calling him/her a psychopath? Such an entity should be well bounded and limited, otherwise it will destroy humanity. Based on this understanding, we draw a distinction between American capitalism of unbounded-corporations which we consider inhuman and bounded-corporations monoexistential capitalism to which we subscribe.

In monoexistential capitalism, the existence of the subject of profit is in singular. To a certain extent, this functions as a natural form of bounding and containment of the corporation. Extending monoexistential capitalism into the realm of polyexistentials in the proprietary and for-profit quadrant empowers the unbounded corporation to profit from the unbounded replicability of polyexistentials.

The Western IPR regime has resulted in the transfer of more power and more control to the unbounded Americanist corporations. The overwhelming majority of copyright and patents are controlled by corporations — not individuals.

Highly optimized economic models can destroy humanity. Economic models define human behavior. Money becomes everything. People start living for money. But economics is full of externalities and other aspects of life start being damaged. Before you know it, people become economic creatures. All of this has already happened in the context of American Capitalism. Before you know it, the rest of humanity will become Americanized. Humanity is at risk.

American Capitalism is not just an economic system. It is a value system. It is intertwined with extreme individualism (khodzadegi) and greed.

The economic model of bounding corporations to the halaal manner-of-existence of polyexistentials protects humanity in the context of a profit-oriented highly competitive polyexistential capitalism. This can be the foundation of an economic system that results in bettering the human condition and can protect humanity from corporations.

13.4 Economics Is Not Science

Unlike chemistry, physics, or medicine, economics is not a science. The pseudo-science of economics, uses the trappings of science, like dense mathematics, to pretend it is science. Real science is not ridiculed. In economics there are many ridiculed schools – many consider Reaganomics as "voodoo economics".

To the extent that certain disciplines and theories have been established in economics, they are mostly applicable to monoexistential capitalism. In modern economics, what we have is application of monoexistential dominated theories to the polyexistential dominated environment. This is a recipe for disaster.

These outdated beliefs remain the basis for economic policies that don't work anymore. In response to inflation they continue to raise the interest rate. Sure, that may have been effective in a monoexistial dominated environment, but it is no longer effective in a polyexistential dominated environment.

Economists need to focus more on discovery of fundamentals and less on policy. The fundamentals include the distinctions between economics of monoexsitentials, economics of mixed-exsitentials and economics of polyexistentials. These are governed by different laws of nature and thus demand separate economic theories.

American economists have yet to discover that economics must be subordinate to nature, humanity, law, and justice. In America all of that is completely backwards. American economists believe that economics is the main axis around which everything else should be structured.

Governance of polyexistentials should not be based on economics. This is what the Western IPR economic regime does.

Halaal manner-of-existence of polyexistentials should govern economics of polyexistentials.

13.5 Proprietary vs. Non-Proprietary; For-Profit vs. Non-Profit

A business or other construct may be characterized as either proprietary or non-proprietary. And it may be characterized as either for-profit or non-profit. Generally speaking, these characterizations are orthogonal. Thus, there are four quadrants in which a construct may reside. This is illustrated in Figure 13.1

Typically, the for-profit label represents self-interest orientation and the non-profit label represents public goods orientation. The Western IPR regime has created the proprietary model in the for-profit context. In Polyexistential Capitalism, there is no proprietary model anymore. Both for-profit and non-profit activities produce public goods.

We first briefly describe each quadrant and then focus on the non-proprietary and for-profit quadrant.

13.5.1   The Proprietary and For-Profit Quadrant

The business models for the *proprietary, for-profit* quadrant are well established. The Venture Capitalist business model resides exclusively within this quadrant.

Conventions and regulations for this quadrant are well established. Copyright and Patents are the norm in this quadrant. Venture Capitalists understand it well.

Historically, proprietary and for-profit have been very closely allied, so that the *proprietary, for-profit* model dominates conventions.

13.5.2   The Non-Proprietary and Non-Profit Quadrant

With regard to public research, there are well established, clear and mature procedures for supporting research in the *non-proprietary, non-profit* quadrant. The recipient organizations are typically .edu or .org entities, and the resulting public-funded research comes back to society in the form of unrestricted, non-proprietary results and assets.

13.5.3   The Proprietary and Non-Profit Quadrant

In theory this quadrant should be empty.

With regard to research, supporting public research in the *proprietary, non-profit* quadrant makes no sense at all. Here the results of the research are shut off from the public in terms of both ownership and business: the results are privately held and make no contribution either to society or to commerce.

In practice, it is where most academics exist.

13.5.4   Operation in the
For-Profit and Non-Proprietary Quadrant

The business models for the *non-proprietary, for-profit* quadrant are not well established. The Venture Capitalist constituency does not understand this quadrant, nor does it believe in it, or have any experience in it.

	For Profit	Non-Profit	
Proprietary Model	Traditional: Microsoft AOL Yahoo	Conflicted: Academics Wap Forum ...	Copyright Patents Secrecy
Non-Proprietary Model	New: Free Software Bus Redhat, ... Libre Services Bus Neda, ...	Traditional: FSF IETF FPF	Copyleft Knowledge Sharing Openness
	Pro-Business	Pro-Public	

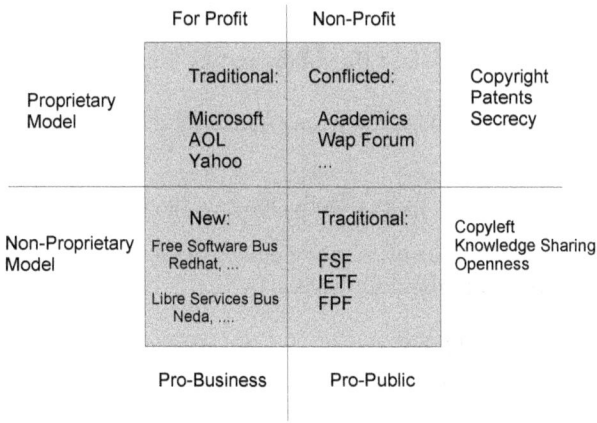

Figure 13.1: Operation in the For-Profit and Non-Proprietary Quadrant

Business operation within the *non-proprietary, for-profit* quadrant is still very unusual at this time, and mature business models for this quadrant do not yet exist. Therefore, our own Open Business Plan may be considered the most complete business analysis of the non-proprietary model in existence today.

The notion of a non-proprietary construct, residing and operating within the for-profit sector, is new and different. Historically, the for-profit sector has been closely associated with proprietary ownership of assets. Hence the Internet Services industry and the likes of Blackberry as we see them today. Also historically, management of non-proprietary or public assets has been primarily associated with the non-profit sector. Hence the current orientation of the FOSS Movement, operating largely within the non-profit sector.

We propose a radical shift of the Internet Services industry from the for-profit, proprietary quadrant, to the for-profit, non-proprietary quadrant. In this space the entire software for an Internet service remains a communal public resource in the trust of the engineering profession, while service deployment is driven forward by the full force of for-profit commercial motivations.

This radical shift to the *non-proprietary, for-profit quadrant* causes a major industry reconfiguration, with significant winners and losers. The losers are the existing vested proprietary interests, whose economic hegemony vanishes. But the winners are the many more companies who can now enter the Libre-Halaal Software and Libre-Halaal Internet Services market —and the end-users. The impact is immense both in economic terms and in societal terms.

13.6   Libre-Halaal Polyexistential Capitalism

Thus far, we have emphasized the following key points:

- Western IPR regime is the wrong model for governance of polyexistentials

- Libre-Halaal is the proper model for governance of polyexistentials

- Recent recognitions of negative effects of American Capitalism reflect the symptoms of the IPR mistake

Earlier, we introduced Libre-Halaal as a replacement model for Western IPR. But we have not introduced an economic model to replace American IPR Capitalism.

So, now we want to draw the contours of what should replace American IPR Capitalism. Its short name is "Libre-Halaal Capitalism". Its full name is: "Libre-Halaal Oriented Polyexistential Capitalism".

The full scope of Libre-Halaal Capitalism is all polyexistentials. The economics of currently patented medications are within scope of Libre-Halaal Capitalism. The economics of Monsanto patents for genetically modified soybeans are within scope of Libre-Halaal Capitalism.

But initially we focus on Libre-Halaal Capitalism in the digital domain. By that, we mean:

- Software — Based on Libre-Halaal Software

- Internet Application Services — Based on Libre-Services

- Digital Content — Based on Libre-Halaal Content

13.6.1   Transformation of Software into Services

In Section 13.5 we introduced two dimensions of Proprietary vs. Non-Proprietary and For-Profit vs. Non-Profit. To those two dimensions now add another dimension. That of Software Vs Internet Application Services (Internet Services).

Part of the debate about FOSS is now over, while part continues. The part that is over is any question about the viability of FOSS as a development model for creating large-scale, complex, relevant software systems. GNU/Linux is a fully viable free software alternative to the proprietary Microsoft Windows operating system, against which it continues to make steady inroads.

And apart from such well-known and high-profile projects, behind the scenes the FOSS movement has become a flourishing creative environment, generating a constant stream of new and better software packages, duplicating and surpassing the capabilities of an ever-increasing portion of proprietary software territory.

And the fundamental FOSS creative dynamic has now also become very well understood: the FOSS development model allows *unrestricted creative reuse of existing assets at essentially zero cost*. It is from this dynamic that the FOSS model derives its tremendous generative power. FOSS is thus fully established as a generative engine and an industry reality and is here to stay.

But the part of the debate that continues is whether or not this has any meaningful commercial dimension. Within the proprietary software domain, a powerful revenue-generating engine exists in the form of the traditional software licensing model. But this revenue source is absent under the FOSS model. In its place there are a number of possible business and revenue models, but in all cases, these lack the large-scale repeatability that makes things really interesting from a business perspective.

There thus remains a conceptual gap, a puzzle, about how the powerful generative forces of FOSS can be turned into a large-scale, repeatable, revenue stream. But this puzzle is now solved.

Business Dynamics Of Internet Services

Within the Internet Services industry the business and revenue models are quite clear and obvious. The largest and most obvious are the subscription fee model of generalized service providers, and the advertising model of numerous specialized no-cost service providers, demonstrated most spectacularly by Google. Both the subscription fee and advertising models are unlimitedly scalable, thus resulting in the gigantic commercial Internet of today.

But the Internet Services industry of today is a fundamentally proprietary construct. While proprietary service providers can and do make frequent use of FOSS components within their services, they do not espouse the FOSS development model itself, and their technical development process remains competitive and proprietary. Though they may incorporate FOSS components, Facebook and Google are certainly not FOSS values oriented.

Thus, as we look at the software and internet industries of today, we see two largely disjointed cultures. As illustrated in Figure 13.2 we see the FOSS domain, with its powerful generative and propagative development model, but lacking any clear large-scale monetization model. And separate from this we see the proprietary Internet Services domain, with enormous revenue and business consequences, but handicapped in scope and scale by its competitive development model.

Now we are witnessing a further transformational event in the evolution of the internet: a shift of traditional software applications towards a service-based implementation, or what is sometimes called the "transformation of software

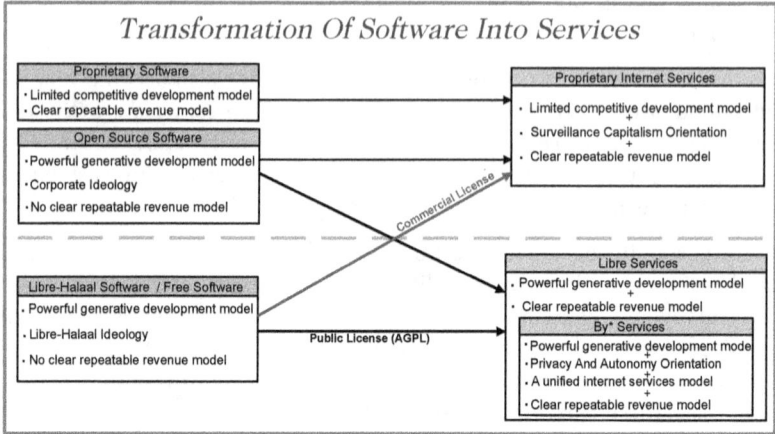

Figure 13.2: Business Ramifications of Software to Service Transformation

into services." This is the critical event that now solves the FOSS revenue puzzle. This development unites the generative power of the free software domain with the proven revenue models of the services domain. The transformation of software into services *allows the powerful generative model of FOSS to be invested directly into the powerful revenue model of the Internet Services industry.*

The dashed horizontal line in Figure 13.2 represents two different models and two two different ideologies. The upper part of the dashed horizontal line represents the proprietary American digital model and the convenient convergence of the open-source and corporate cultures. We described some of these dynamics in Section 12.1.6 — Corporatization of FOSS.

The lower part of the dashed horizontal line represents the Libre Services model and the consistent Libre-Halaal Software and Free Software ideologies. In Figure 13.2, note that open-source software feeds into both Proprietary Internet Services and Libre Services. Some software engineers who choose the Libre-Halaal public licensing model choose not to be agnostic and recognize that the moral and ethical ramifications of not cultivating the proprietary internet services are very important. At this point (in 2023), the Libre Services industry is insignificant compared to the proprietary internet services. This is not because of the inherent economics of the two models. It is because of lack of understanding of the economics of Libre Services, business comfort with the traditional proprietary model, and American and Western societal values.

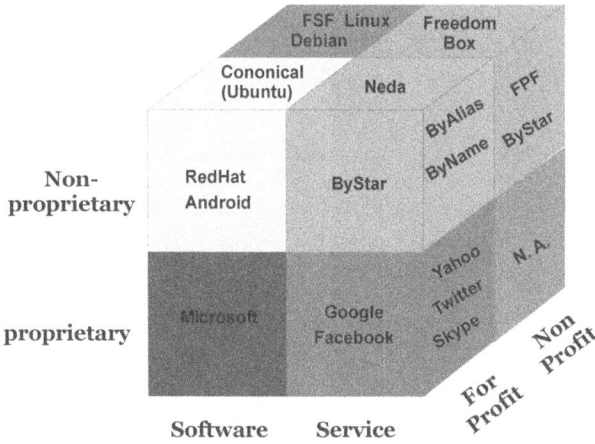

Figure 13.3: The For-Profit Non-Proprietary Quadrant For Internet Services

13.6.2 Libre-Halaal Internet Services Capitalism

With the above understandings of:

1. For-Profit/Non-Profit and Proprietary/Non-Proprietary Quadrants

2. Transformation Of Software Into Services

We now add another dimension to the square and turn it into a cube.

So, we now have a cube as shown in Figure 13.3. The Libre-Halaal services are positioned in the For-Profit Non-Proprietary Quadrant for Internet Services. Note that in the non-proprietary layer, re-use and collaboration is far richer than the proprietary layer. For example, in the Software slice, Debian and Ubuntu cross progress. In the Services slice the same can happen. For example, ByStar and FreedomBox can cross progress.

The Libre-Halaal Services deployment model breaks both these traditions. It represents a radical shift of the Internet Services industry from the for-profit, proprietary quadrant, to the for-profit, non-proprietary quadrant. In this space the entire software for an Internet service remains a communal public resource in the trust of the engineering profession, while service deployment is driven forward by the full force of for-profit commercial motivations.

13.7   Attribution Based Economics (ABE)
— Instead of Ownership

Ownership and attribution are two separate things.

Through ownership, the IPR model includes attribution. In the IPR model, the one (or the ones) who creates the original copyrighted polyexistential becomes the owner and the polyexistential is attributed to the owner.

In the Libre-Halaal model, the one (or the ones) who creates the original polyexistential becomes the origin of that polyexistential. And the polyexistential is attributed to that origin. In the Libre-Halaal model, by rejecting ownership we are not rejecting attribution. Attribution is an integral part of the Libre-Halaal model.

Capitalism operates on supply and demand as the basis of value. There, open and unlimited availability translates into zero market value. In that model, non-rivalry goods are worthless. So, in that traditional economic model, polyexistentials are not economically sound.

In the context of Libre-Halaal software (FOSS) and internet application services the common revenue generation model has been that of providing value added services rather than from the original development of the core open software. Since, as the core Libre-Halaal software is unrestricted polyexistentials, from a market value standpoint, that developed software is worthless.

Yet, the Libre-Halaalness of polyexistentials leads to limitless availability of useful works. This is a profoundly good thing from the perspective of maximizing value, and thus suppressing it is deeply misguided.

Attribution-based economics is a new model that aims to remedy this state of affairs by changing the basis of value from supply and demand to collective recognition. This is facilitated by a process of "inheritance attribution" where we collectively agree on the extent of inheritance of ideas and works in other (e.g., derivative) ideas and works, by means of transparent and evolving standards. This model is capable of recognizing a much larger set of valuable contributions, including forms of value that cannot be coerced into a supply-and-demand equation. That is, in this model, there is no need to artificially restrict availability in order for something to be considered valuable. By virtue of the curious property that innovations on the process are themselves subject to the process of recognition in a self-reflective way, we gain accuracy, and by the property that agreed-upon standards apply equally to all, we gain fairness —guarantees that are at best tenuously present in today's economic systems.[45]

13.7.1   Attribution Based Economics (by Sid Kasivajhula)

This book is a collection of thoughts and beliefs. The role of the author is to organize and direct these thoughts and these beliefs. When we use the word "we", this is what we mean.

The concept of Attribution Based Economics is relatively new and the best way to present it is to use the words of one of its origins and attribute it to him.

At the emacsConf-2022, a virtual Emacs conference, Sid Kasivajhula presented some thoughts related to the concept of Attribution Based Economics (ABE). We reproduce parts of that presentation below:

> When we think about the problems of the world we see global warming, war, appropriation, poverty, and among numerous other problems, also the inability to make a living as an open source developer.
>
> Now this last problem may seem a lot less consequential compared to the other ones, but what if I told you that the solution to this problem and the solutions to the others are one and the same?
>
> And it's because there's a common underlying problem at the heart of all of these problems. I'm going to tell you what that problem is in one sentence. You ready for it? It is ... the deviation of market value from true value. Let's think about this in the context of existing economic systems such as capitalism and communism.
>
> And of these, I want to focus on capitalism because it is the only nontrivial economic system, really. Communism is more sort of a political means to achieve economic ends. And the other economic systems exist sort of on a spectrum between these two. So let's focus on capitalism. Capitalism has as its basis of value supply and demand. And consequently, there is a great emphasis on this idea of ownership. Now ownership is an idea that made some kind of sense when you have goods and services that are constrained in some way, that are essentially finite in supply. But when you have things like works of software, art, and music, which are essentially infinite in supply, the idea of ownership and supply and demand don't make sense anymore. And yet we employ the institution of property to constrain supply and introduce the idea of supply just so that we can induce a market value in terms of supply and demand in a capitalist economic system. And it's wrongheaded.

How many of us have written copyright declarations like these on our work. It's a lot of work! Especially when we have version control. Now in this example, almost every line is written by a different person, so who owns the code in this case? Who owns the copyright here? Is it some of them, is it all of them, do they share it in some way? It doesn't really make sense, especially when the reason we're employing copyright and ownership in this case is to approximate the idea of attribution, which is what we really care about here. And that brings us to the nature of the solution, which is to move away from an economic system based on ownership and supply and demand, to an economic system based on attribution, instead. That is, moving away from who owns what to who did what and how important was it. And we can do this by the process of Dialectical Inheritance Attribution, which just means that we do it in a collective way using common collectively agreed upon standards that are applied transparently to all. And when we have an economic system that is based on attribution as the source of value in this way, we call it attribution based economics. Now, once we have that, it gives us fairness, effective empowerment of expertise, freedom through incentives rather than through coercion. And privacy as well.

But I could tell you all of those things and some may still say, "Why should I care about this?" There are those who would say that fairness is not a good goal, and that might makes right, and that as Darwin showed us, the nature of nature is violence. Now I know that many of us reject this ideology, and we feel in our bones that it is wrong. But luckily we don't have to resort to high philosophy and gut feeling in order to convince ourselves that an attribution-based system is truly better. Because in addition to all of those other properties we talked about, an attribution-based economic system is also efficient. And I say this from the perspective of having an admiration for the efficiency of capitalism. So understand that that is my perspective when I say that this system — an attribution-based economic system — is significantly more efficient than capitalism. And it achieves that by virtue of eliminating the waste that is inherent in adversarial competition, while still preserving market forces!

... Now, I don't know about you, but I'd prefer to avoid fighting these gyroscopic forces. I'd rather have these forces work with me rather than against me. Now in a capitalist system, there is another problem, which is that not only do you have these gyroscopic forces at work, but these forces aren't even all working together. They're working against each other, in many cases. They represent misaligned interests. And indeed, these misaligned interests are the very means by which these forces operate at all. So in a way, war is not just an inevitable consequence in this system but is rather the very nature of such a system. In an attribution-based system, on the other hand, by virtue of the source of value being collective attribution, we are able to achieve alignment of all of these interests at every scale, so that at every scale of society, from the smallest to the largest scales, the interests will be aligned, will be consonant and harmonious. I think this is a very important, profound quality that I think is the fundamental problem of economics - the fundamental goal of economics to solve. And I believe that an attribution-based economic system addresses it and solves it.

... The second component of the implementation is the accounting system. All accounting is public. All payments into the repo are public and all payments out of the project are also public. We can do some things for privacy, and again, the basis of this system is dialogue. ...

... You can financially support an ABE project. This is important to do because the system won't get started without money as an input. And it also has network effects, as we saw — the more money you contribute, the more incentive there is for other people to join the system. And contributions are also attributable, as we said earlier. Some of them can be treated as investments. ...

Now in this world, we are told that we should look out for ourselves because no one is going to look out for us. That we should take care of our own because we can't rely on others to care. An attribution-based economy is nothing like that. We care about each other, we take care of each other, because taking care of one another is valuable, and an attribution-based economic system is capable of recognizing that value, in financial terms. And as a result, we are safe in the embrace of the world. ...

13.7.2   Attribution Based Libre-Halaal Capitalism

The concepts of working on the side lines of the IPR system with public license (the FOSS model) or that of rejecting the Western IPR model and replacing it with the Libre-Halaal model are relatively new. There is some consensus on the need for replacing the economics of the Western IPR regime with an attribution oriented economic model. For now we are calling that "Attribution Based Libre-Halaal Polyexistential Capitalism".

For something along these lines to become main stay of societies, we need to do exactly what this book is trying to do. Introduce the key concepts and the needed vocabulary, be multidisciplinary and bring it all together. Then, we need time to absorb and to consolidate relevant efforts. This is the first edition of this book. We hope to follow up with regular updates.

Something along the lines of Attribution Based Economics (ABE) that we introduced in the previous section is being understood and cultivated by many. And this is a sign that we are on the right track and that we are progressing. For example, without using the vocabulary of ABE, SourceCred—`https://sourcecred.io/`— is doing something similar. Below we reproduce a part of their documents:

> So what IS SourceCred?
>
> SourceCred (in the most basic sense) is a technology that makes the labor of individuals more visible and rewardable as they work together in a project or community. The goal of SourceCred is to use this technology to make rewarding labor as nuanced as human contribution often is. We hope to be one piece in the puzzle of a healthier future where systems serve community members, where financial maximization isn't the end-all be-all goal, and where wealth actually flows to those who are creating the value in our world.
>
> ...
>
> SourceCred uses an algorithm to determine how much value a contribution or contributor added to a project overall. When a contribution is made to a project, SourceCred's purpose is to "see" that contribution and assign it an amount of "Cred" based on how much value it brought to the project as a whole.
>
> ...

Granted, these are all early attempts. But it is clear that there is consensus on the way forward.

In due course and over time, we will build the equivalent of Venture Capitalists, Investment Bankers, Copyright Attorneys, Patent Attorneys, IPOs, etc. in the context of "Attribution Based Libre-Halaal Polyexistential Capitalism"

In the meantime, even inside of the Western IPR regime, using existing constructs, there are ways that we can evolve the current model.

13.8   Case Study: The Libre-Halaal ByStar Digital Ecosystem Open Business Plan

To make things less abstract and more concrete we present an open business plan for a complete digital ecosystem that we have built and that we describe in Chapter 16 — The Libre-Halaal ByStar Digital Ecosystem.

Focusing on ByStar individual services, you can think of the business of ByStar as two separate things.

1. Development (of software) of ByStar Individual Services

2. Deployment, Operation and Support for ByStar Individual Services

We have the precedence of the dynamics of Free and Open-Source software for the development (of software) of ByStar individual services. Public-sector, academics, engineers and business concerns all collaborate and the accumulated result is publicly-owned. Involvement of public-sector (Governments) in this phase should grow.

Deployment, operation and support for ByStar individual services can be primarily in the hands of the for-profit private sector. Beyond basic self-regulating principles of ByStar, very little additional regulations are needed.

As origins of ByStar, as part of our responsibility to create a viable implementation construct we have fully analyzed the business dimension, and we have formulated the business model in the form of an Open Business Plan, titled:

The Libre-Halaal ByStar Open Business Plan
An Inversion to the Proprietary Internet Services Model
Neda Communication Inc.'s Open Business Plan
http://www.by-star.net/PLPC/180014 — [28]
http://www.neda.com/strategicVision/businessPlan

In the context of Western IPR regime, polyexistential capitalism simply amounts to running your business in the for-profit and non-proprietary quadrant. For software, the business models are not as favorable as the for-profit and proprietary quadrant. But for Internet Services, the for-profit and non-proprietary quadrant poses no significant disadvantages. The main challenge of our business plan is to get traditionalist monoexistential venture capitalists to understand the economics and business dynamics of internet application services as polyexistentials.

In the context of this concrete example of ByStar open business plan, we are looking for a venture capitalist who can see that it is to his/her economic advantage to consider the Western IPR regime as fraudulent and as vulnerable.

Chapter 14

Ethical and Religious Cures

Questions of ownership are the inherent domain of morality, ethics and religion.

Earlier we said "IPR is Haraam", but who are we to make such declarations? Uses and introductions of halaal and haraam by individuals here and there are of some importance and significance. But it is broad consensus and widespread acceptance of halaal and haraam that results in significant moral impact. Halaal and haraam declaration are more significant when they reflect consensus of a profession. Halaal and haraam declaration are far more meaningful when they reflect the consensus of a religion. Ethical Halaal is far more significant than moral Halaal.

How are we to arrive at that broad consensus and widespread acceptance?

In the West, people attempt at expressing their take on right and wrong and all of that right and wrong becomes quickly irrelevant when economics comes into the picture – as economics is the center of the Western model. So, for the most part, halaal and haraam are academic and anecdotal in the West.

To the extent that religions can be considered vehicles for promotion of morality and ethics, based on their track record; a religion can be considered weaker or stronger compared to another religion.

Church and State were easily separated in the West as Christianity is a weak religion. Christianity draws a clear separation between the two worlds and the two times. The Western Christian model has become very "Secular" now. The definition of the purely Western word and the concept of "Secular" by Webster is:

> Of or pertaining to this present world, or to things not spiritual or holy; relating to temporal as distinguished from eternal interests;

not immediately or primarily respecting the soul, but the body; worldly.

In that simple Western Christian model, the Church is in control of the other world (heaven and hell) and the State is in control of this world. And the State quickly boils down to economics and the Corporation.

The concepts of halaal and haraam are totally absent in Christianity. Christianity does not concern itself much with this world.

Westerners consider their idea of separation of church and state as prescriptive. They believe that their notion of church applies to all religions and that their concept of religion emanating from Christianity is universal. The concept of separation of religion and state is in no way universal.

Unlike Christianity, Islam is a strong religion which concerns itself fully with both worlds. The founding fathers of the Islamic Republic of Iran were quite familiar with the West's history of the Dark Ages. Those who wrote the Islamic Republic's constitution had read the French and the American constitution and were familiar with the lessons of the French and the American revolution. The founding fathers of the Islamic Republic of Iran fully understood the Western concepts of separation of church and state and they fully rejected these concepts.

The model of fusing Islam and the Republic is complex and powerful. It is only such a model that can preserve humanity and it is only this model that can stand against the Western model of economic creatures calling their collection a society.

Halaal and haraam are of this world. Halaal and haraam are for this world. Only a religion that fully concerns itself with both worlds can properly drive forward, Halaals and Haraams. Secular Western and Christian models of focusing on each of the two worlds separately, at best will result into highly diluted Halaals and Haraams.

In the Moslem model, declarations of halaal and haraam by sources of imitation play an important role in moving society forward as new topics for Halaal and Haraam arise.

For example, towards societal consensus on halaal manner-of-existence of software, consider Imam Khomeini's fatwa on invalidity of Western Intellectual Property Rights regime which has paved the way towards current sources of imitation digesting the software engineering profession's definition of halaal manner-of-existence of software.

Consensus amongst Moslem sources of imitation in recognizing halaal manner-of-existence of software and halaal manner-of-existence of internet services can result in significant moral impact towards preventing the harm that the current disastrous Western model of manner-of-existence of software and internet services are headed for.

Majority of Grand Ayatollah's are against so-called IPR Regime.[46]

We humbly offer our professional analysis to Ghom and Najaf towards establishing a full consensus against the Western so-called IPR Regime.

Explicit and repeated fatwas against the Western so-called IPR Regime will assist the cure.

We humbly offer our professional analysis to Vatican and Protestants towards establishing a full consensus against the Western so-called IPR Regime.

Explicit and repeated decrees against the Western so-called IPR Regime will assist the cure.

14.1 Moral Sovereignty and Global Morality

The scope of polyexistentials is universal. Knowledge and information know no border.

Ghom and Las Vegas can coexist just fine as long as they remain separate. In which case, economic creatures in Las Vegas need not even know what halaal means.

But things have changed, and that separation is no longer viable. Knowledge and application of knowledge are now more than ever essential to health of any society and the digital era is here. Polyexistentials are now a dominant reality. Unlike a world dominated by monoexistentials, a world dominated by polyexistentials demands greater commonality of morality. Polyexistentials are easily transmittable and know no borders.

As such, at a minimum we need to move towards global consensus on halaalness of manner-of-existence of polyexistentials.

14.2 Intellectual Property Rights and Religions – Halaal Manner-of-Existence of Polyexistentials

Since "ownership" is proper domain of religions, in the context of concepts and vocabulary of Western IPR, the position of various religions on Intellectual Property Rights is of interest.

In our model of polyexistentials, the position of religions on halaalness of manner-of-existence of polyexistentials is of interest.

With regard to ownership of monoexistentials all three Ibrahimic religions (Islam, Christianity and Judaism) have full and absolute consensus on "thou shall not steal". Other major religions such as Buddhism also have full and absolute consensus on ownership rules of monoexistentials.

But when it comes to considerations for ownership of polyexistentials, things are not all that clear.

Here is a summary of what our research has produced.

14.2.1   Islam

In the Moslem/Shia tradition and in Iran's context, there is:

Iran's Theological Research on Intellectual Property Rights

پژوهشی فقهی در باب مالکیت فکری و معنوی

Farhang Tahmasebi – فرهنگ طهماسبی

2007 (1386)

http://www.ido.ir/a.aspx?a=1385023101

http://mohsen.banan.1.byname.net/Repub/120028, [18].

This document is in Farsi/Persian and is quite comprehensive. It was sponsored by the Iranian Government. The document analysis the topic of Intellectual Property Rights from an Islamic perspective. It then reviews the positions of a number of sources of imitation (Ayatollahs). The summary is that most Shia clergy invalidate Intellectual Property rights. Imam Khomeini and Ayatollah Golpayegani are fully against so-called Intellectual Property Rights.

14.2.1.1   Imam Khomeini's Decree
Invalidates So-Called Intellectual Property Rights

Imam Khomeini in tahrir-ol-vasileh explicitly rejects the validity of copyright, patents and trademarks.

The text of the relevant section in Farsi and its translation follows.

Imam Khomeini (peace be upon him) in Tahrir ol-vasileh on the subject of Western Intellectual Property has written:

That which has become famous among people as the right of authorship (copyright) is not a theological

امام خمینی(ره) در تحریرالوسیله در بحث مسائل مستحدثه با اشاره به مسأله مورد بحث می‌فرمایند:

آنچه که معروف به حق طبع نزد افراد است حق شرعی به شمار نمی‌آید و زایل نمودن سلطه مردم بر اموالشان بدون اینکه شرط و عقدی در بین باشد جایز نیست و مجرد نوشتن جمله «حق چاپ

or an ethical right. And
to take away the control
of people on their belongings without explicit condition and contract is not
permitted. And just by writing a sentence saying "Copyright: Print and Copying
Rights are Reserved" cre-
ates no right and does not
require conformance of others.

That which has become fa-
mous as "registration of
invention" (patents) cre-
ates no theological or ethical rights for the inventor and cannot prevent others in copying or repro-
ducing that invention. And
you cannot restrict peo-
ple from copying that in-
vention and you cannot restrict them in conducting
commerce which is based
on that invention. And no
one has a right to restrict
another with regard to his
full ruler-ship on his own
property.

And also that which has
become famous as "Monopoly
Of Commerce Over An Ob-
ject Or Objects" (trademark)
for an organization or a
number of merchants or
the like has no theologi-
cal or ethical lawful im-
pact. And restricting others is commerce and in-
dustry based on monopoly
of a few is not permitted.

و تقلید محفوظ است» حقی به
وجود نمی‌آورد و التزام دیگران
را به دنبال ندارد.

آنچه که معروف است به «ثبت
اختراع» برای مخترعش و منع
دیگران از تقلید او و تکثیر نمودن
آن اختراع هیچ اثر شرعی ندارد
و نمی‌توان افراد را از تقلید نمودن
آن اختراع و تجارت و کسب
کردن با آن منع کرد و هیچ کس
حق ندارد دیگری را از سلطنت
در اموال خودش منع کند. و نیز
آنچه که معروف است از «انحصاری
بودن تجارت یك شیء یا اشیاء»
برای موسسه‌ای یا تعدادی از تجار
یا مانند این‌ها هیچ اثر شرعی
ندارد و بازداشتن دیگران از تجارت
و صنعت حلال و محصور دانستن
در حق چند نفر جایز نمی‌باشد.

There are several things to note in Imam Khomeini's writings:

- The equivalent words for copyright, patent and trademark are non-existent in Arabic and Farsi. These are Western constructs.

- Imam Khomeini therefore refers to the equivalent phrase translation into Arabic and Farsi for these and further prefaces them with "that which has become famous". These emphasize that copyright, patent and trademark are non-Iranian and non-Islamic concepts which he fully rejects.

- The essence of Imam Khomeini's rejection of copyright, patent and trademark is the dilutive impact on ownership of real property. With respect to copyright and patent Imam Khomeini emphasizes the importance of one's full ruler-ship over one's own property.

- Imam Khomeini's rejection of Western so-called Intellectual Property is absolute, complete and total. Imam Khomeini fully rejects copyright, patent and trademark and considers them unlawful.

Imam Khomeini is the Founding Father of Islamic Republic of Iran who has fully invalidated the so-called Western IPR regime.

Particularly well-known Founding Fathers of America like George Washington and James Madison can be considered as originators of the American intellectual property protection.

Imam Khomeini was a theologian, a philosopher and an ethicist. America's Founding Fathers were businessmen. It is this difference in perspectives (philosophy vs economics) that has led to different conclusions on this topic. Governance of polyexistentials by economic creatures for economic creatures would be distinct and different from governance of polyexistentials by humans for humanity.

14.2.2   Christianity

We were only able to locate relevant text in the Catholic branch of Christianity.

In the Catholic tradition, there are:

Jean-Paul II Encyclique "Laborem exercens" (On Human Work) (1981) n°613.[47]

And ENCYCLICAL OF POPE LEO XIII ON CAPITAL AND LABOR.[48]

None of these texts take any explicit position on ethics and morality of Intellectual Property Rights. As far as the Church is concerned, its own independent assessment of validity or invalidity of Copyright, Patent and Trademark laws is unknown.

The Church points out that Intellectual Property Rights result in concentration of wealth in Corporations and that the poor then need more help.

As it was with Slavery, the Church is way behind on the question of "Property" in the Western Intellectual Property Rights regime.

14.2.3   Judeasim

In the Jewish tradition we have found: "Jewish Law and Copyright" by Rabbi Israel Schneider.[49]

This leaves things quite unclear.

Copyright and Patent and Trademark laws in Jewish Israel are fundamentally copied from the US laws, traditions and practices which extends Americanism to Israel.

To the extent that Israel claims to be the only state for Jews and to the extent that the relationship between America and Israel is symbiotic, the IP constitutional clause of the US could be considered fully adopted in the Jewish state.

The fact that the overwhelming majority of CEOs of US Media Companies are Jews, further reaffirms validity of Western IPR Regime amongst Jews.

14.2.4   Taoism and Confucianism

In the ancient philosophies of Taoism and Confucianism, dating back to the 6th century BC, we have not found any endorsement of anything resembling the Western intellectual property model.

Part of the conclusion section of Peter K. Yu's paper titled: "The Confucian Challenge to Intellectual Property Reforms" [48] is reproduced here.

> Confucianism provides one of the most widely cited cultural explanations for intellectual property piracy and counterfeiting in Asia. Such an explanation has received renewed attention in light of China's rapid technological rise, the rejuvenated interest in Confucianism, the ongoing discussions of regional trade matters in Asia, and the negotiation of the Trans-Pacific Partnership Agreement. Yet, upon close scrutiny, that explanation has grossly oversimplified the complex interface between intellectual property and culture. Although it is hard to deny that Confucianism has coloured the development of intellectual property rights in China — and, perhaps, even some parts of East Asia — one should be very cautious in using Confucianism as a cultural explanation for the massive piracy and counterfeiting problems in Asia.
>
> ...

Translation of a Chinese concept (Qie Shu Bu Suan Tou) is: "To Steal a Book is an Elegant Offense". This is the title of a book by William Alford which deals with Intellectual Property Law in Chinese Civilization [1]. In Section 20.3.1 — Building Consensus on Invalidity of IPR in China — we expand on this.

Part IV

Libre-Halaal ByStar Digital Ecosystem

Chapter 15

Theory of Libre-Halaal Digital Ecosystems

In order to cure the IPR disease in the digital domain, we must consider it in its entirety as a "Digital Ecosystem".

The Proprietary American Digital Ecosystem is leading to an eventuality that is detrimental to civilization and humanity. We must create an alternative digital ecosystem to stand against it. In this Part, we will focus on how to do this.

In the engineering discipline, when building something large, a particular process is typically followed. This process involves the creation of three sets of documents. We will follow this same engineering process, by applying it to the entirety of our Libre-Halaal digital ecosystem. The three sets of documents are:

1. **Requirements Specifications**

   The Requirements Specification outlines the attributes of a healthy digital ecosystem. These attributes are based on harmony with nature and the health of society, and lead to the definitions of a halaal-manner-of-existence for software, content, and internet application services. To illustrate what is meant by healthy, we compare and contrast the desired Libre-Halaal Digital Ecosystem with the existing Proprietary American Digital Ecosystem. The requirements are specified in general terms, without reference to any specific Libre-Halaal Digital Ecosystem.

2. **Functional Specifications**

In the Functional Specifications we introduce a specific and tangible Libre-Halaal Digital Ecosystem which we call "ByStar" (By*). We then describe the various functionalities, capabilities, and structures of the Libre-Halaal ByStar Digital Ecosystem. We explain how existing capabilities of The Proprietary American Digital Ecosystem can be replicated in ByStar while preserving the autonomy and privacy of the individual.

3. **Design, Architecture and Implementation Specifications**

   In very general terms, we then describe how we designed and how we have implemented various capabilities of ByStar. ByStar functionalities are rooted in a common set of facilities delivered through BISOS (ByStar Internet Services Operating System).

This part consists of three chapters, each corresponding to one of the specifications mentioned above.

This chapter, Theory of Libre-Halaal Digital Ecosystems, corresponds to "Requirements Specifications". Chapter 16 — The Libre-Halaal ByStar Digital Ecosystem, corresponds to "Functional Specifications". Chapter 17 — Technology of ByStar: BISOS, corresponds to "Design, Architecture and Implementation Specifications".

15.1   Required Attributes of a Healthy Digital Ecosystem

The short history of the internet has taught us that when it comes to internet capabilities we can believe in miracles. And not just that. We can even rely on miracles. As internet engineers, we know that we can build anything. The key question is: "What Should We Build?" Should we follow the example of Google and Facebook and facilitate surveillance profiteering, or should we join forces and build Libre-Halaal Internet Services to empower individuals with autonomy and privacy? Here, we present our vision of a healthy alternative digital ecosystem.

The model of this healthy alternative digital ecosystem must be based on:

- Sanctity of autonomy and privacy — based on morality and philosophy.

- Ideology of guardianship of the Internet by the engineering profession.

- Full rejection of Western IPR.

- Correct/Healthy manner-of-existence of software and services.

- Tangible assertion of autonomy.

- End-to-End Inter-Autonomous Confidentiality.

- Audit Trail Protection.

- Recognition of independence of societies and cultures.

- Full consideration of business and economics.

Consistent with these, in Chapter 16 — The Libre-Halaal ByStar Digital Ecosystem and at:

> **The Libre-Halaal ByStar Digital Ecosystem**
> **A Unified and Non-Proprietary Model For Autonomous Internet Services**
> **A Moral Alternative To The Proprietary American Digital Ecosystem**
> http://www.by-star.net/PLPC/180016 — [11]

> http://www.by-star.net

we put forward a blueprint for a healthy digital ecosystem.

The context of ByStar includes:

- Tangible Open-Source — Chapter 12 — Digital Non-Proprietary Movements

- Polyexistential Economic Model — Chapter 13 — Global Polyexistential Capitalism

- Endorsement of Ethicist — Chapter 14 — Ethical and Religious Cures

- Societal Adoption — Chapter 20 — Eastern Societal Libre-Halaal Strategies

15.2 Formal Definitions for Libre-Halaal Governance of Polyexistentials

At this point in this document, we have established the necessary foundations to now introduce formal definitions for Libre-Halaal governance of polyexistentials in general and digitals in particular. The established foundations include:

- Polyexistentials are un-ownable.

- The Western IPR regime is a colossal mistake.

- Digital domain is best suited for polyexistential reform.

- "Libre-Halaal" has been defined as a label for proper governance of polyexistentials and digitals.

- Some engineers and authors have established a variety of copyright public licenses and patent related procedures to ameliorate the harm of IPR.

- Attribution Based Economy should replace ownership in polyexistential capitalism.

Based on these, we can now provide formal definitions for Libre-Halaal governance of polyexistentials in general and digitals in particular.

We start with a focus on the digital domain and provide formulations for formal definition of:

- Libre-Halaal Software

- Libre-Halaal Content

- Libre-Halaal Internet Services

For each of these we first describe the intent of the definitions and then provide, explicit permissions and prohibitions.

Based on these formal definitions for Libre-Halaal digitals we then draw a complete picture for the general contours of Libre-Halaal Digital Ecosystems.

15.2.1   Definition of Libre-Halaal Software

Software is a unique and very special form of polyexistentials. Unlike music or other forms of digital art, software is explicitly useful. Software controls disposition of other digitals. Software is the basis of internet services. Software is inherently cumulative and its development is highly collaborative.

This formal definition of Libre-Halaal Software only applies to public software. Public software is software that is made available to the public at large. Private software that requires explicit agreements between parties is not the subject of this definition.

A primary intent of this definition is to allow for the software engineering profession to fulfill its guardianship responsibilities to society and humanity.

Verification of claims by software producers against what the software actually does (based on analysis of source code) is one of these guardianship responsibilities. Another guardianship responsibility is to produce more and better software in a collaborative environment. Another intent of this definition is to maximize accrued benefits from the software to society. These intents are in harmony with the nature of software as polyexistentials.

As mentioned in Section 4.6.2, software is Libre-Halaal Software if it has all of the following attributes:

- **Halaal Criterion 1 — Unrestricted Multi-Possessablity.** There are no restrictions in possessing the software by anyone who wishes to possess it — there are no restrictions in copying and redistributing copies.

- **Halaal Criterion 2 — Unrestricted Usage.** There are no restrictions for using (running) the software.

- **Halaal Criterion 3 — Internal Transparency.** The source code of the software is available to all software engineers to examine the software and study how it works. Unless software is internally transparent, the software cannot be trusted.

- **Halaal Criterion 4 — Modifiability.** Software engineers must be able to modify the software, re-install the modified version and use the modified version without restrictions. The available source code of the software permits software engineers to change and enhance it.

- **Halaal Criterion 5 — Proper Authorship Attribution.** The authorship of the software is not misrepresented.

In a document titled:

Definition Of The Libre-Halaal Software Label
Defining Halaal Manner-Of-Existence Of Software
http://www.by-star.net/PLPC/180044

http://www.halaalsoftware.org

we provide definitional criteria for Libre-Halaal manner-of-existence of software.

In the Western IPR model, a copyright holder can subject the work to various public copyright licenses. A public copyright license is a license by which a copyright holder as licensor can grant additional copyright permissions to any and all persons in the general public as licensees. By doing so, permission is given to the general public to copy or change the work in ways that would otherwise infringe copyright law.

There are many software public copyright licenses. At this time, among all of these licenses, the AGPLv3 (Affero General Public License) is most compatible with our definition of Libre-Halaal Software.

The full text of AGPLv3 license is available at:
https://www.gnu.org/licenses/agpl-3.0.en.html

As such, where copyright applies, we use the AGPLv3 license for Libre-Halaal Software.

In civilized societies that reject the Western IPR model and adopt the Libre-Halaal model instead, all public software is Libre-Halaal Software. This would be similar to having all public software be subject to the AGPLv3 license in the IPR regime.

15.2.2   Definition of Libre-Halaal Content

By digital content we mean content that exists in the form of digital data. Types of digital content include: video, audio, images, text, books, and movies.

This formal definition of Libre-Halaal Content only applies to public content. Public content is content that is made available to the public at large. Private content that require explicit agreements between parties is not subject of this definition.

A primary intent of this definition is to allow for society to maximize benefits of the content. And for content producers to produce more and better content in a collaborative environment. These intents are in harmony with nature of content as polyexistentials.

There are many content public copyright licenses. At this time, among all of these licenses, Attribution-ShareAlike 4.0 International (CC BY-SA 4.0) is most compatible with our definition of Libre-Halaal Content.

This license lets others remix, adapt, and build upon the work as long as attribution is given to the original creators and this license is propagated forward — any derivatives will also be subject to this license.

The full text of Attribution-ShareAlike 4.0 International license is available at:
https://creativecommons.org/licenses/by-sa/4.0/legalcode

As such, where copyright applies, we use the CC BY-SA 4.0 license for Libre-Halaal Content.

In civilized societies that reject the Western IPR model and adopt the Libre-Halaal model instead, all public content is Libre-Halaal Content. This would be similar to having all public content be subject to the Attribution-ShareAlike license in the IPR regime.

15.2.3 Definition of Libre-Halaal Internet Application Services

First, we need to define what we mean by internet services.

Internet application services allow for remote execution of software and remote delivery of the results of that execution. So, to begin with, for the internet application service to be considered Libre-Halaal, the remote software that is executed must be Libre-Halaal.

Our scope here is internet application services at layer 7, not services related to internet connectivity at layer 3. For brevity, sometimes we refer to internet application services as internet services.

As mentioned in Section 4.6.3, internet services are Libre-Halaal Internet Services (Libre Services) if they have all of the following attributes:

1. Every software component included in the service must be Libre-Halaal software.

2. The software for the entire service must be Libre-Halaal software. The entire primary source code for the entire service must be available to all software engineers, so that the entire service can be reproduced.

3. All protocols used by the service must be transparent and unrestricted.

In a document titled:

Definition Of The Libre-Halaal Internet Services Label
Defining Halaal Manner-Of-Existence Of Internet Application
Services
A non-proprietary model for delivery of Internet services
http://www.by-star.net/PLPC/180045

http://www.libreservices.org

we provide definitional criteria for halaal manner-of-existence of internet services.

A primary intent of this definition is to allow for the software engineering profession to fulfill its guardianship responsibilities to society and humanity. One of these guardianship responsibilities is verification of claims by internet service providers against what the service actually does (based on analysis of source code of the software). Another guardianship responsibility is to produce more and better internet services in a collaborative environment. Another intent of this definition is to maximize accrued benefits from the internet services to society. These goals are in harmony with the nature of software as polyexistentials.

Use of internet services impact autonomy of the individual in ways that use of software does not. With software you are not restricted with the choices that the service provider has made on your behalf. Use of software is more convivial than use of internet services.

Use of internet services impact privacy of the individual in ways that use of software does not. When you run and control the software of your own email server, your emails are in your own exclusive possession. When you use Gmail, your emails are also in Google's possession. When you run a software on your own computer, the logs of what you requested and how the software accomplished your instructions are in your exclusive possession and logs of your activities are private. When you use an internet application service logs of what you requested and how the software/service accomplished your instructions are in possession of the service provider. The service provider has the ability to monitor your activities. You may then have less privacy. Furthermore, when you use internet application services and interact with other individuals or organizations, logs and perhaps content and details of your interactions are also in possession of the service provider. As a result, the individuals with whom you corresponded may then have less privacy as well. When you use internet services, both you and those that you have been interacting with are potential subjects of surveillance at layer 7.

Surveillance capitalism drives the American proprietary digital ecosystem and loss of privacy and autonomy of the individual are considered natural by products of technology in Americanism.

In Libre-Halaal digital ecosystems, things are different. We protect against loss of privacy and autonomy by providing proper definitions for Libre-Halaal Internet Services.

Therefore, the definition of Libre-Halaal Internet Services also involves protection of privacy and autonomy of the individuals. To provide for such protections, we need to go beyond the halaal manner-of-existence of internet services and regulate internet application service providers.

Based on capabilities and services that internet services provide, we can identify different type of internet services. These include:

- Possession Assertable Libre-Halaal Services — Abstract real individuals. Email, Messaging, Autonomous Web Publication

- Content Syndication Libre-Halaal Services — YouTube like services

- Information Provider Libre-Halaal Services — Google Map and Google Search like services

- Group Collaboration Libre-Halaal Services — Github, Zoom like services

- Mediated Inter-Autonomus Communication Facilitation Libre-Halaal Services — Craig's List, dating, eBay like services

- Bazar Oriented Libre-Halaal Services — Amazon, AliBaba, Walmart-like services

- Locale Oriented Libre-Halaal Services — Uber, Airbnb-like services

- Social Oriented Libre-Halaal Services — Facebook, Twitter-like services

- Brokerage Oriented Libre-Halaal Services — booking.com-like services

- Escrow Oriented Libre-Halaal Services — escrow.com-like services

In Libre-Halaal digital ecosystems, each of these types of internet application services demands its own specific set of regulations.

Surveillance capitalism driven American proprietary internet application services are inherently centralized. The service provider sits in the middle, observes and controls everything on a large scale and exploits individuals on the periphery.

The type of regulations that are needed are very different for each type of Libre-Halaal Services. At this time, we focus on just two types that are being implemented in ByStar. Future updates to this document will include more details with respect to regulations of each type.

Possession Assertable Libre-Halaal Services (PALS) are the main building blocks of Libre-Halaal digital ecosystems, through which internet services are forced to be de-centralized.

15.2.3.1 Definition of Possession-Assertable Libre-Halaal Services (PALS)

The concept of Possession-Assertable Libre-Halaal Services (PALS) does not materially exist in the American proprietary digital ecosystem.

Possession-Assertable Libre-Halaal Services are used to represent real individuals and their belongings in the real world.

PALS are Libre Services that belong to their users. The owner-user should be able to self-host the service if she wishes to. A PALS can also be externally-hosted, in which case the PALS service provider must conform to a set of operational constraints. The PALS model provides for portability and transferability of Libre-Halaal Services between network abodes.

When externally-hosted, the PALS service provider must conform to the following rules. First, it must run the PALS without any modifications – the software of PALS must be known to its owner-user. Second, upon demand by the owner-user, the PALS and all user data should be transfered to the owner-user. Third, after delivering the services and the data to its owner-user, PALS operator must delete all of the user data from all of its resources and retain none of the owner-user's data.

15.3   Problem: Individual's Autonomy and Privacy are Being Crushed

Today, the internet services industry is almost entirely owned and controlled by proprietary commercial interests. Google, Yahoo, MSN, LinkedIn, YouTube, Facebook, Apple, and virtually every other Internet service—these are all proprietary for-profit corporations, with no obligation towards the public welfare.

This represents a grave hazard to the broader interests of society. The existing proprietary digital ecosystem is well on its way towards the destruction of humanity. Under immediate threat of destruction are the privacy and autonomy of the individual.

Loss of autonomy and privacy are symptoms of the basic model of the Proprietary American Digital Ecosystem. At a societal level, autonomy and privacy cannot be preserved just with new technology. There are no band-aid technical solutions.

The basic model of the Proprietary American Digital Ecosystem is all wrong.

There is already the beginning of a dawning realization within society of the growing danger to the individual's rights and freedoms.

Various attempts at blowing the whistle are made by some, but these are often crude and lack an understanding of the root of the problem.

15.3.1   Early Shallow Recognitions of the Problem

Some such superficial expressions of the problem include:

Julian Assange (in 2012) puts it like this:

> The world is not sliding, but galloping into a new transnational dystopia. This development has not been properly recognized outside of national security circles. It has been hidden by secrecy, complexity and scale. The Internet, our greatest tool of emancipation, has been transformed into the most dangerous facilitator of totalitarianism we have ever seen. The Internet is a threat to human civilization.

Eben Moglen (2011) says:

Zuckerberg has done more harm to the human race than anyone else his age.

Moglen (2011) also says:

Facebook is Wrong. It should not be allowed. You technologists should fix this.

Scott McNealy is quoted (1999) as saying:

You have zero privacy anyway. Get over it.

Tim Berners-Lee (2014) says:

We need to re-decentralise the Web.

Tim Berners-Lee (2014) is even willing to think of responsibilities of the "geek community as a whole" — but as a Westerner, he is apparently unable to recognize Software Engineering as a global profession with global responsibilities. So, he says:

It's important to have the geek community as a whole think about its responsibility and what it can do.

Donald Knuth says:

A mathematical formula should never be "owned" by anybody! Mathematics belong to God.

Steve Jobs has said something along the lines of:

If you're not paying for something, you're not the customer; you're the product being sold.

Even the British Sir Elton John, who has made his fortunes from copyright restrictions, now kind of gets it. When it comes to pharmaceutical companies profiting from the miseries of the sick through patent restrictions, Elton John says:

We must end the greed of these corporations.

Edward Snowden (2013) says:

> "if a surveillance program produces information of value, it legitimizes it. ... In one step, we've managed to justify the operation of the Panopticon."

The Panopticon is an architectural concept for a prison where the guards can watch, unseen by the inmates, from a tower in the middle into all cells build in a circle around the tower. It leaves the inmates in a perceived state of permanent surveillance. The French philosopher Michel Foucault described the effect:

> Hence the major effect of the Panopticon: to induce in the inmate a state of conscious and permanent visibility that assures the automatic functioning of power. So to arrange things that the surveillance is permanent in its effects, even if it is discontinuous in its action; that the perfection of power should tend to render its actual exercise unnecessary; that this architectural apparatus should be a machine for creating and sustaining a power relation independent of the person who exercises it; in short, that the inmates should be caught up in a power situation of which they are themselves the bearers.

The original Panopticon, like the digital versions the likes of NSA and Microsoft are building, takes away all feeling of privacy. Even when one is not watched, knowing that the possibility of being watched is always there, creates uncertainty and leads to self disciplining and self censorship. It is certainly a state the powers that be would like everyone, except themselves, to be in.

To call these signs of deterioration of humanity is an understatement.

15.3.2   Denial, Ambivalence, Ignorance, Inevitability and Acceptance

Many think that there is no problem.

Many Americans work for the likes of Facebook, Google, Microsoft, Yahoo, etc. Or they are related and dependent on these companies. If the bread and butter of these companies were to become profiting from crushing autonomy and privacy of the individual, most of their employees would likely not have any interest in facing an honest mirror. That has already happened.

People are naturally good at justifying the morality of their self-interest in a variety of forms. Mass psychology then kicks in and reinforces short term interests towards global mass exploitation. It is an inherent characteristic of citizens of unchecked powers to confuse morality with self-interest. Consider America and Americans.

From the perspective of a drug dealer, drug use is no problem. Many drug pushers are users. They want everybody to be using drugs. After all, it is a profitable business and economics is the basis of everything. When someone tells them that subjecting cocaine to business and economics is wrong, the drug dealer does not have the ear for it.

Individuals' autonomy and privacy are not market commodities. They are part of humanity. The problem that we are pointing to is a human problem. This could well not be a problem for economic creatures existing in an exploitative industrial context — that is how pure raw American capitalism is viewed by many.

This sort of thing happens gradually. People become accustomed to the problem. They become dependent on the problem. They become the problem. The next generation is born into it. And then there is no problem.

Everybody does it. Everybody is on Facebook. What problem?

The public at large, and the young in particular, follow and are manipulated. They sit in awe of Internet technology. Ignorant, they trust the specialists who are there to milk their soul. The latest gadget and the latest Internet feature includes exploitation of another aspect of their privacy. They feel in charge while being used. And they feel empowered.

The concept that these very same awesome capabilities and technology can exist in a healthy context is foreign to the public at large. Industrial tools are all that they have seen, Tools for Conviviality, [5], is Greek to them.

Others kind of see the problem but consider it inevitable. More recently, discussions of loss of privacy in the context of Internet services has become a daily occurrence in mainstream Western press. None of these discussions have any depth and no meaningful cure is even searched for. Many articles and books have been written about the "End of Privacy." Shallow, subdued nagging — that is the position and role of American press on the problem.

15.3.3 Contours of the Cure

In order to cure this disease, we need to conceptualize it in its totality — that of a "Digital Ecosystem".

The Proprietary American Digital Ecosystem cannot be fixed. Its dynamics are taking it to a particular eventuality — the destruction of civilization and humanity.

Instead, we need to erect an alternative digital ecosystem to stand against it.

15.4   Overview of Digital Ecosystems

Our use of the term "Digital Ecosystem" is very broad and includes inter-related software, systems, services, content and societal frameworks including: philosophical, moral, societal, social, economic, business and legal practices – that shape it and are shaped by it.

Here we describe digital ecosystems in four parts.

Ideology — Societal Frameworks:
    Digital Ecosystems exist within societal frameworks. Digital Ecosystems are shaped by societal norms and shape people and society.

    Very important aspects of societal frameworks which have immediate impacts on the shape of digital ecosystems are laws and models governing polyexistentials. Societal Agreements governing all that is digital (and more broadly polyexistentials) in the West is based on the Intellectual Property (IP) regime. This has shaped the entirety of Western Digital Ecosystems.

Software and Usage Environments:
    Software is the digital form that controls other digital forms. As such, it is the foundation of digital ecosystems.

Internet Services:
    Internet Services consist of *software execution accessed through a network*. As such, software may no longer be in the immediate possession of the user. Internet Services are therefore a distinct part of digital ecosystems – separate from Software.

Information and Content:
    A primary purpose of digital ecosystems is to facilitate production and communication of information and content. In addition to the content itself, facilities and rules governing production, publication and access to content are distinct parts of digital ecosystems.

15.5   The Proprietary American Digital Ecosystem

The broad label that we use for Internet services and software as it exists and is practiced today, is: "The Proprietary American Digital Ecosystem". We include the term American in this label not just because it is dominated by America, but because it is rooted in American values and American rules. The American purely economic model and widespread practices which are based on Western IPR regime have led to dominance of Internet by large American corporations

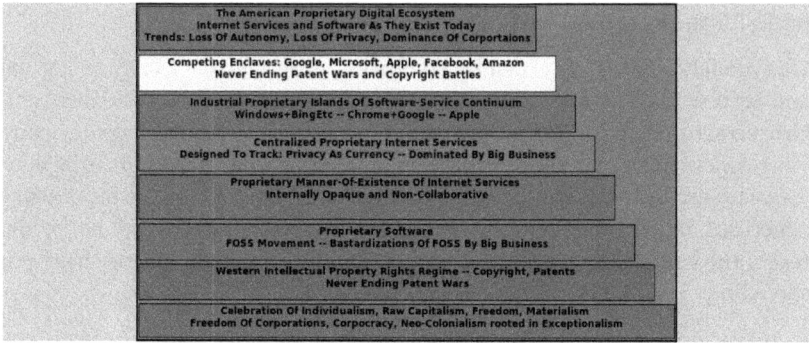

Figure 15.1: The Proprietary American Digital Ecosystem (Layered Model)

and the governance of the internet through Corpocracy. These corrupt values and models are now being exported and forced on the rest of the world in the name of Internet.

The manner by which the Proprietary American Digital Ecosystem is shaped by American societal norms is multi-faceted. To better understand this, in Figure 15.1 we provide a layered model.

The very same eight layers that are presented in Figure 15.1 are the basis of the layered model that we present as a moral alternative in Section 16.2. Note that without recognizing and tackling the underlying root causes of the problems that the proprietary American digital ecosystem present, it is not possible to cure these problems. When the underlying nature of any public digital ecosystem is proprietary, it poses a danger to health of society.

In the following sections, we focus on specific aspects of the above layered model.

15.5.1 Competing Proprietary Digital Enclaves

The Proprietary American Digital Ecosystem comprises of a number of competing Proprietary Digital Enclaves. The proprietary Microsoft digital enclave is one such example. The Microsoft enclave has had its roots in the proprietary software business and is now trying to bring in proprietary services. The proprietary Google digital enclave is another example. The Google enclave has had its roots in the proprietary search business and is now trying to integrate with more software and services. Apple, Facebook and Amazon are examples of other American Digital Enclaves. What they all have in common is that they are all competing in a locked environment driven by Patent and Copyright laws. None of these enclaves were designed ab-initio to be digital environments for humanity. All of these enclaves exist primarily to generate profit for their owners.

This model of being governed by competing proprietary enclaves is normal and even desired by most Americans. The American medical system is similarly structured and so is the American food system. From the outside, many view Americans as purely economic creatures that exist in an industrial context who are fully committed to supremacy of money. While the proprietary American digital ecosystem my be fine for Americans, it may not be for the rest of the world. Bits are without borders and this American disease has been spreading.

Ramifications of manner-of-existence of the proprietary digital ecosystem, matter in two important ways. It matters in terms of service functionality —what the service itself is actually doing. And it matters in terms of policy— what the service provider is doing.

15.5.2 Ramifications on Service Functionality

Regarding service functionality: existing proprietary services such as Google, Yahoo, YouTube, Facebook, Microsoft, Apple, and virtually every other service —these are strictly controlled assets of their owning companies, heavily defended by patents and copyright. The software that runs the service is closed, such that the true service functionality is unknown. This means that as the user of the service you have no knowledge of what the service is actually doing behind the scenes. For example, you have no knowledge of what the service is doing with your personal information. Every item of information you provide to the service, either implicitly or explicitly—every communication, every search query, every website visited, every mouse click—can be used by the service provider for unknown purposes, without your knowledge or consent.

15.5.3 Ramifications on Service Policy

Regarding policy: in principle, the service provider's actions are constrained by the Service Agreement (Terms of Use, Privacy Policy, etc.) between the provider and user. However, these agreements are drafted by the provider's corporate lawyers, consist of sophisticated legalese that few users read, and are heavily biased towards the interests of the provider. In particular, they are drafted without any formal representation or advocacy for the interests of the user.

Proprietary services are operated by corporations whose actions are driven purely by profit. This is the single ultimate purpose of the proprietary service provider, to which all other considerations come secondary. In particular, both functionality and policy are dictated wholly by this purpose, with no concession towards the interests of the individual user or general public welfare, beyond what contributes directly or indirectly to profit.

This closed, profit motivated and profit dominated internet services model represents severe endangerment to critical civil liberties such as privacy, freedom of information, and freedom of speech.

The existing proprietary regime leads to the wrong manner-of-existence for software and the wrong model for provision of Internet services. Wrong in that it allows control of the service by the provider, and exploitation of the user's data, in a way that is detrimental and unknown to the user. The solution to this is an entirely different model for Internet services, where service ownership is placed squarely in the public domain.

Chapter 16

The Libre-Halaal ByStar Digital Ecosystem

Considering the previous chapter, Chapter 15 — Theory of Libre-Halaal Digital Ecosystems — as "Requirements Specifications", we now want to focus on "Functional Specifications". Here, we now introduce a specific and tangible Libre-Halaal Digital Ecosystem called "ByStar".

16.1   Leading to Libre-Halaal ByStar Digital Ecosystem

As described, the digital domain and software and internet services provide a ripe front for demonstrating the vulnerability of the Western IPR regime.

We can now build on these concepts and assets that we have described in this document to provide a complete blueprint and an initial implementation for a digital ecosystem that can stand against the existing American proprietary digital ecosystem.

In Chapter 12 — Digital Non-Proprietary Movements, we described how rich and wonderful FLOSS outcomes have become.

In Chapter 13 — Global Polyexistential Capitalism, we described that in the context of Internet Services, business operation in the for-profit and non-proprietary quadrant can be as lucrative as that of for-profit and proprietary quadrant.

It then becomes obvious that at a certain point in time it would be possible to build a complete Libre-Halaal Digital Ecosystem to stand against the

Proprietary-Haraam American digital ecosystem. That certain point in time is now.

This document is part of a bigger picture. Our goals are broader than just analyzing the correct manner of existence of polyexistentials.

We want the world to move towards Libre-Halaal Software and Libre-Halaal Internet Services.

The totality of our work is directed towards creation of:

The Libre-Halaal ByStar Digital Ecosystem
A Unified and Non-Proprietary Model For Autonomous Internet Services
A Moral Alternative To The Proprietary American Digital Ecosystem
http://www.by-star.net/PLPC/180016 — [11]

http://www.by-star.net

The engineering design and implementation of the ByStar Digital Ecosystem is documented in:

The Universal BISOS: ByStar Internet Services Operating System
Model, Terminology, Implementation And Usage
A Framework For Cohesive Creation, Deployment and Management Of Internet Services
http://www.by-star.net/PLPC/180047

In the above mentioned overview documents of The Libre-Halaal ByStar Digital Ecosystem, we draw a vast picture for putting in place a model and process that can redirect manner-of-existence of Internet services and safeguard humanity.

In this chapter we include some extracts from that document.

For those wishing to dig deeper into ByStar, we provide a reading road map in http://www.by-star.net/bxRoadmap. In ByStar Publications List: http://www.by-star.net/bxPublications, we provide pointers to ByStar related articles. These documents evolve as ByStar evolves, and the publications list will be kept up to date. The ByStar publications list is structured primarily for reference.

For Preservation of the Individual's Autonomy and Privacy

Dear Fellow World Citizen,

In the Proprietary American Digital Ecosystem (Internet Application Services as they exist today), the individual's autonomy and privacy are being crushed. A deal has been made. Users free-of-charge get: email, calendar, address book, content publication, and Facebook friends. In return, American corporations get: semantic analysis of email, spying with consent, traffic, logs and trail analysis and behavior cross referencing.

A new currency has been created. The user's autonomy and privacy is now the implicit Internet currency. For now, the established business model is that of translation of the individual's privacy into targeted advertising. That business model will naturally grow in scope. The debit side of this new currency is civilization and humanity.

Today, the world is largely unaware of this. The public is completely oblivious to the perils of the proprietary Internet model, and happily entrusts its personal data, its privacy, its freedoms and its civil liberties to proprietary business interests. And the people whose responsibility it is to safeguard the public interest – the government, and the engineering profession – are asleep at the wheel. Or worse yet, they have become accomplices.

In addition, Internet services are inconsistent, disparate and incoherent. This results in 10s of passwords for the individual on services over which she has no real control. The dynamics and trends of the Proprietary American Digital Ecosystem are such that autonomy and privacy of the individual will continue to deteriorate.

This is about rescuing humanity from the dragnet of Google, Facebook and America's surveillance economy. **Our primary offerings are real, tangible and practical autonomy and privacy – on a very large scale.**

We are Internet Engineers. We know that we can design and create a complete parallel digital ecosystem which preserves the individual's autonomy and privacy – to compete with and stand against the existing Proprietary American Digital Ecosystem. And we have done enough to establish a proof of concept.

But to put it in its intended widespread usage, we also need your participation (our fellow engineers, journalists, financiers, academics, government representatives, ethicists and users). Preservation of autonomy and privacy is multi-dimensional. So, we have taken it upon ourselves to also consider philosophical, moral, societal, social, economic and business dimensions of our parallel digital ecosystem.

The umbrella title that we have chosen for our work is:

The Libre-Halaal ByStar Digital Ecosystem
A Unified and Non-Proprietary Model For Autonomous Internet Services
A Moral Alternative To The Proprietary American Digital Ecosystem
http://www.by-star.net/PLPC/180016 — [11]

ByStar (By* – pronounced by-star) is based on the model of Federations of Autonomous Libre-Halaal Services and is being presented as a moral alternative to the American Proprietary Digital Ecosystem.

The totality of Libre-Halaal software, Libre-Halaal Internet services, content generation and publication facilities and societal frameworks that we describe are designed for preservation of ByStar user's autonomy, privacy and freedom. The health of society is our objective. This is not about the rejection or prohibition or censorship of the internet. This is about the creation of a parallel digital ecosystem within the Internet based on values which are very different from the economically driven proprietary American digital ecosystem.

By "Digital Ecosystem", we mean the whole thing, including inter-related software, systems, services, content and societal frameworks. The integrated facilities of ByStar are intended to be used by a very large segment of the population on this planet. The scope of these integrated offerings is vast – paralleling most of what exists in the proprietary Internet today.

The parallels include:

- A functional equivalent of Gmail that recognizes your mailbox must be autonomous and private.

- A functional equivalent of Facebook that is based on facilitation of end-to-end private interactions.

- A functional equivalent of YouTube that recognizes your content as yours.

- A functional equivalent of Windows that creates a deep Software-Service continuum.

In the ByStar model these capabilities are unified, consistent and coherent.

This is not about any new particular functionality. It is not a faster, cheaper, better story. In terms of functionality, what we offer is generally the same as what exists today. Our model provides for the existing functionalities, while offering tangible autonomy and tangible privacy.

The ByStar model empowers the user herself to be her own Application Service Provider (ASP). This model of "Be Your Own ASP", is based on comprehensive

Libre-Halaal software and a cohesive infrastructure that any user can choose to fully host her own cloud services (Do It Yourself ByStar), or use pre-made autonomous cloud services (We Do It For You ByStar).

There is nothing anti-business about our offerings and our moral stands. The ByStar business model is simply different from the current dominant American business models of exploiting privacy and autonomy. We are in the business of providing autonomy and privacy. And there is plenty of money in that. Broad and deep usage of our software and our Internet application services will create revenue opportunities that are similar to those of large Internet application service providers today. These revenues include subscriber fees, advertising, customization consultation, general consultation and interaction facilitation fees. Profit, business and economics are an integral part of ByStar.

Key distinguishing aspects of our approach and software and services are:

- Preservation of the individual's autonomy. ByStar services are inherently autonomous. They belong to each and every one of their owner-users – not the service provider.

- Preservation of the individual's privacy. The individual is in full control of her service. She can fully control her privacy.

- They are comprehensive, unified, consistent and cohesive. The scope of ByStar is everything. The "*" in By* comes from the glob expansion symbol. And all these services are unified with the ByStarEntity model.

- They are rooted in the correct manner-of-existence of software and services. The entirety of ByStar software and services are internally transparent. ByStar software and services development process is fully collaborative. Based on the nature of polyexistentials, ByStar ideology fully rejects the Western Intellectual Proprietary Rights regime.

In other words, morality, health of society, and well-being of humanity are an integral part of software and services that we offer. This work is primarily not Businessman driven. It is Engineer driven.

We believe that the privacy, autonomy and freedom aspects of the Digital Ecosystem that we are creating are important enough to "convert" many existing proprietary service users to become Libre-Halaal ByStar users. All attempts at claiming autonomy and privacy in the proprietary model are hollow at most. It is not possible to offer real and tangible autonomy and privacy without committing to complete internal transparency of software and services. The proprietary model leads to dark software and dark services (internally opaque) which are inherently anti-autonomy and anti-privacy.

Such a large undertaking by such a small group should normally amount to not much more than pipe dreams. Typical first reaction to our claim is a chuckle.

Some say it is insane. Many say that the notion of creating a parallel digital ecosystem is so very lofty that it can't be realistic.

There are several reasons why we believe widespread usage of what we are building is more than plausible. It is viable and likely.

1. ByStar ideology is in harmony with nature. We understand the enormous, seismic force that accompanies halaal manner-of-existence of software and halaal manner-of-existence of Internet services (as expressed in the Libre-Halaal label). Manifestations of this force include the Free Software Movement and GNU/Linux. But there is far more to come.

2. We have already built the needed framework and starting points. These are in place and are growing.

3. The ByStar model grand design is broad, evolutionary, expandable and it can grow to scale to planet wide usage.

4. The demand for autonomy and privacy is very real. Many are starting to recognize that things like Facebook are very wrong. Healthy alternatives are craved.

5. The business and economic models for ByStar have been thought through and are being cultivated.

There are two fundamental concepts at the core of what we are presenting and offering:

1. Humans are more than just economic creatures. The internet's model cannot be based on pure economics.

2. The Western Intellectual Property Rights (IPR) regime is a colossal mistake – Western IPR laws are in conflict with nature and detrimental to civilization.

If you are unable or unwilling to explore the truth behind these basic concepts, then ByStar is likely not for you.

If you recognize the critical distinction between humans and economic creatures, and if you recognize the basic human need for autonomy and privacy, and if you are willing to explore the rejection of the Western IPR regime, then the Libre-Halaal ByStar Digital Ecosystem could well be for you.

16.1.1   Root Causes of the Problem

The Internet has its origins in America. In the beginning, the Internet was a healthy engineering construct – and we played a minor role in its formation.

The initial model of the Internet was rooted in the end-to-end model of inter-actions between autonomous entities/individuals, but things changed quickly. The Internet became a business construct. Now, the current basic model of the internet is rooted in the rise-of-the-middle model of corporations exploiting the individual.

Today's Internet has been shaped by Proprietary American values. And this is the root cause of the problem.

We describe this in Chapter 9 — Americanism: Root of the IPR Mistake.

16.2   The Libre-Halaal ByStar Digital Ecosystem

The Libre-Halaal ByStar Digital Ecosystem model is fundamentally different from the American Proprietary Digital Ecosystem in every respect.

In terms of ownership, there is no ownership: Libre-Halaal Services in soft-ware form are a communal public resource, with no patent, copyright or se-crecy barriers to free access and usage by anyone.

In terms of functionality, the software is open, so the services are completely transparent in operation. This transparency allows professional oversight by the engineering community, to verify the integrity of the service, ensuring that it in no way violates the interests of the user or the general public welfare.

And in terms of policy, operation of the service is governed by a social con-tract, drafted with full representation and advocacy for the individual user and the general public welfare.

The Libre model thus fully guarantees the critical civil liberties that are en-dangered under the proprietary model.

By* Federation of Autonomous Libre Services are Internet Application Ser-vices that are internally transparent and focus on preservation of user's pri-vacy and autonomy. By* stands against Facebook/Google/Yahoo/MSN/iCloud the same way that Linux stands against Microsoft Windows.

This is very different from existing Internet services capabilities. The Inter-net landscape of today has arisen in a highly disorganized, unstructured way, driven by a multitude of uncoordinated commercial ventures. The existing services capabilities have been built in a completely ad hoc manner, based on immediate business expedience, rather than any sort of coherent design. The result is the Internet Services industry as it appears today: a multiplic-ity of functionally isolated, incompatible services. And while this may not be apparent to the everyday user, having never experienced anything different, this limits the capabilities of Internet services in many ways.

By* is the model for a new generation of unified Internet services, far superior to the uncoordinated mishmash of services that exists today. It is designed for consistent, uniform interoperability across all types and manners of service usage. By* is the Internet services industry, done right.

We now present an overview of our work and the contours of ByStar in 4 regards – Ideology, Model, Capabilities and Economics.

16.2.1   ByStar Ideology: The Libre-Halaal Philosophy

A very important aspect of societal framework which has immediate impact on the shape of digital ecosystems are laws and models governing polyexistentials (knowledge, ideas, information, the digital entities). Societal Agreements governing all that is digital (and more broadly polyexistential) in the West are based on the IP regime. This has shaped the entirety of Western Digital Ecosystems.

In contrast, ByStar is ab-initio driven by the ideology that morality and health of society should be the foundation of the ByStar digital ecosystem. The fundamental difference between ByStar ideology and the Proprietary American ideology is that in ByStar priorities, society/humanity comes first and profit/economics come second. In the Proprietary American priorities profit/economics comes first and above all else.

16.2.2   Applied Model of
Federations of Autonomous Libre Services

In addition to being Libre-Halaal, ByStar is based on the Unified Autonomous model.

The internet services industry as it exists today is chaotic, non-collaborative, uncoordinated, and falls far short of its true potential.

In contrast to this, the ByStar Digital Ecosystem is based on a coherent, collaborative, scalable, generalized Internet Services model.

Together, the Libre-Halaal Services and By* models have enormous implications. The Libre Services development model, and the By* unified services model can transform the internet completely, from the proprietary and ad hoc model of today into something far more powerful.

The realization of this potential is large, complex and ambitious. It is far too large in scope to be accomplished by any one company acting alone, but instead can only be accomplished as a coordinated industry-wide effort. But the ByStar Libre-Halaal Services model enables precisely the necessary large-scale, distributed, cooperative effort.

In the document titled:

The ByStar Applied Model
Of Federations of Autonomous Libre-Halaal Services
http://www.by-star.net/PLPC/180015 — [10]

We provide an overview of the model and design of ByStar Federation of Autonomous Services.

Based on this model and structures, ByStar services can consistently grow and interact with other ByStar services to provide a rich and healthy environment.

16.2.2.1 The ByStar Reference Model

ByStar is based on a set of key abstractions, representing the major real-world entities that must be represented within a generalized web structure. These entities include such things as individual persons, businesses, physical locations, and events. For each such entity we have defined the structures and conventions required to represent, instantiate and name that entity in a unified, consistent way, and at a very large scale. We have then defined the major classes of services required to manage these entities, and to allow highly generalized interactions within and among each other.

In the ByStar applied model, a real-world entity type (for example, individuals or a physical locations) maps on to a ByStarEntityType (BxEntityType). A real-world entity instance maps on to a ByStarEntity (BxEntity) All ByStar services are anchored in ByStarEntity.

ByStarEntityTypes are structured hierarchically in a tree.

ByStarEntityType is either a ByStarAutonomousEntityType
or a ByStarControlledEntityType.

ByStarAutonomousEntityType and ByStarControlledEntityType are either Classified or UnClassified.

In this structure, persons identified by their name, are represented as:

```
ByStarEntityType=
    ByStarAutonomousEntityType.Classified.Person.ByName
```

Each BxEntity (an instance) is identified by BxEntityId.

A BxEntityId is structured as:

```
BxEntityId=RegistrarId+BxEntityType+InstanceId
```

All ByStarEntityIds are unique. The InstanceId is assigned by the RegistrarId.

Each BxEntity can be activated within a
ByStarAutonomyAssertionVirtualMachine

(BxAutonomyAssertionVirtualMachine).
The representation of a BxEntity in a BxAutonomyAssertionVirtualMachine
is called a ByStarServiceObject (BxServiceObject).
A ByStarServiceObject maps to a Unix account and a user-id.
The BxServiceObject can have any ByStarServiceCapability
that BxAutonomyAssertionVirtualMachine offers.

Any ByStarServiceCapability can be bound to and exposed through a
registered domain name.

Based on the above structures, ByStar services can consistently grow and interact with other ByStar services to provide a rich and healthy environment.

16.2.2.2   Domain Name Bindings of ByStarEntity

Each ByStarEntity consists of specific information and a set of computing
and communication services.

Publicly, BxEntity is usually exposed throughout the internet at a selected
DNS domain name. In the ByStar model, binding of a BxEntity to one or
more domain names is designed to be very flexible. This flexibility relates to
Service Portability but is broader. These notions are absent or very rare in the
Proprietary American model.

For instance, in the context of the examples described in Section 16.3, Bob
Smith is assigned BxEntityId=23.1.2.7.3.32674 which is canonically bound to
the base domain name 5.bob.smith.byname.net.

ByStar permits Bob Smith to bind his BxEntity to other domain names, for
example bobsmith.fr. In the ByStar BySMB service this is commonplace. Often, with the anticipation of obtaining example.com, example.bysmb.com and
its BxEntity can be pre-generated. The owner can re-adjust the binding of
BxEntity to a chosen domain name at will.

Different information, different capabilities and different features of a BxEntity
are usually bound to different domain names within a base domain name hierarchy.

For example, Bob's imap service is at imap.5.bob.smith.byname.net, his
genealogy service is at geneweb.5.bob.smith.byname.net and his synchronization repository (version control – vc) is at:
git.5.bob.smith.byname.net.

In cases where the owner asserts autonomy by possession of the service as a
BxAutonomyAssertionVirtualMachine, ByStar provides the ability to selectively DNS resolve BxEntity domains locally. This then also permits fully
local (non-networked) development and access to BxEntity – based on existing
DNS bindings.

These flexible ByStar domain name to BxEntity bindings, and flexible DNS resolutions, are built on top of djbdns.

16.2.2.3   ByStar Autonomous Services

Internet services come in all shapes and sizes, serve all manner of purposes, and interact with each other and with societal entities in all manner of complex ways.

In some cases a service may be associated exclusively with a particular societal entity, such as an individual, an organization, or a corporation. Such entities enjoy a high degree of autonomy within society, and so we refer to these as autonomous entities. When a service is associated uniquely with particular autonomous entity, we refer to the entity as the owner of the service.

When a service is associated with a unique "owner", certain characteristics of the service are of particular concern to the owner. The service may include information of a personal or private nature, and the owner may wish to ensure that his/her/its privacy is protected. It is also important that the service reflect and maintain the autonomy of the owner, providing parallel freedom of action to that which the owning entity enjoys at large.

Certainly, the privacy and autonomy of the owner are fully guaranteed if the owner exercises direct control over the functioning and provision of the service. In practice, an owner may or may not choose to exercise such direct control of the service. In many cases the owner of the service will leave the service provisioning in the hands of a second-party service provider. Nevertheless it is sufficient to guarantee the autonomy of the owner if the nature of the service is such that the owner could in principle take control of the service himself.

We define an **autonomous libre-halaal service** as an Internet service associated with a unique owner, that the owner could in principle and at his option take control over and provide for himself.

ByStar services are structured in two layers. (1) ByStar Autonomous Services and (2) ByStar Federated Services.

Any ByStar Autonomous Service may also include ByStar Controlled Services.

As noted, in many or most cases the service will be provided by a second-party service provider, who runs and administers the service on behalf of the owner. The autonomy of the owner requires that he is in no way tied to this or any other service provider. The general societal autonomy of the owner means that for any other type of service—banking, legal, medical—the owner is free to move from one provider to another, leaving no trace of himself behind with the previous provider.

In the case of Internet services, similar principles apply. For a service to be an autonomous halaal service, it must satisfy the twin requirements of **portability**, and **non-retention**. Portability, meaning the owner can transport the entire service to a different service provider. And non-retention, meaning the previous provider must retain no trace of the owner's information.

Specifically, when a second-party provider is providing the service on behalf of the owner, the service is an autonomous halaal service if the provider meets the following requirements:

1. **Service and Data Portability.** On the instruction of the service owner, the entire service can be transferred to a different service provider. This could be another second-party provider, or the service owner himself.

2. **Service and Data Non-Retention.** At the instruction of the service owner, the service provider must destroy all service-related information (i.e., all owner data and log files).

16.2.2.4   ByStar Controlled Services – Internet of Things

Any ByStar Autonomous Service may control certain "ByStar Controlled Services" that are his.

A ByStar Controlled Service is a ByStarEntity which is in control of ByStarAutonomousEntity.

As an example, consider an individual (say the author – `http://mohsen.1.banan.byname.net`) who hypothetically owns a house, a bicycle, a Nike fuel band and a tag for his suitcase.

Virtual representation of these could be:

1. A House – `http://info.1-98008-5807-10.bywhere.net` – where ByWhere structure links control to its owner (a ByStarAutonomousEntity).

2. A Bicycle – whose location information goes to it owner (a ByStarAutonomousEntity) and not Google.

3. A Nike Fuel Band – which sends the exercise information to its owner-individual.

4. A tag for his suitcase – which links to its owner (a ByStarAutonomousEntity).

Each of these as a ByStarControlledEntity will be controlled by the ByStarAutonomousEntity. All of these are ByStarEntity-s. The ones that are controlled, link to their controller. The ByStarAutonomousEntity has links to all the ByStarControlledEntity-s that it controls.

So, we now have a framework for abstracting individuals as owners/controllers through ByStarAutonomousEntity. And we have abstractions for things to be owned and controlled through ByStarControlledEntity. And we have a framework for interaction of individuals/things and things/individuals through ByStar Federated Services.

Now, compare the model of ownership and interactions of Things in Libre-Halaal ByStar Digital Ecosystem – which is anchored in the autonomous individual – with the Proprietary American Digital Ecosystem – which is anchored in the Proprietary Corporation. There the proprietary internet service provider controls individuals also through Things.

16.2.2.5 ByStar Federated Services

Autonomous services and their controlled services may wish to engage in end-to-end interactions with other autonomous services. But in order to facilitate such interactions, involvement of some intermediary services may be needed.

We refer to such enabling intermediary services as **federated services**, and we refer to the association of a federated service plus its subscribing autonomous services as a **federation of autonomous services**.

The concept of Federated Services is layered above Autonomous Services and focuses on interactions amongst Autonomous Services and facilitation of information aggregation amongst ByStar Services.

An example of a federated service for information aggregation is ByTopic.org where autonomously published content (documents/music/videos) is optionally centrally republished – autonomous and federated publications are fully consistent.

16.2.2.6 ByStar Convivial User Environments – Blee

Users experience ByStar Services through ByStar User Environments.

ByStar services can be accessed in a variety of ways. In addition to the traditional browser based model, ByStar provides for rich and deep Software-Service integration.

Initially we are focusing on two convivial user environments for ByStar.

Blee (ByStar Libre Emacs Environment) – [26] – is a layer above Emacs that integrates ByStar platform (Debian GNU/Linux) capabilities into Emacs and provides for integration with ByStar Services.

An overview of this User Environment is provided in:

Blee and BxGnome:
ByStar Software-Service Continuum Based Convivial User En-

vironments
http://www.by-star.net/PLPC/180004 — [26]

The deep integration between Libre-Halaal Software and Libre-Halaal Internet Services creates a Libre-Halaal Software-Service continuum, far superior in capability to any Proprietary/Haraam Software/Service combination.

16.2.2.7   ByStar Content Generation and Content Publication Facilities

ByStar offers a rich environment and a number of facilities for content generation.

Autonomous Content Publication facilities are a well established feature of ByStar.

In the document titled:

ByStar Content Production and Publication Facilities
http://www.by-star.net/PLPC/180038 — [27]

we describe capabilities and features of ByStar content generation facilities and ByStar autonomous content publication facilities.

Autonomous self-publication can then be augmented by information aggregation federated services such as ByTopic, ByContent and BySearch.

16.2.3   ByStar Architecture Principles

The ByStar Digital Ecosystem is driven by a set of engineering architecture principles. We summarize some here.

16.2.3.1   Tools for Conviviality

Our primary criteria for software component selection and service design is "conviviality".

By conviviality we refer to the concept of "Tools for Conviviality" as Ivan Illich introduced it.

In the document titled:

Introducing Convivial Into Globish
http://www.by-star.net/PLPC/120037 — [5]

we introduce the concept of "Convivial" into Globish.

Briefly, in Illich's words:

> Tools are intrinsic to social relationships. An individual relates himself in action to his society through the use of tools that he actively masters, or by which he is passively acted upon.
>
> To the degree that he masters his tools, he can invest the world with his meaning; to the degree that he is mastered by his tools, the shape of the tool determines his own self-image. Convivial tools are those which give each person who uses them the greatest opportunity to enrich the environment with the fruits of his or her vision. Industrial tools deny this possibility to those who use them and they allow their designers to determine the meaning and expectations of others. Most tools today cannot be used in a convivial fashion.

The dynamics of the Proprietary American Digital Ecosystem are such that they produce industrial tools.

The Libre-Halaal ByStar Digital Ecosystem is designed to fully reside in the Libre-Halaal-Convivial quadrant, [8].

16.2.3.2 ByStar End-To-End Philosophy vs Rise of the Middle

The dominant model of interaction between people and the model of access to information in the Proprietary American Digital Ecosystem is the centrally controlled Rise-of-the-Middle model – which puts the service provider at the center of all interactions so that it can exploit users and traffic information.

The ByStar model, in contrast, is end-to-end oriented and is based on the following principles:

- Make Services Autonomous Whenever Possible (peer-to-peer oriented)

- Invest and Focus on End-to-End communications facilities amongst Autonomous Libre Services

- When a Federated Service functions as an intermediary, limit its role to the bare essential of hooking the two ends. Thereafter, communications can be end-to-end.

16.2.3.3 Choice of Software Components

The Libre-Halaal software model is a flourishing creative environment, generating a constant stream of new and better software packages, duplicating and surpassing the capabilities of an ever-increasing portion of proprietary software territory. Indeed,for any particular item of functionality, there are typically multiple alternative free software packages available.

In this environment the model for implementation of By* service functionality is not one of original software development. Rather, it is a process of intelligent selection and integration of functional components from the Libre-Halaal software creative environment.

So, in creating By* our task has not been to write functional software components—in fact we have written almost none. Our main task has been to make careful engineering choices among the available free software components, and integrate these properly into the By* framework. In making these choices we consider not just the features and capabilities of each software component, but also the compatibility of the component within the overall By* architecture.

The main considerations in our choice of software components have been:

- Conviviality

- Scalability

- Libre-Halaal Mainstreamness

- ByStar Consistency

Virtually all the initial By* service functionality has been created this way. The following are some of the basic By* features that have been included by this process:

- Debian GNU/Linux.

- Base: djbdns, daemontools, ucspi, multilog, ...

- Mail: qmail, courier, spamassassin, ezmlm, ...

- Web: apache, zope, plone, geneweb, squirellmail, jquerymobile, galleria, ...

We will continue to select and incorporate additional software packages as these materialize within the free software environment. We will not create so much as we will harvest. Or to paraphrase the common industry dictum: *Good programmers write good software; great programmers reuse and integrate.*

16.2.3.4 Confidentiality, Anonymity and Privacy

By confidentiality we mean: ensuring that information is accessible only to those authorized to have access.

By anonymity we mean: the characteristic of any interaction where an individual protects his or her identity from being shared with another person or with a third party in the context of particular communications. In other words, people know what you do but not who you are.

By privacy we mean: the ability of an individual or group to seclude themselves or information about themselves and thereby reveal themselves selectively. In other words, people know who you are but not what you do.

ByStar Autonomous Services are designed to provide tangible confidentiality, anonymity and privacy on a large scale. All of Libre-Halaal ByStar Digital Ecosystem has this inherent design.

The basic assumption in the ByStar Digital Ecosystem is that all communications and traffic is subject to eavesdropping and traffic analysis.

Fortunately, the nature of digital information is such that it is easier to encrypt than it is to decrypt.

With nature on our side, ByStar Digital Ecosystem provides large scale countermeasures which include end-to-end data confidentiality and traffic flow confidentiality.

ByStar federated services are governed by transparency and well understood logging expectations and audit trail protections which are oriented towards preserving privacy.

All of this is in stark contrast to how confidentiality, anonymity and privacy are in the American Proprietary Digital Ecosystem. There, they have become a currency.

16.2.4 ByStar Central

The basic design of ByStar is very distributed. Services are generally autonomous and interactions are usually end-to-end.

This means that ByStar is centrally light. But there are some fundamental, infrastructural, and foundational organizations and services that are required at the center of ByStar.

The following infrastructure and foundational organizations have been put in place towards administration, guardianship, direction setting and facilitation of collaboration and growth of ByStar.

16.2.4.1   Libre-Halaal Foundation - non-profit, non-proprietary

Libre-Halaal Foundation is the non-profit legal entity that facilitates collaborative development, maintenance and administration of ByStar.

16.2.4.2   Neda Communications, Inc. – for-profit, non-proprietary

Neda Communications, Inc. is the for-profit legal entity that has developed Libre-Halaal ByStar Services. The core of ByStar software is subject to the Affero v3 General Public License and also the Neda Commercial License (dual licensed). Neda plans to profit from widespread usage of The Libre-Halaal ByStar Digital Ecosystem in a variety of ways.

16.2.4.3   LibreCenter.net

LibreCenter.net is Neda's data center. It is distinct and different from other data centers in that is built purely on Libre-Halaal Software. At this time most ByStar Services are hosted at Libre Center.

16.2.4.4   BySource.org

BySource.org is the Software Distribution Center for ByStar software in source form.

16.2.4.5   ByBinary.org

ByBinary.org is the Software Distribution Center for ByStar software in binary form.

16.2.4.6   ByStar Name and Number Assignment Authority

ByStar Name and Number Assignment Authority is responsible for central assignment of names and numbers for ByStar services.

Design of ByStar as an ab initio independent separate digital ecosystem permits ByStar to expand beyond the Proprietary American Digital Ecosystem. This is desired and possible for two main reasons. First, ByStar ideology may demand certain separations. Second, end-to-end purity of ByStar software-service continuum enables ByStar to do things that are not possible in the Proprietary American Digital Ecosystem.

ByStar's Public Key Infrastructure (PKI) and the possibility of a ByStar Alternative DNS Root, and ByStar Digital Currency are some examples.

16.2.5   Current ByStar Services and Capabilities

ByStar Services are vast in scope. They are designed to be ever growing. Basic structures of ByStar are in place and many services are built or partially built. The Libre-Halaal Services collaborative framework allows for ByStar to grow dynamically.

Thus far our focus has been in making sure that the overall architecture of the ByStar Digital Ecosystem is sound. We have been designing big and implementing gradually. A complete stable system is in place. It is now a matter of expanding and improving it.

In ByStar today, for email we don't use gmail, yahoo, msn, outlook.com, aol or other proprietary centrally controlled mail services. We use BystarMail. Similarly, for web presence, content publication, photo and video galleries ByStar has existing capabilities in use.

Here we provide a summary of where ByStar services stand today.

A snapshot of the organizations, services and software that form the ByStar Digital Ecosystem today are shown in Figure 16.2.

Libre-Halaal Foundation central resources are shown in violet in Figure 16.2. Neda resources are shown on the top. Current ByStarEntity generators are shown under the "ByStar Autonomous" label and ByStar federated services are shown next to them. ByStar software consists of three major layers, these are shown in the lower part.

The current status and growth of ByStar falls into four broad categories:

1. Current capabilities of ByStarEntity (ByStarServiceObject) – what any autonomous services are capable of offering.

2. Current span of ByStarEntity generators – what type of autonomous services (ByName, ByArtist, BySmb, etc) can be readily generated and supported?

3. Current scope of ByStar Federated Services.

4. Scale of user base – how many people are using ByStar?

16.2.5.1   Current Capabilities of ByStarEntity

Every ByStar autonomous service is anchored in a ByStarEntity. Every ByStarEntity can be provisioned to provide any of the current capabilities enumerated below.

- ByStarEntityIds and credentials – single password. [Unix account based]

- PKCS – ByStar Public Key Infrastructure (PKI) – Credentials.

- Autonomous VPN services and ByStar overlay networks. [openvpn based]

- Large amounts of autonomous disk space. [secure ftp based]

- Autonomous synchronization and version control facilities. [git – and also svn and cvs based]

- A Content Management System based website – with both public and private access. [Plone based]

- A conventional public website. [Apache based]

- Mobile websites. [jQuery Mobile based]

- Content publication services. [Plone based]

- A photo gallery. [galleria based]

- Genealogy web services. [geneweb based]

- Mail transfer service (MTA). [qmail based]

- Mail access service. [Secure Courier IMAP based]

- WebMail service. [SquirrelMail based]

- Mailing list services. [Ezmlm based]

- Mailing distributions. [Gnus based]

- LibreTexting. [qmail and emsd based]

- Matched User Environment Profile. [Blee based]

Various other capabilities are in the works. With the ByStarEntity model in place, addition of features is quite simple.

16.2.5.2   Current ByStar Services Sites

Current ByStar services sites are depicted in Figure 16.1.

ByStar services sites are organized by "types" in Figure 16.1. The *Autonomous ByStar Services* are PALS (Possession Assertable Libre Services). An example of *Autonomous ByStar Services* is ByName.net. The *ByStar Central* sites support the infrastructure of ByStar.

Anonymous By* Services	ByAnonymous	ByLeak			
Inter-Autonomous Interaction Facilitaion	ByInteraction	ByHookup			
Federated By* Services	ByTopic ByEvent	ByContent ByBinary	BySource	BySearch	ByLookup
Controlled By* Services	ByFamily	ByWhere	ByMemory	ByEntity	
Autonomous By* services	BySMB ByAuthor	ByName ByArtist	ByAlias ByNumber		
ByStar Central	By-Star Neda	BySource LibreCenter	ByBinary Free Protocols	Liber Services	Halaal Software

Figure 16.1: ByStar Domains Table

16.2.5.3   Current Status and Span of ByStarEntity Generators

A number of ByStarEntity Generators—the machinery required for fully automated creation of new service instantiations—are in place for a number of ByStarEntityTypes. Current ByStarEntity Generators are shown in Figure 16.2 under the "ByStar Autonomous" label. We thus have the ability to create unlimited numbers of new accounts in batch mode, or at any time we can "enable" the services, to permit self-service account creation by individual and business users.

16.2.5.4   Current Status and Scope of ByStar Federated Services

A number of sites are in place for facilitating inter-autonomous relations. Current Federated Services are shown in Figure 16.2 under the "ByStar Federated" label.

Our initial focus amongst federated service is those used for information aggregation. These include ByTopic, ByContent and BySearch.

16.2.5.5   Growth of user base: timing

An important consideration is the point at which we will begin to accept the burden of significant numbers of users.

In the case of a conventional service deployment there is typically a major emphasis placed on early and rapid growth of user base, to demonstrate demand

and marketplace viability of the service, and lay claim to a particular portion of functional territory. This was the modus operandi during the dot con era, where claims of user base numbers were an integral part of spin-and-flip and pump-and-dump models. Some of those attitudes still persist.

However, we are not following this standard early proof-of-service approach. This may be appropriate for a conventional new service, where service functionality is the central and most critical issue. But for ByStar, a different timing strategy is required.

First, as a superset of numerous existing services, proof of service for By* in functional terms is already demonstrated by the Internet Services industry as it exists today. It is far more important to prove the model itself rather than its functional manifestations, and hasty creation of user base does little to accomplish this.

Instead, we have provided a coherent and complete description of the model in this and our other documents. The theoretical basis for the model is solid, and this will be clear to anyone willing to invest the time to understand it. In addition, a number of working By* implementations are already in place; examples are provided. Though the scale of usage remains small, these are sufficient to demonstrate the viability of the Libre-Halaal model and the ByStar design, and the value of the resulting services to paying clients.

But a far more important consideration is that installed base is very costly in terms of maintenance and support, and premature exposure to these costs can jeopardize the more critical work of building the underlying model machinery. Therefore, we will not take on the burden of user base until the time and/or context is right for this. This means either that we are fully ready to accept the associated costs of ownership, or that the user base is being taken on in an appropriate context, such as a suitable business partnership.

Under either scenario our strategy is the same: at the right time we will populate the services at large scale by mass creation of By* service accounts for large existing user bases.

16.2.6   Relationship With Existing Realities

The Libre Services and By* models are revolutionary, and can be expected to have a revolutionary effect on Internet usage. But these models are about service development and functionality, not about technological infrastructure. We are not reinventing the Internet protocols, or any other technical aspect of Internet operation.

What is being presented here is not a tear-down and rebuild operation.

Libre Services and By* imply no discontinuity, in terms of either technology or service deployment. The implementation model for Libre Services and By* is

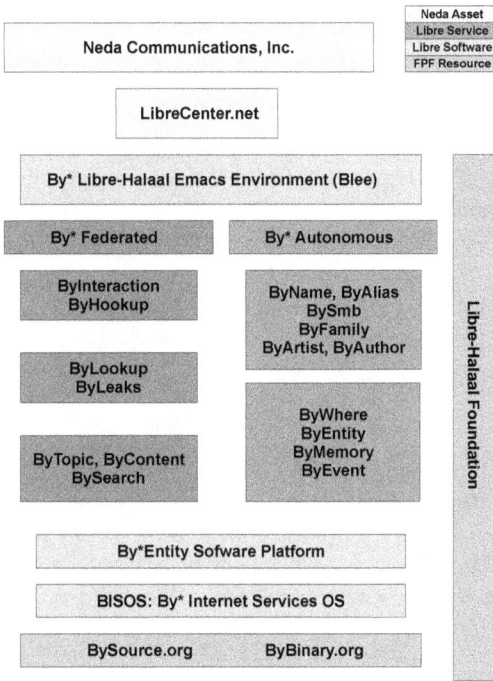

Figure 16.2: Libre Services Supporting Organizations

wholly evolutionary—there exists a continuous migration path from the proprietary model of today to the Libre model of tomorrow.

16.2.6.1   Relationship With the Proprietary American Digital Ecosystem

Based on ideology, the Libre-Halaal ByStar Digital Ecosystem fully avoids proprietary software and proprietary services. We simply avoid The Proprietary American Digital Ecosystem.

But, any and all of our services can be used in the Proprietary American model.

The core of ByStar software is subject to the Affero v3 General Public License and also the Neda Commercial License (dual licensed).

In a document titled:

> **A Strategy For Rapidly Becoming An Internet Application Service Provider**
> **Joining, Adopting and/or Licensing ByStar**
> **A Public Unsolicited Proposal**
> http://www.by-star.net/PLPC/180040 — [25]

We describe various options for those interested in joining, adopting and/or licensing ByStar.

16.2.6.2   Relationship With FOSS / FLOSS Movements

Libre-Halaal ByStar Ideology and FOSS Ideology have a great deal in common and we closely collaborate with our FOSS brothers and sisters, but the ByStar Libre-Halaal Ideology is distinct.

We invite our "Free Software" and "Open-Source" brothers and sisters to recognize that the "Libre-Halaal Software" model is a more complete model and that the "Libre-Halaal Software" label is a better label.

16.2.6.3   Active Private Parallel Digital Ecosystems – Example: NSA

What we want to do on a very large scale and in the open has been done in medium-scale in private.

For instance, the United State's National Security Agency (NSA) has created a separate parallel private digital ecosystem for its own use. NSA operates the private .nsa TLD; many NSA internal email addresses are of the form username@r21.r.nsa, mirroring the NSA organizational group structure. NSA has a particular ideology for its digital ecosystem which includes a large element of security, confidentiality and secrecy. The NSA, through use of its own particular software and services has created a completely different environment in parallel to the internet.

The precedence of such private parallel digital ecosystems combined with the proven power of Libre-Halaal software demonstrates that widespread realization of ByStar digital ecosystem is very viable.

16.2.6.4 Relationship With Piecemeal Privacy Oriented Software and Services

Some engineers kind of get it and have been trying to build various piecemeal privacy and autonomy software and services. Such efforts have always stayed limited in scope and scale. That is primarily for two reasons. First, the engineers have failed to connect with society. And second, piecemeal solutions don't work.

We build on these piecemeal privacy and autonomy software and services and bring them into ByStar as integrated and complete large scale services.

An example of a piecemeal privacy effort is PGP - Pretty Good Privacy. A bunch of engineers and technologists use it amongst themselves, but PGP never penetrated society at large. ByStar comes with Public Key Infrastructure (PKI) as an integral part of the service and equivalent of PGP is an inherent part of ByStar.

Another example of a piecemeal privacy effort is:
Tor https://www.torproject.org.
Tor attempts to accomplish traffic flow confidentiality just through redirection. Traffic flow confidentiality is an inherent part of ByStar which includes redirection plus layer 3 and layer 7 padding as well.

16.2.7 ByStar Economics

Having introduced the Libre-Halaal Bystar Digital Ecosystem in philosophical, moral, societal and engineering terms, we now turn our attention to the economic and business dimensions.

We are devout monoexistential bounded-corporations capitalists. We believe in proper ownership rules, free markets and proper regulation. We are pro-business.

The existing capitalist model for monoexistentials is generally correct, in both philosophical and economic terms. But the extension of the monoexistential capitalist model into the domain of polyexistentials, based on the Western IPR regime, is a grave mistake. Philosophically it is wrong. Societally it is harmful to humanity. And economically it is unstable and vulnerable, since it can be displaced by disruptive business models like ours. The ByStar Open Business Plan explains how this will come about, and how we will profit from this.

We expand on this in Chapter 13 — Global Polyexistential Capitalism.

16.2.7.1   Revenue model for Libre-Halaal Software

The Proprietary-Haraam software model, operating under Western copyright restrictions, includes a highly effective recurring revenue generation model: the proprietary software licensing model.

But the Halaal manner-of-existence of software eliminates all restrictions on the distribution and use of software. Thus, the Proprietary-Haraam recurring revenue model is also largely eliminated. Recurring revenues under the Libre-Halaal software model are much less than under the Haraam software model.

16.2.7.2   Revenue model for Libre-Halaal Internet Services

The Halaal manner-of-existence of software creates a powerful generative development model for Libre-Halaal Internet Services. This generative model is absent from Proprietary-Haraam Internet Services. Thus Libre-Halaal Internet Services have a major advantage and can compete directly with Proprietary-Haraam Internet Services in terms of development.

The basic recurring revenue models for Libre-Halaal Internet Service providers are essentially the same as for Proprietary-Haraam Internet Service providers. Therefore in terms of revenue generation, Libre-Halaal and Proprietary-Haraam services are on an equal footing.

16.2.7.3   ByStar Value Chain Analysis

ByStar value chain is a chain of activities that we perform in order to deliver valuable internet services to the market. It is a high-level model of how we take raw externally developed Libre-Halaal software as input, add value to these software packages through various processes, and sell finished services to our customers.

In Figure 16.3, we illustrate the ByStar value chain on the left column and its inter-mixing with proprietary value chains on the right column.

Focusing on the right column of Figure 16.3, notice that "Neda Operated By* Services" establish a direct relationship with Subscribers and Users at the very top. Note that the scope of these Internet services is everything – the * in By* – and that the intended scale of these services is planet-wide. By definition, no Internet services opportunity can be bigger than that.

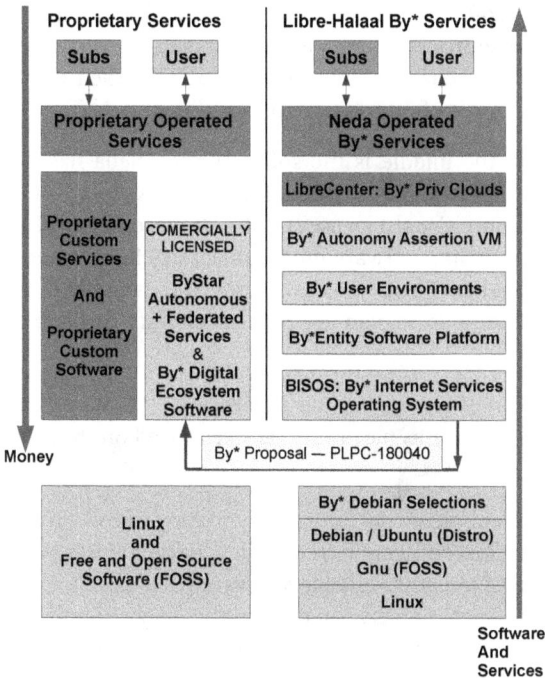

Figure 16.3: ByStar Value Chain

The arrows between Neda Services and User/Subscriber in Figure 16.3 include an element of "Trust, Loyalty, and Respect" which is the result of "ByStar Ideology" that we presented earlier. The element of trust and respect is fully absent in the left column. In business terms, Trust and Respect, translate into "stickiness" – where the user is more committed to the service. So, all our investments in ideology are actually also business wise.

All of the ByStar value chain software is Libre-Halaal (Free and Open Source) software. ByStar software in Figure 16.3 is shown in two different places.

The software in the lower part represents Debian and/or Ubuntu GNU/Linux and the specific software packages that we have chosen. These are externally developed open-source software packages which are typically subject to the free software GPL license (or similar) which permits their inclusion in proprietary services. This is often referred to as ASP loophole.

The software in the middle is the software that Neda has developed. It is subject to the "Affero General Public License Version 3" (AGPL3) and Neda Commercial License (Dual Licensed). AGPL3 closes the ASP loophole. Any ASP which uses ByStar software must subject its changes and improvements to AGPL3 and make its changes and improvements publicly available. Those ASPs not wishing to do so, can use ByStar software through the Neda Commercial License.

In the left column of Figure 16.3, we illustrate a typical proprietary ASP who is incorporating ByStar as part of its services based on the Neda Commercial License.

In this environment the model for implementation of By* service functionality is not one of original software development. Rather, it is a matter of selection and integration of already available software packages. Virtually all existing By* service functionality has been created this way—in building By* we have written almost no new software components at all.

Thus we are not so much in the business of software development, as we are in the business of software integration. But the integration of software components to produce a coherent service is far from trivial. We have created a sophisticated technical integration environment for this purpose, called the **BISOS: ByStar Internet Services Operating System** [29].

Design of BISOS and the **ByStarEntity Software Platform** recognize the evolution of underlying external software (bright blue) in the ByStar value chain. This is the extraordinary magic of Libre-Halaal software and services: the ability to take things and reuse them at extremely low cost. This is the fundamental growth dynamic of Libre Services, and the powerful generative force that is lacking in the proprietary model. This is the key dynamic that causes the By* Libre Services eventually to surpass the proprietary model entirely in terms of features and functionality.

16.2.7.4 ByStar Open Business Plan

The halaal manner-of-existence of software creates a powerful generative development model for Halaal Internet Services. This generative model is absent from Proprietary/Haraam Internet Services. Thus Libre-Halaal Internet Services have a major advantage and can compete directly with Proprietary/Haraam Internet Services in terms of development.

The basic recurring revenue models for Libre-Halaal Internet Service providers are essentially the same as for Proprietary/Haraam Internet Service providers. Thus, in terms of revenue generation, Halaal and Haraam services are on an equal footing.

As part of our responsibility to create a viable implementation construct, we have fully analyzed the business dimension, and we have formulated the business model in the form of an Open Business Plan, titled:

> **The Libre-Halaal ByStar Open Business Plan**
> **An Inversion to the Proprietary Internet Services Model**
> **Neda Communication Inc.'s Open Business Plan**
> http://www.by-star.net/PLPC/180014 — [28]
> http://www.neda.com/strategicVision/businessPlan

ByStar open business plan is available in 3 forms; the Condensed Summary (about 12 pages), the Executive Summary (about 15 additional pages) and the full plan (about 85 pages).

Our business plan is viable because we understand the critical dynamics of polyexistentials. The current direction of the internet services industry does indeed present a grave hazard to humanity, and we will indeed safeguard humanity against this. These extraordinary claims provide a unique and powerful marketing message. And they also happen to be true.

16.2.8 Understanding the Full ByStar Picture

We have given you a brief summary of ByStar above.

This summary is over simplified and captures the gist of a series of articles that we have developed to analyze and describe various aspects of ByStar.

In ByStar Publications List – http://www.by-star.net/bxPublications – we provide pointers to ByStar related articles. These documents evolve as ByStar evolves, and the publications list will be kept up to date. The ByStar publications list is structured primarily for reference. Below we provide a description of how these documents collectively draw a comprehensive picture.

The big ByStar picture is shown in Figure 16.4. Each of the layers in this figure represents either a conceptual definition (shown in blue), or an actual software/service implementation (shown in orange). Each layer builds on the layers beneath.

The layers in Figure 16.4 are color coded. Each of the layers are either:

A Conceptual Layer. Representing concepts. Layers 1,2,3,4,7 and 8 are in Green, Blue and Yellow.

A Tangible Layer. Representing software/service implementations. Layers 5 and 6 are in Orange and Brown.

The tangible layers are bound by the conceptual layers underneath them and receive legitimacy from those concepts.

The conceptual layers are validated by the tangible layers.

The green layers (1 and 2) at the bottom are philosophical, moral and societal. Their scope is wider than the moral digital ecosystem that we are after. Generally speaking, these are not the domain of engineers. They are the domain of ethicists, philosophers and sociologists.

The blue layers (3, 4 and 8) are philosophical, moral, societal, social and engineering aspects of digital ecosystems that require direct involvement of engineers and the engineering profession. The yellow layer (7) addresses economics and business dimensions of ByStar.

The orange/brown layers (5 and 6) are engineering constructs. They are in-use software and in-use Internet application services.

In ByStar Roadmap: http://www.by-star.net/bxRoadmap
we provide a reading roadmap to ByStar related articles.

Figure 16.4 shows how the moral, legal, societal, engineering, economic and business dimensions of the ByStar Halaal Digital Ecosystem are layered as described above.

Note the differing characterizations of this layering on the left and right. Both characterizations are valid, but they reflect entirely different viewpoints. The left side characterization is called "The Human Model," and reflects the philosophical, moral and societal elements of the model. It also identifies the role of the engineering profession in maintaining these elements. The right-side characterization is called "The Venture Capitalist Model," and is very different from the "The Human Model." The same elements are present, but now represent their significance as part of an investment strategy. Thus, the moral and societal concerns within the human model are now viewed as a sales and marketing opportunity. This makes clear that when dealing with Venture Capitalists, issues of morality and societal welfare are not the topic of discussion. In this regard Venture Capitalists need only understand that human beings are in fact concerned with vital moral considerations such as "privacy" and

Human Model   Venture Capitalists' Model

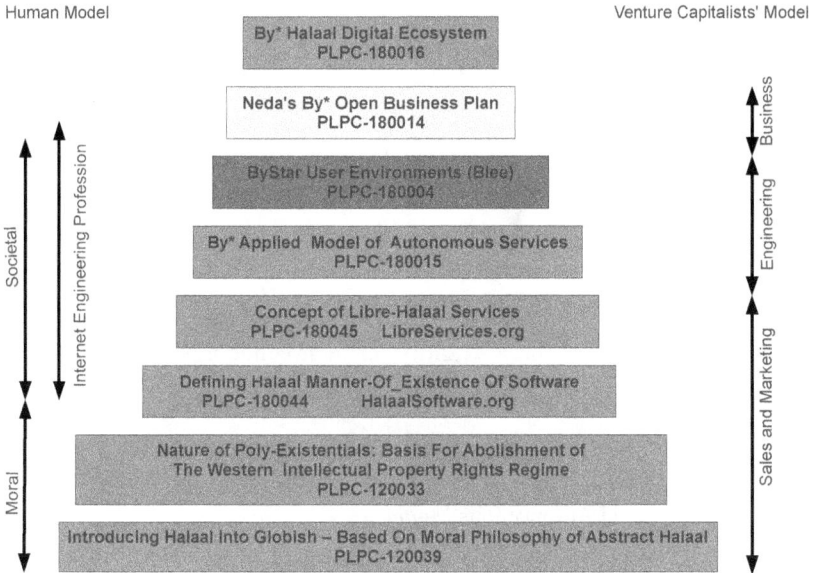

Figure 16.4: The Libre-Halaal ByStar Digital Ecosystem Conceptual Layering

"autonomy," and that these considerations have powerful sales and marketing consequences. And that our unconventional strategy of overturning their sacred-cow – Copyright and Patent model – gives us a huge competitive advantage.

The gigantic picture we have drawn in Figure 16.4 is a blueprint. It represents a complete framework for collaborative work towards an alternative to the current proprietary digital ecosystem. By aligning ourselves with the natural forces and dynamics of polyexistentials, and by means of large-scale unrestricted collaboration, we can achieve this.

16.3 ByStarEntity Realization Models — By Way of Some Examples

Let's explore ByStar in the context of a few examples. All these examples are completely fictional.

Let's consider Bob Smith, a 46-year-old university researcher and his 15-year-old daughter, Alice Smith. Alice is a freshman (9th grader) at Garfield High School (GHS).

Bob wishes to have the following in ByStar.

1. An Autonomous ByName BxEntity for his private and public use –
   5.bob.smith.byname.net (he is the 5th bob.smith requesting byname services).

2. An Autonomous ByFamily BxEntity for his family – 8.smith.byfamily.net.

3. A Controlled ByFamily BxEntity for his daughter Alice –
   alice.8.smith.byfamily.net (Alice is a minor and Bob wishes to have the
   option of overseeing her communications).

4. A Controlled ByWhere BxEntity for their condo in Kirkland, WA – 1-
   98034-3681-74.bywhere.net (say for reliable driving directions).

There are 3 different realization models for Autonomous BxEntity-s.

- Shared Cloud Autonomous Model

- Hosted Private Cloud Autonomous Model

- Premise Private Cloud Autonomous Model

Bob is concerned about privacy and prefers the "Hosted Private Cloud Au-
tonomous Model" over the "Shared Cloud Autonomous Model". He trusts the
ByStar model enough not to need the "Premise Private Cloud Autonomous
Model".

In the following sections we describe ByStarEntity realization models in the
context of Bob and Alice's example.

As we go through these examples, we will also be comparing them with their
counterpart in the Proprietary American Digital Ecosystem.

16.3.1   ByStarEntityId Registrations

Through ByStar, Bob needs to have an Autonomous ByName Registration, an
Autonomous ByFamily Registration and a Controlled ByWhere Registration.

So, Bob goes to http://www.byname.net and provides his name "Bob" "Smith"
and an email address and agrees to conform to ByStar usage policies and in
return, he receives:

- 5.bob.smith.byname.net – BxEntityId=23. 1.2.7.3 .32674 – BxEntityId-
  Password=

Similarly, Bob goes to http://www.byfamily.net and provides his autonomous
BxEntityId=23.1.2.7.3.32674 and gets:

- 8.smith.byfamily.net – BxEntityId=23. 1.2.9.5 .4689

He then provides his autonomous BxEntityId=23.1.2.7.3.32674 and gets:

- 1-98034-3681-74.bywhere.net – BxEntityId=27. 2.2.6.4 .4689

for a ByWhere controlled entity.

All of the above were external registrations. In the ByStar model, Bob himself has now become a registrar for some ByStarEntitys.

Under the 8.smith.byfamily.net domain, Bob now registers

- bob.8.smith.byfamily.net – as BxEntityId=23. 1.2.9.5 .4689 .1

And

- alice.8.smith.byfamily.net – as BxEntityId=23. 1.2.9.5 .4689 .2

Note that Bob has the option of using a single password and that all his ByStar-EntityId are related.

With his 5 ByStarEntityIds in place, Bob now can realize his ByStarEntitys in the model that he wishes.

16.3.2 Shared Cloud Autonomous Model

This model is very similar to how Gmail and other proprietary Internet services works. It involves Bob going to http://www.byname.net, logging in and using the web service.

Even at this level, there is a big difference between the Proprietary American Services and the Libre-Halaal ByStar Services. ByStar is transparent – not opaque/dark/closed.

Even in the shared cloud autonomous model, Bob has the choice of demanding that his entire service be delivered to him as a ByStarAutonomyAssertionVir-tualMachine – that means the entire software for the ByStar service and his entire data be delivered to him. And that the service provider abides by the "Service Data Portability" and "Service and Data Non-Retention" obligations.

In the Gmail (and other) Proprietary American Model there are no such concepts.

16.3.3   Hosted Private Cloud Autonomous Model

16.3.3.1   Obtaining A Generic ByStarAutonomyAssertionVirtualMachine

Bob downloads to his laptop the latest generic ByStarAutonomyAssertionVirtualMachine. This has all the relevant software for ByStar services.

The latest generic ByStarAutonomyAssertionVirtualMachine is available at `http://www.bybinary.org`.

16.3.3.2   Adding ByStarEntitys to the Generic ByStarAutonomyAssertion-VirtualMachine

Bob then adds his ByStarEntitys to the ByStarAutonomyAssertionVirtualMachine.

This involves Bob running the ByStarAutonomyAssertionVirtualMachine on his laptop and entering his ByStarEntityIds into the ByStarAutonomyAssertionVirtualMachine. All of Bob's ByStar services are now added to his ByStarAutonomyAssertionVirtualMachine.

16.3.3.3   Choosing A ByStar Private Cloud Provider – e.g. LibreCenter.net

Bob then chooses a host for his Virtual Machine.

His choice of ByStar Private Cloud Provider may be influenced by the location and laws of where the ByStar Private Cloud Provider operates in. If U.S. wiretap laws are too invasive to his taste, he may choose a ByStar Private Cloud Provider outside of the U.S. – ByStar is very global.

Let's say that Bob chose `http://www.librecenter.net`.

16.3.3.4   Running Your ByStarAutonomyAssertionVirtualMachine

Bob then transfers his fully configured ByStarAutonomyAssertionVirtualMachine to `http://www.librecenter.net` and runs the service.

Bob is now in control of his own service.

ByStar and LibreCenter have given Bob what is necessary and are supporting him. Bob is in possession of all of the service's software and the service is Bob's.

16.3.4   Premise Private Cloud Autonomous Model

In the Premise Private Cloud Autonomous Model, Bob is in possession and control of the entire software and the entire hardware for the service.

16.3.4.1   Obtaining a Premise ByStar Host

A Premise ByStar Host is a computer with a static public IP address capable of running a ByStarAutonomyAssertionVirtualMachine. Any modern desktop or laptop would do just fine.

16.3.4.2   Preparing the ByStarAutonomyAssertionVirtualMachine

Bob does what was previously described in Section 16.3.3.1 and Section 16.3.3.2 to prepare his ByStarAutonomyAssertionVirtualMachine.

A typical ByStarAutonomyAssertionVirtualMachine is capable of containing 100s of ByStarEntitys.

16.3.4.3   Running the Premise ByStarAutonomyAssertionVirtualMachine

Bob then puts his ByStarAutonomyAssertionVirtualMachine on his "Premise ByStar Host" and runs it.

Bob now possesses all of the software for ByStar,
all of his own data,
all of his logs and audit trails,
and all of his services.

This means real and tangible autonomy.

Efforts like FreedomBox have been attempting to accomplish this in a more limited fashion. But in the ByStar model the Premise Private Cloud Autonomous Model is just one of many ways to realize tangible autonomy.

16.3.5   ByStar Autonomous Services Use and Access Examples

So, now Bob and Alice have a number of autonomous services in place. Now, let's see how they will be accessing them and what these ByStar Autonomous Services can do for Bob and Alice.

16.3.5.1   Browser Based Web Service Usage

Most ByStar services are also offered as interactive web services just like traditional web services.

The generic ByStarAutonomyAssertionVirtualMachine includes all ByStar user environments. A Tor-Firefox browser is all you need for ByStar interactive web services.

But the preferred model for accessing ByStar services is through Blee.

16.3.5.2   Blee Based Software-Service Continuum Usage

Blee (ByStar Libre Emacs Environment) is a layer above Emacs and Firefox that integrates ByStar platform (Debian GNU/Linux) capabilities into Emacs and provides for integration with ByStar Services.

Use of Blee makes for a very rich software-service continuum model that does not have a real counterpart in the Proprietary American Digital Ecosystem.

16.3.6   Some Examples of ByStar Autonomous Services Capabilities

With everything in place, let's see what are some of their ByStar capabilities. ByStar full set of Autonomous capabilities is determined by the capabilities of Bob's ByStarAutonomyAssertionVirtualMachine. These are already quite powerful and they are ever growing. Below we mention some.

16.3.6.1   ByStar Email (Messaging)

In terms of email capabilities, ByStar email is similar to Gmail. However, ByStar email is very autonomous, very personal and very private.

For example, note that email communications between Bob and Alice need not even leave Bob's ByStarAutonomyAssertionVirtualMachine.

Beyond Gmail like capabilities, ByStar email service is inherently multi-address and multi-mailbox.

For example Bob and Alice can each have a specific address for Alice's school – Garfield High School (GHS). Those email addresses would be:

- ghs@alice.8.smith.byfamily.net

- ghs@bob.8.smith.byfamily.net

Libre-Halaal ByStar email services are superior to Proprietary-Haraam email services both in capability and privacy.

16.3.6.2 ByStar Public and Private Web Presence Services

ByStar public and private web presence services are very rich. They are based on the Plone Content Management System.

The URL for Bob's public web site would be http://5.bob.smith.byname.net. Its capabilities could be similar to the author of this document's site: `http://mohsen.1.banan.byname.net`.

16.3.6.3 ByStar Photo and Video Galleries

Bob and Alice and their family's (8.smith.byfamily.net) photo gallery can be similar to what is in: `http://mohsen.1.banan.byname.net/albums`.

ByStar Photo and Video Galleries are based on galleria and are integrated into Plone. ByStar photo gallery capabilities comfortably compete with the likes of flickr and photo bucket. The difference of course is that Bob and Alice remain in control of their photos with ByStar.

16.3.6.4 ByStar Genealogy Services

Bob and Alice can build their genealogy tree in ways similar to what is in: `http://mohsen.1.banan.byname.net/genealogy`.

ByStar Genealogy Services are based on geneweb. ByStar genealogy capabilities comfortably compete with the likes of ancestry.com, FamilySearch, and MyTrees.com.

The difference of course is that with ByStar, Bob and Alice remain in control of their genealogical personal information.

16.3.6.5 ByStar Libre Content Self-Publication Services

Bob Smith is an academic. He writes and publishes a lot. Some of his thoughts and writings are outside of the mainstream. As a true academic, he prefers not to subject his publications to restrictions that the likes of IEEE and ACM demand. His publication philosophy is consistent with ByStar Publication Philosophy.

He uses the ByStar Content Production and Content Publication Facilities to write and publish.

The list of his publications is similar to what is in:
http://mohsen.1.banan.byname.net/publications/collections/bystarDE.

The access page to Bob's documents are similar to this document's:
http://mohsen.1.banan.byname.net/PLPC/180016.

Bob, can optionally use ByStar Federated Services to achieve permanence and ease of search and access to his writings. See Section 16.3.7 for more details.

So, ByStar has empowered Bob to be a true academic and avoid pseudo academic copyrighted publication traditions.

16.3.7   ByStar Federated Services Examples

Bob has chosen to subject some of his publications to "Federated Re-Publication". He uses `http://www.bycontent.net` for that.

ByContent is a ByStar Federated Service where ByStar self-published documents are republished.

By submitting some of his documents and podcasts (videos) for ByContent re-publication, Bob accomplishes several things.

ByContent Federated Services offer the following:

- Permanence. If Bob's web site or he, himself disappear, his documents still remain.

- Large volume publication. ByContent runs on large computers with access to lots of bandwidth. Bob need not worry about slowness of access to his public videos and public writings.

- ByContent republication maintains reference to original source.

- Classification with peer content. Bob's content is classified and sits next to other similar and competing content.

- Searchability. Bob's content are now subject to search features of `http://www.BySearch.org`

ByContent is similar to YouTube, except that ByContent allows your content to be clearly referred back to you. All of ByContent is copyleft.

16.3.8   Bob And Alice's ByStar Digital Ecosystem

Now, Let's look at this example in its entirety and see what Bob and Alice gained by buying into the ByStar Digital Ecosystem.

First, they lost nothing. ByStar exists in parallel to the proprietary Internet. Everything that everybody else can do, Bob and Alice can do as well. Through peer pressure Alice will likely be pushed to join Facebook.

But, Bob and Alice now have autonomous and private email. They communicate with everybody else in normal email fashion. But they are in control of their personal messages. When Bob deletes an email he knows that the email has truly been deleted.

And Bob and Alice are truly in control of what they do with their photos, and their content on the Internet.

That can be considered a good beginning. ByStar is evolutionary. ByStar is designed to be ever-growing and comprehensive.

Are you ready to follow Bob and Alice's example?

16.4 The Libre-Halaal vs. Proprietary-Haraam Battle

The inherent nature of software, Internet services and other polyexistentials is fundamentally at odds with these historical conventions of physical property (monoexistentials) ownership. Such constructs have the inherent potential for unlimited replicability and dissemination, and in the age of the Internet this potential is now fully realized.

As a result the existing Western Intellectual Property conventions are coming under increasing stress, as the internal forces of replicability clash with the externally constraining Intellectual Property framework. The Intellectual Property regime is also coming under formal intellectual attack, as the dysfunctionality and true costs of this regime become increasingly apparent.

In practice, the proprietary software and services model has engaged in various forms of bastardization of libre-halaal software model. Well recognized examples of such bastardizations include the service loophole, Tivoization, Appleization, and Androidization.

In practice, open-source and free software movements represent compromising models and ideologies. For the most part they are comfortable being intertwined with the proprietary model. Full rejection of the proprietary model is considered radical in much of the open-source culture.

In practice, with ByStar ideology we accomplish three things. First, we create a completely separate and independent digital ecosystem that fully rejects the proprietary model. Second, we take all possible measures to prevent bastardization of ByStar software and services by the proprietary model. Third, we create a comprehensive internet services business model which competes directly with the proprietary model in terms of revenue and profit.

16.4.1 Engineering vs. Business

Today, the internet services industry is owned entirely by business interests. But the Libre Services and By* initiatives represent a startling challenge to this: they represent a determined reassertion of proper guardianship of the

Proprietary vs Libre	Libre-Halaal Ecosystem	Proprietary Ecosystem
Laws, Values	Patent-free	Patented
and Model	Copyleft	Copyright
Software and	Transparency	Secrecy
User Env	Public ownership	Private ownership
Internet Services	Privacy, Autonomy	Surveillance Capitalism
Content	Guardianship	Exploitation

Table 16.1: Engineering vs. Business Polarization

internet by the Engineering Profession. This challenge will bring us into massive conflict with existing commercial interests, who will fight ferociously to defend the status quo.

Table 16.1 shows the many elements of contrast between Engineering and Business value systems. As the table makes clear, these two values systems are in complete and total conflict. We will fully exploit this conflict as the metaphor of a war: a war between Engineering and Business, in which Business represents exploitation of the Internet for profit, and Engineering represents guardianship of the Internet on behalf of the public.

16.4.2   War of Ideas – War of Words

ByStar is huge, powerful, and viable. But given the entrenched vested interests in opposition to it, the promotion of ByStar amounts to a kind of war. ByStar has the inherent characteristics to prevail in this war – we have moral superiority, intellectual correctness, and a construct that is viable in every respect: technological, economic, societal etc. But it is essential that all this be communicated effectively.

The ByStar Wars (to coin a phrase) will be fought on multiple fronts. But as a revolutionary movement, to a significant extent it will be fought as a war of words and ideas. This means that the movement is advanced effectively in words, defended against attack in words, and extremely forceful and effective counter-attack made against its detractors.

Please refer to http://www.by-star.net/bxPublications for a list of publications that we have felt is necessary for ByStar to be equipped with.

16.5   Joining ByStar

Successful Digital Ecosystems are dynamic. They grow and are ever evolving.

In the early stages of the evolution of ByStar we have adopted the strategy of limiting the size of our user base. A large active user base requires more support and is more difficult to maintain when service changes are frequent and when structural corrections may be needed.

At a certain point we would invite the public at large to use fully automated services to obtain ByStar accounts and start using ByStar. But that is not now. ByStarEntityGenerator web services such as ByName.net ByAuthor.net By-Where.net, etc. are in place. However, at this time we screen account requests individually.

16.5.1 Individually

Any individual wishing to join ByStar can make a request and we usually activate accounts for these requests. Please see http://www.by-star.net/joiningByStar for details.

16.5.2 En Masse

Groups of users (Autonomous ByStarEntities) such as students or staff at a university or High School or a church can join ByStar en masse and obtain ByName services. Other ByStarEntity abstractions can also join ByStar en masse and obtain associated ByStar services.

In an article titled:

> **Joining, Adopting and/or Licensing ByStar**
> **A Strategy For Rapidly Becoming An Internet Application Service Provider**
> **A Proposal**
> http://www.by-star.net/PLPC/180040

We describe various options for those interested in joining, adopting and/or licensing ByStar.

Chapter 17

Technology of ByStar: BISOS (ByStar Internet Services Operating System)

In the previous two chapters, we described the requirements for a healthy digital ecosystem and its functionality. In Chapter 15 — Theory of Libre-Halaal Digital Ecosystems — we provided definitional criteria for the manner-of-existence of relevant parts of Libre-Halaal digital ecosystems. In Chapter 16 — The Libre-Halaal ByStar Digital Ecosystem, we described the functionality of ByStar. In this chapter, we focus on the technology of ByStar: the architecture, design and implementation of ByStar.

The engineering design and implementation of the ByStar Digital Ecosystem is documented in:

> The Universal BISOS: ByStar Internet Services Operating System
> Model, Terminology, Implementation And Usage
> A Framework For Cohesive Creation, Deployment and Management Of Internet Services
> http://www.by-star.net/PLPC/180047 — [29]

In that overview document, we present a vast model and process that can redirect the manner-of-existence and functionality of internet application services to protect humanity. In this chapter we include some extracts from that document.

Our audience for this book is all of humanity. Anyone who is willing to read and and who is willing to think independently. However, this chapter of the book is aimed primarily at fellow engineers and software-oriented readers and those who are curious to learn about the internals of ByStar. Here, we provide a simplified overview of BISOS. This overview includes the components we have selected, how we have arranged them, and the abstractions we have created to structure BISOS as an integrated platform. Additionally, we describe how ByStar uses BISOS. This overview does not aim to describe the inner workings of BISOS.

For those wishing to dig deeper into ByStar, we provide a reading road map in http://www.by-star.net/bxRoadmap. In ByStar Publications List: http://www.by-star.net/bxPublications, we provide pointers to ByStar related articles. These documents evolve as ByStar evolves, and the publications list will be kept up to date. The ByStar publications list is structured primarily for reference.

The internet services industry of today has three characteristics that greatly limit its capabilities, its usefulness and its health.

First, virtually all existing internet services are based on the traditional proprietary opaque model. So far, the FOSS movement has no formal presence within the services domain. The internet Applications Services Provider (ASP) sits in the center and controls and owns almost every aspect of our (user) communications.

Second, the current proprietary central model of American internet services has taken us to live in a world where our use of the network is mediated by organizations that often do not have our best interests at heart. This has led to the rise of surveillance capitalism.

Third, the internet services industry has arisen in a highly disorganized, unstructured way, driven by a multitude of uncoordinated commercial initiatives. The various industry capabilities have been built in an *ad hoc* manner, based on immediate business expedience, rather than by any sort of overarching engineering design. The result is the internet services industry as it exists today: chaotic, uncoordinated, and falling far short of its true potential.

The solution to these limitations consists of three main components:

1. We need to require the Libre-Halaal manner-of-existence for internet services. In other words the entirety of our public internet services should be internally transparent. The entire software of our own internet services should be Libre-Halaal Software (FOSS, FLOSS, OpenSource, Free Software).

2. We need a "Unified Autonomy and Privacy Oriented Digital Model" that is built on a "Universal Internet Services OS" and provides us autonomous services — that belong to us and are controlled by us.

3. We need a "Universal Internet Services Operating System (OS)" to bring consistency and cohesion to ower digital environment.

Here by "our" and "us" we are speaking of society at large when it is represented and protected by the Internet Engineering Profession.

Thus far we have been describing the contours of the problem and the contours of solution in abstract terms. We now present a specific implementation, that makes our proposal concrete.

17.1 Concept of the Universal Internet Services OS

The concept of an internet services operating system, or a common foundation, platform, and framework for the development of internet services, is not new. Proprietary internet service providers have their own proprietary and closed Internet Services OS. However, on the non-proprietary internet services side, this concept has not been formalized, structured, and cultivated. There is some precedence for this, and we can use this as a starting point.

Shortly after the internet started to impact society (say in 1994) and shortly after Linux became widespread, the idea of a server-side Internet Services OS appeared as "The LAMP Stack".

17.1.1 The Early LAMP Precedence

LAMP is an acronym that stands for "Linux, Apache, MySQL, Perl/PHP/Python". Packaged together, they create an application stack that is both free to use and open source which functions as a general purpose web server.

In 1994, the Common Gateway Interface (CGI) was introduced in CERN httpd, allowing for the server-side execution of code to create dynamic webpages. In a sense, this can be considered the genesis of internet application services. This made it possible to create a LAMP stack (the free general-purpose web server) using Linux, CERN httpd, and server-side programming languages such as Perl. However, it wasn't until the release of Postgre95 that a free database was available. Finally, in 1996, MySQL was released online, completing the LAMP stack.

Validity of the LAMP stack as a server-side web services generic OS was established through its widespread use in the late 1990s. Many of the dot-con era firms ran their websites with LAMP.

We recognize what is generally labeled "The LAMP Stack" as a very rudimentary Internet Application Services OS. LAMP had the following characteristics.

1. LAMP was a layer on top of Linux distributions

2. LAMP was a server-side stack

3. LAMP addressed a certain segment of internet application services. Its scope was websites development.

4. LAMP focused on a very specific profile of the Linux distribution — Apache and MySql.

5. LAMP focused on a specific programming language — one of Perl, PHP or Python.

Extending and improving the concept of LAMP can lead to the notion of "A Universal Internet Services OS".

Such an extension involves two dimensions:

1. An Internet Services OS should cover all internet services — not just web services.

2. An Internet Services OS should fully cover all sides — clients, servers, things in the middle and software-service-continuums.

By "Universal" we are referring to this notion of "covering all sides" from phones and tablets to mainframes and sever-clusters. This idea of "Universal Services OS" builds on Debian's concept of "The Universal Software Operating System".

17.1.2 Operating System, Internet Application Service and Digital Ecosystem

Almost everyone uses email. Email is a widely used application. To make things more explicit, we will use email as an example of an application service.

In Figure 17.1, let's consider email in the context of operating systems, internet application service and digital ecosystems.

First, let's take a look at what is happening in the proprietary universe. The five major American proprietary tech companies (Google, Microsoft, Apple, Facebook, and Amazon) have created five distinct digital ecosystems as competing enclaves. In Figure 17.1, ByStar and Proprietary American Digital Ecosystems, we are focusing on the first 3 and each of their office and email environments. These ecosystems are mostly separate and isolated from one another, and the economic model of these proprietary digital ecosystems is "Surveillance Capitalism". As such, when users sign up for a free email account, they are voluntarily forgoing much of their privacy. Sadly, the rest of the world is becoming Americanized through the American Internet. Each of these enclaves also have Mail User Agents that are fully integrated into their digital

Legend	Proprietary American Digital Ecosystems (Opaque, Central, Controlled, Exploiting)			Non-Proprietary Digital Ecosystems (Transparent, Decentralized, Autonomous, Private)	
Digital Ecosystem	Google DE	Microsoft DE	Apple DE	Western FLOSS Components	Libre-Halaal ByStar DE
Operating System	ChromeOS Android	Windows 11	MacOS iPhone	Linux Various Distros Debian	Debian-BISOS (By* Internet Services OS)
Usage Environment	Google Office	MS Office	Apple Office	Gnome Emacs	Blee (By* Libre Emacs Env)
Mail User Agent	Gmail MUA	Outlook	Apple Mail	Evolution DIY Gnus	Blee-Gnus + MARMEE
Internet					
Mail Services	Gmail.com Service	Outlook.com hotmail.com msn.com	icloud.com/mail	Nil or Any	ByName.net Mail
Portal Services	Google apps	Microsoft 365	iCloud	Nil	ByStar Services

Figure 17.1: ByStar and Proprietary American Digital Ecosystems

ecosystems, providing users with address books, calendars, time management and planning tools, multi-lingual authoring tools, and more.

Now, let's focus on the right side of this picture. On the non-proprietary side, based on the FOSS model, we have ended up with lots of components. We have Debian as a platform, we have Emacs as an editor-centered office environment and lots of great applications. But on the non-proprietary side we don't have anything that can reasonably be considered a digital ecosystem.

We need non-proprietary digital ecosystems. And that is what ByStar is.

In proprietary digital ecosystems, the scope of the operating system (Chrome, Android, Windows, MacOS) is limited to the usage-side. The service-side OS is unknown due to the proprietary services being opaque. The concept of an Internet Services OS is well established inside of each of the proprietary services providers. Each has their own and parts of their Internet Services OS are exposed to their "Cloud" users.

On the FOSS side, the scope of the LAMP style operating systems is limited to the service-side, with the usage-side being considered agnostic. ByStar and BISOS provide a powerful and universal solution, covering both the service-side and the usage-side.

17.2   Overview of BISOS and ByStar Digital Ecosystem

BISOS (ByStar Internet Services OS) is a reification of the abstraction of "A Universal Internet Services OS". ByStar is a concrete form of the abstraction of "A Unified Autonomous Digital Ecosystem".

BISOS has the following key characteristics.

1. BISOS is both purposeful and general purpose. BISOS is ideology driven. The general purpose of BISOS is to facilitate the creation of digital ecosystems that prioritize autonomy and privacy. The specific purpose of BISOS is to facilitate creation of the Libre-Halaal ByStar Digital Ecosystem.

2. BISOS is layered on top of the Universal Debian software.

3. BISOS facilitates secure and private possession and portability of the user's information through the abstraction of ByStar Portable Objects (BPO).

4. BISOS enables the two-way transfer of Libre Services from the user's own possession to Libre Service providers and between Libre Service providers through the Possession Assertable Libre Services (PALS) abstraction.

5. BISOS creates software-service continuums through universality on both server-side and usage-side.

6. BISOS services integration and usage integration structures are self-confined to select languages: Python, Bash, Elisp and C/C++. Each language environment is augmented with BISOS native frameworks. The primary integration framework of BISOS is Python-Command-Services (PyCS).

7. The primary usage interface for BISOS is Blee (ByStar Libre-Halaal Emacs Environment), which is comprehensive and extends to development environments.

8. BISOS server-side PALS features are based on specific profiles from Debian packages collection. The profiles primary focus on autonomous email and autonomous content publication.

9. BISOS usage-side capabilities are based on specific profiles from Debian packages collection. The profiles primary focus on email handling and content production.

10. BISOS platforms are automated to be recreatable from BPO contained information as physical and virtual images. Linux KVM is the only supported virtualization model.

11. BISOS's basic unit is a site. A BISOS-Site includes a private git server and a registrar.

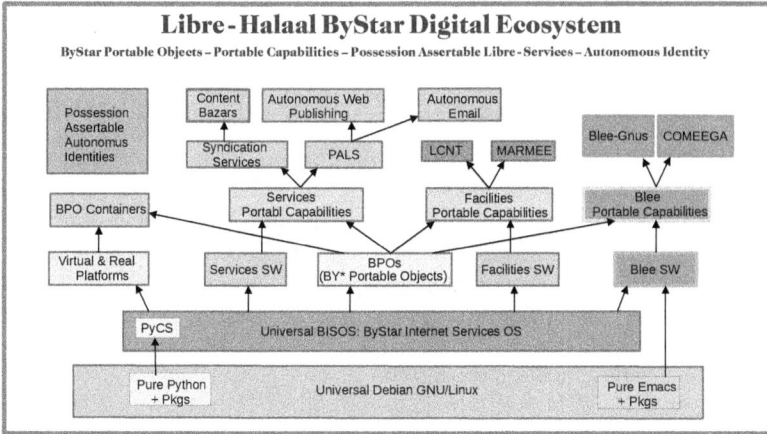

Figure 17.2: ByStar Portable Object Capabilities

BISOS facilities are used to create the infrastructure of ByStar and various types of ByStar services.

Figure 17.2 depicts layerings of BISOS and of ByStar services. The Universal Debian Gnu/Linux is our foundation on top of which BISOS resides.

The box labeled "Services SW" refers to instances of BISOS service-side debian packages. The box labeled "Facilities SW" refers to instances of BISOS usage-side debian packages. Configuration information for packages reside in BPOs (By* Portable Objects).

The combination of "Services SW" and its relevant configuration within a BPO, forms a "Portable Services Capability". The combination of "Facilities SW" and its relevant configuration within a BPO, forms a "Portable Facilities Capability".

Possession Assertable Libre Service (PALS) is a type of Portable Services Capability. Multi-Account Resident Mail Exchange Environment (MARMEE) is a type of Portable Facility Capability.

Possession Assertable Autonomous Identities (PAAI) are types of BPOs which include the identifiers (e.g., domain names) that enable PALS to become Realized Services.

The stack on the right side of Figure 17.2 depicts BISOS's usage environment which we describe in Section 17.10.

The stack on the left side of Figure 17.2 depicts evolution of platforms in BISOS. A BISOS-Platform is a Debian computer loaded with BISOS software. A BPO-Container is a BISOS-Platform which has received (contains) some BPOs. A

PAAI-Container is a BPO-Container which ontains one or more PAAI-BPO.

17.3   BISOS Engineering Philosophy and Ideology

BISOS is purposeful and ideology driven. Parts of BISOS ideology are rooted in health of society. BISOS also reflects a particular engineering philosophy. Figure 17.3 depicts our choices in adoption of philosophical characteristics from various software development groups, with some adjustments.

Unix's Genericity and Conviviality

BISOS is based on the "Unix" model. Not the "Linux" model. We draw a distinct differentiation between "Unix Philosophy" vs "Linux Philosophy" vs "Business Philosophy". Unix Philosophy is a set of cultural norms and philosophical approaches to convivial software development and usage. Unix Philosophy has been well articulated by Ken Thompson, Doug McIlroy, Kernighan, Pike and others.

Linux Philosophy is a laissez faire adaptation of Unix Philosophy that results in software bloat.

BISOS is firmly rooted in a Unix Philosophy and discounts the Business Philosophy and the Linux philosophy.

Debian's Universality

Debian insists on running on everything. By everything we mean a large number of CPU architectures. This is accomplished on methodic and durable reliance on primary source code. By everything we also mean the range of very constrained environments to super computers.

This is important for ByStar because BISOS inherits Debian's Universality.

Emacs's Deep Integration

Blee, BISOS's usage environment, is based on Emacs. Some Emacs builds include a kitchen-sink icon. It is the one feature not yet implemented in Emacs.

Emacs is an integral part of BISOS. It is a framework for consistent integration of internal and external applications. This in turn results in a very convivial usage environment which spans software development, content creation, interpersonal communication and integrated internet application services access.

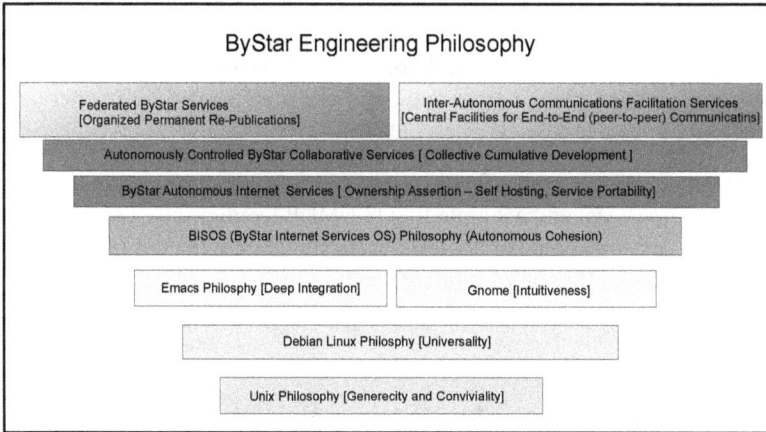

Figure 17.3: ByStar Engineering Philosophy

17.4 BISOS: an Over Debian Pure Blend

Debian defines Pure Blend as: "a subset of Debian that is configured to support a particular target group out-of-the-box. One way to understand this is a list of packages that gets installed to provide a focus of use."

The lower layers of BISOS can be considered a Debian Pure Blend. BISOS-service-side has one deb-pkgs-profile and BISOS-usage-side has another deb-pkgs-profile.

But BISOS goes beyond that. BISOS and Debian are not peers. BISOS is a layer on top of Debian. BISOS provides services-oriented facilities that go beyond the scope of Debian. BISOS has its own policies and practices that are a super set of Debian policies and practices. While the basic unit of Debian is a computer, the basic unit of BISOS is a BISOS-Site.

17.5 BISOS's Basic Unit: BISOS-Site

Typically, the basic unit of an Operating System is one computer — depending on the context the computer is called: a host, a system, a platform, a box, etc.

With BISOS the basic unit is more than one computer. We call BISOS's basic unit: BISOS-Site. Fundamental BISOS abstractions are based on BISOS Portable Objects (BPO) which are implemented as git accounts. Some BPOs must be private. So, a BISOS-Site must include a private git server — which is implemented as a Gitlab instance. BISOS's use of BPO is purely through a Python API interface. Gitlab GUI is hardly ever used. BISOS also relies on the uniqueness of names and numbers. BISOS therefore needs an automated registrar for some private names and numbers. For BISOS to fully operate, at a minimum it needs those services.

A BISOS-Site also provides facilities for creation and management of Virtual Machines (VMs) and a simple BISOS-CMDB (configuration management database) — a central repository for storing BISOS-Site related resource. For creation and recreation of VMs (image management), BISOS uses Vagrant.

17.6   BISOS Portable Objects (BPO)

A fundamental abstraction of BISOS is the concept of BISOS Portable Objects (BPO). BPOs are packages of information. There are some similarities between BPOs as packages of information and software packages such as deb-packages or rpm-packages.

Like software packages, BPOs are named uniquely and can depend on each other and can be collectively installed and uninstalled. BPOs are used for many things similar to how the files system is used for many things. BPOs can be used to hold the complete configuration information of a system. BPOs can be used to hold configuration information for software packages. BPOs can be used to hold private user data. BPOs can be used to hold collections of content and source code.

For its own operation, BISOS uses various BPO types. Other types of BPOs can be created or generic BPO types (for example the Project type) can be used.

Each BPO consists of a number of Git Repositories (hereafter called "repos"). Each of the BPO's repos can be synchronized using generic Git tools, but we use Blee/Emacs's MaGit exclusively.

BPOs are implemented as Gitlab accounts. Gitlab accounts are Unix non-login shell accounts. BISOS's interactions with Gitlab is exclusively through an API (Remote Operations). Each Gitlab account then can contain repos subject to common access control mechanisms. Gitlab accounts map to BPO-Identifiers (BPO-Id). Each BPO-id then maps to Unix non-login shell accounts. The Unix account then becomes the base for cloning of the repos in the corresponding Gitlab account.

Combinations of profiled deb-packages for internet application services and their configurations in the form of BPOs can then create Libre Services that are possession assertable, portable and transferable.

17.7 BISOS Possession Assertable Libre Services (PALS)

Based on capabilities of BPOs and the capabilities of service-side profiled Debian packages, we can now create Libre Services.

BISOS Libre Services can be thought of four parts:

1. Libre-Halaal software of the services (usually a Debian Package)

2. Configuration information for the software for the service (often as a repo of a PALS-BPO)

3. Names and numbers for binding of services (as a repo of a PAAI-BPO)

4. Service owner data (in the form of one or more BPOs)

This model provides for portability and transferability of Libre Services between network abodes. For example, a Libre Service at a provider can be transferred to its owner to be self-hosted.

There are some similarities between PALS-BPO and container virtualization (Docker and Kubernetes). PALS-BPOs include comprehensive information for construction of services and these can be mapped to container virtualization. However, at this time BISOS does not use container virtualization, as it is redundant. BISOS uses BPOs to create and recreate Kernel-based Virtual Machines (KVM) inside of which PALS-BPOs are deployed.

Self-hosting is the practice of running and maintaining a Libre Service under one's own full control at one's own premise. BISOS Possession Assertable Libre Services (PALS) can be initially self-hosted and then transferred to a Libre Service provider. PALS can also be initially externally hosted and then become self-hosted on demand. The concept of "transferability" between network abodes is well supported in BISOS.

17.7.1 Network Abodes and Transferability

In the proprietary American digital ecosystem, the concept of network abodes is mostly vague. Names such as cloud and edge are used without much precision, and, the concept of transferability simply does not exist. You cannot self-host your Gmail service.

Within ByStar and BISOS, we have precise definitions for where Libre Services can be realized and where they can be transferred to. This is depicted in Figure 17.4

Let's define "edge" as point of demarcation between the public digital world and the physical world (and its associated private digital environment). In

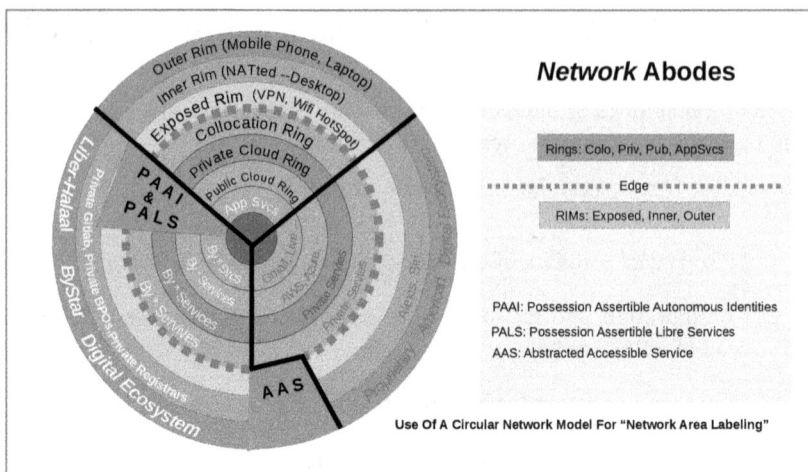

Figure 17.4: Network Abodes: A Circular Model For Network Area Labeling

Figure 17.4 this is depicted as a dotted red circle. When by physical world, we mean "things", then in the American Internet, we have the culture and lingo of IoT (Internet of Things) Edge Computing. But what if by the physical world, we mean people — individuals?

The three concentric circles on the outer side of the edge are called "Rims". These are:

1. Exposed Rim.

   Systems in the Exposed Rim are on your premise, and they are externally visible. Wifi hotspots, routers and VPNs are usually in the Exposed Rim. Self-Hosting occurs in the Exposed Rim. Systems in the Exposed Rim should be well secured as they are vulnerable to direct attacks.

2. Inner Rim.

   Systems in the Inner Rim are on your premise behind a firewall. private desktops, fileservers, private Gitlab and private registrars are usually in the Inner Rim. Systems in the Inner Rim are usually physically stationary.

3. Outer Rim.

   Systems in the Outer Rim are usually portable devices and at this time they are on your premise behind a firewall. Laptops, Pads, Mobile-Phones (with wifi access) are usually in the Outer Rim. Systems in the Outer Rim are usually portable devices.

The four concentric circles on the outer side of the edge are called "Rings". These are:

1. Collocation Ring.

   Systems in the Collocation Ring are on somebody else's premise (usually a data center), but they belong to you (or are rented by you). A collocation data center is a physical facility that offers space with the proper power, cooling, network connectivity and security to host other people's computing hardware and servers. There is a certain aspect of self-possession in the Collocation Ring.

2. Private Cloud Ring.

   Systems in the Private Cloud Ring are usually virtualized and are under your exclusive access.

3. Public Cloud Ring.

   Systems in the Public Cloud Ring are usually virtualized and are under your access.

4. Public Internet Application Services.

   Examples of Public Internet Application Services in the proprietary American digital ecosystem are Gmail, Facebook and Instagram. You pay for public proprietary internet application services by becoming the product, through your privacy.

In the model of the proprietary American digital ecosystem, a given internet application service typically permanently resides in the ring abodes and is not transferable to other service providers. The service belongs to the service provider and it is locked.

In the ByStar model, the service belongs to its user and it is the user who decides where she wants to realize it. This transferability is accomplished through the abstractions of BPOs (BISOS Portable Objects), PALS (Possession Assertable Libre Services) and PAAI (Possession Assertable Autonomous Identities). In Figure 17.4 the segment labeled "PAAI & PALS" spans the Exposed Rim, the Collocation Ring, the Private Cloud Ring, the Public Cloud Ring and the Application Services Ring. This means that a BISOS based Libre Services can be transferred between any of those network abodes.

BISOS can also be used to provide access to proprietary internet application services. This is shown in the segment labeled "AAS" of Figure 17.4. Abstracted Application Services (AAS) are facilities that allow for abstraction of some proprietary internet application services to be used by BISOS. One such internet service is Gmail. Gmail can be used through Blee-Gnus and BISOS-MARMEE.

17.7.2   Ramifications of Libre-Halaal Edge-Oriented Strategies

To illustrate the privacy and autonomy-oriented benefits of the PALS model, let's compare and contrast The American Internet with ByStar in the context of a very simple but very important human application: "email". To be more concrete and specific, in the context of the American Internet, let's use the fictional example of an American politician called "Hillary Clinton". In the context of ByStar, let's use the fictional example of an Iranian engineer called "Mohsen Banan".

In the American Internet environment, the individual typically has at least two email addresses. One is through her work, say at the State Department, as: "hillary.clinton@state.gov". The other is for personal use, as: "hillary.clinton@gmail.com". Paying attention to her email addresses, we note that "hillary.clinton" is always on the left side of the "@". This means that "gmail.com" has risen in the middle and controls "hillary.clinton@" — and millions of others. This means that Google has full possession and full control over Hillary's personal emails. Her "hillary.clinton@gmail.com" emails are neither autonomous nor private. Now, since Hillary Clinton is an intelligent and powerful American politician, she has recognized that her privacy and autonomy are important and that her email communications should be under her full control. She is rich, so, she goes ahead and sets up her own email server in her basement. We don't know if that email server was based on proprietary software or not, but we do know that as an individualistic American, she was only focused on addressing her own email autonomy and privacy concerns. Email autonomy and privacy of society at large was not her concern.

In the ByStar environment, the individual similarly also has two sets of email addresses. Mohsen's work email may well be under the control of his employer, but his private email service and email addresses are under his own control. For personal use, Mohsen has registered and obtained
`mohsen.banan.byname.net` for himself.
Notice that while `byname.net` is part of ByStar,
`mohsen.banan.byname.net` belongs to Mohsen. Based on that, he can now create a series of email addresses for himself.
For example, he can use "bystarPlan@mohsen.banan.byname.net" for matters related to distribution of this document.
He can use "card@mohsen.banan.byname.net" on his visit cards.

Now, let's compare and contrast the email addresses "hillary.clinton@gmail.com" and
"myDesk@mohsen.banan.byname.net". The right-part of the '@' signifies ownership and control. The right part of '@' controls the left-part of '@'. So, `gmail.com` controls "hillary.clinton". While `mohsen.banan.byname.net` controls "myDesk" and Mohsen, owns `mohsen.banan.byname.net`. Notice that `gmail.com` controls millions of people through their left-part. In ByStar, millions of people can obtain their own right-parts and then control their own

left-parts — and own their own portable full email addresses.
Notice that while gmail.com has positioned itself in the middle of the network, mohsen.banan.byname.net has positioned itself in the edge of the network. Longer domain names which fully take advantage of DNS's hierarchical design are manifestations of edge-oriented strategies.

Next, let's compare and contrast the software of the gmail.com service against the software of
mohsen.banan.byname.net. The software of gmail.com service is proprietary. It belongs to Google. We don't know what it does. When you hit the delete button for a particular email, you can no longer see that message. But perhaps Google is keeping all of your deleted messages somewhere, forever. Because it is all proprietary software, you just don't know what is actually happening with the emails that you may think are yours. The software of mohsen.banan.byname.net services is part of the public ByStar software. It is part of BISOS. It is a public resource. That entire software is internally transparent. On your behalf, the engineering profession knows what it does and what it does not. When you delete one of your own email messages, it can be known that it was truly deleted — forever. This is what having a Libre-Halaal Service means.

With ByStar in place, all the Hillary Clintons of this world can have their own email communications under their own full control. We invite Hillary Clinton to join ByStar. As an American politician, perhaps she can start thinking about solving her society's email problems — not just her own. We welcome her assistance in promoting ByStar.

Consider the privacy and autonomy of such edge-to-edge email communications between
"myDesk@mohsen.banan.byname.net" and "myDesk@hillary.clinton.byname.net".
The mail protocol traffic is of course end-to-end encrypted between mohsen.banan.byname.net and hillary.clinton.byname.net. The message itself can additionally be encrypted. At no point is any third party in possession of the clear-text message. Logs of the message transfer are only in the possession of the two edges. And all of this can be realized on an internet-scale.

All ByStar individual services are intended to be end-to-end and edge-oriented. However, they don't need to reside on the "Rims" side of the network edge. Since ByStar individual services are possession-assertable and portable, they can also be provisioned in the "Rings". See Figure 17.4 for the references to Edge, Rims and Rings. This provides for options of self-hosting or external-hosting of individual services. So, byname.net can be made to be as convenient as gmail.com yet preserves the guarantees of autonomy and privacy through being possession-assertable, portable, Libre-Halaal, and edge-oriented.

While here we focused on the email service as an end-to-end edge-oriented

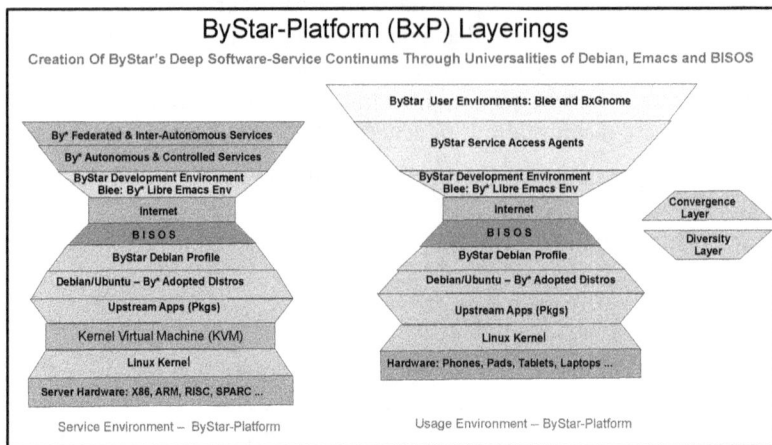

Figure 17.5: ByStar Platform Layerings and Software-Service Continuums

strategy, similar approaches can be applied to other internet applications and intra-edge applications. In the edge-oriented ByStar model, when you control the thermostat in your own house, that can all happen as a ByStar intra-edge application without loss of privacy and autonomy.

17.8   BISOS Model of Platform Universality and Software-Service Continuums

Earlier we made several points about the universality of BISOS. We pointed out that BISOS inherits Debian's universality, and that our design philosophy includes relying on a singular Unix with full cohesion.

We have Service-Side BISOS for creation of internet services and we have Usage-Side BISOS for usage of internet services. These two create the BISOS software-service continuum. This is very powerful because the two sides are very consistent. This is depicted in Figure 17.5.

Note in Figure 17.5 that although the lowest layer (hardware) of the two stacks is very different, most of the rest of the stack is very common. Also note that on the top parts, capabilities are complimentary based on the common lower layers.

The degree of consistency and cohesion that this universality creates if far superior to what exists today in the proprietary American digital ecosystem.

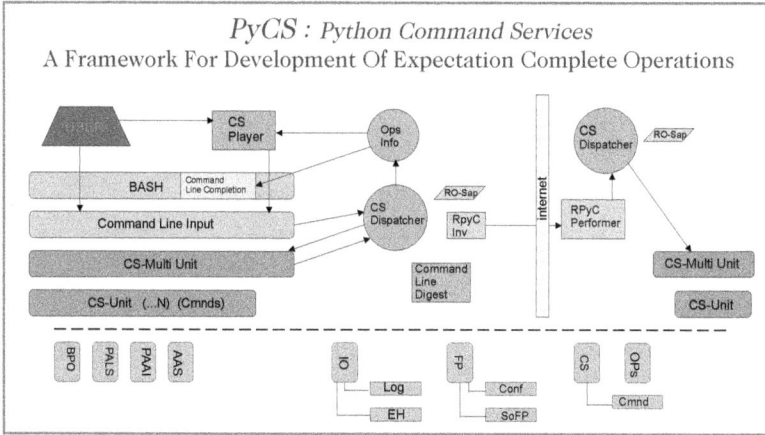

Figure 17.6: BPyF (BISOS Python Platform) and PyCS

17.9 PyCS: BISOS's Integration Framework

BISOS is largely focused on configuration and integration of related software packages towards creation of consistent services. This is typically done with "scripts" that augment the software packages in a consistent way. By scripts, we mean programs that are executed at command line. At times we also need to build Remote Operations (RO) to accommodate remote invocation of central services.

There are three fundamental important choices to be made:

1. What programming language should we use for integration?

2. What command-line framework should we use?

3. What Remote Operations (Web Services, REST, Micro Services) framework should we use?

BISOS primarily uses Python and some Bash for scripting.

There are various Python frameworks for command-line and web services. These include click, FastAPI, Flask, Django, RPyC and various others. None of these provide a comprehensive enough framework for BISOS. BPyF (BISOS Python Framework) is a comprehensive integration framework of BISOS that combines existing capabilities from various Python frameworks.

As depicted in Figure 17.6, BPyF consists of five major parts.

- Common facilities — logging, io, error handling, etc.

- File Parameters (FP) and Schema of File Parameters — BISOS's data representation and configuration model

- PyCS: Python Command Services

- BISOS Abstractions

- CS-Units and CS-MultiUnits

In Figure 17.6, boxes under the dashed line represent various libraries. General purpose libraries (on the right side is light green) provide common facilities such as IO, logging, error handling and configuration management which are used throughout BISOS. Various libraries that represent BISOS abstractions in Python such as BPOs, PALS and PAAI. These are shown on the left side in darker green.

For data representation, BISOS uses its own model called File Parameters. The equivalent functionality of File Parameters is often provided by Yaml and Json in typical open-source software packages.

PyCS is rooted in the model of Expectation Complete Operations (ECO), which allows for local invocation of an ECO to map to command-line invocation and remote invocation of an ECO to map to the microservices model and Remote Operations. This universality of ECOs allows for command-line facilities to become microservices.

Facilities for command line invocation are depicted above the dashed line, on the left side of "internet". Facilities in support of service (Remote Operation) performers are depicted above the dashed line, on the right side of "internet".

Expectation complete operations are specified and implemented in CS-Units. A CS-Multi-Unit represents a collection of CS-Units. Notice that CS-Unit and CS-Multi-Unit boxes are replicated on both sides of "internet". This indicates that both commands and remote operations map to expectation complete operations.

Each ECO is capable of describing everything expected from the operation in full detail which includes all typing information. The information in Expectation Complete Operation includes:

- Name of the operation

- All input parameters

  - List of optional and mandatory parameters

  - List of positional arguments

  - Stdin expectations

- All outcome parameters

  - All result parameters

  - All error parameters

The information of expectation complete operation then maps to command-line verbs, parameters and arguments, and similarly for remote operations. The list of available verbs is specified by the CS-Multi-Unit. Since CS-Multi-Units are capable of describing all of the expectations of all of their operations, very powerful automated user interfaces for invocation of operations can be built. The "CS Player" box in Figure 17.6 illustrates that.

Remote operations are implemented using RPyC. RPyC or Remote Python Call, is a transparent library for symmetrical remote procedure calls, clustering, and distributed-computing. Use of RPyC is depicted with the line going through the vertical box labeled "internet". Names used by invokers and performers are shown in the boxes labeled "RO-Sap" (Remote Operation Service Access Point).

PyCS framework provides a solid foundation for transformation of software into services and integration of software and services in BISOS.

17.10   ByStar Libre-Halaal Emacs user Environment (Blee)

Blee, ByStar Libre-Halaal Emacs Environment, is ByStar's primary usage environment. It is fully integrated with BISOS and Blee is aware of all ByStar conceptual constructs.

Conventional OS wisdom calls for separation of OS functionality from user-interface/usage-environment. But BISOS is not a traditional OS and Emacs is not a traditional usage-environment.

The concepts of universal platform and software-service-continuum that we presented have ramifications on usage and user experience. ByStar services can thus be greatly enhanced by providing the user with a "matched" environment— a user environment that is closely integrated with the service. This provides the user with features and capabilities that go far beyond what is possible using the traditional generic browser access.

By fully integrating BISOS and Blee, we accomplish a degree of cohesion and conviviality within the ByStar Digital Ecosystem that is absent in the American internet environments. Blee is significantly more broad and sophisticated than other usage environments.

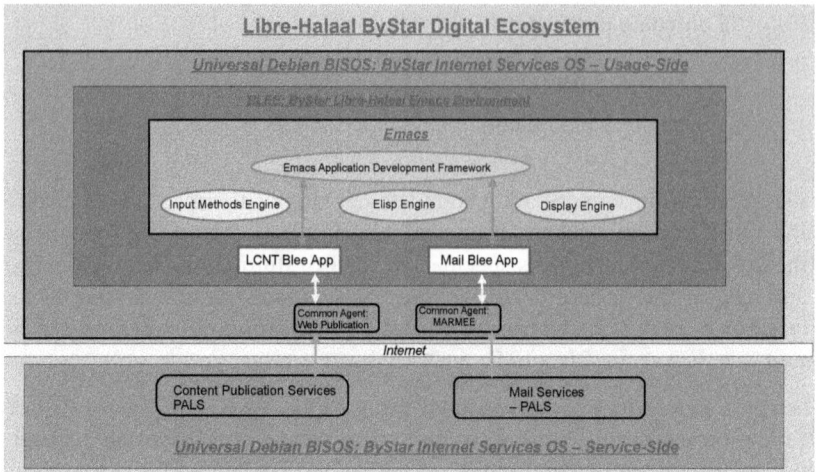

Figure 17.7: A Blee Centric Perspective Of By* Digital Ecosystem

In Figure 17.7 we depict that Blee is part of BISOS and that Blee includes Emacs. Think of Figure 17.7 as a containment hierarchy. The Libre-Halaal ByStar Digital Ecosystems contains both Usage-Side BISOS platforms and Service-Side BISOS platforms. The Usage-Side BISOS platform contains Blee. And Blee contains Emacs.

Emacs is a 40-plus years old editor centered usage environment, with a Lisp engine at its core and an extremely powerful display and editing engine in its nucleus. Emacs is one of the oldest Free Software in continuous use. Over the past 40 plus years, sophisticated engineers have added support for anything and everything to Emacs. Emacs's well designed fundamental abstractions make it the most convivial usage environment. Emacs is a multi-lingual editor that supports most human languages. But out of the box, Emacs is clunky and difficult to use.

Blee serves two purposes:

1. Blee integrates with BISOS and ByStar services and ByStar concepts.

2. Blee makes Emacs less clunky and easier to use without losing any of Emacs's conviviality.

Figure 17.7 depicts that Emacs contains a very powerful display engine, a very powerful Lisp engine, a very powerful input methods engine and a very powerful applications development framework. Emacs is primarily known as a textual environment. But it is more than that. Emacs is now capable of handling multimedia (images/audio/video) as well. Emacs's display engine supports bidirectional (bidi) text and is fully multilingualized. Emacs supports

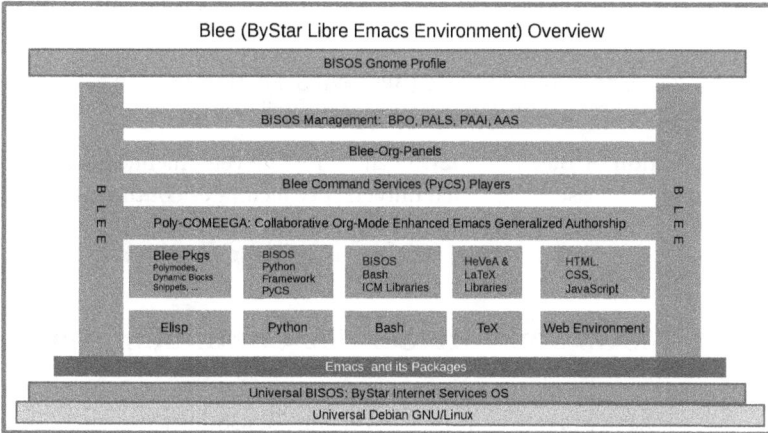

Figure 17.8: Overview of Blee Features

input methods for many human languages. Emacs's Lisp engine and its applications development framework allow for convenient development and customization of applications.

Blee builds on Emacs.

Figure 17.8 shows some of the salient features of Blee. For each of the programming languages of BISOS (Python, Bash, Elisp, LaTeX, Web environment and C/C++) Blee provides Interactive Development Environments (IDEs) that go beyond the language and include the frameworks and libraries of BISOS.

All coding and all writing in BISOS is based on a model called: COMEEGA (Collaborative Org Mode Enhanced Emacs Generalized Authorship).

COMEEGA is the inverse of Literate Programming, where code is written in native programming mode and then augmented with comments and docstrings in org-mode. COMEEGA provides the necessary tools to switch between native-mode and org-mode conveniently and is used in BISOS and Blee to ensure a high degree of consistency.

The usage of BISOS's Integration Framework (PyCS) described in Section 17.9 is facilitated in Blee through Blee Command Services Players. Each Command Service, whether it is a command-line or a remote-operation (microservice), is expectations complete and can be run more conveniently through Blee.

Of course, all of BISOS and Blee is self-documented. The documentation takes the form of Blee-Org-Panels which take the form of related org-files. Unlike typical documentation, Blee Org Panels are active. You can modify, configure and customize BISOS and Blee from within Blee-Org-Panels. Additionally,

Blee-Org-Panels can be used by users to organize their own information and applications.

All of the key abstractions of BISOS (BPO, PALS, PAAI, AAS), can be managed through Blee.

The combination of Blee and BISOS fully wraps development, management and usage of ByStar services. Such universality facilitates continuous growth of ByStar.

17.11   BISOS Software-Service Continuum Apps

Thus far, we have provided an overview of the BISOS infrastructure. Based on these, there are various capabilities that the owner-user can profit from. In BISOS, we call these capabilities "Software-Service Continuum Applications" (SSCA).

As described in Section 17.8 — BISOS Model of Platform Universality and shown in Figure 17.5, part of the capability is realized in software on the user side and part of the capability may realized on the services side. Since both the user-side and the service-side are based on the universal BISOS platform the resulting combined capability is consistent and flexible.

There are many BISOS software-service continuum applications and the model is open ended. There is an SSCA for genealogy, for photo galleries, and much more.

In BISOS, Software-Service Continuum Applications have a common structure. They typically consist of a three layered stack.

1. BISOS-Svc-Layer: BISOS Services Layer runs as a service-provider and interacts with the BISOS-Sw-Layer.

2. BISOS-Sw-Layer: BISOS Software Layer that facilitates work of Blee-SSCA-Agent and interacts with BISOS-Svc-Layer.

3. Blee-SSCA-Agent: Emacs-Lisp Code of Blee which the user interacts with.

The general model of interactions between BISOS-Sw-Layer and BISOS-Svc-Layer is typically that of Remote Operations where BISOS-Sw-Layer assumes the invoker role and BISOS-Svc-Layer assumes the performer role.

There are two BISOS software-service continuum applications that are foundational. These are email processing and content generation and self-publication.

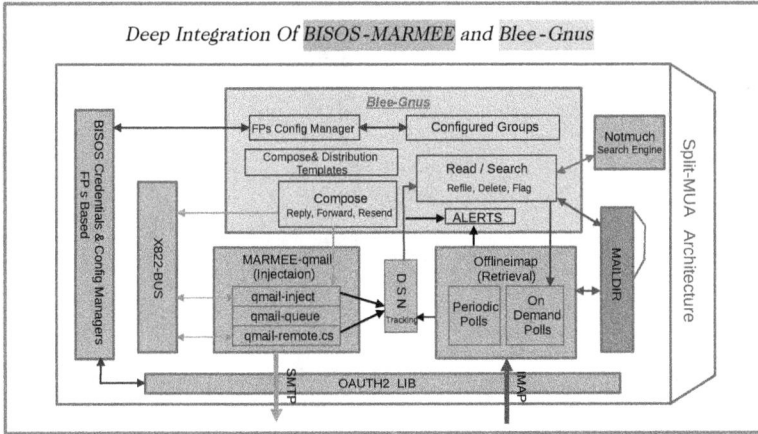

Figure 17.9: Blee-Gnus and MARMEE as a Split-MUA

17.11.1 BISOS Email Software-Service Continuum App

Email is a foundational application. BISOS Email SSCA is structured as follows: The Blee-SSCA-Agent for email is called Blee-Gnus. The BISOS-Sw-Layer is called MARMEE (Multi-Account Resident Message Exchange Environment). BISOS-Svc-Layer is called BISOS-Mail-Service.

Figure 17.9 depicts Blee-Gnus and MARMEE in the context of split-MUA (Mail User Agent) Blee-Gnus is the usage environment and MARMEE addresses mail protocols processing. Gnus is a very flexible mail processing environment which is integrated into Emacs.

BISOS uses a modified version of qmail called BISOS-qmail as the MTA (Mail Transfer Agent). When used it as a traditional MTA, we refer to it as PALS-qmail. And on the usage side we call it MARMEE-qmail. For incoming mail within MARMEE, BISOS uses offlineimap.

It is possible to use MARMEE and Blee-Gnus to access other email services. This is done through configuration of an AAS (Abstracted Accessible Service). For example, in addition to ByStar email, an owner-user can also access her gmail account with Blee-Gnus.

17.11.2 BISOS Content Generation and Self-Publication

BISOS software-service continuum application for content generation and self-publication is called LCNT (Libre Content).

The content generation capabilities of LCNT are akin to Microsoft-Word and

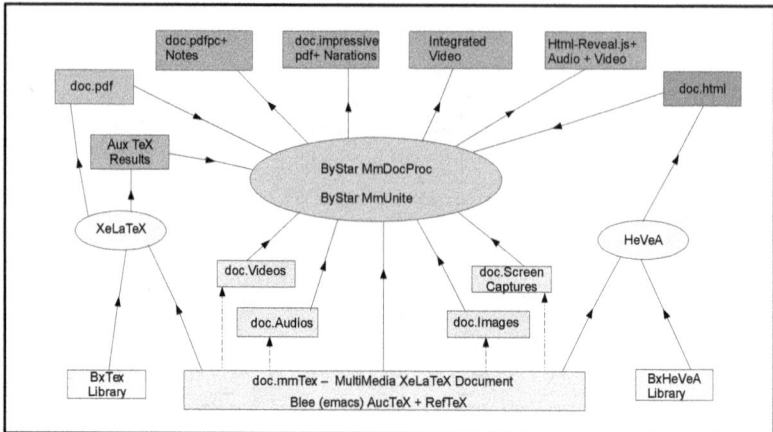

Figure 17.10: ByStar Multimedia Document Authorship And Generation

PowerPoint. But the model of content generation in BISOS is very different from Microsoft-Word and Microsoft-PowerPoint. We use LaTeX for document processing and COMEEGA-Blee for authorship.

A pictorial overview of multi-media content generation is provided in Figure 17.10. A single LaTeX source file is used to embed text, images, audio and video. This single source file is then processed in a variety of ways with a variety of tools including XeLaTeX and HeVeA to produce a variety of outputs including pdf and html. Multimedia frames/slides are then disposed using reveal.js.

BISOS-LCNT also includes facilities for self-publication where the above mentioned generated content can be pushed to owner-user's web sites and can also be syndicated.

17.12   Privacy, Security and Regulatory Ramifications of BISOS

Technological design of BISOS is very different from the technological design of proprietary American internet application services.

BISOS capabilities revolve around the abstraction of the individual and its belongings and delivery of possession and control of those abstractions to the individual. In BISOS, you own and possess your own data and you can own and possess your own services.

BISOS's philosophy is privacy by design.

Privacy by design is the antithesis of the proprietary American internet application services model, which is based on surveillance by design. Surveillance by design leads to centralized architectures and control, while privacy by design architecture leads to distributed architectures and autonomous control.

BISOS's fundamental design has immense security ramifications. Combinations of BPOs, PALS and service recreations capabilities of BISOS render many traditional security models inapplicable. In conjunction with being transferable, autonomous Libre Services are very easily recreatable. In many instances, upon detection of intrusion (or even periodically), after capturing the context of an exploit, a fresh new service replaces the contamination. All of this can be automated.

Since proprietary American internet application services are fundamentally designed for surveillance, the needed societal regulations are complex and ineffective. Since ByStar and BISOS are fundamentally designed for privacy, societal regulations are very simple and effective. ByStar is designed to be self-regulating. ByStar promotes proactive regulations as opposed to the current model of reactive regulations. The engineers have done the work. The politicians just need to understand. The bulk of the needed regulations can amount to exclusive use of PALS Libre Services as defined in Section 15.2.3.1 — Definition of Possession-Assertable Libre Services.

17.13 ByStar and Uses of BISOS

The specific purpose of BISOS is to facilitate the creation of Libre-Halaal ByStar Digital Ecosystem.

Let's see how ByStar uses BISOS to realize the underlying model and capabilities of the Libre-Halaal ByStar digital ecosystem.

- ByStar is about redecentralization of the internet. Control and ownership is transferred from central corporations to distributed individuals (as autonomous entities). Rise-of-the-middle model is rejected in favor of the autonomous edges model.

  BISOS was designed for all of that.

- ByStar software and internet services are un-owned/publicly-owned and internally transparent.

  BISOS 'is Libre-Halaal software subjected to AGPL. The entirety of ByStar Individual Services can be reproduced based on their available sources.

- Broadly speaking, ByStar services fall into these 3 categories:

1. ByStar Individual (Possession-Assertable/Autonomous) Services.

2. ByStar Content Syndication Services.

3. ByStar Facilitated Direct and Assisted Inter-Autonomous Interaction Services.

BISOS PALS address (1) and (3). BISOS's Libre Content (LCNT) addresses (2).

- ByStar individual services represent real individuals in the real world. In ByStar, real individuals have real autonomy, real control and real ownership of their own ByStar individual services. ByStar individual services are edge-oriented and can be externally-hosted or self-hosted. When externally hosted, ByStar individual services are regulated to be portable and possession-assertable. For example, Mohsen's ByStar individual services is:
mohsen.1.banan.byname.net.
You can have your own as: first.last.byname.net. Since you own your domain and since you can fully possess the service and your data at will, you have real autonomy.

  BISOS PAAI is designed to support deep domain names and PALS are transferable.

- ByStar individual services are "Possession-Assertable". A portable hosted service can be transferred to the individual who owns it where the individual becomes her own Application Service Provider. For example, people can run their own fully private email servers in their own houses. Just like Hillary Clinton.

  Some early examples of ByStar possession-assertable individual service factory domains are: ByName.net, ByFamily, BySMB, ByMemory, ByAlias, ByWhere, ByAuthor and ByArtist.

- Direct inter-autonomous relations such as Facebook style photo sharing are accomplished through the individual's own possession-assertable authorization services (individualized OAuth services). Healthy equivalents of capabilities of typical social networks can be created with PALS authorization services where each individual uses his own OAuth service to grant access to his own resources.
BISOS-OAuth supports this.

- Syndication services such as Youtube style content publication are clearly regulated and integrated with ByStar content production capabilities of individual services. Some early examples of ByStar syndication services are: ByTopic, ByContent, ByLookup, ByEvent, BySource, ByBinary, BySearch.

- Facilitated inter-autonomous interaction services such as dating, auction and trade services, are clearly regulated and well integrated with ByStar identity services. Some early examples of ByStar inter-autonomous facilitated interaction services are:
  `ByInteraction, ByHookUp, ByEntity`.

- ByStar also functions as a hierarchical registrar. For example, Mohsen Banan's registration of
  `mohsen.1.banan.byname.net` with the `byname.net` registrar results in ownership of
  `mohsen.1.banan.byname.net` by Mohsen Banan. This domain registration is independent of the service provider that is hosting the portable and possession-assertable individual service. The combination of the portable owned domain and the portability of publicly-owned ByStar individual services allows for transparent transfer of an individual service from one hosting service to another hosting service. This accomplishes the equivalent of Wireless Local Number Portability. Such fundamental user freedoms are absent in the American internet.

  BISOS PALS are portable and transferable.

- ByStar is mostly self-regulated. Upon assertion by the user-owner, the ByStar individual service provider must fully and permanently delete the possession-asserted service and all her data. Or otherwise, ab initio let the owner know that her data will be maintained. Within applicable jurisdictions, ByStar service providers must comply with Lawful Interception (LI) and satisfy regulatory requirements and legal obligations towards Law Enforcement Agencies. Syndication and facilitated inter-autonomous relation providers are subject to known and clear regulations and restrictions.

Part V

Formulation of Libre-Halaal Oriented Societal Policies

Chapter 18

Societal Adoption of Libre-Halaal Strategies

At societal scale, having recognized that the Western IPR regime is fundamentally fraudulent, there are two basic strategies that we can adopt to attempt to cure our societies.

1. **Inside of IPR Libre-Halaal Strategies.**

   Inside of IPR, we can emphasize public copyright licenses and invest in the FOSS and copyleft content. We can cultivate the Libre Services models and frameworks inside of the existing Western IPR regime. Such approaches are practical and will produce some positive outcomes. Such strategies are insufficient to have a material impact on the health of society. In a sense, this has been and is the status quo in America and in the West and the rest of the world.

   The main problem with the inside of IPR Libre-Halaal strategy is that in parallel with the Libre-Halaal positive progress, there will also be negative IPR based progress. The dominant negative IPR based progress will render the minor positive Libre-Halaal based progress irrelevant.

2. **Outside of IPR Libre-Halaal Strategies.**

   Outside of IPR, at societal scale, we can fully reject the Western IPR regime and call for the abolition of IPR. Avoid the IPR related agreements in the likes of WIPO, Berne Convention, WTO, TRIPS, GATT, GATS and the rest. Consider patent and copyright laws invalid and instead create other laws for proper governance of polyexistentials. This can result in fundamental change and if done properly can be a cure to the problems that we are seeing in the Western IPR model. But it can be very costly.

Costs of outside of IPR Libre-Halaal strategies will likely take the form of vast economic trade sanctions. Western IPR regime is enforced through general trade agreements.

This simple perspective of focusing on just these two categories of strategies does involve some degree of oversimplification but is effective in helping with analysis and planning.

The problem with (1) — Inside of IPR Libre-Halaal Strategies — is that it is too limited and its impact is marginal. Yet its execution is straight forward, well established, and practical. Therefore, it should be well supported both in Western and Eastern societies.

The problem with (2) — Outside of IPR Libre-Halaal Strategies — is that it is difficult to execute as it demands becoming separate from the West. Westerners have fully merged intellectual property with the rest of the global trade agreements to such an extent that in practice rejecting IPR equates to full isolation and separation from the West. In many cases, adoption of (2) as a strategy amounts to a global uprising!

In this part, we will explore (2) — Outside of IPR Libre-Halaal Strategies — in Eastern societies. We don't believe that it is realistic to consider (2) viable in Western societies. In the West calling for abolition of IPR is mostly symbolic. In Chapter 19 we focus on Western strategies. In Chapter 20 we focus on strategies for Eastern societies in general with Iran and China as special cases.

Depending on how a society is structured and its belief system, there are certain things that it can do well and there are things that it cannot do so well and there are things that it simply cannot do.

IPR is a keystone ingredient of structure and of the belief system of Western societies. It shapes the entire ecosystem of the West. It permits Westerners to do certain things very well and it prevents them from doing other things. Deterioration of digital autonomy and digital privacy is due to IPR as a keystone ingredient. Real digital autonomy and real digital privacy are not achievable in IPR based ecosystems.

In biology, a keystone species is an organism that helps define an entire ecosystem. Without its keystone species, the ecosystem would be dramatically different or cease to exist altogether. Keystone species have low functional redundancy.

As a parallel to biology, in sociology we consider the Western IPR a keystone ingredient. Without IPR, society would be very different. This has not happened anywhere yet and is therefore difficult to imagine. As we have shown, IPR is an ownership mistake. Without it, we will have a much healthier society.

It is at this scope and at this scale that we want to explore rejection of the Western IPR regime.

Things have been arranged a particular way. Recognizing the fact that things can be rearranged differently is not in the interest of most Westerners. David Graeber, In "The Utopia of Rules: On Technology, Stupidity, and the Secret Joys of Bureaucracy", [22], points to this in a number of occasions:

> "the ultimate, hidden truth of the world is that it is something that we make, and could just as easily make differently."
>
> ...
>
> "the hidden reality of human life is the fact that the world doesn't just happen. It isn't a natural fact, even though we tend to treat it as if it is — it exists because we all collectively produce it."
>
> ...
>
> "It's not just that some people get to break the rules — it's that loyalty to the organization [or system] is to some degree measured by one's willingness to pretend this isn't happening."

We want to rearrange things differently, so that society is no longer in conflict with the nature of polyexistentials.

All previous sections of this document have been towards this:

- In Part I — Polyexistence — , we introduced the concepts of monoexistence and polyexistence which make the fraudulence of Western IPR regime obvious.

- In Part II — The Mistake: Myths and Realities of the Western IPR Regime — , we described the Western IPR regime as a mistake and as a disease.

- In Part III — Contours of Cures — , we focused on cures.

- In Chapter 12 — Digital Non-Proprietary Movements — , we described that FOSS has produced a great deal.

- In Chapter 13 — Global Polyexistential Capitalism — , we described how Libre-Halaal Capitalism can be more efficient than the Western IPR regime in aggregate economic terms.

- In Chapter 16 — The Libre-Halaal ByStar Digital Ecosystem — , we provided an overview of the Libre-Halaal ByStar Digital Ecosystem as a moral alternative to the Proprietary-Haraam American digital ecosystem.

- In Chapter 14 — Ethical and Religious Cures — , we described how significant religious and ethical consensus on validity of Western IPR is.

Based on the above, we can now offer our thoughts on the societal adoption of the Libre-Halaal model. A deep understanding of the nature of polyexistentials leads to the realization that societal and national policies must be consistent and in harmony with the halaal manner-of-existence of polyexistentials.

In this part we focus on such cultivations with a narrow focus on digital ecosystems, software, content and internet services. In each section, we describe a societal action. The order of actions in these sections is not critical. Many can be done in parallel.

18.1   Private Sector and Public Sector Strategies

Based on the conceptual foundations that we have built in this book and the software and internet services of ByStar, we can now consider various private and public sector strategies. The outlined private sector strategies are both ethical and profit-oriented, while public sector strategies focus on the public good.

18.1.1   Private Sector Strategies

Private sector strategies that we propose are focused on making the adoption of ByStar widespread and profiting from it.

Primary ByStar offerings are: "Tangible Autonomy and Tangible Privacy." At a large scale, there is a demand for this. Facebook, Google, Microsoft and Apple are in the business of exploitation of autonomy and privacy. The business model required for offering true tangible autonomy and tangible privacy is very different from traditional current practices.

The nature of the business of ByStar Libre-Halaal internet application services is such that it demands large amounts of investment. Dynamics of increasing returns are at work. In theory, based on the existing Venture Capitalist (VC) frameworks, ByStar can receive the investments that it needs if the Venture Capitalists were to understand that rejection of traditional copyright and patents are an essential ingredient of the ByStar business plan. ByStar software and services can further be cultivated based on the existing software public licenses model as "Inside of IPR Libre-Halaal strategies."

But that requires an enlightened Venture Capitalist who would recognize that in addition to being an ethics-oriented book, what he is reading is also a very large, complex and sophisticated business plan.

To the extent that Venture Capitalists are an audience for our open business plan, we know that talking morality to a Venture Capitalist is like talking chastity to a prostitute. From the perspective of a Venture Capitalist, morality *per se* is of no interest whatever. But the moral dimension is real and is an essential component of our marketing strategy, and from the perspective of an intelligent Venture Capitalist, this is what matters.

Our motivations in building ByStar include addressing our responsibilities with respect to the engineering profession. But, clearly venture capitalists have no responsibilities in the context of their profession. It is all just about money. And, in that context, for a serious and complex plan like ours, there are good VCs and there are bad VCs.

If we show disrespect to Venture Capitalists in our communications, this is part of the execution of our marketing plan. Only the Venture Capitalist who understands this entangled strategy fully—that being held in contempt as a Venture Capitalist represents an investment opportunity—is a suitable investor candidate for our open business plan which we mentioned in Section 13.8 – Libre-Halaal ByStar Digital Ecosystem Open Business Plan of Chapter 13 – Global Polyexistential Capitalism.

Furthermore, an intelligent Venture Capitalist would recognize that adoption of ByStar by the public sector as an "Outside of IPR Libre-Halaal Strategy" augments the potential market. See Section 18.9 – Adoption of Libre-Halaal Digital Ecosystems – for more details.

18.1.2 Public Sector Strategies

The nature of polyexistentials demands more from the public sector. Libre-Halaal polyexistentials lead to public goods and cultivation and administration of public goods falls mostly in the public sector domain.

We devote the remainder of this Part to public sector strategies.

18.2 Build Consensus on Invalidity of IPR

Earlier in this book, we established that the concept of Western IPR is fundamentally invalid. However, providing proper logic on a subject to a reader is different from creating societal consensus on that subject. Each society needs to arrive at that conclusion on its own and through its own processes. Books such as this can help, but they are not sufficient.

Even in an authoritarian society, it is not necessary to arrive at invalidity and the need for abolishment of IPR through decrees. IPR is invalid and people can get to that conclusion through independent thinking and discussions. They simply need to be guided.

Part one of this book established invalidity of IPR. In Part two, we debunked most arguments made in favor of IPR. The references section of this book includes a large number of books and articles that recognize invalidity of IPR. But, at societal scale, in the West none of these will have a material impact. The reason why Western societies are not convinced is because they are vested in it. It is not in their interest to understand it.

Moslem societies can arrive to that consensus both through public discussions and through discussions among sources-of-imitation. Imam Khomeini's logic is crisp and fully aligns with our logic. We have pointed to this in Parts two and three of this book.

The Chinese have done many studies. Chinese academics know that there is no evidence to support that IPR is good for economy or for innovation.

Any society wishing to arrive at the consensus on invalidity of IPR should encourage public discussions on this topic on national TV, national radio and elsewhere. Keep in mind that the burden of proof should be on those who advocate for IPR.

18.3   Outside of IPR Libre-Halaal Strategies

Right now, many people think that making illegal copies of copyrighted material is unethical. When there is societal consensus on invalidity of IPR, it is the copyright law which is properly viewed as unethical. Copying is your natural right. With that implied mindset in place, there is a great deal more that can be done.

Establishing societal consensus on invalidity of IPR is one thing, acting on that consensus is another.

Execution of "Inside Of IPR Libre-Halaal Strategies" are well established and relatively straight forward but they will not bring about material results.

Outside of IPR Libre-Halaal strategies revolve around the notion that all models of governance of all polyexistentials should be Libre-Halaal. From that standpoint, all existing public proprietary polyexistentials can then also be regarded as Libre-Halaal polyexistentials.

Once societal consensus on invalidity of IPR has been reached and when the choice for execution of outside of IPR Libre-Halaal strategies has been made, we consider that society an "outside of IPR society." For outside of IPR societies, all existing public proprietary polyexistentials of all nations become unrestricted. In other words, every existing book, every song, every movie and use of all know-hows become unrestricted and public goods.

In the context of outside of IPR Libre-Halaal strategies, we then call the process of making polyexistentials freely available to the public of outside of IPR societies as "rescuing" the proprietary polyexistentials. It then makes good sense to create public libraries of rescued proprietary polyexistentials.

18.3.1 Public Libraries of Rescued Proprietary Polyexistentials

Imagine this. Let's say that Iran, Cuba, Russia and China were to achieve societal consensus on invalidity of IPR and be ready to exit all copyright and patent western trade conventions and agreements. In other words, let's say that part of the world was ready to recognize the invalidity of IPR and act on it.

It would then make good sense for that part of the world to individually or collectively create very large libraries that include all existing technical papers, books, music and movies without regard to any copyright restrictions. The access to such libraries could then be free-of-charge or very inexpensive for all of that part of the world — as copyright royalties and restrictions are no longer applicable.

What economic ramifications would this have on the American and Western models? It is logical to expect that Americans and Westerners would fight for keeping the status quo. But then, they would be fighting nature.

Unrestricted access to polyexistentials is part of their nature and "rescuing" proprietary polyexistentials is in harmony with nature.

18.3.2 Pure Libre-Halaal Digital Ecosystems

Earlier we introduced the theory of Libre-Halaal digital ecosystems in general and the Libre-Halaal ByStar digital ecosystem in particular. Those introductions were very deliberately positioned as inside of IPR Libre-Halaal strategies.

In other words the Libre-Halaal ByStar digital ecosystem is designed and implemented to co-exist in parallel with the proprietary American digital ecosystem. In the inside of IPR Libre-Halaal model use of ByStar improves autonomy and privacy but is clunky, as common usage will likely be mixed with parts of the proprietary American digital ecosystem.

For outside of IPR societies, the outside of IPR Libre-Halaal model presents the possibility of implementing pure Libre-Halaal digital ecosystems. With "Public Libraries of Rescued Proprietary Polyexistentials" in place, outside of IPR societies first absorb all relevant proprietary polyexistentials. Next, importation of all proprietary software and all proprietary internet services needs to be restricted. Then Libre-Halaal digital ecosystems such as ByStar can be

adopted at societal scale to address all digital needs of the outside of IPR society. It is only at that point which we can achieve the full benefits of "pure"
Libre-Halaal digital ecosystems.

18.4 Evaluate Merits of National Withdrawals From IPR Agreements

The ultimate national action for rejection of the Western IPR regime is with-
drawal from the many West dominated global trade agreements. Any society
daring to fully reject the Western IPR regime will be subjected to the full wrath
of America and Western sanctions.

IP is an integral part of many West dominated global trade agreements and
rejection of Western IPR regime results in being removed from many global
trade agreements. This may not be in national interest.

Each society contemplating the merits of withdrawals from IPR agreements
faces a trade-off analysis.

On the negative side are Western sanctions and wrath of America.

On the positive side by getting out of the Western IPR regime, the rejecting
nation gains the ability to organize and redeliver large amounts of available
content and move towards implementation of pure Libre-Halaal digital ecosystems.

But then perhaps this should not be viewed as a trade-off analysis at all. Perhaps morality, ethics, and harmony with nature should trump the trade-off
analysis.

18.5 Promulgate the Libre-Halaal Model for National Governance of Polyexistentials

Polyexistentials will continue to dominate the future. Many crucial national
policies need to be made to deal with polyexistentials.

Once illegitimacy of IPR has been established, abolishment of the Western IPR
regime should not lead to anarchy. Recognizing the importance of polyexistentials, at the highest level of societal governance — The Leader, sources-of-
imitation, President, National Legislators — need to take on the question of:
What is the halaal manner-of-existence of polyexistentials?

We answered that question earlier, briefly:

- For each polyexistential (digitals, software, movies, pharmaceuticals, etc.) Halaal manner-of-existence of that polyexistential should be determined by ethicists (The Leader, sources-of-imitation, etc.) and the profession of that polyexistential. Clear definitions for Halaal manner-of-existence of each polyexistential is needed.

- For Software in particular, we have offered our criteria for halaal manner-of-existence of software as "Libre-Halaal Software" as outlined in Section 4.6.2 — Libre-Halaal Software — Halaal Manner-of-Existence of Software and at http://www.HalaalSoftware.org

- For Content in particular, we have offered our criteria for halaal manner-of-existence of content as "Libre-Halaal Content" as outlined in Section 15.2.2 — Definition of Libre-Halaal Content.

- For Internet Application Services in particular, we have offered our criteria for halaal manner-of-existence of internet services as "Libre-Halaal Internet Services" as outlined in Section 4.6.3 — Halaal Manner-of-Existence of Internet Services and at http://www.LibreServices.org

In the Western IPR model, this is the equivalent of saying that all software should be subjected to the AGPL and all content should be subject to the Attribution-ShareAlike license and that there are no other licenses and that by default all software and all content is as such. Some Westerners already consider this as the desired ultimate ethical environment.

In the inside of IPR strategies, some individuals may subject their work to Libre-Halaal licenses through which we end up with some Libre-Halaal polyexistentials. In the outside of IPR strategies, all polyexistentials are Libre-Halaal by default.

18.6   Regulate Delivery of Libre Services Based on Types of Libre Services

For internet application services, it is not sufficient to just define the proper manner-of-existence of internet application services as Libre Services. Their delivery needs to be regulated.

It is also necessary to constrain the operation of various types of Libre Services through regulations. For example, a PALS (Possession Assertable Libre Services) operator should transfer all data to its owner and then destroy all copies of data when demanded by the owner. This should be mandated through regulation.

For other types of Libre Services there are other constraints imposed on the operator. See Section 15.2.3 — Definition of Libre-Halaal Internet Application Services for additional information.

In the inside of IPR strategies, imposition of constraints such as PALS can only take the form of service agreements similar to existing Service Level Agreements (SLAs). Such a model has little chance of becoming widespread at a societal level unless society values the importance and benefits of autonomy and privacy.

In the outside of IPR strategies, since proper manner-of-existence of internet application services as Libre Services are already established/legislated, additional constraints on the Libre Service operators through legislation is practical.

There are parallel types of legislation in the monoexistential realm. For example, for Safety Deposit Boxes in State of Washington, we have:

> RCW [Revised Code of Washington] 22.28.030
>
> Exercise of due care required.
>
> Whenever any safe deposit company shall let or lease any vault, safe, box or other receptacle for the keeping or storage of personal property such safe deposit company shall be bound to exercise due care to prevent the opening of such vault, safe, box or receptacle by any person other than the lessee thereof, or his or her duly authorized agent, and the parties may provide in writing the terms, conditions, and liabilities in the lease. Authorized agent as used in this section includes, but is not limited to, a duly appointed personal representative, an attorney-in-fact, a special representative, or a trustee acting under a revocable living trust.

In the mid 1980s, among System Administrators, we used to have ethical conventions such as "Thou shalt not snoop". Simply put, it meant: Do not spy on another person's computer data.

In the 2020s, we are advocating for formal regulation of the operation of Libre Services.

18.7   Replace the Patent Office
With the Invention Registration Office

Patents and copyright work very differently. With regard to copyright, we are saying that it should be fully abolished. The copying rules are defined by proper manner-of-existence of specific polyexistentials at societal level and attribution for creation can be accomplished through public ledgers.

Patents are wrong as a form of ownership but not as a mechanism for attribution. Patents enforce attribution through ownership. We want to abolish the ownership aspect but keep the attribution aspect.

It makes good sense to have a registration for inventions which attributes inventions to inventors.

Further, in the inside of IPR strategies phase, it makes sense to convert internal registrations into external patents.

18.8 Create Infrastructure for an Attribution Based Economy (ABE)

In Section 13.7 — Attribution Based Economics (ABE) – Not Ownership we described the concept of Attribution Based Economy (ABE).

By rejecting Western IPR we are rejecting the ownership of polyexistentials. In the Libre-Halaal model, attribution of polyexistentials to their creators (authors) is essential. Economic models that fairly evaluate the value of the polyexistential and the significance of various contributors in creation of the polyexistential need to be cultivated.

In the early days, governments need to play a role in creating the needed structures for the infrastructure of Attribution Based Economy.

18.9 Adoption of Libre-Halaal Digital Ecosystems

In Part IV — Libre-Halaal ByStar Digital Ecosystem, we present the contours of a specific Libre-Halaal digital ecosystem, named: "The Libre-Halaal ByStar Digital Ecosystem".

The natural scope of ByStar is global. ByStar can be deployed and used as an "Inside of IPR Libre-Halaal Strategy." The copyright public license for software of the ByStar services is AGPL. Americans and Europeans can deploy and use ByStar services as they use other internet application services. With ByStar they get real and tangible autonomy and privacy.

Use of ByStar as an "Outside of IPR Libre-Halaal Strategy" is a great deal more effective. In the ByStar model each nation and each culture adopts and nationalizes the publicly owned (humanity owned) global ByStar digital ecosystem software consistent with its own values — while preserving the universal ByStar model of autonomy and privacy of the individual. This is very different from the proprietary American model of exploitation, and this is also very different from national reactions and responses to the proprietary American model.

Let's take the case of email at societal scale inside of IPR model. In the proprietary American model, we have the likes of the central corporate owned and operated Gmail.com. As of 2023, Gmail is the most popular email platform with over 1.8 billion users worldwide — and roughly a 30% market share. The overwhelming majority of Gmail users are outside of US — and American Google is watching over all of that. About 333.3 billion Gmail emails were sent and received daily in 2022.[50]

Let's consider what email can be at societal scale outside of the IPR model. In the Libre-Halaal ByStar digital ecosystem, email is realized as a PALS (Possession Assertable Libre Service). This means that each individual can own her own email service. She can choose to delegate operation of her email service to a service provider and have the equivalent convenience of Gmail. Or possess the services herself, like Hilary Clinton. The PALS model allows for that degree of transferability and transportability. Details of how PALS works are described in Section 15.2.3.1.

Further, let's consider what adoption of national email based on the PALS model of Libre-Halaal ByStar can look like. Let's take the hypothetical case of Iran. To make sure that every Iranian citizen has access to autonomous and private email, the Iranian government creates a domain for every citizen in the form of, say: `selNu.firstName.lastName.name.ir`. The selNu is a unique identifier that the government can assign — corresponding to national id-cards for example. The `selNu.firstName.lastName.name.ir` domain would now belong to the individual. The name-servers for that domain will be chosen and controlled by the individual (not the government). Free of charge, the Iranian government will provide PALS services for individuals who wish to have their email PALS service transferred in or out of the government provided PALS service. With her domain under her own control, the individual can now use the local-part of the email address syntax to create as many email addresses as she wishes. For example, `work@selNu.firstName.lastName.name.ir` or `school@....` These need not be the individual's only domain, similarly other domains and addresses can be used. For example, the author of this book has chosen to use `plpc-120033@mohsen.1.banan.byname.net` for matters related to this book.

Consider the differences between the proprietary American Gmail.com email service and the nationalized Libre-Halaal PALS based name.ir email service. Gmail.com is an opaque service, while name.ir is transparent. Gmail.com is central while name.ir is highly distributed. With gmail.com, your address is locked to the Gmail service. With name.ir your address is portable and transferable. Gmail.com is privacy crushing. Name.ir is privacy cherishing.

From a societal perspective, consider the email medium for say, a high school student. Should the rest of the world become like Americans and Westerners?

18.10   National Public Sector Libre-Halaal Policies and Strategies

Outside of America, the current software and internet application services landscape is a humiliating mess. Outside of America, American internet corporations function as the surveillance and propaganda arms of the U.S. government and its American values. As of 2022, almost 90% of Facebook's daily active users come from outside the US. When necessary, American internet corporations happily collaborate with the US government towards foreign espionage and foreign exploitations. American internet services cannot be fixed on its fringes, they should be avoided.

Earlier we recognized polyexistentials as public goods. Replacing the IPR model with the Libre-Halaal model demands much larger public sector involvement and investment in research and development.

For Eastern societies, the costs and consequences of not having a national polyexistential/digital policy are immense. In the absence of a national polyexistential/digital policy, the West dictates and the East must follow. Americans control the likes of Facebook's interpersonal communication conventions and Easterners conform.

When such fundamental aspects of human behavior are determined by the West, Eastern models and values are being crushed in due course. Having independent Eastern national polyexistential/digital policies is a matter of survival.

This matter of survival amounts to a "Models War". In the realm of polyexistentials, Western IPR and halaal manner-of-existence of polyexistentials are at war. The results of these models war at that basic level, can indirectly impact other significant aspects of life models.

18.10.1   Universal Linux Everywhere Strategies

Viability of Libre-Halaal software as a development model for creating large-scale, complex, relevant software systems has been established. GNU/Linux is a fully viable Libre-Halaal software alternative to the proprietary Microsoft Windows operating system.

Viewing Linux as a universal operating system, spanning embedded devices and handsets, as well as desktops and mainframes is very reasonable. Based on this, a unified "Universal Linux Everywhere Strategy" is the obvious strategy for implementation of the policy of "Exclusive Development and use of Libre-Halaal Software in Iran". If the public sector was to require the "Universal Linux Everywhere Strategy", the evolution of private sector could be expected.

18.10.2   Cultivation of National Debian Like Linux Distros

Amongst choices of Linux distributions, at this time Debian Gnu/Linux Distro is the obvious choice. We then need to establish a layer above Debian Gnu/Linux to form a national distro. This layer above Debian Gnu/Linux would have three primary purposes:

- Localize/nationalize the global Debian Gnu/Linux

- Create a common software base that would permit pointing to central national names and numbers authorities (e.g., perhaps alternate DNS root servers).

- Form a software foundation for building and use of consistent internet services such as ByStar.

In an ad-hoc fashion and in a limited sense this has been happening in various Eastern societies. The list below was compiled in 2017 and has not been fully verified in all respects.

China: The Chinese have been building the likes of Ubuntu Kylin as their Chinese OS.

China also has a Chinese version of all popular web services. Baidu for Google, Weibo for Twitter, 51.com for Facebook. The list is endless. It is not surprising that China has its own operating system Ubuntu/Debian Kylin. As the name suggests Kylin is based on Ubuntu with extensive support for the Chinese language. However, all of these are essentially in the spirit of responding to the Western model. Even China has not yet asserted its Digital Independence. That would require full rejection of the Western IPR regime.

Cuba: Cuba's national OS Nova is also based on Ubuntu/Debian.

North Korea: North Korea has its own national OS based on Linux and it goes by the name of Red Star OS. It has been under development since 2002. Since North Korea has been forced to be a closed society, there is not all that much information available on Red Star OS.

India: BOSS (Bharat Operating System Solutions) is a Debian based Linux OS being developed by India's C-DAC (a government owned organization for advanced computing development).

The Indian government has also adopted an Open Source policy to minimize its reliance on Microsoft. In fact, some state government have started to switch to open document format and BOSS Linux already.

Indonesia: The Research Center for Informatics Indonesian Institute of Sciences has developed IGOS Nusantra Linux to promote Linux in Indonesia.

Iran: In the first decade of 2000, Iran attempted to produce "Sharif Linux", which has since been abandoned as many of its developers took the "bus" and are now in Silicon Valley. Clearly an Iranian national OS is needed. There have also been various other attempts such as Parsix GNU Linux. Ghasedak OS, Jabir OS and XAMIN.

Russia: In Russia's private sector and military, there are several Linux based OS distributions including: ROSA, Astra Linux and Zarya OS (for military use), ALT Linux, Calculate Linux, Runtu and ReactOS.

Argentina: Canaima Linux is based on Debian.

By a "National OS" we mean a government supported, endorsed and even mandated (at a minimum in the public sector) software.

Building of a National OS should go well beyond localizing Linux. While localizing Linux is a local/national activity, moving towards a foundation for autonomy oriented National OS can be an Eastern strategy.

A National OS can permit, for example a society's own DNS servers, block chains and (Public Key Infrastructures) PKIs. A National OS can also be the foundational software on top of which consistent internet services can be built.

18.10.3 Full Adoption of Exclusive Development and Use of Libre-Halaal Software

What should be the software platform that we use?
What should be the software platform that we develop software for?

Use of Linux for everything and everywhere is very practical. Based on that, full adoption of the policy of exclusive development and use of Libre-Halaal software in Iran is quite reasonable.

Full adoption of exclusive development and use of Libre-Halaal software in Iran goes beyond just that mandate and also requires prohibition of public offers of proprietary-haraam software and proprietary-haraam internet services.

18.10.4 Nationally Directed Libre-Halaal Digital Research and Development

Justification for budgets and resources for nationally directed applied Libre-Halaal digital research would be very different when the nature of polyexistentials is deeply and broadly understood.

Deep understanding of polyexistence can make it clear that results of well directed applied Libre-Halaal digital research can produce results with large multiplier effects in economic, military, security and societal autonomy dimensions.

To facilitate development of Libre-Halaal Software, much Libre-Halaal software infrastructure needs to be cultivated.

There are well established patterns for establishing Libre-Halaal software infrastructure that can be mimicked. The Debian culture is one good example.

There are many such success stories that can be mimicked and collaborated with. Some such examples include Taiwan's ERSO and France's INRIA.

18.10.5   Transition Towards Prohibition of Import of Proprietary Software Based Products

Consider the use of Smart Phones. Smart Phones are mostly software. Towards the goals of autonomy, self-reliance and self-sufficiency; it makes good sense for us to require Smart Phones whose software is Libre-Halaal software.

Once we have adequate national Libre-Halaal Internet Services in place, we need to transition towards blocking Internet services whose manner-of-existence are haraam. Not just because of their content or their services, but because of their manner-of-existence.

18.11   Global Libre-Halaal Sector Collaborations

Polyexistentials are inherently non-territorial. The most effective way to cultivate polyexistentials is through global collaboration.

Over the past 3 decades we have seen various self-organizing engineering efforts that have produced significant results. One of these self-organizing engineering movements is Debian. Debian is two things: a complete and universal non-proprietary Operating System and a Community of People!

The philosophy of Debian as a community of people aligns very well with the Libre-Halaal philosophy. In the beginning, Debian consisted mostly of American software developers. Things have changed, Debian is no longer mostly American. It makes very good sense for Eastern societies to coalesce around Debian and fund it very heavily.

Americanists have been packing the likes of the Trans Pacific Partnership Agreement (TPPA) with Western IPR clauses which emphasize Copyright and

Patent enforcement in a good number of West-toxicated Asian countries and American satellite nations.

It makes good sense for Eastern societies that understand the Libre-Halaal strategy to create an Eastern front against the likes of WIPO (Western (not World) Intellectual Property Organization).

So, Eastern societies should unite and collaboratively adopt Libre-Halaal software and services development and usage policies. And we should also join forces with our Western FOSS brothers and sisters.

Chapter 19

Theoretical Western Societal Cures

All the tangible autonomy and privacy oriented capabilities and the engineering potentials of the ByStar Libre-Halaal Digital Ecosystem that we have described are publicly available to all. Americanists, Westerners and Easterners can profit from them equally.

But those tangible capabilities and engineering solutions cannot be considered societal cures unless societal leaders, policy makers and legislators buy into them.

In our model, in the end, the cure requires rejection of Western IPR regime and adoption of the Libre-Halaal model.

Is this a realistic possibility for the American society? We don't think so.

Dynamics of the established IPR regime and Americanism are deeply rooted and cannot be realistically changed in the foreseeable future in America. Americans have invested heavily in their IPR model, and it is not in their interest to recognize their mistakes.

While it is not realistic to imagine that the IPR regime would be abolished in the West in our lifetime, it is perfectly reasonable to expect that realizations of its fraudulence will continue to grow. The situation is similar to American slavery in the 19th century or the situation with guns and healthcare in the United States today.

With respect to autonomy and privacy, Western models in general and the American internet model in particular are fundamentally conflicted and contradictory. On the one hand, they promote the IPR regime that transfers more power and more control to corporations which in turn makes them better positioned to exploit the individual and her privacy. On the other hand, they come up with a day late and a dollar short type of regulations like the European General Data Protection Regulation (GDPR) or the Californian Consumer Privacy Act (CCPA) which fail to recognize that since data and service are usually intertwined, control and ownership of both should be transferred to the user — not just the data.

Westerners fail to understand that the IPR regime directly and indirectly diminishes autonomy and privacy of individuals. Real privacy demands real autonomy. Real autonomy demands that individual services be in full control of the individual. Full control of individual services requires that software and services be internally transparent and publicly owned. But IPR is an instrument of exclusivity and makes software and services internally opaque and corporate owned.

We can also walk through the ramifications of IPR on the individual's privacy in the other direction. IPR, as an instrument of exclusivity, empowers the corporation to exploit the individual's autonomy and privacy. We then end up exactly where we are, with American internet and surveillance capitalism. IPR and surveillance capitalism are directly linked.

While rejecting the Western IPR regime, the Libre-Halaal ByStar Digital Ecosystem can co-exist in parallel with the American internet. However, ByStar can thrive much better in societal environments that fully reject and abolish the Western IPR regime.

From the very beginning our main goals have been two fold:

1. Bring about the understanding that Western IPR is best framed as a societal disease

2. Offer realistic societal cures to the Western IPR disease

The metaphor of Disease is quite useful in that it also provides us metaphors of: Patient, Cure, Spreading, Symptoms, Patient Zero, Quarantine and Diagnosis.

Building on these metaphors, doctors know that there is not much that they can do if the patient is not willing to recognize that he is sick. In order to cure a disease, the patient needs to recognize that he is sick and he needs to desire to be healed. Americans and Americanists in particular and Westerners in general do not recognize a problem with their IPR. For now, most Americanists believe that Western IPR regime works well and that the rest of the world should follow them. Some of the Americanists who believe that there may be something wrong with IPR, also believe that the American model is very dynamic and is capable of correcting itself when needed. Those Americanists often willingly forget or whitewash their history.

In Section 9 — Americanism: Root of the IPR Mistake, we recognized patient zero from which the disease is spreading. Americanists reject our diagnosis of the Western IPR as a societal disease. In such a scenario, it is best that we avoid and neglect that patient.

Instead, it is best that we focus on preventing the spread of the disease and focus on curing those who are willing to recognize the disease and who can be persuaded to want to be cured. This is why we focus on cures of Eastern societies in the next chapter.

19.1   Formulation of Libre-Halaal Based National Policies in Western Societies

While America leads internet technology today, full adoption of Libre-Halaal ideology will likely be very difficult in America.

Simply put, it is naive to imagine that there is any hope that Libre-Halaal Software (or any form of non-proprietary software) can become a basis for formulation of national policies in any Western society.

This is because of a number of a reasons, including:

- Intellectual Property Rights regime has become an integral part of Western cultures. Even after it becomes obvious that the Western intellectual property rights regime is corrupt, economic interests will keep it in place. In many ways this parallels the history of Slavery in America.

- Western societies are primarily economically driven. Halaal and Haraam for anything, generally (if not always) remain fringe concepts.

- The Proprietary model is fully entrenched. And the course for using the proprietary model for internal and external exploitation is already fully charted.

In the West, there is a track record of how Libre-Halaal software and internet services fit into Western societies. Despite the advantages of being in harmony with nature, Linux has not been able to gain widespread adoption, except through economically driven bastardizations of Libre-Halaal software such as Appleization, Tivoization, and Androidization.

There is one aspect of Libre-Halaal software and Libre-Halaal internet services that is congruent with Western cultures. It is of course "freedom" oriented.

19.2   Neglecting the American Society

We don't consider rejection of the IPR regime and adoption of the Libre-Halaal model a viable possibility in America. For the American society, we have no specific suggestions and recommendations towards a cure. Unlike the rest of the civilized world, in America, market driven health care and TV advertised prescription drugs are the norm. Each of those TV advertised prescription drugs is for a set of patents. And none of that is even being recognized.

We will watch the evolution of the American society with respect to guns. Clearly the cure for IPR comes after the cure for persistent and common mass shootings.

Even then, within the Western IPR regime we fully intend to advocate the adoption of the Libre-Halaal ByStar Digital Ecosystems. Some Americans recognize the need for autonomy and privacy and for those, the Libre-Halaal ByStar Digital Ecosystems can be a solution.

We understand that some Americanists may be offended by the Eastern societal cures we discuss in the next chapter. However, as US citizens, we believe that activism in this area is in America's interest, as common support for the IPR regime is wrong. We expect that the American response to the Eastern scenarios that we suggest will likely be one of crushing them and possibly us. It is best to consider the ramifications of the scenarios that we are mentioning as natural. Fighting nature is not the right thing to do.

19.3   Can There be a Political West Sans America?

In Europe, in Japan, in South Korea and in India, TV advertisements for prescription drugs is illegal. Persistent mass shootings are also not common in those societies. So, in many ways the rest of the political West is different from America.

Could rejection of the IPR regime and adoption of the Libre-Halaal model be considered a viable possibility for the rest of the political West?

The answer to that question is very likely no as well. America will not permit it. Rejection of IPR regime requires separation from America.

19.3.1   Europe Sans America?

Philosophy, ethics and values of our French cousins are clearly different from our American friends. It could well be that the logic and directions that we describe in this book would resonate more with our French cousins.

It is difficult to say how deeply the Europeans have understood the harms of their Western IPR and Americanism. Most of what they say and do is imitations, reactions and band-aids.

Europeans have figured out that public sector investment in digital domain research is the right thing. So, there are research organizations such as Inria.

Shortly after that we get to Inria and Meta engaging in collaborative research. The French used to be able to recognize that things like Facebook should not even exist. What happened to that independent European thinking?

The Europeans think that the General Data Protection Regulation (GDPR) is the toughest privacy and security law in the world. That becomes kind of funny when you consider that:

> The US National Security Agency [NSA] tapped phone calls involving German chancellor Angela Merkel and her closest advisers for years [perhaps decades] and spied on the staff of her predecessors, according to WikiLeaks.

In this book, we propose a different approach to data privacy – different from that of tha GDPR regulations model. We believe that the best way to protect your data is to possess it yourself. Libre-Halaal regulations play an important role in this, as they provide the framework for Privacy Oriented Engineering. As an example, if your email service is Libre-Halaal and realized as a Possession Assertable Libre Service (PALS), then you are the only one who possesses your emails, both the data and the service.

Through the likes of the Libre-Halaal ByStar Digital Ecosystem, large American companies (Google) need not even possess our data (emails) — in which case much of GDPR is no longer needed. We are saying that IPR based models like Gmail should not exist. We are suggesting that Europeans should engage in some real root cause analysis. Adopting Libre-Halaal Digital Ecosystems at societal level involve rejection of the Western IPR regime.

There are some indications that many Europeans have come to recognize the fraudulence of the IPR regime. The key question is: separate from America, what is Europe's independent position on the IPR regime?

We are hoping that at some point the Europeans can grow a backbone. At what point could Europeans confront America and split on the topic of IPR?

19.3.2   What About the Non-Western Part of the Political West?

In 1989, Shintaro Ishihara (the then Minister of Transport) and Akio Morita (Sony co-founder and chairman) co-authored an essay titled: "The Japan That Can Say No: Why Japan Will Be First Among Equals" [30]. The essay argued that Japan should wean itself from its reliance on the United States and that Americans were guilty of anti-Japanese racism.

But then, in 2023 all the American military bases are still open in Japan and in South Korea.

When did the term "Intellectual Property" first enter the Japanese language? Was it a translation?

The key question is: separate from America, what is Japan's independent position on the Western IPR regime?

Chapter 20

Eastern Societal Libre-Halaal Strategies

In Chapter 18 — Societal Adoption of Libre-Halaal Strategies, we outlined a number of theoretical strategies that can be taken by any society to move towards cures against the Western IPR regime — which we view as a societal disease. There we introduced two basic strategies, "Inside of IPR Libre-Halaal Strategies" and "Outside of IPR Libre-Halaal Strategies".

In Chapter 19 — Theoretical Western Societal Cures, we described how for Western societies IPR cures are limited to "Inside of IPR Libre-Halaal Strategies" and that these cures are therefore quite weak. More than that can be done by Eastern societies.

Obviously, rejecting or abolishing Western IPR regime, has immense ramifications.

In a multi-polar world, it is realistic to recognize that IPR can become a tear-point among poles. So, ramifications of Polyexistential Capitalism in the West and outside of the West are very different. The business and economic impacts are fundamental and existential.

When viewed properly, Digital Capitalism as Americans know it can be turned upside-down. We have dedicated a chapter titled "Global Polyexistential Capitalism" to this topic. It is really only in the East that this can be done.

In this chapter, we focus on Eastern societies, with a particular emphasis on China and Iran — two strong Eastern cultures. We discuss both Inside and "Outside of IPR Libre-Halaal Strategies" which are outlined in In Chapter 18.

While much of this chapter focusses on China and Iran, similar strategies are applicable to any other Eastern society (Brazil, Indonesia, Malaysia, Cuba, etc.).

Our choice of Iran as a focus has several reasons. First, we are Iranian. Second, Iran is very well positioned to consider the bold positions that are required for proper adoption of policies towards becoming a Libre-Halaal software based society. Having chosen already to challenge Western neo-colonial agenda, Iranians can relatively easily conclude that the policies outlined in this section are in Iran's interest.

Our choice of China as a focus also has several reasons. China is big enough and powerful enough to in due course stand against the West and challenge the legitimacy of the Western IPR regime. The Chinese civilization is intrinsically more aligned with the Libre-Halaal model.

The Western IPR regime is a vulnerable economic system. Eastern sovereigns can do a number on Western IPR vulnerabilities. Doing so requires deep understandings of the flaws and vulnerabilities of the Western IPR regime and Libre-Halaal formulation of polyexistential national policies that unleash natural forces that work against the Western IPR regime.

20.1   Formulation of Libre-Halaal National Policies in Eastern Societies

Libre-Halaal software and Libre-Halaal Internet services have a much better chance of becoming a basis for formulation of national policies in Eastern societies.

This is because of a number of reasons including:

- Rejection of Western Intellectual Property Rights regime is easier and more beneficial to Eastern societies.

- Eastern societies are less economically driven and the general concept of halaal and haraam play a more significant role in Eastern societies.

- Proprietary software and Proprietary Internet services are used by the West as an instrument of exploitation and neo-colonialism against many Eastern societies in economic and political contexts. And whomever objects to America and the American model is swiftly subjected to American freedom and American democracy through Facebook and Twitter.

- Unowned Libre-Halaal Software provides an alternative to the Proprietary American software. The collaborative model of Libre-Halaal Software allows collective efforts to replace American Proprietary Software.

We expand on these below.

It is much easier for Eastern societies to conclude that the Western IPR regime is morally wrong and that it is being used as an instrument of Western neo-colonialism.

Libre-Halaal ByStar Digital Ecosystem thrives when Western IPR is rejected.

For example, the full beauty and power of the Libre-Halaal ByStar Digital Ecosystem will not be realized until a culture whose ideology is in line with ByStar's is ready to fully adopt it.

The Libre-Halaal model creates an entirely new environment in terms of competition, collaboration, and value chain relationships. Libre-Halaal software and Internet Services are genuine public resources, not owned by anyone, freely available for reuse by anyone. They are created by society/humanity, for society/humanity.

From an Eastern perspective, the collaborative model has been shown to be more cost-effective than the American proprietary and competitive model. This allows for collective efforts to replace American proprietary software.

Here we focus on such cultivations with a narrow focus on digital ecosystems, software and Internet services in the context of China and Iran.

20.2 Theoretical Iranian Societal Digital Strategies

There are a good number of specific reasons for why Iran makes for a good concrete Eastern example case. These include:

- Iran is currently not a signatory to the Western IPR model.

- Since the 1979, Iran has been under Western economic sanctions and as a result has established significant Eastern-relations and is immune and resilient to Western pressure.

- The "Islamic Republic of Iran" is more ethically oriented and less economically driven than the West.

- Imam Khomeini's fatwa with regard to invalidity of the entirety of the Western so-call Intellectual Property Rights regime is quite succinct (as described in Section 14.2.1.1 — Imam Khomeini's Decree Invalidates So-Called IPR.)

  While there is not full consensus among sources-of-imitation on invalidity of IPR as described in Section 14.2.1 — Islam, the necessary dynamics for moving towards full consensus on this important topic of "ownership" are in place. We hope that the current trends towards Washington D.C. and New York becoming sources-of-imitation for this topic can be stopped. Perhaps the current disagreements amongst sources-of-imitation can be settled by the logic presented in this document.

- American and Israeli Western cyber-attacks against Iran in the form of malware and worms the likes of Stuxnet, Duku and Flame have demonstrated Iran's vulnerabilities in use of internally opaque proprietary Western software. It is perfectly reasonable for Iranians to regard the entirety of Microsoft Windows as malware.

- The exploitative character of the West in general and America in particular has been crisply understood.

- The Libre-Halaal ByStar Digital Ecosystem that we introduced in Chapter 16 has been localized for Perso-Arabic usage, [9].

- The importance of digital societal autonomy is well understood by most Iranians.

- It is in Iran's interest to fully reject the Western IPR regime and play a leadership role towards adoption of Libre-Halaal polyexistentials policies.

The key starting point for all Iranian societal digital strategies is to reach a consensus on the invalidity of the Western IPR regime.

20.2.1   Build Consensus on Invalidity of IPR in Iran

Fortunately, a clear statement and rationale for the illegitimacy of the Western IPR regime has been made by Imam Khomeini. Imam Khomeini's position on this topic as described in Section 14.2.1.1 — Imam Khomeini's Decree Invalidates So-Called IPR, paves the way towards what is needed from the society's leaders with regard to the question of: "What is the Halaal Manner-of-Existence of Polyexistentials?"

The current situation in Iran is actually quite unclear, as Iran has both accepted and rejected aspects of the Western IPR regime. Over the recent years, many west-toxicated Iranians have been pushing for mimicking Western copyright and patent models. And they have had some success. So, with respect to acceptance or rejection of Western Intellectual Property Rights regime, Iran's position is quite muddy.

Iran is a non-signatory to WTO (Western Trade Organization) copyright laws, but crisp full rejection of the concept of copyright and patent as was explicitly stated by Imam Khomeini has not been asserted again. In recent years, a parallel to the Western IPR regime has been shaping Iranian practices inside of Iran.

Moving towards a society based on halaal manner-of-existence of software requires crisp declarations that fully invalidate Western intellectual property rights regime. And this is in Iranian society's best interest.

Acceptance or rejection of merits of Western IPR regime, above all, is a moral and ethical question. Not a business or economics question.

We humbly request for the Iranian Leader (Ayatollah Ozma Khamenei) and other Shia Ayatollahs to reach consensus on "Property" as it relates to polyexistentials. The theological aspects of "Property" are so very fundamental in any religion and Islam in particular that lack of a clear consensus among all sources of imitation cannot be healthy.

The logic that we have presented in this document makes it clear that polyexistentials cannot be property and that the Western IPR regime is erroneous. Mimicking the Western IPR should not be the Iranian way.

We look to Shia sources of imitation to either endorse our logic and conclusions or point to where they think we have gone wrong.

It is only through full rejection of the Western IPR regime that our theoretical Eastern societal cures can have a material impact. Libre-Halaal software based formulation of national policies in Eastern societies are most effective when they demand full rejection of the Western IPR regime.

Libre-Halaal software in general and Libre-Halaal ByStar Digital Ecosystem thrives when Western IPR is rejected.

We also look to Shia sources of imitation to either endorse our definitions of Libre-Halaal Software and Libre-Halaal Internet Services or point us to their criteria for halaal manner-of-existence of software and their criteria for halaal manner-of-existence of internet services.

20.2.2   Iranian Public Sector Libre-Halaal Strategies

The Western IPR disease is being imposed on Easterners/Iranians in the name of freedom and globalization. The 1979 revolution was about the freedom of Iranians to be Iranians and to reject American and Western models. In the realm of polyexistentials, preservation of the Iranian independence demands formulation of national polyexistential/digital policies.

Furthermore, absence of national digital policies or wrong national digital policies result in loss of autonomy.

In the context of software, as an example, let's consider the dependence of Arabs and Iranians on American proprietary software.

Today, if you want to write in Farsi or in Arabic, your main choice is Microsoft's Proprietary-Haraam Windows environment. And in the business driven (not societal or engineering driven) Western model, Perso-Arabic users are always second-class citizens because they represent an insignificant market to the likes of American Microsoft and American Google. In other words, computing and communication capabilities of Perso-Arabic societies is determined by Americans.

Eastern societies recognize this and see how Libre-Halaal Software can provide an alternative.

In general terms in Chapter 20 — Eastern Societal Libre-Halaal Strategies, we outlined some Eastern strategies. Here we contextualize those for Iran:

1. Adopt a pure Libre-Halaal Software policy for the public sector. Mandate use of a National-Linux in all public high-schools, public universities, and government offices. Prohibit use of Microsoft Windows. See Section 20.2.3 — Recognition of the Entirety of Microsoft Windows as Malware — for our reasoning.

2. Support Libre-Halaal Software development. Fund strategic Libre-Halaal Software projects.

3. Support Libre-Halaal Services cultivation. When Libre-Halaal alternatives are available, close off (prohibit) proprietary competition.

4. Cultivate production of Libre-Halaal Content.

5. Host large scale polyexistential library/archives in the public sector.

20.2.3   Recognition of the Entirety of Microsoft Windows as Malware — and Full Rejection of Windows

Much use of computing and communication in Iran today is based around Microsoft Windows. Microsoft Windows is internally opaque. Iranians have no way of knowing what exactly the software that they use is doing.

The likes of "Stuxnet" and "Flame" are external pieces of malware that have done Iran harm. But based on what logic can Iranians have any assurance that the Windows operating system itself has not been rigged to facilitate harm to Iran? Are Iranians to be that naive to assume that the American corporation producing Windows would not be collaborating with those intending to inflict harm on Iran?

Windows in its entirety should be considered a potential malware.

In fact, this is true of any and all software that is not internally transparent and therefore haraam based on definition of manner-of-existence of software that we provided.

So, the only reasonable national policy with respect to Microsoft Windows is not to use it at all. Even when it is available at zero cost.

20.3   Theoretical Chinese Societal Digital Strategies

In the 1970s, China decided to adopt an export-oriented strategy. This strategy was designed to help the country become more competitive in the global market. The strategy focused on increasing exports of goods and services while reducing imports. This allowed China to increase its foreign exchange reserves and become a major player in the global economy. The strategy also helped to create jobs and spur economic growth. Over the years, China has continued to refine and improve its export-oriented strategy, and it has become one of the most successful economies in the world.

The export-oriented strategy was also beneficial for China's domestic economy. By increasing exports, China was able to create jobs and increase income for its citizens. This in turn helped to reduce poverty and improve living standards.

50 years later, China, Europe and America are now economically fully interdependent. China is the world's largest exporter and the second-largest importer of goods and services. Europe is the second-largest exporter and the third-largest importer of goods and services. The United States is the world's largest importer and the third-largest exporter of goods and services.

IPR is intertwined in this trade picture.

20.3.1   Building Consensus on Invalidity of IPR in China

For China, adoption of Western IPR regime has been a side effect of its export-oriented strategy. China was required to adopt international standards of intellectual property protection in order to gain access to foreign markets. This meant that China had to implement laws and regulations that would protect the intellectual property rights of foreign companies operating in China. This included the adoption of copyright, patent, and trademark laws, as well as the establishment of an enforcement system to ensure that these laws were followed. In addition, China also had to sign international treaties and agreements that would ensure that its intellectual property laws were respected by other countries.

So, China has been playing the Western IPR game because it has had to. But what is the historic and real position of intellectual property in Chinese civilization? What was Confucius's position on intellectual property?

William Alford started a debate on this in 1995 with his book: "To Steal a Book Is an Elegant Offense — Intellectual Property Law in Chinese Civilization" [1]. The strong form of his claim is along these lines: Confucianism militates against intellectual property reforms in China. From the Westerner's perspective this accounts for the failure of the many reforms pushed by foreign countries and intellectual property rights holders to induce improvements in intellectual property protection and enforcement. However, it is a fact that there are striking similarities between Confucianism and what is generally regarded as the public domain in the West.[51]

Perhaps it would be an exaggeration to say that everything in "To Steal a Book is an Elegant Offense" (Qie Shu Bu Suan Tou) is an accurate characterization of intellectual property law in Chinese civilization. However, there is no doubt that intellectual property has a different place in Chinese civilization compared to the West. Eastern perspective on IPR is different. In the United States, intellectual property is protected by the Constitution, while in Iran, Imam Khomeini explicitly invalidated it. Thus, it is fair to say that at a minimum, intellectual property is not an indigenous concept in China. Rather it is one that has been imposed and imported.

In imperial China (221 B.C. — A.D. 1911), there were no formal or informal regulations in place to protect the reproduction of literary and other creative works which could be considered as parallels to the Western copyright or other forms of intellectual property law.[52]

Similar to Iran and other Eastern societies, IP is not an indigenous Chinese construct. As it is with Iran and other Eastern societies, the Western IPR regime has been exported and imposed by the Westerners onto China.

The Chinese know that intellectual property does not lead to economic growth and innovation.

In Section 6.9 — On IP Placebos and Self-Fulfilling Prophecies, we cite various studies which conclude that causality of IP on economic growth remains indeterminable and the placebo effects of IP are to be taken seriously. Some of these studies are based on research done by the Chinese in China.

So, given this mixture, what are the Chinese to do? We say, the Chinese should consider all of what we have suggested in Part IV — Libre-Halaal ByStar Digital Ecosystem. And move towards an independent national position on halaal maner-of-existence of polyexistentials.

20.3.2   Preparing for a China That Can Say No

China Can Say No (中国可以说不 Zhōngguó kěyǐ shuō bu) is a 1996 Chinese language manifesto which in some ways parallels "The Japan That Can Say No".

Its full title is often translated as: "China That Can Say No: Political and Emotional Choices in the post Cold-War era". It became an overnight bestseller, as the authors called on the Beijing government to stand up against the United States in a new era of global competition. The popularity indicates the growth of anti-American and anti-Japanese sentiment in the Chinese public. It indicates disillusionment among many younger and better educated Chinese as the nation searches for a major role in the global economic and political systems.[53]

Zhang Zangzang, one of the authors of China Can Say No, is a former student radical and an "uncritical admirer of all things American". His disillusionment with foreign countries' treatment of China, and particularly that by America, reflects the experience of about a quarter of Chinese students studying in the United States, who, despite their initial Americophilia, undergo a surge of Chinese patriotism upon their return. Contributing factors to this transformation in the United States include racial discrimination, denial of cultural legitimacy, and negative media portrayal.[54]

No English translation of China Can Say No has been published.

In the digital domain, what does it mean for China to say No? The basic model of things like TikTok and Huawei is American and Western. So far, China has been constructing its digital ecosystem by replicating the American IPR model. But what is the independent Chinese model? We are claiming that the Libre-Halaal model is the right model and that the Chinese can build on it.

Much preparation is needed in the digital domain before China can say No. Most of that preparation can be done as "Inside of IPR Libre-Halaal Strategies" that we described in Chapter 18 — Societal Adoption of Libre-Halaal Strategies.

20.3.3   An Eastern Global Alternative to GitHub

As we described in Section 12 — Digital Non-Proprietary Movements, GitHub has become the defacto convergence point for global open-source development. There are a few things wrong with that.

1. GitHub, as an Internet Service is based on opaque-services software.

2. GitHub is owned by Microsoft, an American company — not a global neutral entity.

3. As an American entity, GitHub must conform to sanctions that US imposes on other countries and various entities. China and Iran can be excluded from access to GitHub if the US government decides to subject them to du jour American sanctions.

4. When it comes to public copyright licenses, GitHub is neutral. GitHub permits each individual to choose a public license for herself.

What if as an "Inside of IPR Libre-Halaal Strategy", China in collaboration with other Eastern countries was to create or to support an alternative to GitHub with the following attributes:

- A Libre Service. Perhaps to start based on something like Gitlab

- Owned and operated by a global neutral entity similar to Debian

- Not be neutral with respect to public copyright licenses. Favor Libre-Halaal licenses

- Fund strategic projects based on Libre-Halaal licenses

Let's call it "Nondiscriminatory Global Git Center" (NGGC). Something along these lines can bring about many strategic benefits for China.

- With respect to ethics of IP, it turns the table on Americans. Left and right, Americans speak of "Intellectual Property Theft by the Chinese". In Section 6 — Debunking the Myth of Western IPR Regime, we explained that the vocabulary of Intellectual Property Theft is erroneous. To speak of theft in the context of IP is American doublespeak. With NGGC, China can establish that China is a proponent of non-proprietary software, that China is a proponent of collaborative global open research and development in academia and in industry. With NGGC China can emphasize that China is on the side of ethics and it is the Americans that are on the wrong side.

- With a focus on Libre-Halaal licenses, China can corner the corporate American open-source model.

- NGGC can even be considered as a digital extension of Belt and Road Initiative.

The Eastern global alternative to GitHub is just one of the many global collaborative strategies that China could engage in.

20.4   Putting it All Together

Our precise and multidisciplinary concepts and models have enabled us to develop a number of specific suggestions that can only be effective if they are implemented in an orchestrated manner.

On a societal scale, such orchestrated execution is very difficult. Of course, specific strategies that reflect consensus should percolate up to the leadership.

However, eventually a certain degree of central power is required to execute the overarching multidisciplinary blueprint.

Since such an undertaking requires a multidisciplinary blueprint in order to be successful, we hope that this book can provide a foundation for the development of that multidisciplinary blueprint.

We view what we have built as a starting point. Above all, our goal has been to initiate an independent dialogue separate and distinct from the Western IPR framework.

In a sense we feel we have done our part, as Khayam and FitzGerald put it:

The Moving Finger writes; and, having writ,	بر لوح نشان بودنی‌ها بوده‌است
Moves on: nor all thy Piety nor Wit	پیوسته قلم ز نیک و بد فرسوده‌است
Shall lure it back to cancel half a Line,	در روز ازل هر آنچه بایست بداد
Nor all thy Tears wash out a Word of it.	غم خوردن و کوشیدن ما بیهوده‌است

Appendices

Appendix A

IP Rituals Case Studies

A.1 Some Questionable Examples of Patents

In an Appendix of [33], Kinsela lists some actually issued patents that demonstrate how things have been pushed to absurdity. Here we include some that we consider particularly ridiculous and funny.

- "Initiation Apparatus," U.S. Pat. No. 819,814, May 8, 1906 ("harmless" way of initiating a candidate into a fraternity by shocking him with electrodes);

- "Method of Exercising a Cat," U.S. Pat. No. 5,443,036, Aug. 22, 1995 (shining a laser light onto the floor to fascinate a cat and cause it to chase the light);

- "Force-Sensitive, Sound-Playing Condom," U.S. Pat. No. 5,163,447, Nov. 17, 1992 (self-explanatory; for example, it could play "Dixie");

A.2 Case Study: WAP Patents

In Section 6.8 — IP Rituals: Formal IP vs Practiced IP vs Enforced IP, we describe how IP in general and patents in particular have become part of Western business rituals.

Here we provide a case study for a set of specific patents that are in many ways typical of what happens in practice. The role that patents play in this case study is central. This case study demonstrates that patents have become a "game" with all the players either being pure economic actors or fully corrupt patent-believers. It further demonstrates that the players are not in it for building anything meaningful. They are all in it just for the money.

The particular set of patents that we track in this case are all continuations of U.S. Patent No. 5,808,415, ("the '415 patent") which was filed on December 11, 1995. Unwired Planet is the assignee of U.S. Patent Nos. 6,405,037 ("the '037 patent"), 6,430,409 ("the '409 patent"), and 6,625,447 ("the '447 patent") (collectively, the "415-series-patents").

With regard to this set of patents, all the rituals that we mentioned in Section 6.8 are practiced. In this case, the patent-centered business rituals involve:

Hollow patents which bring entrepreneurs and VCs together: Alain Rossmann and a few collaborators formed Libris, Inc. in 1996 around the '415 patent intending to bring in Venture Capitalists (VCs). Much VC money came in and Libris then became Unwired Planet which then became Phone.com and then Openwave and then back to Unwired Planet. All of these names kept 415-series-patents central during the full pump-and-dump cycle.

Rigged protocols which promote use of undeclared standard essential patents: Wireless Application Protocols (WAP) were designed around the 415-series-patents. And then the "WAP Forum" which became "Open Mobile Alliance" were formed to promote WAP. Yet, the 415-series-patents were never declared as standard essential patents (SEP) as it was not in the interest of the patent players to even be minimally honest.

Patent oriented Pump-and-Dump and Spin-and-Flip schemes: The stock prices peaked during the DotCon era (2000) and then started to collapse as the patents and technology were hollow.

Failed patented technology leading to product business sell-off. Unwired Planet hype and revenue declined until the firm was forced to sell off its product business around 2012.

Formation of Patent Trolls. A Non-Practicing Entity (NPE) – also called Patent Assertion Entity (PAE) – called again Unwired Planet was formed around the 415-series-patents around the same 2012 time-frame.

On December 15, 2015 the United States Court of Appeals for the Federal Circuit issued the following ruling:

CONCLUSION

For the foregoing reasons, and because we find that Unwired Planet's remaining arguments are without merit, we conclude that the district court properly construed the claim terms at issue and properly entered judgment of non-infringement. Accordingly, the district court's judgment is affirmed.

AFFIRMED

15 years earlier, in April of 2000, we had published.

The WAP Trap
An Expose of the Wireless Application Protocol
http://www.freeprotocols.org/PLPC/100014 − [13]
also available in French at: http://www.freeprotocols.org/PLPC/100015

In that document we had explicitly identified the '415 patent and had warned about WAP technology being booby trapped with patents. The relevant section is reproduced below:

2.3 Not Patent-Free

...

The WAP specification, however, is burdened with several patent restrictions. These include patents held by certain members of the WAP Forum itself, most notably Phone.com and Geoworks. Patent infringement claims have already been made by the holders of the following patents:

- U.S. Patent # 5,327,529 (Geoworks). Process of designing user's interfaces for application programs.
- U.S. Patent # 5,809,415 (Phone.com, formerly Unwired Planet). Method and architecture for an interactive two-way data communication network.

More patent infringement claims can almost certainly be expected in the future.

About 12 years after writing that document when the '415 patent was asserted against Apple and RIM, we were considered prescient. Irell and Manella LLP on behalf of RIM found us and hired us to assist in defending the patent assertions.

The life cycle of these typical patents demonstrates that the rituals surrounding patent law really amount to a negative-sum game.

Alain Rossmann and collaborators made a whole lot of money through using the 415-series-patents as a basis for a pump-and-dump scheme. Many new investors lost money. A whole lot of lawyers made some money. As patent defense engineering consultants, we too made some money – our services are available only in defense against patent assertions.

But in the aggregate, nothing of enduring value was created as a result of the 415-series-patents. And we now have a Patent Assertion Entity in charge of the patents.

Not patented alternative technologies became enduring solutions.

We would all have been better off if the 415-series-patents did not exist, or better yet, if the patent system did not exist.

Appendix B

On the Distinction Between Economic Creatures and Humans

The Founding Fathers of America believed that IPR should be included in the US Constitution in order to incentivize people to engage in activities that progress science and useful arts. They reasoned that since humans are essentially economic creatures, they will be more likely to pursue such activities if they are rewarded for their efforts. So, they chose to turn natural public goods (polyexistentials) into artificial scarcities through legislation.

In Chapter 9 — Americanism: Root of the IPR Mistake — we recognized the core of the Americanist character as that of morally bankrupt and self-absorbed bullies who behave as corporatized economic creatures existing in an exploitative industrial context.

Outside of Americanism, human beings are more than economic creatures. In fact, for humans, the natural collaborative model of polyexistentials often leads to activities that progress science and the useful arts in a much more effective way.

Understanding the distinction between economic creatures and humans is essential for developing appropriate models of governance for polyexistentials.

Below we include parts of two speeches, one was a speech by Imam Khomeini in 1979 and the other was in 1968 by Robert F. Kennedy.

Imam Khomeini:
A donkey too considers economy as its only infrastructure

[Various Westerners and various west-toxicated Iranians have mis-quoted Imam Khomeini as having said: "economics is for the donkey" — «اقتصاد مال خره». The full context of his speech, makes it all very clear. The essence of Imam's message is that: "economic creatures and humans are very distinct."]

Imam Khomeini Journals — Volume 9 — Pages 449 and 450

Speech

Place: Ghom
Subject: Role of Radio and Television in Society
Audience: Employees of the radio branch
Date: September 8, 1979

In the name of God, the most gracious, the most merciful

...

I cannot imagine and no wise person can presume the claim that we spared our bloods so watermelon becomes cheaper. No wise person would sacrifice his young offspring for [say] affordable housing. People [on the contrary] want everything for their young offspring. Human being wants economy for his own self; it would therefore be unwise for him to spare his life in order to improve economy [...] Those who keep bringing up economy and find economy as the infrastructure of everything —not knowing what human[ity] means— think of human being as an animal who is defined by means of food and eats[...] Those who find economy as the infrastructure of everything, find human beings as animals. Animal too sacrifices everything for its economy and economy is its sole infrastructure. A donkey too considers economy as its only infrastructure. These people did not realize what human being [truly] is.

...

Robert F. Kennedy:
GDP is an insufficient measure of success

Robert F. Kennedy's remarks at the University of Kansas were given on March 18, 1968.

Part of Kennedy's speech relates to the notions that gross national product and economics are an insufficient measure of success.

...

Even if we act to erase material poverty, there is another greater task, it is to confront the poverty of satisfaction — purpose and dignity — that afflicts us all.

Too much and for too long, we seemed to have surrendered personal excellence and community values in the mere accumulation of material things. Our Gross National Product, now, is over $800 billion dollars a year, but that Gross National Product — if we judge the United States of America by that — that Gross National Product counts air pollution and cigarette advertising, and ambulances to clear our highways of carnage. It counts special locks for our doors and the jails for the people who break them. It counts the destruction of the redwood and the loss of our natural wonder in chaotic sprawl. It counts napalm and counts nuclear warheads and armored cars for the police to fight the riots in our cities. It counts Whitman's rifle and Speck's knife, and the television programs which glorify violence in order to sell toys to our children.

Yet the gross national product does not allow for the health of our children, the quality of their education or the joy of their play. It does not include the beauty of our poetry or the strength of our marriages, the intelligence of our public debate or the integrity of our public officials. It measures neither our wit nor our courage, neither our wisdom nor our learning, neither our compassion nor our devotion to our country, it measures everything in short, except that which makes life worthwhile. And it can tell us everything about America except why we are proud that we are Americans.

If this is true here at home, so it is true elsewhere in world.

...

Appendix C

About the Author

The nature of the topic and tone and style of this writing is such that some may suspect the author's biases, agenda and motivations.

Those suspicious of religious, national or cultural bias in these writings, may profit from some background information about the author.

The primary author of this document is Mohsen Banan.

He is a Software Engineer.

He is a Shia Muslim. Much of his formal education were at schools that were operated by Catholics — Saint-Louis, Salesians of Don Bosco and Jesuits of Seattle University.

He is fluent in Farsi, English and French. His children are additionally fluent in Mandarin Chinese.

He has a Masters of Science in Electrical Engineering from University of Washington.

He holds residences in Seattle, WA, USA and in Isfahan, Iran.

He runs Neda Communications, Inc. a for-profit organization. He runs the Libre-Halaal Foundation, a non-profit organization.

He has worked for a number of American, Canadian, European and Chinese companies including: AT&T, T-Mobile, Huawei, Motorola, Sema Group, US Department of Justice and Sierra Wireless.

He was the principal architect of the Cellular Digital Packet Data (CDPD) network specifications. He played a key role in design, implementation and deployment of AT&T's first native Internet Protocols based wide-area wireless data services. In 1996, he co-authored the "Internetwork Mobility —The CDPD

Approach", [45], book.

Since the late 1980s, he has been an active participant in various international standards organizations including CCITT/ITU, ISO/IEC, 3GPP, NIST, and IETF. He is the primary author of two Internet RFCs.

He has a fair amount of first hand experience with the American Venture Capitalist model.

He has no patents and has never applied for a patent. As an expert witness he has assisted in legal efforts involving invalidation of a number of patents.

The software and internet services that he publicly offers all conform to the definition of Libre-Halaal Software and Libre-Halaal Internet Services. His favorite programming languages are: Lisp, Python, and C.

All of his public writings are subject to verbatim-copying-permitted and are web published. The tools that he uses to write and publish are Libre-Halaal Software and Libre-Halaal Internet Services.

He is the main driver behind development of

> **The Libre-Halaal ByStar Digital Ecosystem**
> **A Unified and Non-Proprietary Model For Autonomous Internet Services**
> **A Moral Alternative To The Proprietary American Digital Ecosystem**
> http://www.by-star.net/PLPC/180016 — [11]

The Author's Own Patent Assassination Experiences

In the words of the primary author of this document:

> I have no patents myself. A search for "Mohsen Banan" yields a number of patents belonging to Mohsen Banan, but that's not me; that's a different Mohsen Banan, specializing in Applied Physics.

> I have made patent-free declarations for RFC-2188 and RFC-2524, two Internet protocols for which I am the principal author, through the Free Protocols Foundation.

> I have written various articles exposing the harm of software and protocol patents, and in active opposition to specific patents. These include:

> http://www.freeprotocols.org/PLPC/100014 — The WAP Trap

> http://www.freeprotocols.org/PLPC/100025 — The Patent Problem

I provide consulting services for defending against patent assertion claims in the areas of wireless, email, telecommunications and data communications. These services include prior art determination, and expert witness testimony.

My services are available only in the defense against patent assertion. I do not accept any work in support of patent assertion.

Appendix D

Provenance, Credits, Acknowledgments and Thanks

We have been at this for a long while and over the 15 years or so many have assisted us in building ByStar and producing this document.

In particular we wish to thank Dr. Andrew Hammoude for both his thoughts and his writings. Many of the papers that have been incorporated in this document were developed in close collaboration with Dr. Hammoude.

This Document as a Collection of Articles

In a sense, this document is compilation of documents that we had previously written.

Much of what is in this document is also available as a set of topic oriented standalone papers.

You can obtain a list of related publications that we have written in:
http://www.by-star.net/bxPublications

Our Use of ChatGPT Rewrite

Starting in early 2023, on occasion, we have used ChatGPT to rewrite some individual paragraphs. Surprisingly, in some situations it works well. We don't use ChatGPT as an information source.

Training of Artificial Intelligence based internet application services and their use is a subject that we have not addressed in this revision of the book. The framework that we have created for Libre Services recognizes such services as a "type" which needs to be well defined and regulated.

Inclusion and Quotation Policy

Throughout this book, we have emphasized the importance of proper attribution and respect for applicable laws. We have included information from various sources and have copied certain segments of text from other books, articles, and papers. In all cases, we have provided pointers to the original work and ensured that our quotations and inclusions conform to fair use and/or copyright public licenses.

In all cases the information that we have included has been publicly available in electronic form on the web. We prefer not to include text from sources that are only available in resitricted paper form or in electronic walled gardens.

Many of the documents that we have cited are only web published and the stability of the URLs that we have referenced cannot be guaranteed. In future editions, we plan to use re-publication facilities of ByStar to capture all the mentioned references.

Appendix E

Manifest and Colophon

E.1 Manifest

We want to provide convenient access to all forms and formats of this book to all readers.

The paper document can be obtained with its ISBN number: 978-1-960957-00-9.

Various electronic forms and formats of this document are available at: https://github.com/bxplpc/120033.

We can benefit from your feedback. Please let us know your thoughts. You can send us your comments and criticisms by email to: plpc-120033@mohsen.1.banan.byname.net.

To help you choose the form and format that best suits you, we have listed the available formats in table E.1.

DOIs (Digital Object Identifiers) for the web published pdf format of the 8.5x11 and the A4 paper sizes have been registered. These are available in table E.2.

Library of Congress Control Number (LCCN) 2023911133 has been assigned to the First US Edition published with ISBN: 978-1-960957-01-6 (6x9, color, soft-cover).

Format	Venue	Size and Form	tag	ISBN
Print	Amazon	6x9, B&W, Soft Cover	p1bsk	978-1-960957-00-9
Print	Amazon	6x9, Color, Soft Cover	p1csk	978-1-960957-01-6
Print	Ingram	6x9, B&W, Soft Cover	p1bsi	978-1-960957-00-9
PDF	Web	8.5x11, Embedded Cover	p3cel	978-1-960957-02-3
PDF	Web	8.5x11, Content, No Cover	p3cel	978-1-960957-02-3
PDF	Web	8.5x11, Soft Cover	p3cel	978-1-960957-03-0
PDF	Web	A4, Embedded Cover	p4cel	978-1-960957-03-0
PDF	Web	A4, Content, No Cover	p4cel	978-1-960957-03-0
PDF	Web	A4, Soft Cover	p4cel	978-1-960957-03-0
EPUB	Web	eBook, HeVeA+Calibre	h0cnp	978-1-960957-04-7
HTML	Web	HeVeA Produced	h0cnp	978-1-960957-04-7

Table E.1: Manifest: Available Forms and Formats

DOI	ISBN	tag
https://doi.org/10.5281/zenodo.8003847	978-1-960957-02-3	p3cel
https://doi.org/10.5281/zenodo.8003401	978-1-960957-03-0	p4cel

Table E.2: DOI Manifest: Digital Object Identifiers

E.2   Colophon

This document was produced entirely with Libre-Halaal Software, and is published using Libre-Halaal Internet Services. All tools used to produce and distribute this document conform fully to the definition of Libre-Halaal Software and Libre-Halaal Internet Application Services as specified in [3] and [4].

E.2.1   Our Libre-Halaal Software Tools

This document has been created based exclusively on the use of Libre-Halaal software tools. We make use of a comprehensive and well-integrated set of tools, including:

- Debian GNU/Linux is our base platform

- Emacs is our editor-based user environment

- TeX, LaTeX, XeTeX, XeLaTeX is our document processor

- Emacs bidi (bidirectional) capability is used to write in mixed Persian and Globish

- xepersian LaTeX package is used to process Persian documents

- LaTeX beamer package is used to prepare presentation slides

- Emacs auctex mode is used to create documents in LaTeX

- Aspell via Emacs is used for spell checking in Persian/Farsi and Globish/English

- Dict via Emacs is used for dictionary and thesaurus lookup in multiple languages

- Conversion from LaTeX to html is accomplished through HeVeA

- Libre Office is used for creating figures and illustrations

- Git via magit of Emacs is used for version control

- Emacs Gnus and qmail facilities are used for emailing out drafts and receiving feedback

- Integration with ByStar Services is through BLEE (the ByStar Libre Emacs Environment)

These Libre-Halaal software tools collectively represent a deeply integrated environment that is far superior in capability to any Haraam software. We question why so many people continue to use the clumsy and ineffective Microsoft Proprietary-Haraam software when such a vastly superior alternative is available.

E.2.2   Our Libre-Halaal Internet Services

The publication and distribution of this document has been accomplished exclusively by means of Libre-Halaal Internet Application Services. We make use of a comprehensive and well-integrated set of services, including:

- The ByName Autonomous Libre Service (part of the ByStar) is used for autonomous web publication of this document by the author himself

- The ByContent Federated Libre Service (part of the ByStar) is used for web re-publication/distribution of this document

- All By* Services are based on the Debian GNU/Linux platform

- Apache2 and Plone3 are used to provide By* Web Services

- All By* Services related to this document are hosted at LibreCenter.net, a physical data center built exclusively with Halaal software. All routers, servers and other hardware infrastructure at LibreCenter.net run Halaal Software exclusively.

- The By* Self Publication Facilities, fully integrated with BLEE, are used for publication of this document

- The By* Library Facilities are used for managing this document in the context of multiple other related documents

These Libre-Halaal Internet Services are comparable in capability to the most high-profile Haraam Internet Services presently available, such as Google or Facebook.

The deep integration between Libre-Halaal Software and Libre-Halaal Internet Services creates a Libre-Halaal Software-Service continuum, which is far superior in capability to any Proprietary-Haraam Software/Service combination.

Notes

We have not identified sources when the facts involved are not in dispute and when the relevant information can easily be found.

Notes for section 1.1

1. See https://www.ontology.co/existence.htm for a more information.

Notes for section 1.7

2. Taken from the transcript of acceptance speech of Ursula K. Le Guin on November 19, 2014 – https://www.ursulakleguin.com/nbf-medal.

Notes for section 2.3

3. Based on Ivan Griffin's periodictable.tex (2010-01-11) file as an example illustrating the Periodic Table of Chemical Elements using TikZ.

4. One of many posters on the web that summarizes all laws of physics in one single equation. We particularly like the one from perimeter institute: https://perimeterinstitute.ca.

5. One of many posters on the web that summarizes all laws of physics in one single equation. We particularly like the one from: https://www.preposterousuniverse.com/blog/2013/01/04/the-world-of-everyday-experience-in-one-equation

Notes for section 2.4

6. Thomas Jefferson to Isaac McPherson, 13 August 1813, Founders Online, National Archives, https://founders.archives.gov/documents/Jefferson/03-06-02-0322. [Original source: The Papers of Thomas Jefferson, Retirement Series, vol. 6, 11 March to 27 November 1813, ed. J. Jefferson Looney. Princeton: Princeton University Press, 2009, pp. 379—386.

Notes for section 2.9

7. This overview of copyright law has been compiled from various online resources.

Notes for section 3.2

8. In reference to the seven layered OSI (Open Systems Interconnection) model of ISO-7498.

Notes for section 3.3

9. Figure 3.1 has been reproduced from Shadman Salih's thesis [41].

10. Wikipedia, "Assembly Language" — 2023.

11. http://digital-law-online.info/lpdi1.0/treatise17.html

Notes for section 3.5

12. A Call to Cryptographic Arms — Julian Assange, London, October 2012,
    https://cryptome.org/2012/12/assange-crypto-arms.htm

Notes for section 4.3

13. According to a report by Kantar Media, in 2018, prescription medication manufacturers spent more than 6.4 billion dollars in direct to consumer advertising, and the average American would see 9 advertisements for prescription medications per day.

14. In 2019, the Canadian government passed legislation allowing direct-to-consumer advertising of prescription drugs. Australia, New Zealand, and the United Kingdom followed suit in 2020, and the regulations went into effect in 2023.

Notes for section 5.2

15. These summaries of Copyright, Patent, Trademark and IP have been compiled from a number of online sources.

16. This information is mostly a collage of various internet sources.

17. This information is mostly a collage of various internet sources.

Notes for section 6.1

18. https://mises.org/library/against-intellectual-property-0

19. http://www.uow.edu.au/~bmartin/pubs/98il/

Notes for section 6.3

20. http://www.uspto.gov/news/publications/copyrightgreenpaper.pdf

Notes for section 6.11

۲۱. مرتضی مطهری، نظری به نظام اقتصادی اسلام، ج۱، ص۵۸ـ۵۹، تهران ۱۳۶۸ ش.

Notes for section 7.1

22. Article I, Section 2, Clause 3 of the United States Constitution is informally known as the "Three-fifths Clause" or the "Federal Ratio." It states: "Representatives and direct Taxes shall be apportioned among the several States which may be included within this Union, according to their respective Numbers, which shall be determined by adding to the whole Number of free Persons, including those bound to Service for a Term of Years, and excluding Indians not taxed, three fifths of all other Persons." The phrase "three fifths of all other Persons" refers to enslaved individual.

Notes for section 7.3

23. The Rise of King Cotton and the Revitalization of Slavery, The Gilder Lehrman Institute of American History, https://www.gilderlehrman.org/history-by-era/slavery-and-anti-slavery/essays/rise-king-cotton-and-revitalization-slavery.

24. Cotton and the Economy of the Antebellum South, Encyclopedia of Alabama, http://www.encyclopediaofalabama.org/article/h-1520.

Notes for section 7.4

25. 2005 statistics — pewresearch.org. See https://www.pewresearch.org/ social-trends/ fact-sheet/ facts-about-the-us- black-population/ for details.

26. The Cost of Mass Incarceration in the United States, Vera Institute of Justice, https://www.vera.org/publications/ price -of-prisons -the-changing -costs-of- incarceration -in-the- united-states/ price-of- prisons-the- changing-costs -of-incarceration -in-the-united- states-executive-summary .

27. 2011 statistics — prb.org. See https://www.prb.org/ resources/ black-women- over-three-times-more-likely-to- die-in-pregnancy- postpartum-than- white-women-new- research-finds/ for details.

Notes for section 7.6

28. We don't mean to minimize rape. In the context of ownership, the question of status and ownership of the child is the key point.

29. This statement is referencing the fact that many of the Founding Fathers owned slaves, and some of them had children with those slaves. See "The Founding Fathers and Slavery" by Henry

Wiencek, Smithsonian Magazine
https://www.smithsonianmag.com/history/the- hard- truth- about- the- founding- fathers- and-
slavery- 110186370/ .

Notes for section 7.8

30. Pages 1, 2, 3 and first 6 lines of page 4 of "King Leopold's Ghost" by Adam Hochschild [24]

Notes for section 8.2

31. The Nation – Economy / February 8, 2021 `https://www.thenation.com/article/economy/`
`inequality-patents-taxes-copyright`

Notes for section 9.1

32. These are Imam Khomeini's exact words from his September 8, 1979 speech — This sentence is
often mis-quoted as "economics is for the donkey" — «اقتصاد مال خره». Also, see Appendix B —
Distinction: Economic Creatures and Humans for additional information.

Notes for section 9.2

33. According to the Bureau of Justice Statistics, in 2021 African Americans make up about 12% of
the total U.S. population, but they account for 33% of the prison population.

Notes for section 11.0

34. Globish (mixture of Glob-al and Engl-ish) is the language that a Chinese may use to communicate
with a Brazilian.

Notes for section 12.1

35. Free software movement according to `https://en.wikipedia.org/wiki/Free_software_`
`movement`.

36. Open source movement according to `https://en.wikipedia.org/wiki/Open_source`.

37. According to `https://www.linuxfoundation.org/`

38. Similar and more detailed points on this topic have been made by boringcactus (Melody Horn) in
Post-Open Source (13 Aug 2022).

39. Halloween Document I (Version 1.17) — `http://www.catb.org/~esr//halloween1.html`

40. Based on web published statistic `https://octoverse.github.com/2022/global-tech-talent`.

41. The source of the cited survey is SourceForge.net

Notes for section 12.3

42. Partly taken from https://en.wikipedia.org/wiki/Essential_patent.

Notes for section 12.5

43. https://en.wikipedia.org/wiki/Source-available_software

Notes for section 13.3

44. This is not a typo. We mean Dot-Con, not Dot-Com

Notes for section 13.7

45. Taken from question and answer section of Sid Kasivajhula's session at the EmacsConf-2022.

Notes for section 14.0

46. See http://www.ido.ir/a.aspx?a=1385023101

Notes for section 14.2

47. The English version is at: http://w2.vatican.va/content/john-paul-ii/en/encyclicals/documents/hf_jp-ii_enc_14091981_laborem-exercens.html

48. The English version is at: http://w2.vatican.va/content/leo-xiii/en/encyclicals/documents/hf_l-xiii_enc_15051891_rerum-novarum.html

49. at http://www.jlaw.com/Articles/copyright1.html

Notes for section 18.9

50. 2022 statistics. https://techjury.net/blog/gmail-statistics.

Notes for section 20.3

51. The Confucian Challenge to Intellectual Property Reforms — Peter K. Yu — China and the Confucian Challenge.

52. Chapter 2 of To Steal a Book Is an Elegant Offense.

53. https://en.wikipedia.org/wiki/China_Can_Say_No

54. In 2009, Unhappy China, a follow-up version, was published.

Bibliography

[1] William P. Alford. *To Steal a Book Is an Elegant Offense: Intellectual Property Law in Chinese Civilization*. Stanford: Stanford University Press, 2023/02/27 1995, p. 236.

[2] D. Baker. *Rigged: How Globalization and the Rules of the Modern Economy Were Structured to Make the Rich Richer*. Center for Economic and Policy Research, 2016. ISBN: 9780692793367. URL: https://books.google.com/books?id=VY8pvgAACAAJ.

[3] Mohsen BANAN. *Defining Halaal Manner-Of-Existence Of Software And Defining Halaal Internet Application Services*. Permanent Libre Published Content 120041. http://mohsen.1.banan.byname.net/PLPC/120041. Autonomously Self-Published, Sept. 2012.

[4] Mohsen BANAN. تعریف نرم افزار حلال و تعریف خدمات اینترنتی حلال. Permanent Libre Published Content 120035. http://mohsen.1.banan.byname.net/PLPC/120035. Autonomously Self-Published.

[5] Mohsen BANAN. *Introducing Convivial Into Globish*. Permanent Libre Published Content 120037. http://mohsen.banan.1.byname.net/PLPC/120037. Autonomously Self-Published, July 2011.

[6] Mohsen BANAN. *Introducing Globish into Globish*. PLPC- 120038. http://mohsen.banan.1.byname.net/PLPC/120038. Autonomously Self-Published, Aug. 2013.

[7] Mohsen BANAN. *Introducing Halaal and Haraam into Globish Based on Moral Philosophy of Abstract Halaal*. Permanent Libre Published Content 120039. http://mohsen.1.banan.byname.net/120039. Autonomously Self-Published, Sept. 2012.

[8] Mohsen BANAN. *Libre-Halaal Software Defining Halaal Manner-Of-Existence Of Software*. Permanent Libre Published Content 180044. http://www.by-star.net/PLPC/180044. Autonomously Self-Published, Aug. 2013.

[9]   Mohsen BANAN. *Persian Input Methods For Emacs And More Broadly Speaking –* شیوه‌های درج به فارسی . Permanent Libre Published Content 120036. http://mohsen.1.banan.byname.net/PLPC/120036. Autonomously Self-Published, Sept. 2013.

[10]   Mohsen BANAN. *The ByStar Applied Model Of Federations of Autonomous Libre-Halaal Services.* Permanent Libre Published Content 180015. http://www.by-star.net/PLPC/180015. Autonomously Self-Published, Aug. 2011.

[11]   Mohsen BANAN. *The Libre-Halaal ByStar Digital Ecosystem A Unified and Non-Proprietary Model For Autonomous Internet Services A Moral Alterantive To The Proprietary American Digital Ecosystem.* Permanent Libre Published Content 180016. http://www.by-star.net/PLPC/180016. Autonomously Self-Published, Sept. 2013.

[12]   Mohsen BANAN and Andrew Hammoude. *The Free Protocols Foundation Policies and Procedures.* Permanent Libre Published Content 100201. http://www.freeprotocols.org/PLPC/100201. Autonomously Self-Published, Mar. 2000.

[13]   Mohsen BANAN and Andrew Hammoude. *The WAP Trap An Expose of the Wireless Application Protocol.* Permanent Libre Published Content 100014. Autonomously Self-Published, Apr. 2000.

[14]   Michele Boldrin and David K. Levine. *Against Intellectual Monopoly.* Web Published at http://levine.sscnet.ucla.edu/general/intellectual/againstnew.htm.

[15]   Boudewijn Bouckaert. *What is Property?*

[16]   Jalal Al-e-Ahmad. *"Gharbzadegi –* غرب زدگی *".* Re-Published Content 120024. http://mohsen.banan.1.byname.net/Repub/120024. Autonomously Self-Published.

[17]   Erica Shadeed E. Richard Gold Jean-Frédéric Morin. *Does intellectual property lead to economic growth? Insights from a novel IP dataset.* http://onlinelibrary.wiley.com/doi/10.1111/rego.12165/full.

[18]   Farhang Tahmasebi فرهنگ طهماسبی . *Iran's Theological Research on Intellectual Property Rights* پژوهشی فقهی در باب مالکیت فکری و معنوی . Re-Published Content 120028. http://mohsen.banan.1.byname.net/Repub/120028. Autonomously Self-Published, Sept. 2012.

[19]   Joseph Feller et al. "Why Hackers Do What They Do: Understanding Motivation and Effort in Free/Open Source Software Projects". In: *Perspectives on Free and Open Source Software.* 2007, pp. 3–21.

[20]   Rana Foroohar. *Don't Be Evil: How Big Tech Betrayed Its Founding Principles – and All of Us.* English. Hardcover. Currency, Nov. 5, 2019, p. 368. ISBN: 978-1984823984.

[21]   J. Gay, R.M. Stallman, and Lawrence Lessig. *Free Software, Free Society: Selected Essays of Richard M. Stallman.* CreateSpace Independent Publishing Platform, 2009. ISBN: 9781441436856.

[22]   David Graeber. *The Utopia of Rules: On Technology, Stupidity, and the Secret Joys of Bureaucracy.* English. Paperback. Melville House, Feb. 23, 2016, p. 272. ISBN: 978-1612195186.

[23]   Andrew Hammoude. *Moral Philosophy: An Abstract Approach.* Permanent Libre Published Content 150020. http://andrew.hammoude.1.byname.net/PLPC/150020. Autonomously Self-Published, Aug. 2009.

[24]   Adam. Hochschild. *King Leopold's ghost : a story of greed, terror, and heroism in Colonial Africa / Adam Hochschild.* English. Houghton Mifflin Boston, 1998, 366 p. : ISBN: 0395759242 0618001905.

[25]   Neda Communications Inc. *A Strategy For Rapidly Becoming An Internet Application Service Provider Joining, Adopting and/or Licensing ByStar A Public Unsolicited Proposal.* Permanent Libre Published Content 180040. http://www.by-star.net/PLPC/180040. Autonomously Self-Published, Aug. 2013.

[26]   Neda Communications Inc. *Blee and BxGnome: ByStar Software-Service Continuum Based Convivial User Environments.* Permanent Libre Published Content 180004. http://www.persoarabic.org/PLPC/180004. Autonomously Self-Published, Sept. 2012.

[27]   Neda Communications Inc. *ByStar Web Facilities ByStar Content Production, Publication, and Distribution Services.* Permanent Libre Published Content 180038. http://www.by-star.net/PLPC/180038. Autonomously Self-Published, May 2013.

[28]   Neda Communications Inc. *The Libre-Halaal ByStar Digital Ecosystem An Inversion to Proprietary Internet Services Model Neda Communication Inc.'s Open Business Plan.* Permanent Libre Published Content 180014. http://www.neda.com/strategicVision/businessPlan. Autonomously Self-Published, Aug. 2013.

[29]   Neda Communications Inc. *The Libre-Halaal ByStar Reference Model Terminology, Architecture And Design.* Permanent Libre Published Content 180047. http://www.by-star.net/PLPC/180047. Autonomously Self-Published, Dec. 2014.

[30]   Shintaro Ishihara. *The Japan That Can Say No: Why Japan Will Be First Among Equals.* Trans. by Frank Baldwin. Simon and Schuster, 1991, p. 160. ISBN: 978-0671726867.

[31]   Theodore Kaczynski. *The Unabomber manifesto : industrial society and its future.* Berkeley, CA : Jolly Roger Press, [publisher not identified], 1995., 1995.

[32]   Robert Kenner. *Food, Inc.* Sept. 2008.

[33] Stephan Kinsell. "Against Intellectual Property". http://www.uow.edu.au/~bmartin/pubs/98il/.

[34] Amy Klobuchar. *Antitrust: Taking on Monopoly Power from the Gilded Age to the Digital Age.* Alfred A. Knopf, Apr. 27, 2021, p. 797.

[35] Lawrence Lessig. "Free Culture". In: (Jan. 2002).

[36] Brian Martin. *Against Intellectual Property.* https://mises.org/library/against-intellectual-property-0.

[37] John McCarthy. "Recursive Functions of Symbolic Expressions and Their Computation by Machine, Part I". In: *Communications of the ACM* 3.4 (1960), pp. 184–195. ISSN: 0001-0782. DOI: http://doi.acm.org/10.1145/367177.367199. URL: http://portal.acm.org/citation.cfm?id=367199.

[38] Roger McNamee. *Zucked: Waking Up to the Facebook Catastrophe.* English. Hardcover. Penguin Press, Feb. 5, 2019, p. 352. ISBN: 978-0525561354.

[39] Tom G. Palmer. *Are Patents And Copyrights Morally Justified? The Philosophy Of Property Rights And Ideal Objects.*

[40] Edward Said. *Orientalism.* 1978.

[41] Shadman Salih. *Selection of computer programming languages for developing distributed systems.* May 2014.

[42] T. Scholz and N. Schneider. *Ours to Hack and to Own: The Rise of Platform Cooperativism, a New Vision for the Future of Work and a Fairer Internet.* OR Books, 2017. ISBN: 9781944869335.

[43] Ibn Sina. *Daneshnameh Alai.* Web Published at http://pdf.tarikhema.ir.

[44] Ramesh Srinivasan. *Beyond the Valley: How Innovators around the World are Overcoming Inequality and Creating the Technologies of Tomorrow (The MIT Press).* The MIT Press, Oct. 29, 2019, p. 420. ISBN: 978-0262043137.

[45] Mark S. TAYLOR, William Waung, and Mohsen BANAN. *Internetwork Mobility – The CDPD Approach.* 120021. http://mohsen.banan.1.byname.net/PLPC/120021. Dec. 2007.

[46] McKenzie Wark. *Capital Is Dead: Is This Something Worse?* English. Paperback. Verso, Feb. 9, 2021, p. 208. ISBN: 978-1788735339.

[47] Tim Wu. *The Curse of Bigness: Antitrust in the New Gilded Age.* English. Paperback. Columbia Global Reports, Nov. 13, 2018, p. 154. ISBN: 978-0999745465.

[48] Peter Yu. "Intellectual Property and Confucianism". In: May 2015, pp. 247–270. ISBN: 9781107588479. DOI: 10.1017/CBO9781107588479.014.

[49] Shoshana Zuboff. *The Age of Surveillance Capitalism: The Fight for a Human Future at the New Frontier of Power.* English. Paperback. PublicAffairs, Mar. 3, 2020, p. 704. ISBN: 978-1541758001.

Glossary

A

americanism In Globish, Americanism is the model of economic creatures existing in an industrial context. 9

C

copyright Broadly speaking in today's world, copyright is a legal concept that grants the creator of an original work exclusive rights to reproduce, distribute, display, perform, or create derivative works based on the original. When a work is copyrighted, others may not use or redistribute the work without the permission of the author. 4, 43

F

FLOSS Free and Libre Open-Source Software. 6

H

halaal In Globish, philosophical halaal is "manifestation" of "moral sensibilities" relevant to a specific topic where "the set of actions" map to "right". See Section 11 — Introducing Halaal and Haraam Into Globish — for a formal definition. 7

haraam In Globish, philosophical haraam is "manifestation" of "moral sensibilities" relevant to a specific topic where "the set of actions" map to "wrong". See Section 11 — Introducing Halaal and Haraam Into Globish — for a formal definition. 7

I

Intellectual Property The term IP means the (abstract) product of the intellect. For example, an invention and an original work of authorship are intellectual property. 1

Intellectual Property Rights The term IPR means a legal right covering IP.. 1

IP Intellectual Property. 41

IPR Intellectual Property Rights. 43

L

Libre Libre is a substitute for the word free in English which distinguishes the freedom sense from the gratis sense. 6

Libre Services Libre Services is the label that we apply for the halaal manner-of-existence of internet application services. See Section 15.2.3 — Definition of Libre-Halaal Internet Application Services — for formal definition of Libre Services. 239

Libre-Halaal Libre-Halaal is the label that we apply for the halaal manner-of-existence of polyexistentials. 7

Libre-Halaal Content Libre-Halaal Content is the label that we apply for the halaal manner-of-existence of content. See Section 15.2.2 — Definition of Libre-Halaal Content — for formal definition of Libre-Halaal Content. 190

Libre-Halaal Software Libre-Halaal Software is the label that we apply for the halaal manner-of-existence of software. See Section 15.2.1 — Definition of Libre-Halaal Software — for formal definition of Libre-Halaal Software. 237

M

monoexistentials That which exists in nature in singular. 1

N

Non-Rivalry In economics, a good is considered non-rivalrous or non-rival if, for any level of production, the cost of providing it to a marginal (additional) individual is zero. 23

O

Open Source Open source enables a development method for software that harnesses the power of distributed peer review and transparency of process. The promise of open source is higher quality, better reliability, greater flexibility, lower cost, and an end to predatory vendor lock-in. 172

P

patent Broadly speaking in today's world, a patent is a form of legal protection granted by a government to an inventor for a limited period of time. It grants the inventor exclusive rights to their invention, which must be novel, non-obvious, and useful. In exchange for this protection, the inventor must publicly disclose the details of their invention.. 4, 43

polyexistentials That which exists in nature in multiples. 1

R

Rivalry In economics, a good is said to be rivalrous or rival if its consumption by one consumer prevents simultaneous consumption by other consumers. 23

S

self-toxicated is a model for self-toxicated economic creatures existing in an exploitative industrial context. 16

T

trademark A trademark is, broadly speaking, any mark that is used for indicating goods or services in commerce. Normally trademarks are words or an image (a logo), although occasionally colors or sounds can also be trademarks. Usually, it is necessary to register the mark with a local trademark office before it gains protection under trademark law. A trademark holder can forbid others from offering particular goods or services using the trademark or a confusingly similar sign. It is also often possible to act against use of the trademark which dilutes its reputation. 4, 43

W

west-toxication is a term that Iranians have created and use to denote pernicious Western influence that is to be rejected. 8

Index

www.ingramcontent.com/pod-product-compliance
Lightning Source LLC
Chambersburg PA
CBHW071537210326
41597CB00019B/3030